INSIDERS' GUIDE® TO

TULSA

HELP US KEEP THIS GUIDE UP TO DATE

We would love to hear from you concerning your experiences with this guide and how you feel it could be improved and kept up to date. Please send your comments and suggestions to:

editorial@GlobePequot.com

Thanks for your input, and happy travels!

INSIDERS' GUIDE® SERIES

INSIDERS' GUIDE® TO

TULSA

ELAINE WARNER

INSIDERS' GUIDE

GUILFORD, CONNECTICUT

AN IMPRINT OF GLOBE PEQUOT PRESS

All the information in this guidebook is subject to change. We recommend that you call ahead to obtain current information before traveling.

To buy books in quantity for corporate use
or incentives, call **(800) 962–0973**
or e-mail **premiums@GlobePequot.com.**

INSIDERS' GUIDE®

Project Editor: Ellen Urban
Layout Artist: Kevin Mak
Text design by Sheryl Kober
Maps by Design Maps, Inc. © Morris Book Publishing, LLC

Library of Congress Cataloging-in-Publication Data is available on file.
ISBN 978-0-7627-5348-2

Printed in the United States of America
10 9 8 7 6 5 4 3 2 1

CONTENTS

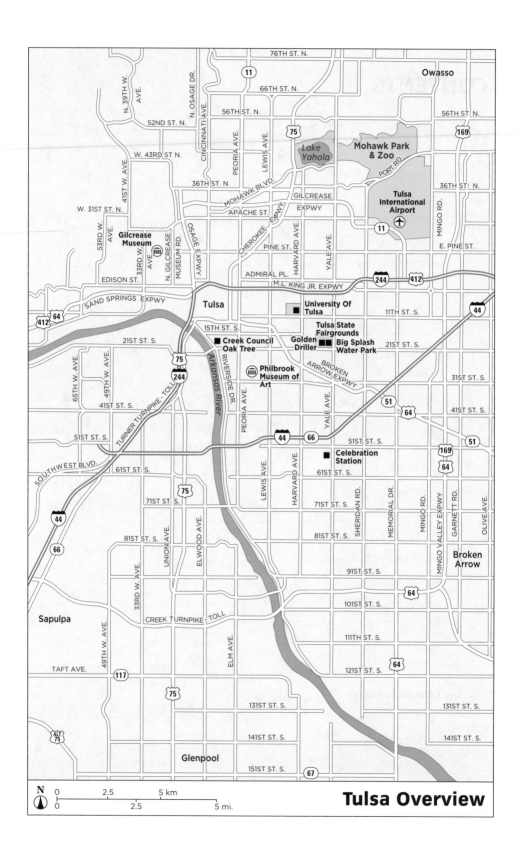

Tulsa Overview

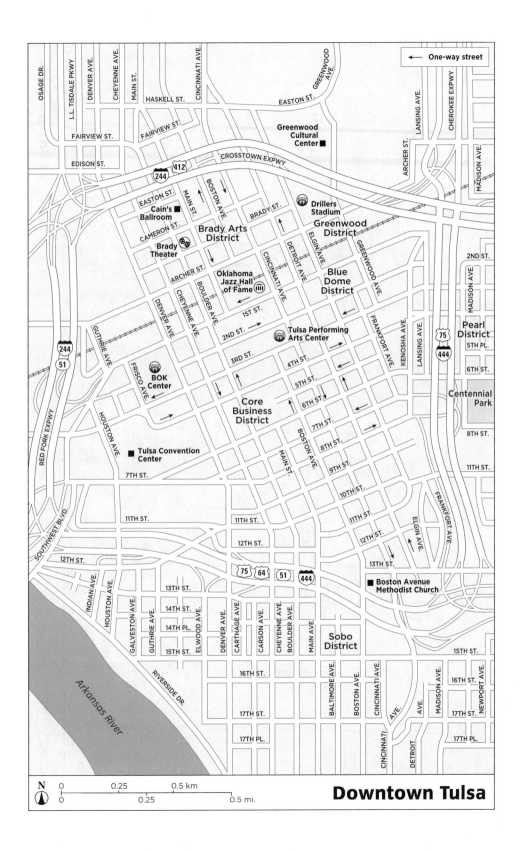

One-way street

OSAGE DR.
L.L. TISDALE PKWY
DENVER AVE.
CHEYENNE AVE.
MAIN ST.
HASKELL ST.
CINCINNATI AVE.
EASTON ST.
GREENWOOD AVE.
LANSING AVE.
CHEROKEE EXPWY
MADISON AVE.

FAIRVIEW ST.
FAIRVIEW ST.
Greenwood
Cultural
Center ■
EDISON ST.
CROSSTOWN EXPWY.
ARCHER ST.

412
244

EASTON ST.
MAIN ST.
BOSTON AVE.
BRADY ST.
Drillers
Stadium
Greenwood
District
2ND ST.

Cain's
Ballroom ■
CAMERON ST.
ELGIN AVE.
MADISON AVE.

Brady
Theater
Brady Arts
District
DETROIT AVE.
Blue
Dome
District
GREENWOOD AVE.

ARCHER ST.
CINCINNATI AVE.
Oklahoma
Jazz Hall
of Fame
FRANKFORT AVE.
Pearl
District

DENVER AVE.
CHEYENNE AVE.
BOULDER AVE.
1ST ST.
KENOSHA AVE.
LANSING AVE.
75
444
5TH PL.

GUTHRIE AVE.
2ND ST.
Tulsa Performing
Arts Center
6TH ST.

244
51
FRISCO AVE.
3RD ST.
4TH ST.
Centennial
Park

BOK
Center
5TH ST.
6TH ST.

HOUSTON AVE.
Core
Business
District
7TH ST.
8TH ST.

RED FORK EXPWY
BOSTON AVE.
8TH ST.
9TH ST.

Tulsa Convention
Center ■
MAIN ST.
10TH ST.
11TH ST.

7TH ST.
11TH ST.
FRANKFORT AVE.

SOUTHWEST BLVD.
11TH ST.
11TH ST.
ELGIN AVE.

12TH ST.
12TH ST.
12TH ST.

13TH ST.
75 64 51 444
13TH ST.

INDIAN AVE.
HOUSTON AVE.
GALVESTON AVE.
GUTHRIE AVE.
ELWOOD AVE.
13TH ST.
Boston Avenue
Methodist Church ■

14TH ST.
DENVER AVE.
CARTHAGE AVE.
CARSON AVE.
CHEYENNE AVE.
BOULDER AVE.
MAIN ST.

14TH PL.
15TH ST.
Sobo
District
15TH ST.

RIVERSIDE DR.
16TH ST.
BALTIMORE AVE.
BOSTON AVE.
CINCINNATI AVE.
MADISON AVE.
NEWPORT AVE.
16TH ST.

Arkansas River
17TH ST.
17TH ST.
17TH PL.

17TH PL.
CINCINNATI AVE.
DETROIT AVE.
AVE.

N
0   0.25   0.5 km
0   0.25   0.5 mi.

Downtown Tulsa

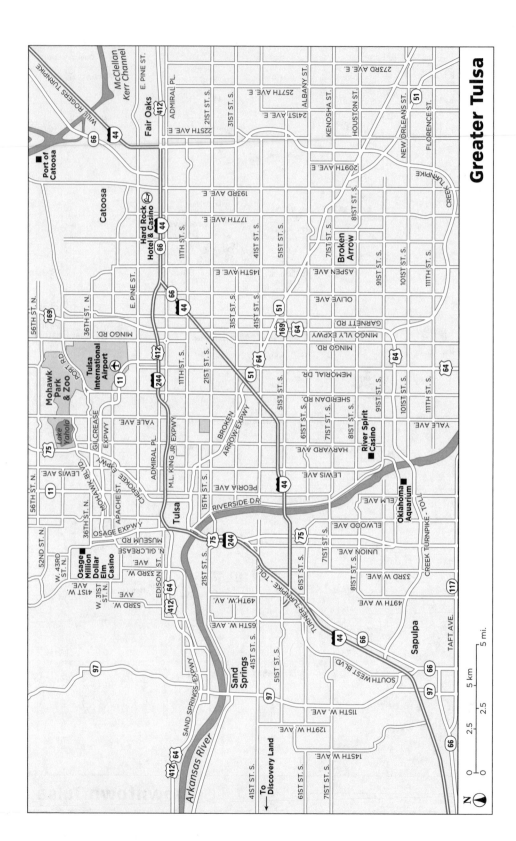

Greater Tulsa

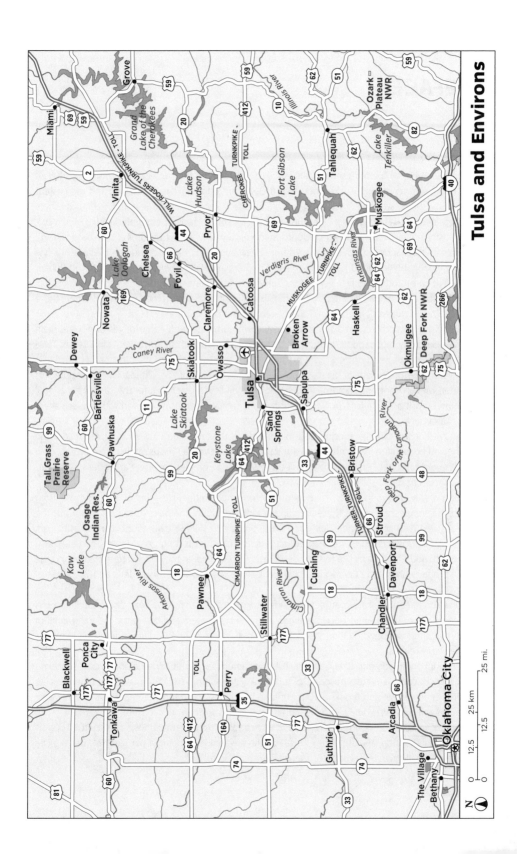

Tulsa and Environs

PREFACE

Welcome to Tulsa, Oklahoma's second largest city. Outranked by the state capital, Tulsa nevertheless takes a back seat to no one. Tucked between the western edge of the Ozark Uplift and the eastern border of the thickly wooded Cross Timbers, the city's site is a pleasant mixture of rolling hills, forests of deciduous trees, and short-grass prairie. Tulsa is noted for spring landscapes painted with a Monet palette of pastel azaleas, dogwoods, and redbuds; summers awash with vivid greens and colorful blooms; and falls with trees sporting leaves in shades from deep purple to brilliant orange and yellow.

Early inhabitants included nomadic tribes of hunters and, later, members of the Mound Builder culture. Not surprisingly, the first permanent settlers were Indians—a group from the Creek Nation, moved forcibly from Alabama. One of Tulsa's most significant landmarks is the Council Oak where these settlers rekindled the embers brought from their former home.

With white settlement, Tulsa became a cow town complete with cattle drives down the main street and Saturday night shoot-'em-ups. All that was forgotten with the discovery of oil when Tulsa turned into a boomtown. Fortunes were made and lost, and when the dust settled, names like Skelly and Phillips were prominent in establishing Tulsa as "Oil Capital of the World." The city saluted its reputation with an enormous gold-painted statue of an oil-field worker built for the 1966 International Petroleum Exposition. Art it isn't, but like a slightly dotty family member, it's viewed with amused affection by Tulsans.

The oil industry brought moguls and millionaires to the area; Route 66 brought the rest of the country. And both influences continue to attract visitors. Tour Waite Phillips's Italianate mansion, now the Philbrook Museum of Art, then slake your thirst with home-brewed root beer at Weber's, a 75-year-old Tulsa institution that still satisfies.

You won't be bored in Tulsa. The community has a rich cultural life—lots of art and music from opera to jazz to western swing. There are parks aplenty, including the miles-long park that fronts the Arkansas River. With playgrounds; disc golf; hiking, biking and skating trails; fountains; and public art, this park is the crown jewel of Tulsa's outdoor venues. Tulsa isn't resting on its laurels, however, and continues to add new spaces like the Linnaeus Teaching Gardens at the Tulsa Garden Center and the work-in-progress Oklahoma Centennial Botanical Garden with 60 acres of gardens and 240 acres of preserved prairie and forestland.

Tulsa's architecture is a big attraction. Tulsa ranks right up with New York City, Miami, and Los Angeles for the number of art deco buildings. And the city's latest addition is the stunning Bank of Oklahoma Center designed by internationally famous architect Cesar Pelli, known for Kuala Lumpur's Petronas Twin Towers.

For shoppers, in addition to large malls, Tulsa has a number of charming neighborhood shopping areas. Shady Utica Square hosts upscale stores like Saks Fifth Avenue and Williams-Sonoma, and smaller areas like Cherry Street and Brookside offer unique boutiques and trendy eateries. Restaurants range from mom and pop–type diners to haute cuisine and food choices from catfish to calamari.

Short of an ocean or mountains, Tulsa has it all. In addition to top attractions, varied cultural opportunities, exciting eating, and shopping, Tulsa has the advantage of being a bargain. You get big-city amenities at small-town prices and less traffic to contend with.

Visitors find Tulsans to be friendly and helpful, and new residents find it easy to get involved. Tulsa offers a blend of sophisticated city and down-home hospitality. There's so much to see and do—it would take a book to describe it all. And so we wrote one! Enjoy!

ACKNOWLEDGMENTS

There are so many people who helped me write this book:

- Nancy Phillips with the Tulsa Convention and Visitors Bureau, for her tireless efforts on my behalf, answering endless questions, arranging itineraries, and providing me with contacts all over town. And she has the fastest phone finger in the west—no sooner did I ask for a contact's phone number than she had called them and they were calling me!
- Tom Green, Dfest founder, who girded his loins and took me barhopping.
- Bill Waller, writer, retired businessman, and former chairman of the Tulsa Chamber of Commerce, who read the History chapter and gave me excellent suggestions, even though I didn't follow all of them.
- James Wagner, senior transportation planner, Indian Nations Council of Governments (INCOG), my transportation guru, bicycling expert, and supplier of all sorts of useful information.
- Jackie Sheckler Finch, who's done a number of these guides and who encouraged me when I felt overwhelmed.
- Jack Warner, faithful chauffeur, sometime traveling companion, cheerleader, and best friend for 48 years
- Globe Pequot editors Amy Lyons and Ellen Urban who were delights to work with
- And, finally, all the restaurant owners, chefs, hotel managers, museum staff members, school officials, and total strangers who offered information and help.

Tulsa is a gracious, beautiful, and generous city, and doing this book helped affirm that conviction.

HOW TO USE THIS BOOK

Welcome to *Insiders' Guide to Tulsa*. Inside these pages we have compiled everything (or pretty close to everything) you need to know to enjoy this beautiful jewel of a town—whether you're here for just a weekend getaway or a long-term stay.

How is the information in this book different from the information you could find in the brochures and booklets you can get free from the local convention and visitors' bureau or the state department of tourism? We're allowed to be opinionated. We're beholden to no one—and it's all based on personal experience and backed up by a number of resources. Whether you're traveling for business or pleasure, passing through or considering relocation, we hope this book will be your new best friend—something to help you get a feel for the city, and to help you feel at home. We'll bring you the straight scoop without the advertisements.

This isn't a novel or a step-by-step, how-to book, so feel free to jump in anywhere. We have attempted to organize it logically—to give you some basic background information, then to provide sections on areas of interest. Arts and culture, sure; enjoying the great outdoors, you bet; and the town is a shopper's delight. Whatever you like to do when you travel, you'll probably find it here——unless you insist on snow skiing or deep-sea fishing!

Travel, like life, isn't easy to compartmentalize—bits and pieces are bound to overlap. We've tried to cross-reference as much as possible, so if, for example, you like art museums, you'll find the Philbrook Museum of Art in the Arts chapter. But you'll also find it under Attractions, as one of the city's most important assets, and under Kidstuff, for its many programs designed to introduce new audiences to its treasures. You'll even find it under Shopping, for its excellent gift shop.

Close-ups will give you even more background on people and places plus extra information that, hopefully, will enhance your experience, or at least make you feel more of an insider. Insiders' Tips range from "helpful to know" to "trivia, but fun"—these are marked with an 🄸.

We've worked hard to make this guidebook as accurate and useful as possible. Please keep in mind that things can change quickly—new restaurants open, management changes at hotels, and attractions change hours and prices. That's why we've given general guidelines rather than specific information. It's always a good idea to call ahead to be certain. Even Web sites can be wrong—it depends on how assiduously they are updated.

Finally, do with this book what you were taught never to do. Dog-ear the pages; write in the margins; make notes on your visits. And feel free to share your thoughts with us. Books in the Insiders' Guide series are regularly revised and we value your input.

Contact us at:
The Globe Pequot Press
Reader Response/Editorial Department
P.O. Box 480
Guilford, CT 06437-0480
Or e-mail editorial@GlobePequot.com

AREA OVERVIEW

Tulsa comes as a big surprise to a lot of visitors. Let's face it: Many people have a mental image of Oklahoma that combines Laurey and Curly and the surrey with the fringe on top, Indians galloping across the plains, and the Joads heading for California. At some time, in some places, these images may have had a kernel of truth but they're as out of date as high-button shoes.

Tulsa is Oklahoma's most cosmopolitan city. Skyscrapers tower over a downtown area that is undergoing revitalization. Bikers, hikers, and skaters zip down miles of tree-lined paths along a river that is broad and beautiful. And the closest you'll get to a surrey is at Discoveryland!—the national home of Rogers and Hammerstein's *Oklahoma!* in nearby Sand Springs.

Tulsa's major attractions are scattered throughout the metropolitan area. But fortunately, Tulsa's easy to navigate. And, of course, the city's more than its museums and amusement venues. It's all the places where Tulsans live, work, play, and pray.

With the revival of downtown, lofts and city living are becoming more popular. With the westerners' sense of space, most residents, however, opt for single-family dwellings in neighborhoods of small, postwar bungalows, larger homes in historic districts, or new developments in suburbs like Broken Arrow, with 90,000 residents, a city in its own right.

Though known for petroleum and natural gas, other major industries include aerospace manufacturing and transportation, health care, and telecommunications. Tulsa's economic diversification has helped the area weather the economic downturn more easily than many other destinations.

Tulsa's lifestyle also provides stress relief—a slower pace, an emphasis on family, and lots of outdoor and recreational opportunities. Some of Oklahoma's most popular lakes are within easy driving distance—Grand Lake, Keystone Lake, Lake Oologah, Tenkiller Lake, and Fort Gibson Lake. Nearby state parks offer accommodations and camping, and Tulsa itself has beautiful parks and green spaces for everyday getaways. It's also a mecca for the country's best golfers. Southern Hills Country Club has been the site of three U.S. Open championships, four PGA championships, and seven other major championships.

Religion is an important part of community life in Oklahoma, and visitors looking for a service won't have to look far. Some of the city's most stunning architecture is in its houses of worship.

And the architecture is a big attraction. Fueled by oil money in the '20s and '30s, Tulsans built amazing buildings in the art deco style. Visitors come from all over the world to examine the genre in variations from early zigzag, middle Public Works Administration (PWA), and late streamline versions.

All in all, Tulsa is a great place to visit—and it's a great place to live.

SITTING PRETTY (GEOGRAPHY AND CLIMATE)

If you took a map of Oklahoma, chopped off the panhandle, and divided the pan into quarters, Tulsa would be in the middle of the northeast section. Most of this area, including Tulsa, is known as Oklahoma's "Green Country," an area of rolling hills, blackjack oaks, tall maples, magnolias, and sweet gums, and swaths of short-grass prairie.

Oklahoma's diverse terrain encompasses 11 eco-regions, 12 if you consider the urban landscapes separately. Tulsa is on the border of two of these regions—the Central Irregular Plains and the Cross Timbers. The Central Irregular Plains region is characterized by a mosaic of grasslands and forests. The Cross Timbers forms a narrow buffer between the forested eastern part of the state and the nearly treeless Great Plains. Parts of the Cross Timbers once featured wooded areas so dense that they were almost impenetrable. These rugged areas are characterized by close-grown, stubby post oaks, many of them centuries old, and red cedars. It was this area that Washington Irving described in his 1835 *A Tour on the Prairies:* "I shall not easily forget the mortal toil, and the vexations of flesh and spirit, that we underwent occasionally, in our wanderings through the Cross Timbers. It was like struggling through forests of cast iron." Today's travelers can actually hike that same terrain in the Keystone Ancient Forest Preserve in nearby Sand Springs.

Less historic but also interesting terrain for hikers and bikers can be found in the Turkey Mountain Urban Wilderness Area situated on a wooded ridge overlooking the Arkansas River. About the term *mountain*—Tulsa's elevation at the airport is 677 feet above sea level. Tulsa's average elevation is 700 feet. Turkey Mountain soars another 104 feet above the Arkansas. You work with what you have! Though Oklahoma does have several points that meet mountain standards—2,000 feet above the surrounding terrain—Tulsa has only hills with big egos.

Tulsa's most striking geographical feature is the Arkansas River. Until the 1960s, when Keystone Lake and Dam were built about 15 miles upriver from Tulsa, the river was a mixed blessing. Depending on the season, it carried too little or too much water. Sometimes flooding occurred, destroying homes and businesses. Since the installation of flood-control measures, the Arkansas forms a watery border to one of the city's most significant play areas, River Parks.

With a moderate climate, outdoor activities are pursued year-round. That's not to say that the weather can't get interesting. Tulsa is located in what is called "Tornado Alley." Tornado season is generally between March and August, but tornadoes can form any time the weather conditions are right. Your chances of being hurt in a tornado are miniscule, but every Oklahoman knows to keep the radio or TV on when the clouds get ominous and to follow safety precautions.

January is usually the coldest month of the year with an average low of 26 degrees Fahrenheit and a high of 46 degrees Fahrenheit. July is the toastiest month with an average high of 93 degrees and a low of 72 degrees. Averages are deceiving, however, because the weather can change quickly and drastically. It's not unheard of to have a sunny, 70-degree February noon with a 50-degree drop before dinner. Winter temperatures occasionally fall below zero but rarely stay there long. From July to September, temperatures reaching the century mark aren't unusual, but with relatively low humidity and a prevailing southerly breeze, the heat is bearable. Will Rogers is often quoted as saying, "If you don't like Oklahoma's weather, wait a minute and it will change." And, to paraphrase Oscar Hammerstein, the wind frequently does come sweeping across the plains.

For the most part the weather in Tulsa is nice, with lots of sunny days—approximately 230 per year, with a 216-day average growing season. Spring is the wettest time of year. In an average year, Tulsans get two or three snowfalls a year; usually not deep and not lasting more than a couple of days. The biggest winter hazard is ice. With daytime temperatures generally above freezing, falling nighttime temperatures, combined with drizzle or rain, can turn the streets into skating rinks. When that happens, Tulsans simply stay off the streets until they melt—and that usually doesn't take long.

In general, Tulsa has short winters, lovely springs, sunny summers, and glorious autumns.

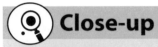 **Close-up**

Tornado Safety

Staying at a hotel? Ask about tornado warnings and shelter.

Listen for sirens; monitor television and radio reports.

At home, have a designated "safe" area—lowest floor, interior, no windows, perhaps a bathroom, closet, or under the stairs.

Keep a shelter kit in the safe area—flashlight with extra batteries, radio with extra batteries, bottled water, nonperishable food items, first aid kit, any necessary medicines.

A mattress, heavy blankets, sleeping bags, bicycle or work helmets—these may protect you from flying debris.

A bathtub may offer some protection.

Minimize injuries by wearing closed-toe shoes, long pants, and shirts with long sleeves.

ON THE GO (TRANSPORTATION)

Tulsa's grid system of surface streets makes orienting yourself easy. Multilane expressways make getting around faster. I-44 cuts across the middle of the city from east to west. The highway goes from Wichita Falls, Texas, through Oklahoma City and Tulsa, and on to St. Louis. Other major highways include US 75, which runs from Dallas to the Canadian border in Minnesota; US 64, which goes from North Carolina to Arizona; and US 169, which stretches from Tulsa to the city of Virginia, Minnesota.

Historic Route 66 is a Tulsa icon. Supplanted by I-44, there are still stretches of original pavement, and a number of remnants of the heyday of the Mother Road can be found on Tulsa surface streets like 10th, 11th, 12th, and Southwest Boulevard.

Like in the rest of Oklahoma, the car is king in Tulsa, and public transportation, while available, is limited in the number of routes it serves and handicapped by long waits between buses. Planning committees are studying ways to improve and expand service.

Tulsa International Airport (TIA) is served by American, Delta, Continental, Northwest, Airlink, Southwest, and United Airlines. TIA (airline code TUL) was the 11th airport in the nation to install whole-body imaging machines and the first to use them for primary passenger screening. R.L. Jones Airport serves as a reliever airport for TIA, handling a great deal of the general-aviation and training-facilities traffic and leaving TIA more room for the major commercial airlines. The R.L. Jones Airport is the busiest airport in the state and the seventh busiest general-aviation airport in the nation.

Tulsa has no direct passenger rail service. The only passenger train in Oklahoma is the Amtrak Heartland Flyer, which runs between Fort Worth and Oklahoma City. The hours of service are not convenient for Tulsans. There is a lot of enthusiasm for rail service and there's always the hope that Amtrak will expand service to this area.

A unique element of the area's transportation network is barge traffic, which starts at the nearby Port of Catoosa, the northernmost port on the McClellan-Kerr Arkansas River Navigation System. Beginning at the Port of Catoosa, barge traffic travels through locks and lakes, down the Verdigris River, the Arkansas River, the Arkansas Post Canal, and the White River, into the Mississippi River at Montgomery Point, Arkansas. From there barges travel south to New Orleans, a total trip of some 600 miles. The port handles about 1,300 barges with a total of over two million tons of cargo annually.

Tulsa Vital Statistics

Founded: 1836 by members of the Lochapoka Creek community, originally from Alabama. The town was incorporated on January 18, 1898.

Population: City of Tulsa: 383,768 (2008 estimate)

Tulsa metropolitan statistical area: 906,870 (2008 estimate)

Counties in MSA: Tulsa, Osage, Pawnee, Creek Okmulgee, Wagoner, Rogers (Washington County, directly north of Tulsa County is not included.)

Area: City of Tulsa: 182.65 square miles. Tulsa MSA: 6281.5 square miles

City government: Three elected elements: mayor, city auditor, city council members (currently nine)

Major airport/code: Tulsa International Airport (TUL)

Major employers: Tulsa Public Schools, St. Francis Healthcare System, Wal-Mart/Sams, American Airlines Maintenance Base, St. John Medical Center, Hillcrest Healthcare Systems, City of Tulsa, Cherokee Casino, U.S. Postal Service, Reasor's, Bank of Oklahoma, Broken Arrow Public Schools, NORDAM

Famous Tulsans: Born or lived in Tulsa: Gene Autry, William "Hopalong Cassidy" Boyd, Garth Brooks, Roy Clark, Paul Harvey, Daniel Patrick Moynihan, Tony Randall, Jeanne Tripplehorn, Alfre Woodard, J. J. Cale, Bob Wills, Daniel J Boorstin, John Hope Franklin, Judy Woodruff, Wes Studi, Kristin Chenoweth

Major colleges: Tulsa University, Oral Roberts University, branches of Langston University, Northeastern State University, Oklahoma State University, and the University of Oklahoma

Newspapers: Daily: *Tulsa World, Broken Arrow Ledger, Journal Record.* **Weekly:** *Tulsa Business Journal, Hispano de Tulsa, Urban Tulsa Weekly.*

Sales tax: State: 4.5 percent. **City:** 3 percent.

Driving laws: Vehicle operators and front-seat passengers must wear seat belts. Children under 6 must use child-restraint seats; children 6 to 13 must use child-restraint seats or seat belts. Oklahoma's open-container law is very strict—no unsealed bottles of alcohol or open containers inside the vehicle.

Liquor laws: Beer and wine coolers sold in grocery or convenience stores must contain no more than 3.2 percent alcohol by volume. Stronger alcoholic beverages can be purchased only by the unrefrigerated bottle at licensed liquor stores or, in bars or restaurants, by the drink. Alcohol cannot be purchased by anyone under the age of 21, and people under this age are prohibited from being in liquor stores or within a designated bar area. Liquor stores, open between 10 a.m. and 9 p.m., are closed on Sunday, and alcohol may not be sold on New Year's Day, Memorial Day, the Fourth of July, Labor Day, Thanksgiving, or Christmas. Bars in Tulsa County are allowed to sell drinks on Sunday, but no alcohol can be sold between the hours of 2 a.m. and 10 a.m. Don't be surprised by a larger tax charge on your mixed drinks—there's a "sin tax" in Oklahoma.

Time zone: Central Standard Time, Central Daylight Time

SAVING SPACES (CONSERVATION AND ENVIRONMENTAL CONCERNS)

Tulsa leads the state in use of green technology and long-term environmental planning. The Tulsa Parks Department oversees 6,000 acres of green space including nature centers, gardens, the zoo, golf courses, tennis facilities, and many more community assets.

Planning for more green space is a priority, both for aesthetic value and environmental benefits. Organizations like Sustainable Tulsa and Up with Trees work actively on not only green space but other facets of green living.

One of the biggest efforts underway is the PLANiTULSA program, a comprehensive plan for growth and sustainability. The year-and-a-half-long process, which began in July 2008, involves workshops on key planning issues and opportunities for significant citizen input.

Sustainable Tulsa also provides educational workshops, offers volunteer opportunities, and produces the Tulsa Area Green Directory, a listing of businesses and organizations that promote good living choices in the community.

Up with Trees promotes and preserves Tulsa's urban forest. With the help of volunteers and donors, they plant trees along streets and trails, in neighborhoods and parks, at schools, and in public areas.

The city, under Mayor Kathy Taylor, moved its offices into an amazing new facility called One Technology Center. Consolidating scattered city offices, reducing paper usage by 40 percent, and buying CNG vehicles has not only helped the environment but also the city budget. Special features of One Technology Center include a solar well, recycling systems on each floor, an exterior glass curtain, limited night lighting, and electronic systems for displaying public announcements and storing the city legal department's law library.

i Keep up with what's happening in city government by following city oftulsagov on Twitter.

In addition, Tulsa has one of the most sophisticated storm-water drainage plans in the country. Part of the solution included building retention areas that in normal times serve as parks and ball fields but help hold water when needed. Because of the extensive work done in this area, folks in Tulsa get some of the nation's best deals on flood insurance.

Planning also includes preservation, and great strides are being made to bring housing back into the center of town. Some of Tulsa's grandest old buildings are now being turned into apartments, lofts, and condos, not only saving architectural treasures but putting people closer to their work and to public transportation.

One of the premier examples of the city's efforts involved century-old Central Park, just east of downtown. The surrounding area had once been one of Tulsa's first urban neighborhoods. By the '50s, the flight to the suburbs had taken its toll and the area was run-down and blighted.

i Tulsa Young Professionals, www .typros.com, is an organization with over 5,000 members. Its primary purpose is to attract and retain a youthful and energetic workforce.

The City of Tulsa purchased blighted properties on the south side of the park and asked for bids from developers who were interested in rebuilding the area. Today the park has been reinvigorated with waterfalls, fountains, and a community center. The adjacent townhouses are all occupied or under contract, and more new units are being added. In 2001 the Oklahoma chapter of the Sierra Club awarded the development, called The Village, the Earthcare Award for overall quality and for imaginative contribution to reducing urban sprawl.

Oklahomans are going green and Tulsa's leading the way.

POCKETBOOK ISSUES (ECONOMY)

Currently, the nation's economic outlook is as unpredictable as Oklahoma weather. No one's sure what the future will bring. Tulsa has, so far, escaped much of the turmoil plaguing many areas of the country. No one's looking for an economic boom in the short term; however, many of the city's business leaders are cautiously optimistic that losses will be minimal. Some industries, like the telecommunication and energy industries, see opportunities in present difficulties. Banks here have been carefully managed and are strong. Business diversification is also a plus.

Tulsa's cost of living is 11 percent below the national average, and the cost of doing business, 7 percent below the U.S. average. In March 2009, Manpower, Inc., surveying 31,800 employers in the top 200 metropolitan areas, named Tulsa 10th best in the nation for jobs. And in 2004 Tulsa was named one of America's most livable large cities by Partners for Livable Communities, an organization that makes these awards once a decade. And in 2009 *Forbes* magazine listed Tulsa fifth on a list of "America's Most Livable Cities." It also selected Tulsa as Number 47 out of 200 cities included in "Best Places for Business and Careers." In an earlier article, the same magazine listed Tulsa as the fifth-best city in the U.S. to ride out the recession.

So Tulsa's a good place to work, a great place to live, and a super place to visit. Your tourist dollar will go farther here and you'll find all the big city amenities without the crowds.

i Bank of Oklahoma has a large presence in Tulsa, from the towering BOK Tower, the tallest building in the state, to the massive BOK Arena. The red BOK symbol is known locally as "the meatball."

i In 2009 Forbes.com rated Tulsa the nation's fifth most livable of the nation's largest metropolitan statistical areas. Factors taken into consideration included: five-year income growth, cost of living, a "leisure/culture index," crime, and unemployment figures.

LOOKING AHEAD

Although Tulsa was the home of some of the nation's first aviators, Tulsans are no longer flying by the seats of their pants. Goal setting and long-term planning are part of Tulsa's look forward. And decisions are not just made at the top—Tulsans are stepping up and participating in the process.

Tulsans look forward to better economic times and a community that balances quality of life with environmental concerns. And they look forward to sharing the many attractions of their city with visitors from all over—including you.

GETTING HERE, GETTING AROUND

As you might expect in a city built on oil, the automobile is still the number one way of getting around Tulsa. And if you want to get to Tulsa, driving or flying are your best choices.

For a city that's not a major airline hub, Tulsa's quite accessible. Again, thanks to the oil boom and the business people it brought to Tulsa, the city has a long history of airline service, with some of the nation's most notable aeronauts, including Oklahoma native Wiley Post, flying in and out of town.

However you get here, expect to spend time on the roads. Things are spread out, but traffic is rarely a problem and most destinations, even from one side of town to the other, are less than a 30-minute drive.

ROADWAYS

Tulsa was laid out logically on a grid system using the Frisco railroad tracks as a baseline. This tipped the town site off a true north/south, east/west alignment. The only deviation the original planners made was to make a slight detour on East 3rd St. to avoid destroying an orchard. As the city grew, the extended streets were curved to make them conform to a strict north/south, east/west orientation.

Today, I-44 is the major highway going through Tulsa. The portion of I-44 from Oklahoma City east follows the famous Mother Road, Route 66, which ran from California to Chicago. As the highway enters town, it splits into I-44, also known as Skelly Drive, and I-244, known as the Crosstown Expressway or M.L. King Jr. Expressway. These two roads join again on the east side of town.

US 75 runs north and south on the west side of town, while US 169 (Mingo Valley Expressway) runs north and south on the east side. Coming into town from the west, OK 51, becomes the Broken Arrow Expressway and runs from downtown southeast to Broken Arrow. The Creek Turnpike, off I-44, offers a quick route around the south and east sides of the city.

Check the Insiders' Tip for help navigating downtown. The logic of that system falls apart as you get away from the center of the city. People will tell you that numbered streets generally run east and west. And that's true—except when they don't! So they add directional numbers—except when they don't. And sometimes, they add two directions—but not combined, i.e., SW or NE.

Baseline streets are Main Street (which runs north and south) and Admiral Avenue (which runs east and west). Generally, numbered streets that go east and west will be called "Street." North/south streets are usually designated "Avenue." So you might see an address like East 41st St. South and you'll know it's an east/west street and that the address is east of Main Street and 41 blocks south of Admiral Avenue. South 79th East Ave. goes north and south, and is south of Admiral and 79 blocks east of Main. Or get a GPS and hope it can figure it out!

i To get around downtown, remember that from Main Street, parallel streets to the east are named alphabetically for cities east of the Mississippi—Boston, Cincinnati, Detroit, etc. From Main west, the streets are alphabetical west-of-the-Mississippi cities—Boulder, Cheyenne, Denver, etc. From the Frisco tracks south, the streets are numbered. North, they are named alphabetically for Tulsa pioneers—Archer, Brady, Cameron, etc.

AIRPORTS

HARVEY YOUNG AIRPORT
1419 S. 135th East Ave.
(918) 437-2877
Small, with one paved and one grass runway, Harvey Young is still a popular choice with some general-aviation customers for its convenience to Tulsa's east side. And you can fly into Harvey Young without flying into the Tulsa Air Traffic Control area. About 60 planes are based here. Mechanics and fuel are available but there are no courtesy shuttles. This is an intimate enough airport that if you fly in Monday through Friday, you still have a chance of catching a ride into town with someone; otherwise, you'll have to call a cab.

R.L. JONES/RIVERSIDE AIRPORT (RVS)
8605 S. Elwood Ave.
(918) 299-5886
www.tulsaairports.com
Surprisingly, this 700-acre airport is the fifth busiest general aviation airport in the nation. About 500 planes are based here, as are six flight schools. With 40 different tenants on-site, pilots will find a full range of services. There is no terminal; there are no rental cars, but courtesy cars are available. The airport is about 20 minutes from downtown Tulsa.

TULSA INTERNATIONAL AIRPORT (TUL)
7777 E. Apache St.
(918) 838-5000
www.tulsaairports.com
Just 5 miles northeast of downtown, Tulsa's main airport is an easy drive from anywhere in the city. Served by five carriers, the airport hosts about 3,200,000 travelers a year and sees approximately 130 arrivals and departures a day. Travelers can find connecting flights anywhere but can fly direct to 15 U.S. cities, including Atlanta, Chicago, Cincinnati, Dallas, Denver, Detroit, Houston, Los Angeles, Las Vegas, Memphis, Minneapolis/St. Paul, Newark, Phoenix, Salt Lake City, and St. Louis.

The airport includes a variety of food choices and even offers a couple of spots—The Great American Bagel Company and Starbucks—in the pre-security area.

There are children's play spots in waiting areas, a military and veterans' resource lounge, and two chair-massage stations post-security. Pre-security, there is a chair-massage station and the Hairport, a beauty and barber shop. If you should be changing planes here, you'll have to go in and out of security to take advantage of this service, but, for the majority of travelers, this is the final destination.

One of the nicest features is all of the seating areas available in the airport—great when that flight you're meeting is delayed. In the main lobby are display cases with interesting items from local museums or exhibits of historical artifacts from Tulsa's oil legacy. If the artifacts don't remind you of Tulsa's great debt to black gold, the 56-by-13-foot mural displaying a panorama of the petroleum industry from exploration to final distribution will. Colorfully painted by Del Jackson (1915–1982) it originally belonged to the Smithsonian Institution but was acquired by the Gilcrease Museum in 1997 and installed in the airport in 1998.

Eight car rental companies have operations at the airport: Alamo, Avis, Budget, Dollar, Enterprise, Hertz, National, and Thrifty. See contact information under Rental Cars.

Parking is no problem. The first half hour is free—a nice amenity for those who are picking someone up.

PUBLIC TRANSPORTATION

TULSA TRANSIT
(918) 585-1195
www.tulsatransit.org
Oklahomans cling to their cars—approximately 2 percent of Tulsans use public transportation. Although there are 20 bus routes that reach a

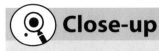

Close-up

Tulsa's First Airport

Duncan McIntyre is honored with the title "Father of Tulsa Aviation." New Zealander McIntyre arrived in Tulsa in 1919 and in 1923 created the city's first commercial airport, located about 2 miles from where Tulsa's International Airport now stands. It was one of the best natural airfields in the country and boasted several hangars and a lighted runway

McIntyre Airport hosted both the Ford Reliability Tour and Charles Lindbergh and his *Spirit of St. Louis* in 1927. Art Goebel, the pilot of the *Woolaroc,* which won the Dole Race from Oakland to Honolulu, flew into McIntyre Airport to see Lindbergh come in, the only time in history that the two ocean fliers, the *Spirit of St. Louis* and the *Woolaroc,* would be together on the same airfield.

A replica of McIntyre Airport is the subject of one of the exhibits at the Tulsa Air and Space Museum.

number of areas of town, the buses don't run on Sunday and the routes serving some of the most popular tourist attractions run infrequently. One route runs from downtown to the airport and is considerably less expensive than a taxi, but service is limited with about an hour between buses and no late evening or Sunday service.

Like many cities, Tulsa is looking at innovative ways to make public transportation useful and cost effective. Fares range from free for seniors 75 and over to $1.50 for adults and $2.50 for lift service. Day passes and multiple-ride passes are offered at reduced prices. The Tulsa Transit Authority is making great efforts to serve its customers with special programs like their Lift Program, curb-to-curb service for clients determined to be eligible for Americans with Disabilities (ADA) Paratransit. Call (918) 582-2100 or check the Web site for more information.

All Tulsa buses have bike racks that accommodate two or three bicycles. If the bike and ride program becomes too popular, that could be a problem, but for now it seems to be adequate. There's also a program for Tulsa residents to borrow bikes from the downtown Denver station, but an advance application must be filled out and filed.

In 2009, stimulus funds enabled the transit system to replace a number of their big buses and all of their Lift Program minibuses with vehicles that run on compressed natural gas

(CNG). This change alone is estimated to cut 320,000 pounds of pollutants from the air. The savings won't be noticed immediately because delivery times on the CNG vehicles can be as long as two years.

> **i** Looking for a tour of town? Alice Foreschle (fresh-lee) has been conducting group tours of Tulsa and the surrounding area since 1987. The maximum-size group is 25, but she will do smaller groups, even families. The price is calculated by the hour. Check her Web site at www.bandanatours.com or call (918) 760-7783.

BUSES AND TRAINS

GREYHOUND BUS TERMINAL
317 S. Detroit St.
(918) 584-3713
Greyhound buses connect with most U.S. cities, but the most popular route is from Tulsa to Oklahoma City. The company offers six trips a day, both ways.

There's no direct passenger rail service from Tulsa; in fact, the only passenger line in Oklahoma runs from Oklahoma City to Fort Worth, Texas. Amtrak provides bus service that connects with the Oklahoma City station, but the hours are so inconvenient—leaving Tulsa very early and returning very late—that few people use it.

i The YIELD sign was invented by Tulsa policeman Clinton Riggs. The first sign, which read YIELD RIGHT OF WAY, was installed in 1950 at the intersection of South Columbia Avenue and East 1st St. In six months the intersection dropped from being the most dangerous in Tulsa to seventh most dangerous. The idea quickly spread across the country and eventually across the world.

TAXIS, RENTAL CARS, AND LIMOUSINES

There are a number of taxi services in town, though several are allied with one another. Rates vary from company to company and can make a difference of several dollars on a trip of 10 miles, so ask about rates before you commit. Some companies add bag charges. Most of the companies take credit cards. A trip from the airport to downtown Tulsa will cost approximately $25.

While you can easily catch a cab at the airport, Tulsa isn't a place where you can expect to hail a cab on the street. Call ahead and give yourself plenty of time. Some of Tulsa's companies include: Yellow/Checker, (918) 582-6161; American/Executive/City, (918) 582-8294; and Tulsa Airport Taxi, (918) 834-2400.

Rental car companies include:
- Alamo
  (800) 462-5266 or (918) 835-8673
  www.alamo.com
- Avis
  (800) 352-7900 or (918) 838-5148
  www.avis.com
- Budget
  (800) 527-0700 or (918) 836-3761
  www.budget.com
- Dollar
  (800) 800-3665 or (918) 838-5236
  www.dollar.com
- Enterprise
  (800) 264-6350 or (918) 832-1818
  www.enterprise.com
- Hertz
  (800) 654-4173 or (918) 838-1015
  www.hertz.com
- National
  (800) 227-7368 or (918) 838-3372
  www.nationalcar.com
- Thrifty
  (800) 847-4389 or (877) 283-0898
  www.thrifty.com

Most of these companies also have phone numbers for other offices in different parts of town.

Limousine services for either business or pleasure include:
- First Class Limousine
  (918) 610-5466
  www.firstclasslimotulsa.com
- Galaxy Limousine and Executive Charter
  (918) 481-3374
  www.galaxy-limo.com
- Oil Capital Coach
  (918) 794-9009
  www.oilcapitalcoach.com
- VIP Limousine
  (918) 492-5984
  www.viplimo.net

i For time, temperature, and the weather forecast, call (918) 743-3311.

BICYCLES

There are people who bicycle to work in Tulsa. They are very brave. While there are lots of places to ride recreationally, bicycling as an alternative form of transportation is in its infancy here. But it is on the radar screen, and according to city councilman Bill Martinson, "Our goal is to ensure that there is a long-term perspective when looking at infrastructure that includes alternative modes of transportation like bicycles." So keep your helmets handy.

Although there are only a few areas in town where bike lanes are marked on the pavement, a number of routes, 41 miles in all, have been designated as bicycle routes. These routes utilize less-busy surface streets. For maps, go to www.incog.org/transportation/trails.htm. Of course, almost all routes are, technically, bicycle routes but not all motorists appreciate that. A lot of education is necessary and it's important to remember to ride safely and keep in mind that you're more vulnerable than the driver of an automobile.

But there are bright spots. One of the downtown churches offers shower facilities for those not having access to showers at their places of employment. One of the major downtown employers not only provides showers and lockers but also free, garaged bike parking. Tulsa is making such a big effort to go green, expect to see more accommodations made for bicyclists.

For information about bike trails and recreational biking, check the Outdoors chapter.

HISTORY

It is what it is—except when it isn't. History is subjective—the story of happenings from differing points of view. This is a quick look at over 150 years of Tulsa history. You'll get a condensed version of how the city grew from a small Indian settlement to a modern metropolis.

Like the history of our country, there were bumps along the way. When times were tough, Tulsans were tougher. And neighbor helping neighbor has always been a way of life here.

Tulsa, both past and present, has been blessed with visionaries. That's why, today, Tulsa is moving forward with green initiatives and concern for the environment, promoting responsible development, continuing its unwavering support of the arts, embracing diversity, and making the city a great place to live.

EARLY DAYS

Most people, even most Oklahomans, think of Oklahoma as a new state. It wasn't admitted to the union until 1907, but a lot of history happened before that.

In the beginning were the Indians. The area was home to Native American tribes, some with permanent villages and others with temporary camps as they followed seasonal cycles. Coronado came through in 1541 and planted the Spanish flag.

The British king Charles II, ignoring the Spanish claim, awarded the colony of Carolina to some of his noblemen in 1663. His definition of that colony included a belt of land, the width of the present states of North and South Carolina, stretching from the Atlantic Ocean to the Pacific—including present-day Oklahoma.

British and Spanish claims notwithstanding, the French explorer Robert de LaSalle claimed for his country all the lands drained by the Mississippi—again including Oklahoma. The first recorded Frenchman actually to visit the area was Bernard de la Harpe in 1719. The French ceded their claim to Spain in 1762; the Spanish gave it back in 1800, and in 1803 Napoleon, who needed money for his wars in Europe, sold the Louisiana Territory to the United States. That purchase encompassed all of the present state of Oklahoma. The Oklahoma panhandle went back to Spain later, but that's another region and another story.

One of the tasks of the Lewis and Clark expedition was to determine how many Indians lived in the territory and where they were concentrated. President Thomas Jefferson understood the movement of westward expansion and knew that it would not stop. He was, of course, right.

By 1808 plans were made to begin moving Native Americans out of their homes and relocating them in a "colonization zone" in the Louisiana Purchase lands. Pioneers moved faster than the government, however, and the area reserved for the Indians became smaller and smaller. By 1830 the reserve consisted of lands between the Red River (Oklahoma's southern border) and the Platt River in Nebraska. By 1854 only the Oklahoma portion remained. Between 1820 and 1880, approximately 60 tribes were moved into the area, joining the indigenous Osages, Caddoes, Kiowas, Comanches, Wichitas, and Quapaws.

The government succeeded, by hook or by crook and treaties not worth the paper they were written on, in persuading a number of Indians to migrate on their own. Recalcitrant groups were moved forcibly. The Cherokees termed their forced march *Nunna daul Tsuny,* or "Trail Where They Cried," but Trail of Tears could refer to any of the numerous removals.

In the 1820s some of the Creeks began arriving in Oklahoma, and by 1830 approximately 300 lived near Broken Arrow, a present-day Tulsa suburb. Among the later arrivals, survivors of their Trail of Tears, a small group of Lochapoka Creeks traveled up the Arkansas, stopping on a rise above a river bend. There, beneath an oak tree, they, as was their tradition, rekindled embers they had brought from their Alabama home. The name "Tallassee" or "Tallasi" was attached to the settlement, though whether by the Creeks themselves or by agents of the government is not certain. Neither is it settled whether it was the Creeks or whites struggling with the pronunciation who began calling the community "Tulsee Town." The word *tul* in Creek means "town." The name later morphed into "Tulsa."

The Creeks settled in and built their town and farms. The area was almost exclusively Indian. An exception was the presence of white missionaries who had come to work with the Creeks and establish missions.

One of the earliest arriving Creek families, coming in 1828, was the family of Benjamin Perryman. He settled with his family near Muskogee. The Perrymans had been prominent and prosperous in their Alabama community. In 1848 Lewis Perryman, one of Benjamin's sons, and his family moved to the Tallasi settlement.

All was well with the Creeks, but the coming Civil War would prove disastrous. A number of Creeks, particularly those who held slaves, allied with the Confederacy. As was the case in many areas, families were split in their loyalties.

In the end, it really made no difference who was on which side. The fact that any of the Indians fought against the Union was all the excuse the government needed for reneging on treaties that promised the Indians that the land would belong to them "as long as the grass grows or the water runs...." The Perrymans and other Creeks who were able to return to Tallasi found their homes and property destroyed. They rebuilt homes but nothing would be the same, and while technically still Indian Territory, the population was looking whiter and whiter.

In March of 1879, the U.S. government designated the house belonging to George Perryman, one of Lewis's sons, as the Tulsa Post Office, thereby settling the question of the name once and for all. George's brother Josiah served as the city's first postmaster. At one time, a good portion of the area that is now the city of Tulsa belonged to members of the Perryman family.

The railroad arrived in 1882 and railroad workers set up a tent city on a site just a couple of miles from the original Creek town. Through intermarriage, federal fiat, shady leasing agreements, and just plain chicanery, the Indians were losing more land, more rights, and more of their way of life.

Entrepreneurs moved in to provide services for the railroad workers. Sources differ on details. One story posits that brothers James and Harry Hall were among those employed by the railroad to supervise construction. Because there were no places to buy supplies between Vinita and Tallasi, James maintained a small stock of necessities, which he sold from a tent that he moved as the construction crew moved.

In another version, Harry traveled with the railroad, selling needed items to the workers, but the brothers were not railroad employees.

The railroad was scheduled to take a slightly northern route into Cherokee territory. Cherokees did not allow anyone who was not an Indian, or the spouse of an Indian, to do business in their territory. Creek laws were more lenient. It is said that Harry persuaded the railroad company to change the route to the south and Creek land.

At any rate, the rails went south and Tulsa was then the end of the line. The Hall brothers got a license to trade with the Indians. James opened one of Tulsa's first mercantile stores and Harry was given the soubriquet "Father of Tulsa."

The Halls weren't the only businessmen to see a future in the little settlement. Cattle became big business and Tulsa was a preferred shipping point to the hungry markets in the East. Merchants and other types of purveyors found the cowboys and railroad workers as profitable a clientele as the Indians.

Over the next few years, Tulsa was as wild as any western cow town. Outlaws and thieves like the Doolins and the Daltons were frequent visitors. But a more reputable portion of the population was also growing. Churches and schools were being established. .

The cow town was starting to feel like a city and was incorporated on January 18, 1898. Tulsa was on its way, on a path of broken promises, to becoming an oil boomtown and, in less than a century, a major metropolitan area.

OIL CAPITAL OF THE WORLD

The first oil strike in the area occurred on June 24, 1901, across the river from Tulsa in Red Fork. Though a small well, it caught the attention of the press and brought speculators and workers to the area. Like the San Franciscan who never prospected for gold but made a fortune selling shovels to miners, Tulsans profited from the boom by supplying services to the incipient oil industry. James Hall was one of the prime movers in organizing the Tulsa Commercial Club, which later became the chamber of commerce.

With the 1905 discovery of the Glenn Pool, south of Tulsa, the boom became an explosion! Derricks sprang up like weeds and the ground was soaked with oily residue. Tulsans, meanwhile, kept their town tidy and their banks busy. Tulsa became headquarters for oil companies large and small, and Tulsa businessmen and entrepreneurs were involved in all facets of the industry from exploration to export.

In the meantime, western parts of Oklahoma were opening to settlement, several sections with land runs, others with lotteries. Oklahoma was now divided into two sections, Oklahoma Territory and Indian Territory. Leaders of both of the Twin Territories, as they were called, met and drafted a state constitution, which was ratified by a vote of the people on September 17, 1907. On November 16 the Oklahoma statehood proclamation was signed by President Theodore Roosevelt.

Tulsa, occupied with its burgeoning fortunes, was busy touting the town to all who would listen. And with the growing importance of oil, lots of folks were listening. People with names like Mellon and Rockefeller, oilmen like Harry Sinclair, William Skelly, and Jean Paul Getty, and companies like Standard Oil and Royal Dutch/ Shell Group were coming to town.

Oklahoma's oil history is full of great stories of down-and-outers who struck oil and became up-and-comers overnight. A favorite is the story of Tom Slick, a wildcatter with such a poor record his nickname was "Dry Hole." He lost that moniker in February 1912 when he discovered the Cushing Field—at that time the world's largest and richest find. Again Tulsa, with its business base and oil acumen, cashed in.

By the late '20s, Tulsa was home to 1,500 companies involved in the oil industry and sat in the center of a region that supplied two-thirds of the nation's oil. Its downtown sported high-rises and embraced modernity with then–avant garde art deco embellishments.

DIFFICULT DAYS

It's a little-known fact that following the Native Americans, African Americans were the next group of permanent settlers in Oklahoma. Several of the Five Civilized Tribes were slave owners and brought African Americans with them on their trek west. Following the Civil War, many of the black freedmen stayed in the area. Following the opening of Oklahoma for settlement, many black southerners came to the area seeking new opportunities. More than twenty all-black towns were established in Oklahoma.

As Tulsa grew, so did its black community. On the surface, things looked rosy. In 1911 Tulsa even had a black policeman. There were a number of black-owned businesses along Greenwood Avenue, a black school, and a black newspaper.

But by 1921 there were two Tulsas—one for whites and one for blacks. With an expanding black population—about 11,000—black businesses were thriving. The community was well served by black lawyers and doctors; there were two theaters, three fraternal lodges, two newspapers, and a public library. The business corridor along Greenwood was dubbed "Black Wall Street" for the order and prosperity found there.

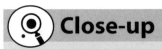 **Close-up**

Recovery and Reconciliation in Greenwood

It would be comforting to think that, like the Phoenix, the Greenwood community was resurrected more vibrant than before, but it wasn't. The citizens did rebuild but many left. By the 1950s, the Crosstown Expressway cut across part of the community and cast a noisy shadow on the area. But there were, and are still, strong leaders in Greenwood. There are thriving businesses, along with the campuses of Oklahoma State University–Tulsa and Langston University–Tulsa, in the area.

For decades, students studying Oklahoma history learned little about the 1921 riot. Finally, in 1997 the Oklahoma Legislature established the Oklahoma Commission to Study the Tulsa Race Riot of 1921. Their mandate was to locate survivors of the race riot; interview witnesses, gather information, and study documents to develop an accurate (as accurate as possible) historical record of the event; and to make recommendations that would lead to reconciliation and healing.

Several of the recommendations have been implemented with varying degrees of success. A scholarship program for children of families affected by the riot was short-lived. The Greenwood Area Redevelopment Authority was established. The legislature allotted a sum of money to build the John Hope Franklin Reconciliation Park.

Future plans include the John Hope Franklin Reconciliation Center, a venue for study, research, and dialog on divisive issues. A number of universities—including Oklahoma State University, Langston, Duke, the University of Chicago, and North Carolina Central (local schools and those associated with Dr. Franklin)—will cooperate on the project.

Greenwood and the Tulsa Race Riot are also being assessed by the National Park Service for inclusion as a possible national historic landmark or historic area.

All that ended on May 30, 1921. A young shoeshine boy, Dick Rowland, was taking an elevator to reach one of the few "colored" restrooms available downtown. He stumbled and bumped the elevator operator, a 17-year-old white girl named Sarah Page. One later report says he stepped on her sore toe. What actually happened is not known, but the combination of a screaming white girl and a fleeing black man was instantly interpreted as attempted rape. Dick was identified and arrested the next morning.

By Tuesday, newspaper articles spread the story and there were rumors of an attempt to lynch Rowland. A white crowd began growing around the courthouse and a small group of black citizens, fearing for Rowland, went, armed, to the courthouse to offer the sheriff assistance in defending the place. They were assured that all was well in hand and they went back to Greenwood.

Some members of the white crowd, upon seeing armed blacks, went to their homes to retrieve guns and recruit their neighbors. The Tulsa National Guard commander was distressed by the situation and ordered his men to the armory. There they held off part of a group that was trying to break in to steal weapons. The adjutant general of the National Guard and the governor, both in Oklahoma City, were alerted. The Tulsa police chief, John Gustafson, downplayed the problem.

By now, the white crowd had swelled to nearly 2,000 people. The black community was tense and nervous, and another contingent, this time between 50 and 75 black men, returned to the courthouse and again offered to help. Again, they were refused. As they turned to leave, a scuffle ensued and shots were fired.

This was the opening salvo in one of Oklahoma's darkest and most shameful moments.

Although shooting was short-lived, 20 people, both black and white, were wounded or killed in this first melee. The outnumbered blacks beat a hasty retreat

More were injured or killed on their way back across the tracks. Cars of whites drove through the streets firing on any black they saw.

Throughout the night there was sporadic fighting. The first fires in the Greenwood District were set around 1 a.m. When firemen responded, they were waved away by white arsonists.

Martial law was declared at 3 a.m. One hundred and nine National Guardsmen from Oklahoma City arrived in Tulsa by train the next morning. By the time they organized, the majority of Greenwood's black residents had fled and two-thirds of their community had been burned. Perpetrators included not only mob members but, often, the authorities who should have been protecting Tulsa's black citizenry.

Shortly after noon, the state troops (Oklahoma National Guard) arrived in the Greenwood District and began disarming whites and sending them out of the embattled area. Other troops were rounding up any blacks they could find and herding them into internment areas, leaving the ruined community with no defenders. Businesses and homes that hadn't been looted and burned were easy prey.

While the mob ruled, there were still some people who failed to go along with the crowd. Some Tulsans hid black employees from roaming bullies. The Red Cross also had a major presence both in treating injuries during the riot and in relief efforts after.

By the end of the riot, 35 blocks of the Greenwood area were destroyed—the entire business district and 70 percent of the residential area. Approximately 1,256 buildings were burned and another 314 buildings, including 215 residences, were looted but not burned.

After the violence ended, a grand jury was convened. When members of a blue-ribbon panel, commissioned by the Oklahoma Legislature in 1997, studied the riot, they discovered that none of the criminal acts—murder, arson, looting—"was then or ever has been prose-cuted or punished by government at any level, municipal, county, state, or federal." Insurance companies denied claims. The exact number of human victims will never be known. Thirty-eight victims were identified but the actual number is estimated to be much higher.

And what happened to Dick Rowland? Sarah Page refused to prosecute and the charges were dropped.

It has been over three-quarters of a century since these events occurred. There is still much controversy over the "facts." Even commission members disagreed on a number of points. Few people remain who remember the actual event. The population in 1921 was about 70,000. Today Tulsa has over five times that many people, many of whom moved to Tulsa with no knowledge of the riot. The building of the John Hope Franklin Reconciliation Park is as much a monument to what the community is now as an acknowledgement of what happened then.

PLANES, TRAINS, AND AUTOMOBILES

The coming of the railroad had transformed transportation in the West. It was faster and easier to take the train than the wagon trains or stagecoaches of earlier times. But the automobile was becoming less of a novelty and more of a necessity and the nation turned its attention to roads.

And no one was more committed to establishing a system of interconnected roads to cross the nation than Tulsan Cyrus Avery. Elected president of the Associated Highways Association of America in 1921, in 1923 he was appointed Oklahoma state highway commissioner. As a leader in the American Association of State Highway Officials, he was involved in a 1924 petition to the U.S. secretary of agriculture requesting action on the design of a network of interstate highways.

Avery was one of the most influential participants in studying the various roads and determining which were most logical to tie into a major highway system. And that's how Route 66—the Mother Road—was born. And, thanks to Avery, that road went through Tulsa.

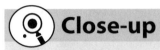

Close-up

John Hope Franklin (Jan 2, 1915–Mar 25, 2009)

John Hope Franklin, one of the nation's most respected authors, educators, and civil rights leaders, was born in Rentiesville, one of Oklahoma's historic black towns. His father, B. C. Franklin, was one of the first black lawyers in Oklahoma; his mother was a schoolteacher and community leader.

B. C. Franklin moved to Tulsa in 1921 to establish his practice and he expected his family to join him at the end of the school year. The riot destroyed those plans—along with B. C.'s office and all his belongings. It was four years before the family was living together again.

Franklin graduated from Tulsa's Booker T. Washington High School, valedictorian of his class. He planned to study law but was inspired by a professor at Fisk University to pursue a career in history. After receiving a Bachelor's Degree at Fisk, he earned both his master's degree and doctorate at Harvard.

His 1947 book, *From Slavery to Freedom: A History of African-Americans,* now in its eighth printing, is considered the definitive text on the black experience. In the '50s he helped prepare Thurgood Marshall's brief that led to the *Brown v. Board of Education* decision.

In his lifetime he received more than 130 honorary degrees and countless other honors. President Bill Clinton appointed him chairman of his Initiative on Race. He also received the Presidential Medal of Honor, the highest civilian award given by the U.S. government.

The Reconciliation Park in the Greenwood District is named in his honor.

In 1919, Duncan McIntyre, a dark-haired, pencil-mustached pilot from New Zealand, came to Tulsa. He saw that airplanes were already being used by oilmen to shuttle parts and people to the oil fields and he decided there was a future here for him. Operating his own airport, he hosted notables like Charles Lindbergh. The Ford Reliability Tour, established in 1925 to promote "commercial aviation as a means of transportation," stopped at McIntyre Airport in 1927. While complimentary of McIntyre's facility, representatives emphasized the importance of a municipal airport for the city's future.

Oilman William Skelly, who, like McIntyre, had arrived in Tulsa in 1919, also developed an interest in airplanes. He bought out a small company that was producing a plane called the Spartan C3. He was among the leaders who built the first municipal airport in Tulsa in 1928. Skelly moved his business, Spartan Aircraft Company, close to the new airport, and later founded the Spartan School of Aeronautics.

i In 2008 the aerospace industry in northeast Oklahoma contributed $3.3 billion to the economy. Over 300 companies provided 32,000 jobs and an annual payroll of $960 million.

Although the Depression of the '30s hit the rest of the country hard, Tulsa fared better than most cities. A number of business indicators showed Tulsa's economy to be sound—in 1935, *Forbes* magazine named Tulsa as one of the best U.S. cities for real estate sales. By 1937, R. L. Polk listed Tulsa as having the highest per-capita buying power among 153 cities surveyed. Still, when oil prices tanked, several of Tulsa's oil millionaires did, too. Even though Tulsa was still the Oil Capital of the World, larger fields had been discovered in Texas and California. The danger of an economy built on one industry was not lost on the locals.

As the political situation in Europe became strained, Tulsa's entrance into the aircraft industry paid off. On May 2, 1941, ground was broken for

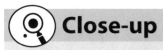 **Close-up**

Waite Phillips (1883–1964)

One of 10 children, Waite Phillips was the youngest of the Phillips brothers who became Oklahoma oil millionaires. Waite's oldest brother, Frank, came to Indian Territory in the early 1900s. Frank had begun his working career as a barber, but after marrying a banker's daughter, began a banking career. Attending the 1904 World's Fair in St. Louis, he ran into an acquaintance who convinced him that oil discoveries in Indian Territory offered rich opportunity. By 1905 Frank and his family had moved to Bartlesville. His brother Lee (L. E.) and his wife followed soon after. Another brother, Ed, had moved to Okmulgee to work in a savings and loan company.

Waite, 10 years younger than Frank, was a twin. He and his brother Wiate had been practically inseparable. At 16, the boys left the family home in Iowa to search for adventure. Over the next two years, they traveled through most of the western states, parts of Canada, the Midwest, and Indian Territory. They worked at whatever jobs they could find—farming, mining, trapping, working on the railroad. They were in Spokane, Washington, working at a hotel, when Wiate began complaining of stomach pains. It was appendicitis. He underwent surgery at a local hospital, but peritonitis had set in and Wiate died.

Waite returned to Iowa, lost without his twin. His older brothers were anxious to help their 19-year-old brother, who took a job as a grocery clerk. Unbeknownst to Waite, the brothers were actually paying his salary. Later, Waite decided to return to school and enrolled in a business college. Upon graduation, he began work as a bookkeeper at a nearby coal company where his brother L. E. was manager and a stockholder. He held a position there until the coal reserves were depleted and the company went out of business.

In the meantime, Frank had moved to Bartlesville, to be joined later by L. E. Together they formed a company, bought oil leases, and were doing well. They encouraged their younger brother to join them. Frank made it clear that Waite would have to start at the bottom. Waite worked with his brothers for a number of years, learning the oil business literally from under the ground up. He and his brother Frank were both strong characters and eventually Waite decided to go out on his own. The parting was amicable, and later Waite merged his company with Phillips Petroleum.

Successful in business, Waite was able to spend more time on real estate and charitable works. He owned a large ranch in New Mexico and was a big supporter of the Boy Scouts. In 1938, Genevieve and Waite Phillips announced their intention to give their 10-year-old residence, Philbrook, to the city of Tulsa to be used as an art museum. Later that year they gave their New Mexico ranch, Philmont, and Tulsa's Philtower to the Boy Scouts.

Waite and his wife had often enjoyed stays in California, and over the next few years Phillips concluded business and tied up loose ends so that by late 1944, the family was ready to make a permanent move. The Phillips lived in Bel Air until Waite's death at age 81. Genevieve lived in the home 15 more years. She died at age 92 in 1979. Although the Phillips are buried in California, a beautiful reminder, Philbrook, stands in Tulsa as a monument to their generosity.

a bomber plant to be located in Tulsa and operated by the Douglas Aircraft Company.

Tulsa would go on to produce planes for World War II, the Korean War, and the Vietnam War. It would also play an important role in America's space program, producing components for several rockets, parts for the Space Shuttle, and even large pieces of the International Space Station. Tulsa aviation workers have been servicing American Airlines equipment since the 1940s, and by 2009 the maintenance facility employees numbered in the thousands.

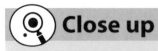

Close up

Thomas Gilcrease (1890–1962)

Thomas Gilcrease's parents came to Indian Territory to receive land through the government's Indian Nations allotment program. His father was French and Scotch-Irish; his mother, one-quarter Creek Indian, made them eligible. Thomas received 160 acres of land south of Tulsa—land that was located atop the rich oil reserve to be named the Glenn Pool.

At the age of 18, Gilcrease married Belle Harlow, a member of the Osage tribe. They had two children. By the age of 21, Gilcrease was a millionaire. In 1914 Gilcrease purchased a home—a modest sandstone residence that still stands on the museum grounds.

He had purchased his first painting, *Rural Courtship* by Ridgeway Knight, in 1912. Though he lacked much formal schooling, he read widely, and in 1925 made his first trip to Europe. Visiting many of the world's great museums, his love of art became a passion.

His first marriage ended in divorce in 1926, and Gilcrease remarried in 1928—this time to a former Miss Tulsa and Miss America, 1926. They had one child, a daughter, before that marriage failed.

Gilcrease began expanding his collection at an accelerated pace—buying not only individual works but whole collections. The accumulation grew to approximately 10,000 works of art, 250,000 artifacts, and nearly 100,000 rare books.

By 1954 he found himself in a financial bind—his debts exceeded his readily available capital. Selling his art collection seemed like the only way out of his predicament. Buyers, including major art museums and universities, were salivating at the prospect of picking up the amazing assemblage. The solution to his problem provided a cultural windfall for Tulsa. A deal was worked out where funds to pay Gilcrease's debts would be covered by money raised by a bond issue and the museum would go to the city of Tulsa.

For the next eight years, until his death, Thomas Gilcrease continued to live in the sandstone home adjacent to the museum. As his financial picture improved, he continued to collect art and artifacts, which, upon his death, were added to the museum collection.

Thomas Gilcrease's love of art and interest in history was practically a lifelong passion. His legacy continues to enrich the life of the city he called home.

i Two of Tulsa's smallest parks are at West 18th St. and South Cheyenne Avenue—the Creek Council Oak site on the north side of West 18th St. and the Creek Stickball Park on the south side.

AND NOW FOR THE REST OF THE STORY

Through the '20s and '30s, prosperous Tulsans had taken pretty good care of themselves. They built beautiful mansions in landscaped neighborhoods and even founded a country club. The downtown skyline was punctuated with impressive buildings. New Deal programs added amenities like the Municipal Rose Garden and architectural gems including the Union Depot and the Fire Alarm Building.

Waite Phillips, one of the band of brothers that spawned Phillips 66, was successful in his own right with his own oil company. He built a palatial Italian-style villa, called Villa Philbrook, south of town and surrounded it with landscaped gardens. In 1938 he donated the home to the City of Tulsa, to become the Philbrook Art Museum.

Another oilman, Thomas Gilcrease, had a passion for American art and history and had begun a collection of art, artifacts, and documents related to these subjects. He had so many items, he built his own museum. Gilcrease spent money about as fast as he made it, and by the

1950s he was in a financial bind. The City of Tulsa passed a bond issue and purchased Gilcrease's museum, giving Tulsa two major art institutions.

By the late '40s, Tulsa had a professional symphony and an opera company to add to the luster of the local culture. Oklahoma-born dancer Moscelyne Larkin and her husband, Roman Jasinski, both formerly with the Ballet Russe de Monte Carlo, returned to Tulsa to raise their son and to open a ballet studio. They founded the Tulsa Civic Ballet (now called Tulsa Ballet). Civic groups worked on public health issues and improving Tulsa's infrastructure.

But there was still one barrier to becoming a great city—segregation. Tulsa, indeed the whole state, was solidly segregated. Oklahoma's constitution, Article XIII, Section 3, stated, "Separate schools for white and colored children with like accommodations shall be provided…." The concept of "separate but equal" had been established in 1896 by the U.S. Supreme Court's *Plessy v. Ferguson* decision.

Following the 1954 U.S. Supreme Court case *Brown v. Board of Education of Topeka, KS.*, Tulsa was ordered to integrate its public schools. It was a drawn-out process with several attempts before the school system, in 1972, arrived at an innovative magnet school concept that has created new opportunities for all students. It's also true that a number of suburban school systems grew much larger during this time.

Oil remains an important element in Tulsa's economy, in spite of the fact that many of the oil companies have moved their headquarters to other cities. The Golden Driller still stands on the Fairgrounds, a monumental reminder that Tulsa was the home of the International Petroleum Exposition. Held in Tulsa from the1920s through the 1970s, it was the largest single-industry trade show in the world.

In the last decade, Tulsa's business and community leaders have devoted themselves to planning for a bright future. Citizen involvement is a large component of these initiatives. The city has weathered trials and tornadoes and seen the economy rise and fall, but the enduring spirit that was kindled with the embers of the Lochapoka tribal fire, the entrepreneurial spirit that arrived with the cowboys and wildcatters, the daring spirit that soared with the air industry, and the noble spirit that produced beautiful buildings, parks, and art collections—that spirit still lives on in Tulsa.

ACCOMMODATIONS

Tulsa is a great place to visit, and you need to stay long enough to get a feel for the city. That means spending the night—or two, three, or four. Listings here include economy accommodations to high-end stays. The delightful thing is that Tulsa's highest-end stays are moderate compared to other cities—and they're every bit as good, if not better, than facilities in much larger metropolises.

The way Tulsa is situated on the river, almost everything you'll want to do will be located in the area east of the river and south of I-244—the southeast quadrant of town—so that's where most of the accommodations listed will be located. Tulsa's a safe place to visit, but as in any large city, some areas have more problems with vandalism than others. It's easy to get from one side of town to the other, so choosing your stay by price and amenities rather than specific location may be the way to go. Bed-and-breakfast establishments follow the hotel listings. Several RV parks are listed at the end of the chapter.

OVERVIEW

As you look through the listings, here are some basics to remember. Most accommodations offer both smoking and nonsmoking rooms. The issue will be mentioned only if the facility is nonsmoking. Assume that parking is easily available at no charge. A few accommodations allow pets—we'll be sure to let you know which ones do, whether or not a deposit is required, and if so, if it is refundable.

Today almost all accommodations are wheelchair accessible—exceptions include historic buildings and some bed-and-breakfasts. If an establishment has added aids like roll-in showers or devices for hearing-impaired guests, we'll note that.

Many travelers feel more comfortable with accommodations with interior halls and entrances. If only outside access is available, it will be stated in the write-up.

The listings include a variety of types of accommodations, from basic to luxurious, in a wide range of prices from economy to money is no object. You'll find motels, hotels, bed-and-breakfast establishments, a resort hotel with casino, and even a ranch with authentic Indian tepees.

Price Code

The price code reflects the average cost of a double-occupancy room during the peak price period. Always ask if any special discounts are available.

$	Less than $75
$$	$76 to $125
$$$	$126 to $175
$$$$	$176 to $225
$$$$$	$226 and up

HOTELS

AMBASSADOR HOTEL $$$$-$$$$$
1324 S. Main St.
(918) 587-8200, (888) 408-8282
www.hotelambassador-tulsa.com

This historic honey is where Tulsa's oil millionaires hung their hats while their palatial mansions were being built. Walking into the lobby is like walking into the elegant living area of an Italian palazzo—richly draped, tall windows, a beamed ceiling with chandeliers, fresh flowers, wood wainscoting, a fireplace, and a tile floor warmed by an Oriental-pattern area rug. Comfortable chairs and sofas add a homey touch.

There are 55 guest rooms including 8 suites, all with amenities too numerous to mention—luxurious linens, laptop-size safes, coffeemakers, robes, flat-screen TVs, lighted, magnifying makeup mirrors, hair dryers, complimentary WiFi, and a fitness center, to name a few. Complimentary airport, midtown, and downtown shuttle service in a Cadillac Escalade or Lincoln Town Car is available from early morning until late evening. Guests can pick up the *Tulsa World, USA Today,* and the *Journal Record,* a local business paper, at the front desk. One of the hotel's strongest draws is the attentive staff, who will make extraordinary efforts to see that guests' requests are satisfied. The award-winning hotel restaurant, The Chalkboard, (see Continental and Fine Dining under Restaurants), serves breakfast, lunch, and dinner every day. Pets are welcome at no extra charge. In addition, the comfortable Hurley Library, named for the hotel's founder, provides a quiet place for reading or complimentary computer access.

A native Oklahoman, Major General Patrick Hurley served as secretary of war under President Herbert Hoover and as ambassador to China under Franklin Roosevelt. He opened the 10-story, Mediterranean-style Ambassador Apartment Hotel in 1929. After 1949 the hotel had a series of owners and finally closed in 1987. Reopening the hotel in 1999, the new owners captured the elegance of a bygone era and added the modern conveniences travelers expect. The Ambassador, a nonsmoking establishment, is a member of the Historic Hotels of America.

BAYMONT INN & SUITES $
4530 E. Skelly Dr.
(918) 488-8777
www.baymontinns.com
With easy access off the Interstate, the Baymont Inn provides the basics at a bare-bones price. The 101 rooms range from standards with a king or two double beds to a two-room suite. Each room has a coffeemaker, hair dryer, and an iron and ironing board. The suites and some standard rooms have fridges and microwaves. *USA Today* is available at a rack in the lobby. A continental breakfast plus make-your-own waffles gets your

day off to a good start. Activity areas include an outdoor pool and a fitness center and, for activity of a more mundane sort, a guest laundry. The Baymont is pet friendly at no extra charge.

BEST WESTERN TULSA INN AND SUITES $$
3212 S. 79th East Ave.
(918) 858-2100
www.bestwestern.com
Of the 62 rooms here, 13 of them are suites. Most suites have one king-size bed and a sofa bed. The Jacuzzi suites have one king-size bed. Children under 12 are free; older children and extra adults in the room will be charged extra. All the rooms have coffeemakers, fridges microwaves, irons and ironing boards, and hair dryers. The newspaper is free in the lobby. The hotel is proud of its breakfast bar—cereals and breads, plus meats, eggs, and a waffle maker. The indoor pool is tiny. There's a fitness center and business center, guest laundry, and airport transportation. They'd really prefer that you leave your pets at home, but ask, because they may make an exception for small, caged animals—with an extra charge. The staff is friendly and helpful and the location is excellent—handy to major highways and next door to Ruby Tuesday's if you want to walk to dinner.

COMFORT SUITES TULSA CENTRAL $$
8039 E. 33rd St.
(918) 622-6300, (877) 424-6423
www.comfortsuites.com/hotel-tulsa-oklahoma-OK109
The manager touts this property as offering "all the amenities you want without paying for those you don't." And she could be right. All the rooms are suites; pay a little more and it gets even sweeter. In the standard rooms, about half have one king bed and sitting area with sofa bed. There are also Jacuzzi suites and executive suites. The executive suites have an ample kitchen area with a two-burner cooktop, a full-size refrigerator, a microwave, coffeemaker, and a dishwasher. There's a small dining table and a desk—all the comforts of home without having to mow the lawn.

All the other suites have coffeemakers, fridges, microwaves, ironing boards and irons, hair dryers,

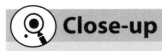 **Close-up**

McBirney Mansion

Washington slept here—no, not that one—Washington Irving. Local legend has it—and there's a good case to be made—that on his tour of the prairies, Washington Irving camped at the spring on the grounds of what is today the McBirney Mansion. If he didn't camp here, chances are still good that his group stopped to water their animals. The spring, close to the banks of the Arkansas River, was a well-known spot to local Indian tribes. Time and construction have lessened the flow of the springs—now all you see are two small, attractive ponds on the grounds of the grand manor.

In the 1920s the land was purchased by James H. McBirney, whose family had immigrated to the United States from Ireland when James was a young boy. He began his working career as a bookkeeper, but he had an affinity for baseball. Having worked for two banks in Kansas, he moved to Tulsa in 1897 to work at Tulsa Banking Company and to pitch for Tulsa's first baseball team. He eventually became vice president of the bank and later, with his brother, started his own bank, the Bank of Commerce.

In 1927 construction began on his mansion, which stands on a rise above the Arkansas. The architects for the project were Biollot and Lauch of Kansas City, with John Long Company of Kansas City doing the actual construction. The end result was a 12,000-square-foot, brick and stone home variously described as Tudor Gothic or Gothic Revival. As with many homes of the period, it's an eclectic blend of a lot of things. Outstanding features of the home include stained-glass elements, beautiful woodwork, a slate roof, and, of course, a magnificent view.

During the McBirney family's tenure in the house, they entertained many visitors, including Amelia Earhart, a friend of the McBirney's daughter Dorothy, who was also a pilot. Today, as a bed-and-breakfast, the McBirney Mansion continues to host visitors from across the United States.

and newspapers at the front desk. The breakfast is an extended continental that includes an egg item, breakfast meat, make-your-own waffles, and fruit, in addition to the usual cold items. Other amenities include guest laundry, airport transportation, a fitness center plus complimentary passes to Gold's Gym, a business center, and WiFi. The pool is indoors and there's a whirlpool. The breakfast room is spacious and pleasant, and in the lobby an unusual streamline-deco–style fireplace is an unusual centerpiece. Twenty-four-ounce mattress toppers make sleeping a treat. If you've forgotten any of your necessary toiletries, check the Suite Shop, where you'll also find cold drinks, ice-cream treats, snacks, and microwaveable food. The hotel has a small conference center, great for small meetings or training sessions. The hotel is a smoke-free facility.

COURTYARD BY MARRIOTT TULSA $$$
3340 S. 79th East Place
(918) 660-0646, (800) 728-2892
www.marriott.com/hotels/travel/tulcy-courtyard-tulsa

Comfortable, clean, accommodating—everything you expect from this chain. There are four categories of rooms in the 122-room facility: Standard rooms include either a king-size bed with a sofa pullout or two queens, the spa king has a whirlpool, and the king suite features its own living room. All rooms have coffeemakers, fridges, microwaves, iron/ironing board, hair dryers, and a newspaper at your door. Several of the rooms are wheelchair accessible. Full breakfast is available for an extra charge. This is one of the more complete buffets, with eggs, meat, biscuits/gravy, waffles, cereals, fruit and yogurts—both regular and light. In addition, if you want your eggs fixed a certain way, the cook can handle it. Don't see your favorite cereal? Ask. They have such a wide variety of selections that not everything is put out every morning. Snacks, sandwiches, even a couple of frozen entree selections are available in the small shopping area by the front desk.

Additional amenities include an indoor swimming pool, whirlpool, fitness center, and computer in the lobby. And the front desk people are knowledgeable about Tulsa, its attractions, dining, etc., and can make good recommendations. Like all Marriotts, this is a nonsmoking environment. No pets, but service animals are welcome.

CROWNE PLAZA $$$-$$$$
100 E. 2nd St.
(918) 582-9000, (800) 2-CROWNE
www.crowneplaza.com

The Crowne Plaza is a 462-room high-rise hotel in downtown Tulsa. The drive-in entrance is on the lower level, and guests enter a sleek space with white marble floors and a black marble fountain around the base of tall escalators leading to the reception lobby. Curtained columns reach from the floor to the ceiling of the next level, and a wave-shaped chandelier hangs overhead.

The look of the reception lobby is softened by a colorful area rug and appealing upholstered furniture including red-velvet wing chairs and a coffee table with a zebra-print base. Originally an Adams Mark, the Crowne Plaza, part of the Holiday Inn family, opened in 2004.

The rooms all have floor-to-ceiling glass on the exterior wall and attractive, dark crown molding. The rooms are painted in soothing shades with accent colors. Amenities include coffeemakers, lighted, magnifying makeup mirrors, hair dryers, irons and ironing boards, and cute, little shimmery bags of sleep aids on the bed—eye mask, lavender spray, and earplugs. The hotel also guarantees that you will receive your wake-up call or your room is free. For ultimate elegance and lots of extra perks, book one of the five suites.

Newspapers are available in the lobby where there's a gift boutique, Starbucks, and The Daily

Grill, the hotel restaurant. If you get hungry any time of day or night, you can buy a sandwich or salad at the reception desk.

The fitness center is open 24 hours a day. There's an outdoor pool, but no hot tub. The Crowne Plaza also participates in an award-winning rewards program.

Other pluses at this hotel include an Elements Spa and an on-site car-rental facility. There is an extra charge for Internet service and the business center also charges. Printing of boarding passes and driving directions is complimentary. The hotel also has a complimentary airport shuttle.

Refrigerators and microwaves are available for an extra charge. Pets under 35 pounds are welcome—but the nonrefundable $100 cleaning fee may not be so welcoming.

DAYS INN $-$$
8888 S. Lewis St.
(918) 299-8511, (800) 325-2525
www.daysinnsouthtulsa.com

You can choose from double, queen, or king-size beds in the Days Inn's 86 rooms. There's a $10 charge for additional guests. Rooms feature coffeemakers, fridges, microwaves, hair dryers, and irons and ironing boards. USA Today is available in the lobby. Guests may help themselves to a continental breakfast. The hotel has a fitness center and a complimentary computer in the lobby. Ask about the hotel's "Evergreen Rooms." These feature air-extraction systems designed to remove irritants, dust, pollen, bacteria, and offensive odors. These rooms also have water-purifying systems.

DOUBLETREE HOTEL TULSA
DOWNTOWN $$$
616 W. 7th St.
(918) 587-8000, (800) 838-7914
www.tulsadowntown.doubletree.com

The sleek, cream marble lobby of the hotel may seem a bit austere, but the warm, chocolate chip cookies add a cozy touch. The hotel has 417 rooms with 13 suites. Standard rooms have a king or two double beds. There are a number of permutations for the suites, with choices includ-ing whirlpool suites, suites with Murphy beds, and kitchens and over-size rooms with king-size beds and the option of adjoining parlor. What-ever accommodation you choose, you'll love the Sweet Dreams bed.

All rooms have coffeemaker, iron and iron-ing board, hair dryers, and the morning paper delivered to your door. The hotel is undergoing a major renovation that began in late 2009. The new fitness center is up and running, and a new fine dining restaurant should be open by the time you read this. There's also the Coffee Con-nection for java and pastries. Other amenities include an indoor pool, whirlpool, guest laundry, and a business center.

Pets are welcome with the payment of a $50 nonrefundable deposit. There is a charge for the hotel's covered parking. The hotel is attached by way of a sky bridge to the Tulsa Convention Center.

DOUBLETREE HOTEL TULSA AT
WARREN PLACE $$$
6110 S. Yale Ave.
(918) 495-1000, (800) 801-1317
www.doubletreehotelwarrenplace.com
This hotel probably has the most attractive set-ting of all of Tulsa's hotels. It sits in an urban office park with lots of trees and even a great walking trail. The lobby is large with plenty of seating areas and a comfortable lounge—a good place for a chat over a drink.

Of the 370 rooms, 16 are suites—executive, conference, or junior—and there is an executive floor with its own concierge lounge, compli-mentary continental breakfast, and evening hors d'oeuvres. Rooms on this floor have turn-down service and bathrobes.

All rooms have coffeemakers, irons and iron-ing boards, hair dryers, and *USA Today* delivered to the door on weekdays. Standard rooms have one king-size bed or two double beds.

Complimentary airport transportation leaves the hotel every hour between 6 a.m. and 11 p.m. Guests can use the complimentary business cen-ter and the fitness center. There's an indoor pool

and whirlpool, sauna, and steam room. Parking in the covered garage is free; valet parking is avail-able at a charge. The hotel also has a Starbucks and a gift shop.

The main dining area is the Warren Duck Club, one of Tulsa's most highly rated restaurants. For more details see the Restaurant chapter.

ECONO LODGE INN & SUITES $$
3217 S. 79th East Ave.
(918) 624-2800, (800) 424-6423
www.econolodge.com
The emphasis here is on the "econo," but you should find that this hotel meets all your basic needs. Of the 58 rooms, 8 are suites, including some with whirlpools. Standard rooms offer sev-eral choices of beds. There is an extra charge for more than two people in a room. Rooms have fridges, microwaves, coffeemakers, hair dryers, irons and ironing boards, and weekday news-papers available at the front desk. In addition, there's an outdoor swimming pool, a compli-mentary business center, and an expanded con-tinental breakfast.

EMBASSY SUITES $$$
3332 S. 79th East Ave.
(918) 622-4000, (800) Embassy
www.tulsa.embassysuites.com
You'll be taken with the lobby as you enter the hotel—Mediterranean tile floors, painted ceramic tile trim, barrel-vaulted brick ceilings. This opens into a garden atrium with a graceful fountain. The facility's 240 two-room suites include king suites, double doubles (two double beds), two-bedroom suites, Jacuzzi suites, and wheelchair-accessible suites. Amenities include hair dryer, iron and iron-ing board, wet bar, fridge, microwave, coffeemaker, flat-screen TVs with cable, in-suite movies and video games, and WiFi access available. The com-plimentary full, cooked-to-order breakfast menu includes a signature omelet—the T-Town Twister. This is an egg-white omelet with diced jalapeños and cilantro, covered in salsa—low-fat and spicy!

And they don't stop there. There's a com-plimentary nightly Manager's Reception with beverages and finger foods, an indoor pool, whirlpool, fitness center, guest laundry, an airport shuttle, and a business center. Their restaurant, Cattleman's, serves lunch and dinner and features Buckhead beef. Be sure and look at the Web site for special packages. If you're traveling with children, check out the Build-A-Bear package. Get this one and your bear (BYOB—bring your own bear) can choose between a spa outfit—terry robe and slippers and a shower kit—or a jammie package—pj bottoms and sleep T-shirt, slippers and a shower kit. Both packages come with a $5 Bear Buck$ gift card and a Build-A-Bear/Embassy Suites branded bag.

FAIRFIELD INN & SUITES $$-$$$
3214 S. 79th East Ave.
(918) 663-0000, (800) 228-2800
www.marriott.com/tulfc
A Marriott economy brand, the Fairfield offers reliability—a clean, comfortable place to stay, some frills, and a good deal for your money. Its 62 standard rooms, all nonsmoking, feature double or king beds, coffeemakers, hair dryers, iron and ironing boards, and newspaper. The 18 suites also have fridges and microwaves and three of them have spa tubs. Room price includes a continental-plus breakfast. Guests have access to the indoor pool, whirlpool, fitness center, and complimentary business center.

HAMPTON INN $$
3209 S. 79th East Ave.
(918) 663-1000, (800) HAMPTON
www.tulsaok.hamptoninn.com
This Hampton Inn has three types of rooms with a total of 162. Standard rooms have either one king or two double beds. The study rooms are a bit larger than the standard rooms and have a fridge and microwave. The suites have two rooms with a microwave and fridge, two televisions and a pullout twin sleeper sofa. Fridges and microwaves are available for a small charge for other room categories. The standard coffeemaker, iron and ironing board, and hair dryer can be found in all rooms. Newspapers are delivered to the door for premium customers—for others, there are newspapers near the breakfast room.

The breakfast room overlooks the outdoor pool. The cardiovascular fitness center has a state-of-the-art treadmill with a built-in television. There's a complimentary business center.

The breakfast buffet is elaborate and the menu choices change daily. There are all the usual items—muffins, bagels, etc.—plus hot items like biscuits and gravy; eggs; bagels topped with scrambled eggs, bacon, and cheese; fruit; and more. The coffee bar is open 24 hours a day, and Monday through Thursday afternoons you'll find a plate of cookies.

Hampton Inn is so sure you'll have a good stay that they offer a money-back guarantee if you're not completely satisfied. They also have a generous honors program—you can get not only hotel points but also airline and car-rental points. If you're visiting in the summer, enjoy the attractive plantings and colorful flowers around the entrance. The lobby is roomy and the staff is friendly and helpful. While pets are not allowed, service animals are welcome.

HAMPTON INN AND SUITES $$
7141 S. 85th East Ave.
(918) 294-3300, (800) HAMPTON
www.woodlandhillssuites.hamptoninn.com
Located across the street from Tulsa's largest shopping mall and sitting on one of the town's restaurant rows, this Hampton Inn is in a busy and popular spot. The lobby is comfy and welcoming and the staff helpful and friendly. A hot breakfast is complimentary—and served in a spacious, well-lighted room overlooking the outdoor swimming pool and whirlpool. The decor features shades of gold, brown, cream, and black.

The small snack stand carries everything from candy bars to microwave meals. About 50 percent of the rooms have microwaves and fridges. All the rooms have coffeemakers, hair dryers, and irons and ironing boards, and USA Today is free in the lobby. There's also a fitness center and a complimentary business center.

The hotel has 74 rooms, including 26 suites. The suites have complete kitchenettes—even a cooktop (no oven). And laundry facilities are available to guests.

HARD ROCK HOTEL AND CASINO $$$
777 W. Cherokee St., Catoosa
(918) 384-7800, (800) 760-6700
www.hardrockcasino.com

Originally the Cherokee Casino Resort, this facility, still owned by the Cherokees, has been re-branded with the Hard Rock imprimatur. The hotel has 350 rooms with suites—from junior to mega-suites. The hotel opened in 1993 and expanded in 2009 with the addition of the Hard Rock Tower. Cherokee symbolism and artwork are prevalent throughout the hotel. Custom-made carpets in the public areas and halls reflect the heritage. Each room features different wall decor. Rooms are spacious, attractive, and comfortable. Amenities include tea and coffeemakers, hair dryers, irons and ironing boards, newspapers, free local calling, in-room safes, flat-screen TVs with cable, HBO and On Demand movies, and games. Microwaves and refrigerators are available on request. King suites feature whirlpool tubs.

In addition, the hotel provides a fitness center, complimentary business center, airport transportation, and pool. There's an attractive piano bar near the lobby—good for drinks and bar food and, of course, entertainment.

The hotel is connected to the casino (see Nightlife), so guests have easy access to 24-hour-a-day dining. Complimentary coffee and soft drinks are available throughout the gaming area. The casino also houses several restaurants, a number of bars, and entertainment six nights a week—everything from jazz to country.

The adjacent golf course (see Outdoor Activities) is an attractive adjunct to the facility

i   When visiting the Hard Rock Hotel and Casino, look for the seven-pointed Cherokee star motif. Each point represents one of the seven clans: Wolf, Blue, Longhair, Bird, Paint, Deer, and Wild Potato.

HILTON GARDEN INN–AIRPORT $$$
7728 E. Virgin Court
(918) 838-1444, (800) HILTONS
www.hgi.com

Location, location, location—if you're flying in or out, this can't be beat. You can choose from a room with a king-size bed or two double beds. All 120 rooms have coffeemakers, fridges, microwaves, hair dryers, and irons and ironing boards. *USA Today* is door delivered. The restaurant serves breakfast, lunch, and dinner. The airport shuttle operates from 4:30 in the morning until the last flight is in. And you can keep track of flights on a monitor in the lobby. The hotel has a fitness center, indoor pool, whirlpool, and complimentary business center. The lobby is spacious, comfortable, and well lighted with a high ceiling. If you get hungry, the Pavilion Pantry is open 24 hours a day.

HILTON TULSA SOUTHERN HILLS $$$
7902 S. Lewis Ave.
(918) 492-5000, (800) HILTONS
www.hilton.com

Right across the street from the Mabee Center, this Hilton is popular with concertgoers and visitors to Oral Roberts University. There are 284 rooms, including a Presidential Suite and seven standard suites. Standard guest rooms feature either king-size beds or two doubles. All rooms have coffeemakers, hair dryers, irons and ironing boards and a weekday morning paper delivered to the doors. Refrigerators and microwaves are available for an extra charge.

The hotel has a restaurant, a coffee shop, a lounge, an indoor swimming pool, fitness center, and a business center (for a fee). Airport transportation is available. Pets are accepted with a $75 nonrefundable deposit.

HOLIDAY INN EXPRESS–JENKS $$-$$$
150 Aquarium Dr., Jenks
(918) 296-7300, (800) HOLIDAY
www.hiejenks.com

This Holiday Inn packs a lot of interest in a small space. The matchbox-size lobby's high ceilings and walls feature murals with an Italian flair and an elaborate chandelier. The hotel has 76 rooms including 19 suites. This is a nonsmoking facility. All rooms have coffeemakers, fridges, microwaves, irons and ironing boards, hair dryers, and complimentary premium movie channels. The hotel also has an indoor pool and spa, steam room, sauna and outdoor tanning deck, a business center, fitness center, small convenience store, and a guest laundry. Some of the suites have kitchenettes. Newspapers are available at the front desk. A short walk south and you're at the Oklahoma Aquarium; a short walk north and you're at the shops, restaurants, and movies of RiverWalk. Ask about discount coupons for the aquarium.

HOLIDAY INN EXPRESS–TULSA CENTRAL $$
3215 S. 79th East Ave.
(918) 665-4242 800 HOLIDAY
www.hiexpress.com/tulsacentral

This Holiday Inn has 62 standard rooms—no suites. Mattresses are double, king, or queen-size. Some rooms have Temper-Pedic mattresses. A large majority of the customers here are on business. They like the quiet hotel and the long-time staff. Room amenities include coffeemakers, fridges, microwaves, irons and ironing boards, hair dryers, and newspapers at the desk. The swimming pool is outdoors and seasonal. The fitness center includes a sauna. The expanded continental breakfast offers hot and cold items, breakfast meats, and egg dishes. Visitors are required to use a valid credit card for checking in.

HOTEL SAVOY $$-$$$
631 S. Peoria Ave.
(918) 347-2869, (866) 347-2869
www.tulsasavoy.com

The Savoy may be tiny—only seven rooms, but the rooms are spacious and feature full kitchens. Each suite is furnished with charming antiques and unusual artwork. A boutique hotel, the Savoy offers concierge service, the *Tulsa World* and *New York Times,* laundry facilities, continental breakfast, laundry facilities and, in four of the rooms, a great view of the downtown skyline. There's no elevator but there are downstairs rooms. If you need wheelchair accessibility, call and ask about the circumstances. The hotel welcomes children and small pets. The rooms are quiet and comfortable; parking is handy in the back, and the location, just east of downtown, is just minutes from the University of Tulsa, Utica Square, and Brookside.

INN AT EXPO SQUARE $$
4531 E. 21st St.
(918) 858-3775
www.innatexposquare.com

Formerly a Microtel, this compact property actually sits on the Tulsa fairgrounds. It has 82 rooms—51 standard and 31 suites. All the standard rooms have either two double beds or two queens. The suites have a queen-size bed and a foldout couch. The new owners began replacing all the beds and furniture in 2009 and expect to have everything new by early 2010. All rooms have fridges, microwaves, and coffeemakers. Hair dryers are available at the front desk. A continental breakfast is served. There's no swimming pool, but Big Splash Water Park is right next door.

Pets are allowed but must be kept on a leash, and there is a nonrefundable deposit. There's no business center but there is a computer for guest use in the lobby. This place is not fancy, but it is clean and friendly and couldn't be handier to the fairgrounds. Book early because it fills up fast for the fair, horse shows, and other special events.

LA QUINTA $$
6030 E. Skelly Dr.
(918) 665-2630, (800) 531-5900
www.lq.com

About half of the La Quinta's 106 rooms are standard rooms with either a king-size bed or two doubles. The other half are suites ranging from one room with a king-size bed and sofa sleeper to two-room suites with one king or two doubles and a sofa sleeper or a Jacuzzi suite . Every room comes with a coffeemaker, microwave, refrigerator, hair dryer, and iron and ironing board. Free morning papers are available at the desk, and a continental breakfast, including waffles and biscuits and gravy, is complimentary. You'll also find free WiFi and a guest laundry, an outdoor pool, fitness center, and business center. Small pets (under 25 pounds) are welcome with no deposit necessary. Staff is capable, helpful, and friendly. Many have been with the hotel for a number of years.

MARRIOTT TULSA SOUTHERN HILLS $$$
1902 E. 71st St.
(918) 493-7000
www.marriott.com/TULSE

With a great location close to the Oklahoma Aquarium, across the street from the Sherwin Miller Museum and near the St. Francis medical complex, the Marriott Southern Hills would be a good choice. Add to that the number of amenities they offer, and the hotel becomes even more attractive. Phil's Smokehouse, their restaurant, serves breakfast, lunch, and dinner, and Starbucks keeps you going in between. They also have two bar areas—a sports bar and a lobby lounge, a gift shop, barber and beauty shop, and a spa.

The hotel has 377 rooms. Six rooms are set up as hospitality suites. Two of the hotel's 11 floors are concierge rooms—with bathrobes and fridges in addition to the usual coffeemaker, iron and ironing board, and hair dryer. Guests on these floors also have access to the concierge lounge, which, during the week, serves a continental breakfast in the morning and offers hors d'oeuvres and goodies in the afternoon.

Other features of the hotel include an indoor swimming pool, whirlpool, sundeck, fitness center with cardio equipment, free weights, and saunas, complimentary business center, a guest laundry, and complimentary airport transportation.

This is a nonsmoking facility. Pets are welcome but you must make a $225 deposit, $150 of which is refundable. The hotel has just undergone a major renovation, so all rooms have new furniture and 37-inch flat-screen TVs.

POST OAK LODGE $$
5323 W. 31st St. North
(918) 425-2112
www.postoaklodge.com

This charming getaway is the process of transitioning from a corporate facility and retreat venue to include tourist accommodations. Built by the Catholic Diocese in the mid-'80s, it was sold to Williams Corporation for their company's use. It was purchased by Persimmon Ridge, LLC, in 2003 and has been serving as a conference and meeting center. The buildings feature a lot of stone and wood and fit into the landscape very well. They are not rustic—they are for people who like to rough it in comfort.

Lodging consists of two large lodges with 18 bedrooms with private baths, and six small lodges with four rooms each. In each of the buildings, there is a shared common area. TVs and other amenities are located in these areas.

Several of the rooms are wheelchair accessible. No smoking is allowed. If there is a group in attendance, meal service may be extended to nonparticipating guests.

The outdoor attractions of the property make sifting through the details of a stay worthwhile. The grounds cover 1,100 acres, offering lots of opportunities for hiking—eventually the walking trail will connect with trails in the nearby Centennial Botanical Gardens. There are areas for basketball, softball, volleyball, and croquet. Catch-and-release fishing is allowed, and there is a swimming pool with two hot tubs.

This might not be the best choice for the typical overnight visitor, but it has real potential for large or small group getaways, weddings, or family reunions. Post Oak Lodge isn't the average accommodation, but it's worth a look.

QUALITY SUITES $
3112 S. 79th East Ave.
(918) 858-9625, 877-424-5423
www.choicehotels.com

This hotel has 69 suites with either two queen beds or one king-size bed. There are also Jacuzzi suites and suites with whirlpool tubs. Children are free but there is an extra charge for more than two adults in a room.

Guest rooms are supplied with coffeemakers, fridges, microwaves, irons and ironing boards, and hair dryers. Newspapers are delivered to Choice Privilege members and are available in the lobby for others. There are a guest laundry, fitness center, business center, and free in-room WiFi. You'll also find an indoor pool and hot tub.

Breakfast is a hot continental with eggs, meats, biscuits and gravy, and self-serve waffles plus the usual cold items. Fresh donuts are delivered daily.

The facility is nonsmoking and has both interior and external room entrances. The staff members are proud of their level of service and have the award to prove it. The assistant general manager was named "Hospitality Champion, 2009" by the Tulsa Hotel and Lodging Association. There's a guest laundry, and while there is no airport transportation, the management has an arrangement with a local cab company that will save you money.

RADISSON HOTEL TULSA $$
10918 E. 41st St.
(918) 627-5000, (800) 395-7046
www.radissontulsa.com

The lobby of this high-rise hotel looks out onto a covered patio and the outdoor pool, giving guests a pleasant vista with their warm welcome. The hotel has 325 rooms, including standards with double or king beds, Jacuzzi and whirlpool suites, club level rooms, junior suites, and the Governor's and Presidential Suites.

A major renovation was scheduled for late 2009, so some of the details may change. As of now, rooms have coffeemakers, ironing boards, and hair dryers, and some rooms have fridges and microwaves. The hotel offers complimentary airport transportation and a free morning newspaper in the lobby. There are two restaurants on-site—Beechwood's, for breakfast and lunch, and Mulligan's Sports and Spirits for dinner.

The hotel also has a business center, a fitness center, and a guest laundry room.

A big attraction for families is the indoor pool for youngsters 10 and younger. Called Leapin' Louie's Lagoon, this mini–water park has slides, water cannons, and a rope bridge. Check the Web site for special package rates.

Pets are allowed but there is a $75 nonrefundable deposit required.

RADISSON INN TULSA AIRPORT $$
2201 N. 77th East Ave.
(918) 835-9911, (800) 395-7046
www.radisson.com/tulsaok

Right on airport property, this hotel is really handy for air travelers. Most of the rooms have either a king-size bed, a queen, or two queens. The executive suites are newly remodeled and feature a king bed, a refrigerator, microwave, and flat-screen TV. Most of the rooms have Sleep Number beds. All the rooms have coffeemakers, hair dryers, and irons and ironing boards. The newspaper is free in the lobby and airport transportation is available, complimentary and on demand. The facility is nonsmoking and allows pets with a nonrefundable deposit. There are fitness and business centers and an outdoor swimming pool. Ask about special weekend rates.

RED ROOF INN $
4717 S. Yale Ave.
(918) 622-6776, (800) RED ROOF
www.redroofinn.com

This inn is on the moderate end of the price scale but it offers good value. There are 100 rooms, including rooms with one queen-size bed, two doubles or two queens, and two Jacuzzi suites with a king-size bed each. The rooms have refrigerators and microwaves, and coffeemakers are available. *USA Today* is available in the lobby, and an expanded continental breakfast is served in the small breakfast area—most people take their breakfasts back to their rooms. The outdoor swimming pool is small but attractive, and there's a guest computer in the lobby. Rooms open on the outside.

Several things make this place a good choice. The staff is friendly and familiar with Tulsa—there's little turnover and that's always a good sign. And the hotel is close to two major malls and about a mile and a half from St. Francis Hospital. Special consideration is given to folks who are staying here because they have family members in the hospital. There is an extra charge for extra people in a room. Pets are welcome but there's a small charge for multiple pets.

RENAISSANCE TULSA HOTEL AND CONVENTION CENTER $$$$
6808 S. 107th East Ave.
(918) 307-2600, (800) 264-0165
www.renaissancertulsa.com

The lobby is attractive, but as you walk through

it, the atrium is stunning. With a skylight 11 floors above, this area features a rambling pond with large koi fish and even turtles. The hotel has been recognized for the level of service it provides, and the physical plant lives up to high standards, too.

Of the 300 rooms, 36 are suites and 6 are wheelchair accessible. Two of the rooms have accessories to accommodate hearing-impaired guests. Standard rooms feature double and king beds. All rooms have coffeemakers, hair dryers, irons and ironing boards, and cable TV. Suites have fridges and microwaves. *USA Today* is delivered to the doors on weekdays.

Other amenities include a restaurant (see Cyprus Grille in the Restaurant chapter), a full-service bar, a Starbucks area, indoor swimming pool, whirlpool, sauna, fitness center, complimentary business center, gift shop, concierge lounge, and mall shuttle. Both valet and self-parking are available and there are self-service laundry facilities. On the Club Level, guests can enjoy a complimentary continental breakfast and nightly appetizers. Pets are allowed with a $250 refundable deposit. This is a nonsmoking facility.

The level of service here really makes this hotel shine—they're used to unusual requests and hustle to fulfill their guests' wishes.

SLEEP INN $$
8021 E. 33rd St.
(918) 663-2777, (877) 424-6423
www.choicehotels.com/ok093

Of the 66 rooms in this compact hotel, there are several suites with whirlpool tubs and several two-room suites. Beds are either full or king. There's an extra charge for more than two adults in one room. Opened in 2000, the hotel is noted for its customer service and cleanliness. All the rooms have coffeemakers and fridges and most have microwaves. All have irons, ironing boards, and hair dryers. The breakfast, included in the room price, is an extended continental with hot items like biscuits and gravy or waffles—no breakfast meats or egg dishes. The hotel offers a guest laundry and airport transportation. The swimming pool is indoors, and there is a fitness

center and business center. The manager hosts a happy hour Monday, Tuesday, and Wednesday afternoons with soft drinks, beer, and appetizers. The facility is nonsmoking.

BED-AND-BREAKFASTS

CEDAR ROCK INN BED
& BREAKFAST $$$-$$$$$
4501 W. 41st St.
(918) 447-4493, (877) 446-4493
www.cedarrockinn.com

The surrounding neighborhood doesn't prepare you for your approach to the Cedar Rock Inn. But once you pass through the stone gates, you could be miles from town. The present property covers 55 acres, part of which was once land belonging to Tecumseh Perryman, a member of the ubiquitous and prolific family that once controlled almost all the land that's now Tulsa.

Tecumseh was one of the more obscure Perrymans—other than the fact that he fought on the side of the South in the Civil War, not much else is known about him. He built a three-room house from native sandstone quarried on the property. That house is now incorporated into the current structure in a most ingenious and attractive manner—most of the outside of the house is now inside. Additions to the house have been carefully crafted so modern materials blend with the older components. Not everything dates back to 1890. Owner Sandi Dittman fought hard to protect the '40s mottled vinyl tile floor in the old kitchen (now the office).

Take note of the wood and cabinetry in the newer areas of the house. Floors and paneling utilize local woods like post oak, pecan, and even blackjack oak. Few people use blackjack because the numerous knots make it more difficult to work with, but the Dittmans think this makes it more interesting and attractive. It took them almost seven years to finish the construction. In addition to the bed-and-breakfast, there's also a conference center. A ¾-mile walking trail takes guests to the top of a ridge overlooking the place.

Each of the five bedrooms has something special to offer. The Cedar Room, downstairs, features

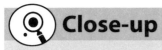 **Close-up**

The Mayo Hotel

When it was built in 1925, the Mayo was the tallest building in Oklahoma. Reaching 18 stories, the Sullivan-style building features two-story Doric columns and false terra-cotta balconies. In its heyday, J. Paul Getty lived here, and Elvis Presley, Mae West, and President John F. Kennedy all visited.

The hotel closed in 1981 and stood vacant until it was purchased in 2000 by the Snyder family, Tulsans, and developers who want to see downtown Tulsa thrive.

Listed on the National Register of Historic Places, the hotel has been lovingly renovated, with the historic integrity holding as much importance as the contemporary amenities. The 76 loft apartments in the building bring a stable and upscale population downtown, while the 102 boutique hotel rooms give visitors a taste of Tulsa oil-boom elegance.

From the red neon sign atop the building to the magnificent grand staircase on the first floor, the Mayo is the same—only much better. In 1925, guests were wooed with ceiling fans and Tulsa's first running ice water. Today's guests are treated to suites with full kitchens, wood floors, separate bedrooms, flat-screen TVs, plus the usual amenities. The hotel has a business center, fitness center, local shuttle service, restaurant, coffee shop, and even a museum. Room rates range from $$$ to $$$$.

The hotel address is 115 W. 5th St.; the phone number is (918) 582-6296; and the Web site is www.themayohotel.com. The hotel reopened in the fall of 2009.

a custom-made, queen-size, cedar bed and has a cedar-lined steam sauna. This room has wide doors for wheelchair accessibility; however, the bed is high and could be difficult to get into without help. Also, the other doors leading to the dining area are in the oldest part of the house, so a guest in a standard-size wheelchair would need to go outside and around to get to the dining area. If you have questions, please call and chat with the manager.

The Sage Room has an en suite fireplace, king-size bed, beautiful blackjack-oak floor, and a patio entrance. Willow, with a queen-size bed, has its own sitting room and can connect to Sage to make a two-bedroom, two-bathroom suite. The Terrace Room has a private patio, and the bathroom features a claw-foot tub and brass shower. The Parkview Room, popular with honeymooners, has a king-size bed, fireplace, balcony overlooking the grounds, a fridge, and a wet bar. The marble and tile bathroom features a two-person whirlpool tub and a large shower.

Arriving guests are greeted with snacks and a cookie jar with fresh, home-baked cookies; coffee and hot water for tea or hot chocolate are always out. Ice and a microwave are easily accessible.

Breakfast is served in the sunny dining area. The meal consists of choices of juices, fruit, usually an egg dish of some sort, breakfast meats, and pancakes with real maple syrup. Guests never leave the table hungry.

Guests are asked to leave their pets and their children under the age of 16 at home. The only exception to the children rule is in cases where a party books the entire house. Smoking is allowed on the property—just not indoors.

This is a charming and interesting property and a great place to get away without going far.

CROW'S REST $$
3405 W. 71st St.
(918) 445-5115
www.thecrowsrest.com

This country getaway is not too far as the crow flies, but the crow is probably glad to rest when he gets here. It's about 10 miles mostly south and a little west of downtown—west of the Arkansas River. The setting is rural, with big trees surrounding a wide swath of green lawn.

Nancy and Don Crow built the property as a bed-and-breakfast. There are five rooms in the main house and a freestanding cottage that will accommodate up to six people.

This place is a special favorite for girls' getaways; they can accommodate scrapbookers, small retreats, or just folks who want a quiet spot to relax but still have access to arts, shops, and amenities in Tulsa.

Several of the rooms have particular themes. The Antique Room has a queen-size, four-poster bed, a chintz-covered wing chair, and wallpaper in a delicate floral print. The Bear Room has cherry-red walls with a valentine-y border, a balcony, and, yep, teddy bears. The European Room has a beautiful mural of Paris on one wall and outstanding black-and-white photographs of familiar European sites on the others.

Both the European Room and the Bear Room have twin beds that can be strapped together to make a king. The Deck Room opens onto the balcony and overlooks the swimming pool.

Downstairs, the Guest Suite, decorated in soft yellows and blues, has a king-size bed, a sitting area, and, in the bathroom, a shower and a whirlpool tub. It also has a private entrance. This room is wheelchair accessible—its bathroom, however, is not large enough to accommodate a wheelchair. For guests with some mobility, this could work fine. Just call and chat with Nancy about your needs.

Don is an advocate of country breakfasts—the meat, eggs, and biscuit school. And Nancy can do that. She also enjoys fixing egg casseroles, omelets, and quiches. She'll ask you about your preferences when you make your reservations. Whatever she fixes, it will be good.

Smokers are allowed to indulge outside—not in the house. And the resident dogs prefer that you leave your pets at home. Nancy takes credit cards, with the exception of American Express.

INN AT WOODWARD PARK $$-$$$
1521 E. 21st St.
(918) 712-9770 (888) 712-9770
www.innatwoodwardpark.com

When Janet and Mark Mobbs found the 1920 midtown Tudor Revival house with possible Craftsman roots and tacky asbestos siding, they were told it was only worth tearing down. But Janet saw something in the old house and was determined to bring it back to life. "It would probably have been cheaper to tear it down," she laughs.

But today, with the original wood restored and repainted, it stands proudly on one of Tulsa's busiest streets, kitty-corner from beautiful Woodward Park. Janet and Mark tore up the old, dark carpet only to discover beautiful hardwood floors, the narrow boards laid in an unusual pattern. A focal point in the living room is an attractive plaster fireplace.

Furniture in the house is a combination of antiques, family pieces, and more modern pieces, but the feel is period. The owners call it a Roaring '20s bed-and-breakfast, and the three guest rooms follow the theme. The front bedroom is the Hollywood Suite. With a blue silk bedspread and chocolate-colored velvet curtains, a chandelier, and a chaise longue, it's reminiscent of a glamorous era. Janet and Mark hoped to put a claw-foot tub in the bathroom, but the original cast-iron bathtub is so heavy that no one would attempt to move it. There's also a stand-alone shower in the bathroom.

The Jazz Room has a queen-size bed. The room is decorated in warm colors with jazz posters. If you feel the need to toot your own horn, there's a tuba in one corner.

The Moroccan Room salutes the intrepid travelers who traveled the world in the '20s, bringing back mementos from exotic climes. It has a queen-size, four-poster bed with shirred curtains that can be pulled to create your own cozy hideaway. The bedspread is a rich red with a gold pattern. In the bathroom is a Jacuzzi for two.

Visitors share the sunroom—a common area. It's a bright, cheerful room with lots of windows. There's a mini-fridge stocked with soft drinks and bottled water. Coffee, tea, or spiced cider is available anytime and there's a basket of snacks in case you get the munchies.

Breakfast is served in the dining room—a pleasant room with colorful Stephen Smith paintings of spring in Woodward Park. Janet may fix you a summer fruit compote with locally grown berries or, in winter, a blend of Rio Grande Valley oranges and grapefruit with a honey-lime dressing. She also does egg dishes, French toast, biscuits, or pumpkin bread. Whatever she fixes, she makes an effort to shop locally. Particularly in the summer, she shops at local farmers' markets and belongs to a food co-op for locally grown meats, fruits, and veggies.

The house is historic and not wheelchair accessible. The bed-and-breakfast is a quiet getaway for adults—no children, no smoking, no pets. (An exception might be made for a family group that books the whole house.) Though the parking is a bit tight, you're right in the middle of Tulsa action at this inn—within walking distance to Woodward Park, the Garden Center, the Tulsa Historical Society, and, in the other direction, Utica Square with its great shops and restaurants. Brookside's just a few blocks away, as is Cherry Street.

KENNEDY MANSION BED AND BREAKFAST $$$$
506 W. Fairview St.
(918) 712-8065
www.kennedymansion.com
Welcome to one of the most venerable homes in Tulsa. Built by one of Tulsa's first physicians and civic leaders in 1925, the brick, three-story mansion was the home of Dr. Samuel G. Kennedy.

Entering the front door, you'll see a grand imperial staircase and Palladian window. Look closely at the craftsmanship and wood on the staircase. It's tiger-cut red gum—no longer available. And it's beautiful. The house is full of interesting touches—like the painting on the wall over the fireplace, done by a German artist, or the outside "speakeasy" stairs.

Previous occupants of the house include the band Aerosmith, who used the third-floor ballroom to record. Today the home is owned by Darell and Françoise Christopher. Darell is a real Renaissance man—talented in many fields. He met Françoise, who is French, when she was living in Germany and he was touring with his band and performing gospel, R&B, and jazz concerts. He holds bachelor's degrees in television and radio and sociology from the University of Tulsa and a master's in theology from Phillips Theological Seminary. Françoise's background is in marketing and merchandising and the hospitality industry. She speaks four languages fluently and can cook international cuisine, too.

The rooms are spacious and comfortable and range from the Osage and Gilcrease Rooms, each with a queen-size bed, to the Country Club Suite with one king and one queen, the Presidential Suite with a king-size bed, and the Cottage with two bedrooms, two queen-size beds, and a full kitchen. Several of the rooms have balconies. The bathroom fixtures are original and charming.

Breakfast is a real treat—the hardest thing is choosing. Some of the options include crepe dishes, either rolled and served with honey or maple syrup or filled with eggs or vegetables. If you're a gal or guy who likes your greens, you'll love the vegetarian omelet with onions, bell peppers, cheese, zucchini, and garlic. And Françoise's homemade croissants are so light you practically have to hold them on the plate. At an extra charge, and with prearrangement, she'll do romantic dinners, also.

The back lawn features a sunken garden with a swimming pool and is frequently the site of weddings.

Because it is a historic property, the mansion is not wheelchair accessible. No smoking is allowed. Some pets are permitted, so ask. There is a resident cat. Be sure and check the Web site for packages. They're up on everything that goes on in Tulsa and can help you plan a very special getaway.

The combination of the house, the Christophers, and Françoise's culinary capabilities make this an extra-appealing stay.

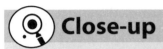 **Close-up**

Dr. Samuel G. Kennedy

Dr. Samuel G. Kennedy and his brother, Dr. James L. Kennedy, moved to the Tulsa area in 1891 and set up practice in the little settlement. Often Dr. Kennedy would travel 35 to 60 miles in a single night to reach patients in the area.

In such a small community, it is not surprising that Dr. Kennedy became involved in local affairs. Although the original charter petition and plat map of Tulsa have disappeared, court documents and local histories reveal that Dr. Sam was one of the original petitioners and town fathers. In 1898 the brothers built Tulsa's first brick building. Dr. Sam was also one of the organizers of the Oklahoma Territorial Medical Association, forerunner of the state medical association.

The brothers married sisters, Osage Indians, and both families acquired large tracts of Osage land immediately north and west of Tulsa. Dr. Sam invested well in real estate and, later, oil, and retired from active medical practice in 1908. That same year he leased 80 acres to a group of Tulsans to establish the Tulsa Country Club and golf course. There's no evidence that he was a member, but several of his seven children were noted local golfers.

In 1925 Dr. Kennedy built his impressive brick mansion, across the street from his business partner's home. He subsequently built substantial houses for several of his children. His first wife had died in 1912. Dr. Kennedy remarried in 1926.

This area of Tulsa is a surprise to those not familiar with its history. Most people are familiar with the historic mansions in the Maple Ridge area of Tulsa. The Kennedy Mansion is actually in Osage County. The story is that Dr. Kennedy got into a dispute with the Tulsa city government about street and utility expansion and refused to sell any of his land, delaying the development of that part of town. Furthermore, he put in his will that none of the land could be sold for 20 years after his death. He died in 1941.

MCBIRNEY MANSION BED AND BREAKFAST $$$$
1414 S. Galveston Ave.
(918) 585-3234
www.mcbirneymansion.com

Want to feel like a millionaire? Try a stay at the McBirney Mansion (see Close-up). This is one of those huge houses, reminiscent of an English manor, where the back door is as impressive as the front. The house was chosen as the 1997 Tulsa Symphony Show Case, and the draperies and a number of the antiques were brought in then. All the beds have recently been replaced with top-of-the-line bedding.

Room sizes range from comfy to spacious—each one is different. Among the amenities, each room has its own small fridge stocked with complimentary bottled water and soft drinks. There are six rooms on the guest-room level, with an additional two junior suites on the top

floor. There is an elevator, so the McBirney is more accessible than many historic properties. No smoking is allowed in the house but there are designated areas outside for smokers. The nature of the property makes it inappropriate for children under the age of 14 unless the booking involves one party taking the entire house.

Every room has its own attractions, and guests often rebook their favorites. Most of the rooms have river views, though the trees are so tall and thick that in summer there's just a glimpse of water. The grounds are so attractive that any view is good. The Poets Porch is a cheery buttercup with fabrics in floral and checked patterns. Riverwalk is roomy with two beds, red walls, white and red toile quilted bedspreads, and red and white striped bed skirts. The Bishop's Suite is a favorite with honeymooners—with a whirlpool tub and shower and a luxurious wrought-iron king-size bed. Whatever room you choose, you'll find charming touches.

Breakfasts are a treat at the Mansion. Whether you eat in the dining room, the breakfast room, or the sunporch, the table will be set elegantly. Breakfast consists of juice, perhaps a fruit/yogurt/granola parfait or a fresh fruit compote, toast, and an entree. Specialties include quiche, an egg casserole, or breakfast burritos with housekeeper Maria's own fresh, homemade salsa. Whatever you have, it will be a while before you're thinking about lunch. And when you head up to bed, have a cookie for a bedtime snack.

MEADOWLAKE RANCH $$$-$$$$
3450 S. 137th West Ave., Sand Springs
(918) 494-6000
(800) 256-5323
www.meadowlakeranch.com
Driving up the winding gravel driveway through cedar and hardwood trees, it's hard to realize that you're just a short distance from the busy city. There are several ways to enjoy this property. It's a bed-and-breakfast, a dude ranch, a day-trip destination, and a great spot for fishing and hunting.

Tom Warren is as versatile as his ranch. A retired chiropractor, he is also involved in an estate business. One of his clients asked one day if he could sell her property. "I'll go take a look at it," he told her. He looked—fell in love with it and decided to buy part of it. He showed the parcel to his wife. He was interested in the area with the lakes. She loved the meadow. They bought both and named their place Meadowlake. Today they have 1,000 acres with five spring-fed lakes, the meadow, and such a variety of habitat that it is a favorite spot with local bird-watchers.

Meadowlake Ranch has some interesting historical features, too. There's an old Indian cemetery on the property and there are remnants of early oil activities, including two original cedar tank batteries.

Accommodations include three lakeside cabins, two bluff-top cabins, and three tepees. The lakeside cabins each have a king-size bed plus a queen-size futon or sleeper sofa in the living area. The cabins are made of Arkansas pine logs and have corner fireplaces and two-person whirlpool tubs, a TV and DVD player, stereo systems, and private patios. They also have kitchens.

The bluff-top cabins are not as fancy but larger—accommodating four to six guests. The complete kitchens include a dishwasher and disposals.

The tepees are Sioux-style and made by the company that created the tepees for *Dances with Wolves*. They're set on concrete pads so you don't have to worry so much about sharing your bed with something creepy. They have padded cots, but bring your own bedding—most people just bring a sleeping bag and a pillow. Each has a *chiminea* for heat on cool nights. There is a modern bathroom with shower and a small refrigerator for each tepee.

For an "awww" moment, visit the little streamside bench closest to the south tepee. At your feet you'll see a piece of concrete with the names Marvin and Betty scratched in the surface. Sue Lynn Warren's dad, Marvin, was killed in Korea. He and her mom, Betty, had put their names on a new sidewalk in Durant when they were in college there. Tom went to Durant and bought that chunk of sidewalk for his wife.

Bed and breakfast guests can enjoy a continental breakfast in the lodge, hike, play horseshoes, or just laze about in a hammock. Dude ranch prices include lodging, three meals a day, and activities like hiking, fishing (yes, you must have a license), canoeing, swimming, horseback riding, shooting (with old-fashioned single-action six-guns or lever-action Henry rifles), or learning to shoot a bow and arrow or throw a tomahawk. Enjoy an evening campfire or a horseback ride. Meals on this plan include a ranch-style breakfast, lunch, and dinner, which is usually something grilled—perhaps buffalo burgers.

RV PARKS

ESTES PARK
1710 S. 79th East Ave.
(918) 627-3150
This was Tulsa's first RV park—built originally as a seniors-only facility. And it still caters to retirees. Tucked into a quiet neighborhood, surrounded

with tall trees, Estes Park may be just what you're looking for if you're looking for quiet and basic amenities. The bathrooms and showers are tiny but clean, and there are guest laundry facilities. They also have a storm shelter—a handy thing in Oklahoma in the spring. Estes Park has 20 full hookups (15/20/30/50 amps). The road through the park and the sites are gravel. There are two pull-through sites. Ask about pets. Estes Park is located north of 21st St., east of Sheridan, near the fairgrounds. Rates for 2009 were $40 per night, 160 per week.

EXPO SQUARE RV PARK
3900 E. 15th St.
(918) 744-1113, ext. 2154
www.exposquare.com
Expo Square RV Park has approximately 370 RV sites and can handle everything from small pop-ups to 50-foot horse trailers, motor homes, fifth wheels, and trailers. All sites have complete hookups and 30- and 50-amp service. Don't look for trees or grass. All sites are paved—actually, it's a giant parking lot. The facilities, however, are great—with modern restrooms and showers, a guest laundry, and Internet service. Pets are welcome. This facility primarily serves folks who need to be at the fairgrounds for horse shows, the fair, car or boat shows, or any one of the myriad activities that take place here. But it also accommodates travelers. Because it is used heavily for big events, call well ahead to check on availability. You'll need to get the reservation form off the Web site—it's under facilities—and mail or fax it

with a one night's deposit. Rates vary by size of unit and whether or not the fair is going on. Rates in 2009 ranged from $25 to $35.

MINGO RV PARK
I-244 and Mingo Road
(800) 932-8824
www.mingorvpark.com
Lots of spaces, lots of trees, and lots of extras here. There are 250 sites with full hookups (20/30/50 amps) including 30 pull-throughs. Amenities include a rec room with a billiard table, arcade games and board games, plus spots just for sitting and chatting and attractive restrooms and showers. Outside you'll find horseshoe pits, a basketball court, playground, and dog run. There's also a laundry room—and if the weather gets scary, a large storm shelter. Free WiFi is available and pets are welcome. In 2009 the standard fee was $28 per night.

TULSA WARRIOR RV PARK
5131 S. Union Ave.
(918) 446-3199
www.tulsawarriorrv.com
On the west side of the river, this park offers 76 sites including 38 pull-throughs, which will accommodate rigs up to 56 feet long, with full hookups. The other spots are back-ins with a variety of amenities, and there are 11 overflow grass sites with electricity only. Laundry facilities and restrooms and showers are available. Ask about pets. Rates here were $28 in 2009.

RESTAURANTS

You've always had choice in Oklahoma, but it used to be what cut of beef or which pieces of chicken. In addition to the more mundane state bird, tree, and flower, Oklahoma legislators designated a "state meal." It brings new meaning to the term "bloated government." It consists of fried okra, squash, corn, black-eyed peas, biscuits, sausage and gravy, grits, barbecued pork, chicken-fried steak, pecan pie, and strawberries. You can still find a good chicken-fried steak in town, and grilled steaks and prime rib will never go out of style. Barbecue—well, that goes without saying. But you'll find so much more variety in Tulsa's cuisine these days.

Innovative chefs are taking old favorites and giving them a new spin—like macaroni and cheese made with cheddar, Gruyère, and Danish fontina cheeses (Daily Grill) or a salmon tamale made with stone-ground jalapeño cheese grits (Polo Grill). And there are plenty of restaurants featuring international cuisines—Italian, French, Mexican, German, Mediterranean, Thai, Vietnamese, and on and on—and fusions, variations, and permutations of many of them. A surprisingly high percent of Tulsa's chefs trained at the prestigious Culinary Institute of America. It's a nice credential but some of the finest food comes from chefs who've learned on the job. And Oklahoma State University at Okmulgee is turning out some super chefs. There's a level of culinary sophistication in Tulsa that would stand up anywhere—at a portion of the price you'd pay in bigger cities.

Times have changed in Tulsa dress-wise, too. Even restaurants that once required jackets and ties have left the dress codes behind. It's just good manners to dress up a bit for dinner, but nice slacks and a collared shirt for men and a Sunday dress or pants suit will be fine for the most upscale places.

Areas like Brookside and Cherry Street have clusters of restaurants. And there are the usual national chains strung along major streets. The chains have been left out of the listings—they're pretty much the same from place to place. Part of the adventure of travel is trying things you don't have at home. Other places are scattered from one end of town to the other. Fortunately, nothing's too much of a drive in Tulsa, so go adventuring.

Bon appetit!

OVERVIEW

Restaurants are divided into sections by cuisine or specialties but, as in other sections of the book, you'll find a lot of crossover.

For example, la Villa, the excellent restaurant at the Philbrook Museum of Art, is listed under American Traditional and Contemporary Cuisine but is open only for lunch. It's not listed with other lunch places because the menu tends more to the elegant than the usual sandwich shop. Likewise, a steak place may list a variety of other entrees. Only a couple of restaurants are cross-listed—places like Savoy, outstanding for breakfast and just the place you'll want when you miss mom and need some comfort food. Otherwise, the descriptions should give you an idea of the extent of the offerings.

You can assume that all the restaurants are nonsmoking unless otherwise indicated and parking is mentioned only if it is an issue. Almost all of the restaurants take all credit cards and are wheelchair accessible.

Price Guide

Prices are calculated on the cost of two entrees, no sides, desserts, or beverages. For restaurants open only for breakfast and lunch, prices are calculated from the lunch menu, so be aware breakfast is probably less expensive. For restaurants open for lunch and dinner or all three meals, prices are determined by dinner entrees. Remember that by the time you add an appetizer or salad, beverages, and desserts, you will have upped your total bill.

$. $15 or less
$$ . . . . $16 to $25
$$$ . . . .$26 to 40
$$$$. . . . . $41 to $60
$$$$$. . . . . $61 and over

AMERICAN TRADITIONAL AND CONTEMPORARY

ALBERT G'S BAR-B-Q $$
2748 S. Harvard Ave.
(918) 747-4799
www.albertgs.com

What's more American than barbecue—and barbecue served in an old filling station? Albert G's fills the bill. Of course, the filling station is cleaned up—the only grease you'll find will be on your chin (and not much there). The walls are decorated with gas station memorabilia—signs, even a gas pump in the corner. The chairs are chrome, tabletops are metal, and the upholstery is black fake leather with red piping—ooh, they've got the ambience down pat. There are picnic tables outside—and smoking is allowed there.

The barbecue is slow cooked, overnight, over hickory logs. The brisket and pork ribs are best sellers. The sliced brisket sandwich features thick-sliced slabs of meat, well trimmed so you're not getting a lot of fat. Smoked chicken is offered on Wednesday and Saturday nights, and there are customers who come in then just for that selection. The baked beans are cooked with bits of meat and a touch of cinnamon. You can order combo plates or dinners with two sides or sandwiches. Buy by the pound to take home and

they toss in sauce and bread. All the sides, except potato chips, are made right here. The sauce comes in sweet or hot—it's their recipe but it's produced commercially.

The only alcohol sold is 3.2 beer. All orders entitle you to the pickle, onion, and pepper bar. Albert G's does dine-in, carry-out, and catering. They're open for lunch and dinner, Monday through Saturday.

THE BROOK $$
3401 S. Peoria Ave.
(918) 748-9977

7727 E. 91st St.
(918) 392-9977
www.brookrestaurant.com

Popular with the casual crowd and those with a love of nostalgia, the Brook on Peoria occupies a former theater built in 1945. By no means a movie palace, the building was built in the streamline art deco style. The marquee remains. This laid-back eatery caters to a wide spectrum of the community—from families to the sports bar crowd.

Menu favorites include chicken-fried steak, a mean blue cheese burger, and a good selection of wraps. The menu lists over half a dozen low-carb options, and a kids' menu is available.

There's a full bar and plenty of parking in the back. And enough TVs so that if there's a big game on, everyone can see. Come for lunch or dinner, any day of the week.

The south Tulsa location serves the same menu, has a full bar and lots of TV screens. Same good food—just missing the movie house connection.

CAZ'S CHOWHOUSE $$
18 E. Brady St.
(918) 588-CHOW
www.cazschowhouse.com

Chef/owner Jeff Castleberry, a grad of the culinary school at Oklahoma State University–Muskogee, specializes in comfort food like Mom's Meatloaf and chicken-fried steak. But he's stepped outside the box with specials like his Cuban Sandwich—

sliced pork loin, ham, Swiss cheese, mustard, and pickles, served on French bread and pressed, Cuban style. Go uber-Okie with Jeff's Great Balls O' Fire—calf fries with buffalo hot sauce. And, as a sop to your southern side, order the fried green tomatoes.

Crowds here are diverse, depending on what's going on in town—lots of downtown business people for lunch, concert crowds going to the Brady or BOK, and on Wednesday evening, families enjoying Kids' Night, when children eat free.

The Brady District is undergoing change, and the building housing Caz's Chowhouse has experienced a lot in its history. Jeff isn't sure what it was in its earlier life but he's guessing it housed a business that manufactured oil-field trucks. Some of the elements in the Chowhouse's eclectic decor are leftovers from those days—joined by a pair of longhorn horns. Tables are covered with butcher paper—definitely informal and fun. There's an upper-level loft, and a full bar sits off to one side of the main room.

Street parking is at a premium on busy evenings, but there's a free lot just west of the restaurant. Caz's Chowhouse is open on Mon for lunch only; Tues through Fri for lunch and dinner; Sat, dinner only; and closed on Sun.

THE DAILY GRILL $$$$
100 E. 2nd St. in the Crowne Plaza Hotel
(918) 295-7748
www.dailygrill.com

Named the number one new restaurant in the *Tulsa World* 2008 poll, the Daily Grill is open seven days a week, three meals a day. Patrons enjoy free valet parking at the hotel. Cuisine style is upscale American and the decor has a retro feel with lots of dark wood and walls covered with black-and-white photos of Hollywood stars. The menu salutes classic American grills as the landmark restaurants of the '20s.

The menu is extensive but one of the most requested items is an old-fashioned classic—a chicken potpie the size of a hubcap. The steaks, hand-cut daily, are also great choices.

California wines are featured—stored in a temperature-controlled, floor-to-ceiling, glass-walled "cellar." The full bar also boasts handcrafted cocktails and classic and fancied-up martinis.

The restaurant is popular with hotel guests, the downtown business crew, and concertgoers. And it's becoming known as a destination, so reservations are always a good idea.

There's patio dining where smoking is allowed. The restaurant overlooks an attractive little park and is just steps away from the Tulsa Performing Arts Center. Open for breakfast, lunch, and dinner, seven days a week.

D'NOVO LEAN GOURMET $$
5982B S. Yale Ave. (KingsPointe Village)
(918) 494-4774 $$
www.dnovoleangourmet.com

From the Latin *de novo,* the name of this restaurant translates as "anew," "afresh," or "from the beginning." And everything about it is new—the look, the food, the concept. Presided over by executive chef Drew Flatt (see more about him under Fine Dining and Continental), no item on the menu is over 500 calories. And the items are wonderful—coconut-marinated chicken over crisp greens with macadamia nuts, mango, and red peppers, lavosh crisp, and orange basil vinaigrette; seared salmon with pecan wild rice, asparagus, and preserved lemon glaze; or an open-faced grilled bison burger with vine-ripe tomatoes, caramelized red onion, and mushrooms on whole wheat foccacia, served with jicama sweet potato fries, for example.

And there are kids' entrees, too, including crunchy chicken tenders with honey mustard and sweet potatoes, grilled cheese panini with fresh fruit, or chicken soft tacos with brown rice. There are even desserts. Almost everything is made in-house. Chef Flatt says, "We pretty much have to create things from scratch to control the calories." Calorie counting was never more fun!

Also new is the blend of order-at-the-counter and serve-yourself beverages with a shockingly elegant, contemporary decor. Stark white and black are softened by gauzy hanging curtains separating some seating areas, and chandeliers with long strings of crystals cast a soft light on the interior.

This new venue, which opened in August 2008, is attracting everybody from new moms working on their post-baby figures to seniors into healthy lifestyles. No bar, but wine and beer are available. D'Novo is open for lunch and dinner Mon through Sat.

5 & DINER $$
3641 S. Memorial Dr.
(918) 828-3467
www.5anddiner.com

Part of a small chain, this funky cafe qualifies for inclusion because it's so cool and it's attached to a small Route 66 museum and a big Harley-Davidson dealership. The decor is everything you thought the '50s looked like and sometimes actually did. Shiny stainless steel reflects red walls and the glitter of red and silver sparkle vinyl upholstery, and each table has its own jukebox.

The menu is extensive and weighted with road food favorites. Beer is the extent of the bar-type beverages. No Okie spot worth its salt would be without chicken-fried steak, and the 5 & Diner doesn't disappoint. Many customers come in just for the homemade meatloaf. Breakfast is served all day and kids' meals are served in cardboard carton re-creations of classic cars. This is a fun spot and the food's good, too.

The crowd's a mix of travelers from the multiple motels nearby, local regulars, and lots of bikers. The 5 & Diner is open from Mon to Sat for breakfast, lunch, and dinner and for breakfast and lunch on Sun.

FULL MOON CAFE $$
1525 E. 15th St.
(918) 583-6666
www.eatfullmoon.com

With its all-American menu plus a soupçon of south of the border, the Full Moon Cafe has been pleasing Tulsans for over 20 years. Favorite items include their "famous" tortilla soup, a thick and creamy soup topped with crispy-fried flour tortilla strips, gobs of cheese, and a dollop of guacamole. Another high-demand item is the Chicken Mar-

garita Salad—a bowl of mixed greens topped with cheddar and Monterey Jack cheese, Roma tomatoes, and a seven-ounce chicken breast that has been marinated in margarita butter. Steaks and burgers are popular and, of course—this is Oklahoma —chicken-fried steak.

Kudos to Full Moon for adding a "Moonlite" section to its menu. Bunless burgers, lite wraps, and grilled tuna and salmon fillets help those who are waist-watching.

Lots of the customers are regulars from the neighborhood. Live music is presented every night except Monday, and in football season Mondays become football nights. Thurs, Fri, and Sat, customers crowd in to enjoy dueling pianos. Taking it to another level, one piano is black with orange Oklahoma State University logos and the other is red with University of Oklahoma emblems. The rivalry is all in fun and the guests really get into the spirit with school songs rivaling the rock 'n' roll.

The Full Moon actually has two complete bars. One is inside, the other out. This is the only place in Tulsa with patio dining and a full bar outside. Smoking is allowed on the patio but not inside.

The Full Moon serves lunch and dinner seven days a week and adds breakfast on Sat and Sun.

LA VILLA $$-$$$$
Philbrook Museum of Art
2727 S. Rockford Rd.
(918) 749-7941 (800) 324-7941
www.philbrook.org

There was no need for elaborate decor to make la Villa a delightful lunch spot. Most of the restaurant walls are glass—overlooking the gardens and the beautiful older section of the museum—the Phillips's amazing Italian villa. The tables are covered with white cloths and the glasses and silver sparkle. This is a perfect spot for a leisurely lunch or Sunday brunch.

Of course, most of the people who eat here are visiting the museum—but not necessarily. Tues through Sat, lunch features soups, salads, substantial sandwiches, or the special pasta, chicken, or seafood of the day. Sunday brunch is an impressive array of breakfast items including made-to-order omelets, Belgian waffles, fruits, breakfast meats, pastries, and grits. Lunch selections include a variety of salads, numerous imported cheeses, seafood, several chafing-dish entrees and a carvery selection, and desserts. There is complete bar service. The price variation denotes the average lunch and the Sunday buffet.

LUCKY'S $$$$
1536 E. 15th St.
(918) 592-5825
www.luckysrestauranttulsa.com

A list of Lucky's regulars reads like a Tulsa's Who's Who. In addition to local notables, you'll find professionals and even a smattering of out-of-towners. The atmosphere is understated and sophisticated in gray, black, and white. The full bar is separated from the rest of the restaurant by a tall planter topped with a healthy stand of sanseveria. Emphasis is on American cuisine with a nouveau twist. It's easy to guess that owner/chef Matthew Kelley and executive chef Scott Van Tuyl are both Culinary Institute of America alums. Look for interesting taste combinations and new takes on old favorites. Popular items include Asian-style pork chop served with house-made mustard, green beans, and smashed Yukon potatoes; bacon-wrapped halibut with spaghetti squash and grilled vegetables with herb-mustard vinaigrette Even the rib eye steak gets spiffed up with sage brown butter and accompanied with creamed spinach and potato and shallot hash.

Opened in 2007, this is one of the newer kids on treat-packed Cherry Street (East 15th St.), but it's built an impressive following. Lucky's serves lunch and dinner Mon through Fri, dinner only on Sat, and brunch/lunch on Sun.

PALACE CAFÉ $$$$
1301 E. 15th St.
918-582-4321
www.palacetulsa.com

Chef/owner James Schrader describes his cuisine as "nouveau American," incorporating traditional favorites with international influences, emphasizing fresh, local products whenever possible.

Regional staples assume gourmet status—like the wood-grilled tenderloin, house-cut, half-pound, certified premium beef, with bleu scallop potato, Bourbon onion, wild mushrooms, and a cabernet glacé. But choices also include lighter dishes and options in portion sizes. "We encourage splits," Schrader says. And they are Tulsa's only bento restaurant—selections of small portions of several items.

Schrader studied at the Culinary Institute of America and is passionate about fine food and healthy choices. The two are not mutually exclusive. If you're watching your weight, ask your server for suggestions. You'll be able to enjoy great goodies and impressive presentation without the residual guilt.

The combination of friendly staff, full bar, great food, and the decor—warm, Chinese-red walls, colorful artwork, and funky lighting fixtures—make the Palace a popular spot with both locals and out-of-towners. And it's brought many local awards, including "Best Brunch," "Best Gourmet Bistro," and "Best Fine Dining." The Palace is open for lunch Tues through Fri, dinner Tues through Sat, and Sunday brunch.

SAVOY RESTAURANT $$
6033 S. Sheridan Rd.
(918) 494-5621
www.savoyfoods.com

Once you've experienced their cinnamon rolls (see Breakfast, Bistros, and Bakeries), you'll want to try lunch. This is about as down-home as you can get. Regular items on the menu—in addition to burgers, sandwiches, and salads—include chicken-fried steak with cream gravy; baked ham; roast beef with brown gravy; and pork chops. Specials change daily and feature items like fried chicken livers, turkey and dressing, and stewed chicken with homemade noodles. Top that off with a piece of home-baked pie. Like going to grandma's—but you don't have to carry your plate to the kitchen.

Open for lunch Mon through Fri. You have to look hard for the restaurant—it's tucked in a strip mall on the east side of Sheridan just north of 61st St.

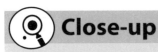 **Close-up**

Waist Not, Want Not

More and more restaurants are catering to customers who want to eat healthy, filling food without a lot of calories and extra fat. Good choices for these diners are the Palace Café, D'Novo Lean Gourmet, Full Moon Cafe, Michael Fusco's Riverside Grill, Eloté, and Ri-Le.

James Schrader, chef/owner of the Palace Café, studied at the Culinary Institute of America during a period of time when they were collaborating with Weight Watchers to create recipes for a cookbook. Schrader liked the challenge and incorporated into it his style of cooking. He can direct you to dishes that are lower in fat and calories. There are also portion-size choices listed on the menu.

D'Novo is directed at people who are monitoring their consumption. Nothing on the menu is over 500 calories. Great care is taken with presentation and seasoning. The food is really as good as it looks—it's got everything but the guilt.

The Full Moon Cafe has a "lite" section on its menu, and Michael Fusco can adapt or portion many of the menu items at his Riverside Grill. Libby Auld at Eloté cuts the fat and ups the seasoning on her offerings.

Ri-Le is a healthy choice because of the large amounts of vegetables offered. And the meats are soy-based. Even fried items are cooked in only small amounts of healthy oils. This restaurant is a vegetarian's delight and it's also good for those who are watching their weight. Most of Tulsa's restaurants will be happy to accommodate special requests and help you with healthy selections. These six make it really easy.

WILD FORK $$$$
1820 Utica Sq.
(918) 742-0712
www.wildfork.com

The Wild Fork is a favorite for elegant eating, breakfast, lunch, and dinner. In tony Utica Square, this chameleon changes character from power breakfasts to a special spot to meet a friend for lunch under the trees or in the sunny, light rooms and, when the sun goes down, a romantic destination. Beignets and biscuits, pancakes, and breakfast pizzas join omelets and other egg specialties on the breakfast menu. Soups, salads, sandwiches, and entrees star on the lunch menu. Longtime crowd pleasers include sherry tomato soup and grilled chicken on flatbread with hummus, onion, mozzarella, lettuce, tomato, and a cream herb vinaigrette dressing. Dinner items include salads, pasta dishes, fresh fish and seafood, and steaks and chops. A full-service bar and extensive wine list are available.

Chef/owners Kim Michie and Julie Woolman have built great reputations for their cuisine, including their homemade breads and desserts. Born-in-Tulsa actresses Amber Valleta and Jeanne Tripplehorn head here when they're in town. The Wild Fork is closed on Sunday.

ASIAN

LANNA THAI $$
7227 S. Memorial Dr.
(918) 249-5262
www.lannathaitulsa.com

Lanna Thai has won *Urban Tulsa* magazine's "Absolute Best of Tulsa" award for Thai food every year since 2000. Whether you get one of their curry entrees, a stir-fry, or a noodle dish, you'll get a plate full of flavor. The appetizer *satay gai*, skewers of chicken marinated in coconut milk and spices, is served with peanut sauce and spicy sweet and sour cucumbers. Too often *satay* chicken has the texture of jerky—not this. It is moist and tender. Dishes are rated from zero for "not hot" to five stars for "extra hot." Believe them.

The presentation is colorful, served on plates with blue-and-white patterned rims and garnished with juicy orange slices. The decor is restrained but there are touches of batik and bamboo birdcages to give it an oriental ambience.

Desserts are yummy and include fried banana crepes sprinkled with powdered sugar and drizzled with honey. The dessert of the day may feature seasonal fruit—like sticky rice with a sugary sauce and a whole peeled and sliced mango.

The waitresses wear attractive long red skirts with gold embroidery around the hems and red jackets. Listen carefully and speak distinctly; sometimes there's a bit of a language barrier.

Lanna Thai has a full bar and an extensive list of domestic and imported wines, beers, and sakes. Friday and Saturday nights, there's live music. The restaurant is open for lunch and dinner.

RI-LE VIETNAMESE RESTAURANT $$
4932 E. 91st St.
(918) 496-2126

This is one of those "book by the cover" spots. Tucked into a shopping strip on the southeast corner of 91st St. and South Yale Avenue, it's easy to miss. Its unprepossessing exterior masks the delight inside. Chef/owner Ri-Le and his fresh, light cuisine have had Tulsans making tracks to his restaurant for 28 years. Plaque after plaque with citations like "Best of the Best" and "Absolutely Best of Tulsa" from reader polls in local publications line the walls.

The decor is pleasant—an ornate moon gate and scrolls with calligraphy, along with a large relief piece featuring the Great Wall of China—complementing the plain tables and floors. The menu has Vietnamese and Chinese favorites but in-the-know diners just ask for Mr. Le's special. Actually all his dishes are special. "These are all my own creations," he says. Favorites include spring rolls with sticky rice and vegetable fillings, tightly rolled egg rolls, and entrees like sesame soy chicken and strawberry soy. While there are some meat items on the menu, even the most confirmed carnivore will enjoy the soy substitutes. Mr. Le says, "Ninety-five percent of my customers prefer soy meat."

Customers also enjoy the fact that Mr. Le uses no MSG (monosodium glutamate), and food is never held over warmers. And even fried items aren't oily. This is a great place for those who are watching their calories but don't want to sacrifice taste.

Ri-Le is closed on Sunday. The menu is the same for lunch and dinner. Ri-Le has built a large following of local customers, and the constant string of awards keeps bringing new people to Mr. Le's door. Ri-Le does not serve alcohol, but if you're a coffee lover, be sure and top your meal off with a traditional Vietnamese favorite—Vietnamese dark roast coffee, slow-dripped in a special individual percolator, mixed with sweetened, condensed milk, and served over ice.

TE KEI'S $$
1616 S. Utica Ave.
(918) 382-7777
www.tekeis.com

TE KEI'S 2
400 Riverwalk Terrace, Ste. 180
(918) 528-6700

Te Kei's original restaurant opened in 2002 and quickly became a favorite with Tulsans looking for Asian food with American flair. Te Kei's 2 opened in 2008. A saltwater aquarium is a nice first sight upon entering this location on the Riverwalk near the Oklahoma Aquarium. In sherbet shades of lime, lemon, and peach with bamboo structures hanging from the ceiling, the casual decor is pleasant without being distracting. Owner Todd Kramer has loaned his initials for the name—and the words mean "special guest."

Thanks to the popularity of the Riverwalk and its proximity to the Oklahoma Aquarium, Te Kei 2's clientele come not only from all over Tulsa, but all over the region.

And they enjoy favorites like the Mongolian beef—sirloin marinated in a secret sauce and stir-fried with mushrooms, red bell peppers, green and white onions, and bean sprouts—and Pearl's Lemon Chicken. The most popular sushi items are the extra-spicy Dragon Roll—tuna, asparagus, cream cheese, chili paste, avocado, wonton crisps, and green onions—and the Ultimate Roll—crabmeat, tempura shrimp, asparagus, and spicy sauce–topped avocado, massago, and fresh yellowfin tuna. Pace yourself because the bread pudding, studded with white-chocolate chunks and topped with buttered rum sauce, is a must.

Te Kei's 2 offers a full bar and patio dining. Sometimes in summer there's late-night sushi and live music. The restaurant is open for lunch and dinner seven days a week.

BREAKFAST, BISTROS, AND BAKERIES

THE BISTRO $$$
10021 S. Yale Ave., Ste. 103
(918) 296-3000
www.tulsabistro.com
An American-style bistro, this restaurant is casually elegant. The decor is subdued—gray, black, and white with red accents. On the far south edge of town, the Bistro attracts most of its customers from nearby neighborhoods, so there are lots of regulars.

Open since 1997, the Bistro is noted for its fillets—served bacon-wrapped, blackened with Cajun spices, or Oscar-style with lump crabmeat and béarnaise sauce. Other favorites include the 'chokes and cheese appetizer; Pasta Yaya, chicken breast and sausage in a spicy cream sauce seasoned with scallions, garlic, white wine, and Cajun seasoning, served over fettuccini; and the Baked Fudge dessert—a gooey walnut brownie served warm with whipped or ice cream.

Enjoy a drink from the complete bar and patio dining when the weather is nice. This non-smoking restaurant is open for lunch and dinner seven days a week.

BLUE DOME DINER $
313 E. 2nd St.
(918) 382-7866
www.myspace.com/bluedomediner
Decor here is definitely diner—open kitchen, Formica-topped tables, chrome and vinyl chairs, worse-for-wear booths, assorted stools at the counter, and a concrete floor with chipped Cherokee-red paint.

And you won't miss the glitz when you try the French toast made with their homemade sourdough, whole wheat bread with delicious eggy crunchies around the edge of the crusts. Don't look for frou-frou entrees—this is pretty much a meat and egg place. The closest you'll get to health-conscious is with the vegetable scrambler, an egg-white omelet, or Grandma's Oats, with brown sugar, walnuts, and raisins. Then again, it's hard to beat homemade biscuits and gravy.

The menu is overseen by chef/owner Brian Prewitt, who got a standing ovation from Robin Williams for the meal he catered for him. Weekdays, lots of business people have breakfast or coffee here, and the rest of the town shows up on weekends.

Popular with the downtown crowd, the restaurant serves up daily lunch specials plus sandwiches and burgers. Surprisingly, you'll find several vegetarian options, including a seared veggie sandwich with lemon-caper aioli. Of the salads on the lunch menu, the Blue Dome Greek Salad would make Zorba weep for joy.

The restaurant is closed on Mon and open for breakfast and lunch Tues through Sun. There's no bar but beer is available. Smoking is allowed in the back room. Bring quarters for the parking meter and prepare to deal with downtown parking.

BROOKSIDE BY DAY $
3313 S. Peoria Ave.
(918) 745-9989
Many Tulsans won't start their days without breakfast at BBD. The place is packed on weekends. Open for both breakfast and lunch, the restaurant offers breakfast items any hour it's open. This place has been around long enough that a second generation is now bringing their kids to eat here.

You can order the usual—eggs, omelets, pancakes, breakfast meats—but try the specialty Murrito. Named in homage to Murray, the owner of the restaurant that used to be here, the Murrito is scrambled eggs, sausage, green onions, and cheddar wrapped in a flour tortilla and served with fresh, house-made guacamole, sour cream, picante, and home fries. Or you can substitute grits if you like a little more South in your Southwest.

Watching your waist? Order a Chickito with chicken instead of sausage.

Lunch items include chicken-fried steak, hot and cold sandwiches, burgers, and a shrimp basket with shrimp flown in from the Gulf by White River Fish Market. No bar, no beer.

Nothing on the menu is over $10. This is the kind of place where you stop for breakfast and stay 'til lunch—very casual, low-key, and friendly.

CRUSTY CROISSANT $-$$
3629 S. Peoria Ave.
(918) 743-2253
www.crustycroissant.com

A bakery and cafe, this is a popular breakfast spot in the trendy Brookside area—but it's also good for lunch. Owner Sean Savage doesn't know the building's history, but the telltale black and white hexagonal tiles on the floor and the shiny black ceramic-tile wainscoting are clues to earlier incarnations. Old-time Tulsans remember when it was the S & J Oyster Company.

Sean's added some Tuscan touches to the place, giving it an eclectic aura. This complements the blend of aromas of fresh-baked cookies, croissants, and quiches. It's possible to eat light here, but you probably won't want to.

The CC's "create your own omelet/breakfast quesadilla" appeals to a lot of customers, while others go for breakfast tacos, French toast, waffles, or crepes. The chicken salad is the most-requested luncheon item, but you won't go wrong with any of their soups, salads, or sandwiches.

In pleasant weather, al fresco is the way to go. With lots of dining and shopping on the Brookside strip, the people-watching is great entertainment.

Parking can be a big issue in this area. Fortunately, the church across the street is very generous with its lot.

The Crusty Croissant is open seven days a week for breakfast and lunch. This is a hot spot for "ladies who lunch," but guys will find plenty to please, too. Wine and beer are available in addition to the usual beverages.

GREAT HARVEST BREAD COMPANY $
5203 S. Sheridan Rd.
(918) 622-1115
www.tulsagreatharvest.com

Just open the door and inhale—heaven! While there are Great Harvest shops in other places, each is unique. The only common denominator is that each buys the finest Montana wheat berries from the same source, and each one mills flour daily. No preservatives are used—you can pronounce every ingredient—and no loaf is older than thirty hours. Honey whole wheat is the best seller, but lots of other varieties are available, including pumpkin swirl bread and cinnamon rolls.

And the best bread makes the best sandwiches. Custom order your favorite ingredients and, if you like, round out the meal with soup, salad, or a cookie. Lunch is the only meal served, and no alcoholic beverages are available. The bakery is closed Sun and Mon. If you'd like to take a tour (Tues, Wed, or Thurs), call ahead.

SAVOY RESTAURANT $$
6033 S. Sheridan Rd.
(918) 494-5621
www.savoyfoods.com

Though the Savoy serves lunch Mon through Fri, it's best known for its breakfasts, served Mon through Sat. There are lots of regulars and they get here early—before the cinnamon rolls or caramel pecan rolls (served Fri and Sat) are gone. And these Tulsans know a thing or two—the cinnamon rolls are melt-in-your-mouth, light, fluffy mega-rolls with just the right amount of icing.

Chef/owner Larry is the third generation in the business, which has been in this location since 1954. His grandfather opened his first restaurant in Tulsa in 1925.

Everything here is made from scratch—even the bread for French toast. The pancakes, biscuits,

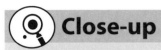

Close-up

Blue Jackalope

306 S. Phoenix Ave.
(918) 582-5344
www.bluejackalope.com

This is one of those off-the-beaten-path places that qualify as a town treasure. It's located in Crosbie Heights, one of Tulsa's oldest neighborhoods. The neighborhood was definitely feeling its age—aging population, aging houses, and no local grocery or services. It met the definition of "food desert"—an area where people have both geographical and financial problems accessing healthy food. Then Scott Smith, a resident of the area, decided to do something about it. He bought the former Church of Christ building, painted it blue and white, and opened a neighborhood grocery store and coffee spot.

If you want to feel the heartbeat of the community, stop in here. The stock's not large—staples plus fresh fruit and vegetables, locally grown when possible.

The coffee's locally roasted. You'll find here not only the immediate neighbors, but folks from all over town who are passionate about Tulsa and concerned about social and environmental issues. You can probably get a discussion going anytime, but Sunday afternoon from 3 to 6 is the "official" coffee-table discussion time.

If you don't want to get that involved but just want to pick up a good sandwich and a bottle of pop, make the stop. The store is open seven days a week, and Scott offers a choice of a vegetarian and two "carnivorian" sandwiches daily. If the avocados meet his standards, one of his best sandwiches is avocado, hummus, and cheese on whole wheat bread. He doesn't sell alcohol or tobacco products. He just provides good coffee, fresh sandwiches, and basic grocery needs, and serves his community.

and other baked goods are super, and there are a variety of other breakfast choices. The decor isn't fancy, but the restaurant is clean, white, and bright, and the waitresses are efficient and friendly. What more can you ask for?

CONTINENTAL AND FINE DINING

ALE HAUS $$$
500 RiverWalk Terrace, Ste. 135, Jenks
(918) 528-6600
www.ale-haus.com

The Ale Haus almost defies categorization. Continental—yes, you'll find European favorites like the signature Beef Wellington, French duck a l'orange, and Spanish paella on the menu. Fine dining—yes, the atmosphere is quietly sophisticated, with its dark wood, stone, and subdued neutral color palette, and soft music. But you'll

also find awfully good pub grub here. The casual signature dish is fish and chips. And the burgers get great reviews—especially the Boondock burger with spinach, Bermuda onion, and spicy Pepper Jack cheese.

In summer the outdoor beer garden is a popular spot. It's a great place to kick back and enjoy people-watching. Smoking is allowed out here.

The clientele is generally 35 and older—looking for good food and low noise level. Children are welcome but they're expected to behave and order off the regular menu. There's no children's menu, coloring sheets, or crayons. It's a good date-night place—not too fancy or stuffy but definitely with an upscale ambiance.

There's full bar service with good lists of wines, beers, and ales. But the Ale Haus doesn't stop at the glass. Try the Guinness Soup, a rich cheesy concoction with a goodly nip of Guinness, or the Bailey's Irish crème brûlée.

The restaurant is open for lunch and dinner Mon through Sat. It's closed on Sun.

CHALKBOARD $$$$
1324 S. Main St.
(918) 582-1964
www.thechalkboard-tulsa.com

Occupying the same space as the restaurant of the same name in the 1950s, the new Chalkboard (open since the renovated Ambassador Hotel reopened in 1999) is a far cry from the old eatery. Check out the photos of the original restaurant in the hotel stairwell leading to the mezzanine. Today's Chalkboard is intimate and cozy—deep rose-colored walls, red banquettes, contemporary art on the walls, and unobtrusive jazz playing. This is sophisticated, adult dining without being stuffy.

Whether you want the latest flavor martini, Moët & Chandon, or choc beer on tap from Krebs, the bar can handle your request. The appetizer crab cakes are a real favorite, along with the Pecan Salad—mixed baby greens tossed with raspberry vinaigrette and topped with dried cherries and apples, candied pecans, and crumbled goat cheese. Longtime customers would balk if the beef Wellington ever went off the menu, but other items change seasonally. The signature dessert is a white-chocolate bread pudding with white-chocolate sauce and fresh strawberries.

The old saw says, "It's an ill wind that blows no good," but New Orleans's misfortune brought a treasure to Tulsa in the form of chef Paul Wilson. Having studied under master chefs there, chef Paul is now firmly entrenched in Tulsa and presides over a cadre of creative cooks, producing everything from their own breads to house-made french fries to go with the Chalkboard Burger.

Through the week, the crowd is mostly business travelers staying at the hotel; on the weekends, locals predominate. For certain special events at the BOK Center, the Chalkboard will serve a preshow buffet and provide trolley transportation so diners don't have to worry about parking downtown.

The Chalkboard offers breakfast and dinner seven days a week, lunch Mon through Fri, and brunch on Sat and Sun. This is one of the few restaurants open on major holidays and is becoming a tradition with less-traditional Tulsans who don't want to cook, and it provides a holiday haven for travelers. Dinner reservations are suggested.

CYPRUS GRILLE $$$$
6808 S. 107th East Ave. (in the Renaissance Hotel)
(918) 307-2600

Open for breakfast, lunch, and dinner, the Cyprus Grille not only caters to hotel guests but is a favorite spot for power lunches, destination dinners, and Sunday-after-church outings. Executive chef William Doyle has created a menu that takes a Grand Tour of the world's cuisines. From Italian *osso bucco* and Moroccan flat iron steak to Greek roasted chicken and the Cyprus burger (shades of the Southwest with Black Angus beef and chipotle barbecue aioli), everyday items take on an exotic flare with his creativity.

Particular crowd pleasers include the Tuscan Chicken Club—grilled chicken, peppered bacon, smoked cheddar, lettuce, tomato on a toasted multigrain bun with roasted red bell pepper aioli—or, for breakfast, the mashed potato, bacon, Swiss cheese, and cheddar omelet.

The ambience is upscale casual, with ample room between cloth-covered tables, chairs, and plush banquettes. Primary color in the room is a deep ruby with buttery-yellow accents.

Full bar service is available. Parking is easy in the hotel lot, or take advantage of the valet service.

LXI $$$
5982C S. Yale Ave.
(918) 340-5244
www.lxitulsa.com

LXI is "61" in Latin and this wine bar/restaurant is in the Kingspointe Village at East 61st St. and South Yale Avenue. Though it almost falls into the bistro category, the extensive bar, in addition to the wine list, and its gourmet cuisine, put it here.

LXI specializes in "small plates," but the most popular offerings are its "tasting flights"—for example, the four-course Latin American flight.

This includes shrimp Culiacan wrapped in bacon with roasted garlic aioli; adobo-rubbed sea bass with avocado cream and mango salsa; ancho relleno with spiced chicken and dried apricots with a carrot sauce; and crème fraiche flan with pepita crust. These flights can also be paired with wines chosen by general manager and sommelier Tyler Mirt.

Executive chef Drew Flatt is a part-owner of LXI and the adjacent D'Novo Restaurant and The Grocer and the Gourmet Market. Trained at the Culinary Institute of America, he has an impressive résumé including the Five-Diamond Marquesa Fairmont Scottsdale Princess and The Grill at the TPC Scottsdale.

Certified sommelier Mirt has an extensive restaurant and bar background and is passionate about his profession. He hosts monthly wine, spirits, and beer education classes at LXI. The restaurant has a long list of signature cocktails—a favorite is the Lavender Lemon Drop made with Absolut Citron, lavender syrup, and fresh lemon with a lavender sugar rim.

The decor here is contemporary with clean lines and a natural color palette accented with contemporary paintings. The seating is a combination of tables and chairs; sofas, chairs, and tables; and bar seating. Smoking is allowed on the patio. LXI is open for dinner only, Mon through Sat.

MICHAEL FUSCO'S RIVERSIDE
GRILL $$$$-$$$$$
9912 Riverside Pkwy.
(918) 394-2433
www.michaelfuscosriversidegrill.com

Training at Johnson and Wales and cutting his Tulsa teeth at Bodean's, Michael Fusco has made a name for himself in the area with his excellent and innovative cuisine. For several years his restaurant, Flavors, was a favorite. In 2007 he got the opportunity to build his own building with a prime view of the Arkansas River.

The decor is clean and uncluttered. Nothing stands in the way of the focus on food. The cuisine is Continental but the restaurant could have easily been listed under Steaks and Sea-

food. Items like Hudson Valley foie gras served with pearl onion marmalade, escargot Provencal, and seared Provimi veal liver push the Continental classification. The Arkansas bacon, smashed potatoes, and fried onions served with the liver make a comfort-food category a possibility. Plus, Michael's Italian heritage shows up on the menu. Michael's tastes—and offerings—are eclectic.

This is one of the few—possibly only—menus in town that indicate gluten-free choices. If you're looking for vegetarian or low-fat dishes, you can be accommodated. As Michael says, "Everything is cooked to order so adjustments are easy." Just don't expect him to make the calories disappear from his spectacular chocolate gateau, made with Callebaut dark chocolate from Belgium.

There is a full bar and outside dining in nice weather. It's open for lunch Mon through Fri and dinner daily. Between lunch and dinner, you can order appetizers at the bar. The restaurant is located just north of the Creek Turnpike and sits in the highest per-capita income zip code in the state. You'll find lots of close neighbors eating here, but the reputation is such that people come from all over town.

i Here's the 411 on smoking: If an establishment sells more alcohol than food, it does not have to be nonsmoking. Restaurants are allowed to have smoking areas, but they must be in separate, ventilated rooms. This is an expensive proposition for most places, so almost all Oklahoma restaurants are now nonsmoking.

POLO GRILL $$$$
2038 Utica Sq.
(918) 744-4280
www.pologrill.com

The restaurant's located in Utica Square, but don't try to find it by driving around. Just come south on South Yorktown Avenue and turn into the shopping area at the entrance across from the Monte Cassino playground. The Polo Grill is tucked into a corner of the first area of shops on your right.

Inside there's a kind of French farmhouse feel—brick floors, lots of wood, accent pieces that have a rustic look. The lighting is subdued, and the colors are ochre, umber, and russet. The menu is Continental but with a definite southwestern twist. The steaks are among the most popular items—the veal reduction used in the sauce takes three days to make. Only prime beef is served, and the bone-in rib eye steak is a favorite choice. The curried chicken salad with a tomato bisque shooter is a good choice for lunch fare.

This is a traditional favorite "nice restaurant" for Tulsans, whether it's ladies who are shopping in the area, business power lunches, or just a great dinner out. It's a quiet restaurant—a good atmosphere for enjoying your food and your dining companion(s).

There's a full bar, and wines are served in handblown Riedel glasses. Save room for dessert. The height of decadence is the baked fudge—it's been on the menu since the restaurant opened. It's a gooey chocolate brownie garnished with a raspberry coulis and chocolate sauce, sprinkled with shaved white chocolate, topped with vanilla ice cream with shavings of dark chocolate.

The Polo Grill is open for lunch and dinner, Mon through Sat.

WARREN DUCK CLUB $$$$$
6110 S. Yale Ave.
(918) 495-1000
www.tulsaatwarrenplace.doubletree.com
Continually receiving kudos for fine dining, the Duck Club also serves breakfast and lunch. Close to a large medical complex, its clientele leans heavily toward professional people and business travelers. It is a 30-plus-year favorite for locals looking for an elegant evening out or a place to bring guests. Service is attentive and accomplished—several of the waitstaff have been with the restaurant since its opening.

The Duck Club's signature dish is Long Island duck, rotisserie roasted, served with rice pilaf and vegetables, and accompanied with a choice of sauces—classic orange, spicy green peppercorn, or ginger soy. Another popular choice is

the blackened beef tenderloin, with a subtle Cajun flavor and served with béarnaise sauce. It's hard to go wrong here. Though the menu does change, these choices are staples. For an unusual appetizer, try the Whiskey Shrimp, jumbo shrimp sautéed with shallots and laced with heavy cream and Jack Daniels.

Many visitors come during the day just to enjoy the view. One side of the restaurant is windowed and overlooks a pleasant park. The decor is one of understated elegance—lots of wood, but not dark. Though there are candles on the table at dinner, Italian light fixtures provide subdued lighting. This isn't one of those so-dark-you-can't-read-the-menu places. The color palette is neutral with pale gold silk coverings on the table for dinner.

The restaurant has an extensive wine list. Wine and other alcoholic beverages can be enjoyed either in the restaurant or the full bar adjacent. The bar also has a limited food menu. Parking is available in the hotel parking garage. Reservations are recommended for dinner.

DELIS, DRIVE-INS, SANDWICHES, AND LIGHT LUNCHES

AMERICA'S INCREDIBLE PIZZA COMPANY $-$$
8314 E. 71st St.
(918) 294-8671
www.incrediblepizza.com
This restaurant really doesn't have a category—but it needs to be in this chapter because if you're traveling with children, you need to know about it. IPC is a one-stop eating and entertainment center. The buffet includes a long list of kid's favorites—and they make almost everything from scratch, including pizza dough. They make over 30 kinds of pizza each day. The salad bar has over 100 items—fruit, veggies, even plain Jell-O for the pickiest eater. Special items are offered each day—could be tacos, burgers, or more substantial entrees. Desserts include cookies, brownies, cobblers, and cinnamon rolls. There's no way this is gourmet fare but it is filling. The cinnamon

rolls are among the most popular items—and if you score one of these gooey glories fresh and hot from the oven, you'll know why.

For kids, the games are going to be more interesting than the menu, so prepare to pay for them to play. The meals will probably be the least expensive part of your visit. For more information check the Attractions chapter.

CONEY ISLAND HOT WEINERS $
123 W. 4th St.
(918) 587-2821

The menu is minimal, the decor even more, but since 1926 Tulsans have been coming downtown for Coney Island hot dogs. Oh, there are a lot of shops with similar names around town, and there are some tenuous ties between a number of them, but the granddaddy downtown is the original Tulsa doggery. Greek immigrant Christ Economou started with a hot dog place back East, was successful, sold it, and moved on. He repeated this move several times before coming to Tulsa. Today this shop is still owned by Christ's son, Jim.

Though you can choose a couple of other items like three-way spaghetti or tamales, most customers come for the dogs. And they bring their children and grandchildren for a real Tulsa mouth-memory. The dogs are smaller than the average wiener. The steamed bun is slathered with yellow mustard. Greek chili with no beans, chopped onion, and the weenie go inside. You can have shredded cheese if you must, but under no circumstances should you ever ask for catsup. With three Coneys, you get a free fountain drink. This is a good deal. These hot dogs are like potato chips—you can't eat just one. Besides, you can get through one in five bites. A real bargain at their original nickel price, even at almost 30 times that price, they still qualify.

You can take your food out, but it's best eaten while the bun is still hot—in an old high school chair with the built-in writing surface on one arm. Even if you didn't grow up in Tulsa, you'll get a big helping of nostalgia with your Coney.

Coney Island is open Mon through Fri for lunch and early dinner.

LAMBRUSCO'Z CATERING MARKET AND
DELICATESSEN $-$$
1344 E. 41st St.
(918) 496-1246
www.lambruscoz.com

Lambrusco'z is a deli and much, much more. Yes, you can buy Boar's Head meats and cheeses and salads here, but you can also get fabulous made-to-order sandwiches, menu-listed sandwiches, and entrees. Eat here or take it to go. The eat-in dinner entrees come with two sides and are a great bargain, but you can also take home enough food to feed a whole party. And it's all made from scratch and good. They're open for lunch and early dinner.

Dinnertime isn't a dine-and-linger affair but it's great for a good meal before an evening event during the week. Their 5 p.m. Saturday closing (two hours earlier than Mon through Fri) probably makes lunch the only meal you would eat in that day—and they're closed on Sun.

As for atmosphere, it's decidedly casual. The decor is negligible—mottled gray and black tile floor and simple tables with bentwood chairs, surrounded by racks of merchandise and cases of goodies. But the food is so good, you won't care. You order at the counter. Choose from a variety of sandwich suggestions, create your own, or have whatever's been prepared for the day—could be cheese enchiladas, grilled chicken breasts, quiche, or any number of choices. A wide variety of salads and sides are available. They make almost everything themselves but they do have a couple of items that are locally made by someone else—like the intriguing savory cheesecakes made by Oodle's and Gobb's. Tasty combos like blue Viva la French onion or Italian sausage and pepperoni pizza can be either appetizers or entrees. Choose your dessert from an array of cookies, pies, and cakes.

Their refrigerator cases are full of freshly made goodies to take home—their white queso dip and the dill chicken salad are among the most popular items, but there are lots more tempting choices. This is the place to stock up for a party—they have lots of different crackers, breads, and chips to go with the goodies. Locals check the freezer for entrees to keep on hand for emergencies—or just because they're so good.

You'd expect to find condiments and other specialty foods on the merchandise shelves—but you'll also find a variety of things from colorful, printed totes made of recycled materials to picnic supplies, cocktail napkins, candles, and body products.

The clientele is mostly local—Lambrusco'z is located on a side street off busy South Peoria Avenue. While lots of people eat in, even more carry out. Nancy, the owner, is generous about giving out recipes. She's not worried about losing business. She says, "Anybody can make these items if they have time; our customers just don't have the time." But these people also like the food they eat to taste as good as if they cooked it themselves. And that's what you get at Lambrusco'z—assuming you're a really good cook.

Nancy's mom started the business in 1987 in her home, doing catering. Today Nancy runs the combo catering company, deli, and restaurant. The business began as a labor of love and continues that way—and it shows in their cooking.

STEVE'S SUNDRY, BOOKS & MAGAZINES $
2612 S. Harvard Ave.
(918) 743-3544, (888) 743-0989
www.stevessundrybooksmags.com
Tulsa's oldest independent bookstore probably has Tulsa's oldest lunch counter, too. Located in the downtown Quaker Drug Store until Steve Stephenson bought it in 1947, this counter has seen a lot of elbows. Order an old-fashioned soda or shake or a vanilla Coke to drink with your homemade chicken salad, egg salad, or pimento salad sandwich.

The counter stools are also original but there are only 12 of them so sometimes there's a wait. There's no other seating, so wheelchair accessibility is difficult.

For more details about Steve's, check under Books in the Shopping chapter.

WEBER'S SUPERIOR ROOT BEER RESTAURANT $
3817 S. Peoria Ave.
(918) 742-1082
www.webersoftulsa.com
Weber's, in business here since 1933, is a Tulsa classic. Great-grandfather Oscar Weber Bilby started the business at the urging of friends who loved the grilled hamburgers he fixed and loved even more his home-brewed root beer. Great-grandson Rick Bilby is still using the same grill. Made in 1891, the 3-foot-by-4-foot, inch-and-a-half-thick pig iron slab takes about an hour and a half to heat up. And Rick, his wife Jennifer, daughter Michelle, and sister Charlotte are still making that famous root beer from the same 14 natural—and secret—ingredients.

Weber's drive-in is tiny—there are 12 stools at a counter inside. Picnic tables outside accommodate 32 more. Many people just order takeout. The hamburgers, made from Angus beef, are still top sellers. And you have to have the root beer—or a root beer float. You can buy the brew in bottles, too.

The french fries are made fresh—Michelle peels about 100 pounds of potatoes a day, and the onion rings are homemade, too. This is Tulsa's oldest restaurant and the grill is just possibly the oldest grill in the United States. The restaurant is closed on Sunday.

GERMAN

MARGARET'S GERMAN RESTAURANT AND DELI $$$
5107 S. Sheridan Rd.
(918) 622-3747
www.margaretsgermanrestaurant.com
Located in The Farm shopping center, Margaret's offers German family fare for lunch Mon through Thurs and lunch and dinner on Fri and Sat. In business for 20 years, owner Margaret Rzepczynski takes Sunday off. A lot of her customers are regulars and come in on the days she serves their favorite specials—maybe Polish pierogies or Hungarian goulash. Purists go for the Kassler rippchen (smoked pork loin) or her Wiener schnitzel.

And they wash it down with German beer (or wine). Whether you just want a sandwich or a whole meal, this is a good spot. Be sure and save room for some of her German chocolate cake or strudel. And you can pick up deli meats, brats, or German specialty items like spaetzle and streusel mix.

ITALIAN

BIGA $$$
4329 S. Peoria Ave.
(918) 743-2442
www.bodean.net/Bigahome.html

Although on the corner of a small mall on busy Peoria, Biga brings a touch of trattoria to Tulsa. Wine, cream, and soft green colors provide a Tuscan background for dining on Italian favorites from many regions. The menu changes during the year, but enduring favorites include the pappardelle with ragù Bolognese, the roast veal chop with Parmesan gnocchi and wild mushroom sauce, and, in the cold months, osso bucco. All the flat pastas and raviolis are made in-house, as is the wonderful country bread.

The restaurant has lots of regulars—it's been here for almost a decade—and the staff stays consistent. Owner and chef is Tucker Curran, whose wife, Kate, manages the restaurant. Curran got his start at Bodean's and is actually partners with the Faulkners. Curran uses as many locally grown or raised products as he can get. The wine list is extensive and there's a full bar. Outside, there's a lovely ivy-covered pergola over a small patio—great for outside dining on pleasant evenings. Biga is upscale, but not break-the-bank so. There is a full bar.

Biga is open for dinner only, Tues through Sun. It is closed on Mon. Because the patio is intimate, there's only one table where smoking is allowed and guests who smoke are expected to defer to nonsmokers' objections.

Watch the Web site for news about special wine dinners. Biga also offers a three-course prix fixe dinner for a very reasonable price.

GARLIC ROSE $$$
3509 S. Peoria Ave.
(918) 746-4900

GARLIC ROSE II $$$
9904 S. Riverside Parkway.
(918) 481-5555
www.garlicrose-tulsa.com

Owned by the family that owns The Chalkboard, the Garlic Rose was named for one of its favorite offerings—a roasted garlic head served with homemade bread and a combination of olive oil and balsamic vinegar—which is complimentary at dinner. While the menu lists some non-Italian dishes, it would be a shame not to try the cannelloni of the day (lunch and dinner) or the ravioli of the day (dinner). The farfalle pasta in pesto cream sauce with red bell peppers, garlic, and spinach and topped with sautéed chicken, pine nuts, and goat cheese is a consistent customer request.

The decor is definitely Italian, with crisp, white tablecloths, clay-colored stucco walls, wine bottles, grapes, and greenery. Full bar service is available.

This place is tricky to find. Although the address is on South Peoria Avenue, the entrance to the little enclave of shops and restaurants where it's located is on 35th St. There's plenty of parking just east of these businesses. The Garlic Rose is open for lunch Tues through Sat and dinner Mon through Sat. It's closed on Sun.

Enjoy the same good menu at Garlic Rose II. The décor's a little sleeker, the bar's a bit bigger, and they have a private wine room. Hours and days are the same, although there is a chance they may add a Sunday brunch.

GINA AND GUISEPPE'S $$
400 RiverWalk Terrace, Suite 100
(918) 296-0111
www.gngitalian.com

With family pictures on the walls, Gina and Guiseppe's has the feel of a nice Italian home. You'll see photos of Grandpa and Grandma Macri—and there you have the inspiration for the restaurant. Grandson Christopher is the chef and, while many of the creations are his own, many of the recipes came from Grandma Gina.

Located on the river, close to the Oklahoma Aquarium, the family-owned eatery has its regulars but draws visitors from everywhere. The biggest seller is the five-layer lasagna, four cheeses, meat, and Grandma Gina's southern Italian marinara. Other favorites include the grilled vegetable salad and grilled chicken parmigiana with angel hair pasta.

The restaurant is open for lunch and dinner seven days a week and offers a full bar. It received "Best New Restaurant 2006," and "Best Italian" and "Best Pizza" in 2008, in local popularity polls.

HIDEAWAY PIZZA $$
1419 E. 15th St.
(918) 582-4777

7877 E. 51st St.
(918) 270-4777

8204 S. Harvard Ave.
(918) 492-4777

8222 E. 103rd St.
(918) 366-4777

1150 N. 9th St., Broken Arrow
(918) 286-1777
www.hideawaypizza.com

Hideaway Pizza has been an Oklahoma institution since it was founded in Stillwater in 1957. After 36 years of one location, the clamor for Hideaway was loud enough that founder Richard Dermer had to franchise. Now there are Hideaways in several Oklahoma cities, including five locations in the Tulsa area.

Hideaway's decor is casual, with large collages on the walls. These are 4-foot-by-6-foot descendants of the wall-sized collage that decorated the original restaurant. Created by kindergarten classes to college students, they were winners in Hideaway collage competitions.

Order salad or pasta if you want; try the spicy mushroom caps, but you must eat the pizza. Try traditional cheese and Hideaway red sauce and you won't be disappointed, but get a little more adventuresome and you're in for quite a treat. Choices include pizzas with kielbasa, pizzas with

pineapple, or pizzas with barbecue sauce. The number one seller is the Paradise Pie—Hideaway Alfredo sauce, mozzarella, smoked provolone, grilled chicken, smoked bacon, fresh sliced mushrooms, fresh spinach, and diced Roma tomatoes.

Hideaway is open for lunch and dinner seven days a week. And if you want wine or beer with your pizza, you'll be accommodated. The 15th St. location offers some patio service, but the entire property is nonsmoking.

TUCCI'S CAFFE ITALIA $$$
1344 E. 15th St.
(918) 582-3456

Welcome to bella Italia and a Tulsa restaurant that will transport you right to a Tuscan trattoria. Black and white tile floor, red walls, subdued lighting, and Italian favorites playing should put you in the mood for a delightful meal.

Staples are pizzas and pasta dishes and a calzone ring that won't ever be taken off the menu for fear of rioting. And they make a lemonata salad dressing here that is so popular that they bottle it and sell it. In this location for 15 years, Tucci's has a faithful following but also attracts lots of out-of-towners. One traveler vowed "I've been all over the world and this is the best Bolognese I've ever eaten."

Parking's scarce here so be prepared to walk a bit. The restaurant has a full bar and outdoor deck seating. No smoking inside or out, please. Tucci's is open for lunch and dinner Mon through Fri, dinner only on Sat, and closed on Sun.

MEDITERRANEAN

HELEN OF TROY MEDITERRANEAN RESTAURANT $$$
6670 S. Lewis Ave.
(918) 794-3322

"What items are so popular that you don't dare take them off the menu?" Owner Sam Senjlawi's answer, "Everything! We can't take anything off the menu and we keep adding more." The most popular items—among all the popular items—are baba ganoush, hummus, and the lamb shanks, which cook for six to eight hours in the oven. And the pita is warm and soft and absolutely great—Sam tasted this pita in Chicago and determined he would serve nothing else.

Helen of Troy is located in a small strip of shops just south of East 61st St. and South Lewis Avenue. Look carefully (on the west side of the street) or you'll miss it. Inside, Middle Eastern, Greek, or Egyptian music plays in the background. The decor is minimal—dark carpet, black wrought iron, and padded, angular, contemporary chairs at plain tables. The walls are a pale sunflower yellow. The ambience is not the point. The food is and this is definitely tasty.

Sam's mother was from Jordan and it's her repertoire of recipes that provides the mainstays of the menu. No alcohol, not even beer, is sold here. Helen of Troy has lots of regulars—diners who crave the garlicky hummus, the gyros, or the cabbage rolls.

The restaurant opened in 2007 and quickly built a reputation. In 2008 *Urban Tulsa* magazine named it the "Absolutely Best of Tulsa Mediterranean Restaurant," and *TulsaPeople* magazine in its 2008 "Food Lover's Guide" named Helen of Troy the "Best Place to Feel Like You're on the Aegean." The restaurant is open seven days a week. Lunch and dinner are served Mon through Sat. Lunch is served on Sun, but not dinner.

MEXICAN, SPANISH, AND SOUTHWESTERN

CAFÉ OLE $$
3509 S. Peoria Ave.
(918) 745-6699
www.cafeoletulsa.com

Don't be fooled by the address—this little restaurant is actually on 35th St. And it's worth finding. Readers' polls have recognized it for Tulsa's best margaritas and best southwestern cuisine. Crowd faves here are the Stacked Blue Corn Enchiladas and the Chicken Verde Enchiladas. Nothing's too spicy. The philosophy is "you can always make it hotter," so if you like your food with plenty of kick, ask your server. While the margaritas are popular, there are few other mixed drinks available—mostly just wine and beer.

The restaurant is small and often crowded inside and out. The patio, with a fireplace and warmers, is used year-round. A small, upstairs area has several tables and some interesting artwork.

Opened over 20 years ago, Café Ole has customers who come in two and three times a week. And each waiter has his own "crowd." But first-timers are welcome, too. Café Ole is open seven days a week and serves lunch and dinner every day. Come in at 10 a.m. on a weekday for huevos rancheros and on Sat and Sun at 9 a.m., when they serve a few other items not on the regular menu.

EL GUAPO'S CANTINA $$
332 E. 1st St.
(918) 382-7482
www.elguaposcantina.net

For a colorful evening, head to the Blue Dome District and El Guapo's for Mexican food and margaritas. The rooftop patio is a big draw in pleasant weather (and for smokers). There's an elevator for those who shy away from the steep stairs that lead to the upper floors in this roomy eatery. You'll find everyone here, from families to the before-the-concert crowd and those who plan to spend the rest of the evening in this burgeoning nightlife area.

The decor is Mexclectic—piñatas hanging from the ceiling, religious art—holy candles on the tables—and folk art on the walls. Some walls are painted bright colors; tables sport wild, colorful oilcloth coverings. Other walls have old brick showing through peeled paint—whether it's old or intentional, the effect is interesting.

The chips and salsa are house-made. The salsa is mild, very tomatoey, with a hint of an afterburn. One of the most popular entrees is smoked steak/cheese flautas. Tacos come with a choice of meats—carne asada (beef), carnitas (pork), and tinga (chicken). One of the more unusual appetizers is the Oaxacan tamale—smoked mole chicken with onions, cilantro, and Mexican crema cooked in a banana-leaf wrapper. .

There's a whole list of margaritas—most 16 ounces. For something a little different, try a Tamarind Margarita—Corralejo Reposado with tamarind and lime—or the Margarita Ponche de Fruta—a fruit puree (choose pomegranate, strawberry, prickly pear, mango, blood orange, or raspberry) mixed into El Guapo's signature Margarita De La Casa, a traditional margarita made with tequila, triple sec, and lime.

El Guapo really shines in the dessert department. A good choice is the Cajeta Chimi—apple wedges, cinnamon, and sugar inside a crisp, light flour tortilla, drizzled with caramel, and served à la mode. Or try the Peaches and Cream Sopapilla Relleno—a gooey goodie with caramelized peaches, honey, and ice cream in a warm sopapilla and topped with whipped cream and strawberries. Sort of makes the flan, fried ice cream, and key lime pie sound mundane. But any of these homemade treats makes a good finish for your meal.

Parking's sometimes problematic, so give yourself time to cruise for a spot. The restaurant is open for lunch and dinner daily and additional brunch on the weekends.

ELOTÉ $$
514 S. Boston Ave.
(918) 582-1403
www.elotetulsa.com
Is the phrase "healthy Mexican food" an oxymoron? Not here. Chef/owner Libby Auld graduated from the culinary arts program at Oklahoma State University–Okmulgee and apprenticed with chef Rick Bayless in Chicago. (He's the owner of several popular restaurants in that city and the author of the definitive *Authentic Mexican: Regional Cooking from the Heart of Mexico*.)

Libby Auld is the face of the future—and it's a smiling one. Her philosophy is good for personal and planetary health. Unnecessary fats are eliminated in cooking—flavor is heightened with spices and fresh herbs. Many of the products she uses in the kitchen are produced locally, and organically, when possible. Produce remnants are shared with community gardens for composting.

And there's more—ask Libby—but let's get to the meat of the subject. The food's great. One of the most popular items is the Puffy Tacos—two puffy flour tortilla shells stuffed with organic roast beef, free-range chicken, or black beans and sweet potatoes, topped with caramelized onions, lettuce, tomato-onion relish, cheese, and crema fresca. Or give the Sustainable Salt Water Halibut a go. The fish is coated with a fresh corn and pecan crust with a honey-tequila vinaigrette and served on a sweet potato flan with local seasonal veggies. The menu is fun and inventive, including traditional offerings and creative combinations. And, in case you wondered, *eloté* is roasted corn, sold from carts on street corners in Mexico—the equivalent of the American hot dog vendor. And you can order *eloté*, too.

Tucked into Tulsa's downtown business district—right across the street from the famous Philcade Building—the restaurant is busy with business people during the week. Evenings, it's full of those same people plus families and people looking for an eating experience that is healthy and eco-responsible.

There's a full bar, but the waiters will suggest you try one of the Eloté house margaritas—agave tequila, lime juice, orange juice, and cane sugar, served on the rocks. The restaurant is open for lunch and dinner Mon through Fri, dinner only on Sat, and closed on Sun. Bring quarters and be prepared to hunt for a parking place on the street. There are several parking lots within a block of the restaurant.

PUB GRUB

JAMES E. MCNELLIE'S $$
409 E. 1st St.
(918) 382-7468
www.mcnellies.com
In an old building on the east end of downtown, James E. McNellie's is so full of customers that you don't notice that the decor is spare. Wood floors and visible wooden rafters give a minimalist pub feel. This place is popular with all ages and counts lots of families among its regulars. Every Wednesday night, from 5 to 11, they serve $3 burgers—a

big draw for students at the nearby University of Tulsa. Of course, the 350 beers, including 60 on tap, also have a lot of appeal.

Big favorites are the burgers but everyone touts the sweet potato fries. They're also particularly proud of their Reuben sandwiches at McNellie's. Entree favorites are the fish and chips and Landlord's Cottage Pie. McNellie's, which opened in 2004, is a leader in bringing more life to downtown. Open for lunch and dinner every day, McNellie's offers a breakfast menu in addition to the regular menu on Sat and Sun—again, ideal for college students who like to sleep in on the weekends.

Even though this is an old building, it is wheelchair accessible. Smoking is allowed upstairs. There's ample parking behind the building and in a lot a couple of doors east of the restaurant.

KILKENNY'S IRISH PUB $$$
1413 E. 15th St.
(918) 582-8282
www.tulsairishpub.com

The appearance of Kilkenny's is closer to the popular idea of an Irish pub than most pubs in Ireland. Dark wood arches and booths, patterned tiles reminiscent of the floor of St. Patrick's Cathedral in Dublin, stained glass, and a faux-smoked ceiling add to the charm. Irish music completes the ambience.

Some of the entrees are Irish in name only—the Ballybello, a grilled, burger-style mushroom on a toasted Kaiser roll, or the Bananas O'Foster—but the colcannon, cottage pie, and boxty will shake your shillelagh. Many first-timers want an authentic Irish dish and often choose the boxty, a grilled potato pancake stuffed with a variety of fillings. Most popular are the Kilmacow—seared beef slow-cooked with portobello mushrooms and herbs and topped with Irish whiskey sauce—or the Chatsworth—tender, slow-cooked chicken breast sautéed with fresh garlic, shallots, mushrooms, and red peppers in white wine, finished with white wine sauce. And the fish and chips is superb.

There's a full bar—and a beautiful bar it is. Parking is available behind the restaurant. Kilkenny's is open for lunch and dinner seven days a week with an added late-morning brunch on Sat and Sun.

STEAK, FISH, AND SEAFOOD

BODEAN'S SEAFOOD $$$$$
3376 E. 51st St.
(918) 749-1407
www.bodean.net/Bodeanhome.html.

Bodean's has come a long way from the poultry and fish market started by Dean and Jackie Carroll back in the late '60s. That business went so well that Dean convinced his childhood best friend, Bob Faulkner, to leave their native California and join him in the business in Tulsa. Jackie talked her sister Mary into coming to help out, too. Mary wound up marrying Bob and the rest is history. Fish customers had long clamored for a restaurant, and Bodean's was born. Dean and Jackie eventually moved on to other projects. Bob and Mary continued with the restaurant. Bob's gone now, but Mary is still a big part of the business—as are other family members.

Bodean's still has a fish market where Tulsans can buy the freshest fish available, flown in several times daily—but many prefer just to let the restaurant fix it. And they do it so well.

Bodean's is located in one of the ubiquitous corner malls that seem to highlight every Tulsa intersection. The ordinary exterior doesn't prepare you for the delight inside. But go through the double doors and you're in for a treat. Floating panels of wavy art glass in blues and greens hang overhead, giving you the feeling of walking on the ocean floor. This is heightened by a large built-in aquarium full of colorful tropical fish. A feature of the main dining room is a large stone fireplace. Colors are in subdued copper and browns. Overhead, shirred, shimmery fabric creates a fanciful accent—reminiscent of billowing sails. Walls are tastefully accented with glazed metallic plaques, and hanging lamps with blown-glass shades in swirling patterns add spots of color.

But the highlight is the food. Overseen by chef Tim Richards, everything is prepared on the property. They used to fly sourdough bread in from San Francisco. Now they make it themselves and it's super—with a soft interior, a nice crust, and that little zing of sourdough. The shrimp and lobster bisque is a staple. Slightly peppery, it's smooth and rich and wonderful. Bodean's is noted for the San Francisco–style cioppino (fisherman's stew), part of the owners' Bay-area heritage. Other favorites include the sesame-crested, Gulf yellowfin tuna and the seared jumbo sea scallops with baby squash, ricotta salatta, port wine, and penne pasta. It would be a shame not to order fish here but their dry-aged steaks are also popular. Do try a dessert. If you're full, the homemade sorbet may be just the thing to cap your meal, but you may not want to pass up some of the weightier offerings just because they sound so good.

Bodean's has been a Tulsa favorite for a long time. Lots of diners came here with their parents and are now bringing their families back. It's a popular spot for special dates, and the question has been popped here more than once. All in all, it's a good choice for the excellence of the cuisine and the consistency and quality of the service. New restaurants come and go—Bodean's is a keeper.

Bodean's has a full bar and parking is no problem. It is open for dinner seven days a week and for lunch Mon through Fri.

ELEMENTS STEAKHOUSE
AND GRILLE $$$$-$$$$$
River Spirit Casino
8330 S. Riverside Dr.
(918) 995-8518, (800) 299-2738
www.riverspirittulsa.com
Stepping into Elements from the busyness of the gaming floor is like walking into a soothing, relaxing retreat. The centerpiece of the entrance is an 8-foot stone fireplace. The emphasis is on neutral colors and shades of chocolate and gold. The candelabras on the table are like little glimmering trees. There's lots of attention to detail in the decor and you know that you'll be dining, not just eating.

Although there is smoking allowed in the gaming area, the restaurant is strictly nonsmoking. The bar is full service and has an extensive wine list that leans heavily toward California vintages. The also carry some great micro beers.

Steaks are the specialty here but there are a number of other entrees that are favorites. Try the apple-wood–smoked, double-cut pork chop with chef's blackberry barbeque sauce or the oven-roasted, sea-salted prime rib with creamed horseradish. The steak and lobster combo is also popular and is sometimes offered at a special price. Save room for the fantastic dessert sampler or the chocolate soufflé.

The restaurant is open Wed through Sun evenings, and reservations are a good idea.

MOLLY'S LANDING $$$$-$$$$$
3700 N. Hwy. 66, Catoosa
(918) 266-7853
www.mollyslanding.com
Northeast of Tulsa, but not that long a drive, is Molly's Landing, as eclectic-looking a spot as you'll find. It started in 1884 with a large log cabin—then grew. Like a giant magnet, it seemed to collect things—on the porch, on the walls, hanging from the ceiling. As you come up the walk—think rustic, with an emphasis on the rust. There are old iron stoves, tools, and barbed wire and metal art. Even the menus have metal covers. Inside, you'll find everything from animal skins and antlers to bowling pins, a water pump, and a model of Westminster Tower complete with Big Ben.

Don't let the decor distract you. You can do some serious eating here. The steaks are tops—try the peppered filet mignon with brandy sauce—and the fish selections range from walleye to Norwegian salmon. Be careful you don't fill up on the excellent bread, and save room for dessert. There's a chocolate cake made with pure butter and egg yolks (none of that nonfat white part) that'll make you want to slap your mama.

The restaurant is open for dinner every evening except Sun.

59

ℹ️ If you eat at Molly's Landing, take time before or after to drive up the road past the restaurant driveway. As you enter the neighborhood, notice the change in pavement. That's original Route 66 Portland concrete. The oldest alignment of the highway curved northwest to the river, where there was a ferry to take cars across.

WHITE RIVER FISH MARKET $$$
1708 N. Sheridan Rd.
(918) 835-1910
www.whiteriverfishmarket.com

The freshest fish is what this place is all about, and the crowds keep coming. In business since 1932 and at this location since '65, White River is a Tulsa fixture. This may be the most democratic spot in town. The clientele ranges from blue collar and employees of businesses around the nearby airport to lawyers from downtown offices, even mayors—past and present.

Ambience—there is none. The restaurant is in a strip of shops in a less-than-fashionable part of town. You order at the counter and, if you want, you can pick your own fish out right there.

Booths, tables, and chairs are ordinary and there's no attempt at decor. The fish is so good that White River doesn't need to depend on anything else to pull customers in.

When possible, the fish is fresh—trout from Idaho, fresh tilapia from Costa Rica. Frozen is used when that's the best way to keep the fish at peak. All the shrimp comes wild from the Gulf—no foreign or farmed crustaceans here. The list of favorites quickly looks like the menu—jumbo shrimp, catfish, halibut, and on Tues and Wed, lobster tail. Another fave—a whole flounder, fried or broiled. Then there's the gumbo—White River sells about 60 gallons a week. Hush puppies, oh yeah, crisp on the outside, cornbread texture on the inside, and a spicy kick to boot.

White River smokes its own salmon, trout, and catfish, and beef brisket for dyed-in-the-wool beef eaters. And they make their own barbecue sauce. If you have room after your entree, try the homemade sweet potato or buttermilk pie.

The restaurant serves lunch and dinner every day except Sunday. If you go for dinner, don't be late—they keep country hours. The market opens early, with lunch service a bit later. You can order wine or beer but leave your smokes at home. The only thing that gets smoked here is the fish.

ATTRACTIONS

Attractions in Tulsa? The city's an attraction. With its amazing collection of art deco buildings, which span the gamut of the genre, Tulsa attracts architecture enthusiasts from all over the country. But there's a lot more to see and do here—for the whole family. Few cities this size can boast two art museums of the caliber of Gilcrease and Philbrook. Interesting areas like Brookside and Cherry Street draw not only shoppers but those looking for good restaurants and a little nightlife. It's hard to divide all Tulsa's attractions into neat categories. Some will be cross-referenced, like Cain's Ballroom, which has historical interest but is also a live-music nightspot. Some places or activities are listed in other chapters like Outdoors or Arts or Kidstuff. So don't stick to one chapter—there are attractions throughout this book—just like there are attractions throughout town.

Price Code

This will provide you with a general guideline for estimating what an attraction costs. The $ symbol represents the standard adult fare. If there's no code, the attraction is free. Some attractions offer occasional discounts not reflected in their prices. If you can count on these price breaks, they will be mentioned. Best advice—always ask about any special deals or promotions.

$.......................$1 to $10
$$ ....$11 to $15
$$$ ....$16 to $20
$$$$ ....$21 and up

ALEXANDRE HOGUE GALLERY OF ART
The University of Tulsa, Phillips Hall
2935 E. 5th St.
(918) 631-2202
www.utulsa.edu/academics/colleges/henry-kendall-college-of-arts-and-sciences/departments-and-schools/school-of-art

Tucked into the University of Tulsa campus, this gallery is a hidden gem. Not a freestanding structure, it occupies a new wing that was added to the 1920s Phillips Building. The gallery is not large but the clean-looking space with its gray tile floor and white walls, along with versatile track lighting, provides a great canvas for the works of art displayed here. The gallery was named in honor of artist Alexandre Hogue, who was the head of the art school from 1945 to 1963.

Shows change from month to month, and the art ranges from students' works to those of widely recognized masters. One of the biggest shows of the year is the annual Gussman Juried Art Show. Established in 1968 by Herbert Gussman—oilman, railroad executive, and arts patron—the show features the works of selected students from the university.

The busy season for the gallery is during the traditional school year, from late Aug until early May. Though the free-to-the-public gallery is open in the summer, there are few shows during that time.

The URL is a doozy but once you get to the site, click on Alexandre Hogue Gallery and you can get to the Arts Calendar. Parking isn't easy—on the street is best. The parking lot immediately north of the Phillips Building is restricted (off-limits); if you park in one of the other lots nearby, you may be ticketed, but you can take your ticket to the gallery and they'll help you.

AMERICA'S INCREDIBLE PIZZA COMPANY $-$$
8314 E. 71st St.
(918) 294-8671
www.incrediblepizza.com

This place is for kids (see the Kidstuff chapter) and kids at heart. It's a combo pizza buffet (see the Restaurants chapter) and indoor amusement park. Dozens of video games flash, ding, and clunk, and there are even indoor bumper cars, go-carts, and miniature golf. This is a great spot to combat museum overload or to add pizzazz to a rainy afternoon.

ART DECO DRIVING TOUR

After you've read the Close-up about art deco and the different styles, why not take this driving (and a little walking) tour to see examples of all three kinds of buildings. Take a good map and several quarters for the parking meters downtown. This tour begins with the **Warehouse Market Building** at East 10th St. and South Elgin Avenue. Park in the lot so you can get a good, up-close view of the attractive terra-cotta medallions. The building was built in 1929 and was known as the "Farmers' Market." Though not as elaborate as some of the examples you'll see soon, this is zigzag vintage.

Head north on South Elgin Avenue and turn west on East 5th St. You'll want to find a parking place as close to Boston as possible. On the northeast corner of East 5th St. and South Boston Avenue, go into the **Philtower Building.** The Philtower was built in 1927 for oilman Waite Phillips. It's an interesting combination of Gothic Revival with art deco embellishments. The lobby ceiling features fan vaulting and is illuminated by elaborate chandeliers. Notice the "WP" on the elevator doors. Interior materials include mahogany and travertine marble. Outside, over the South Boston Avenue entrance, you'll spot two gargoyles. Look for the one holding a replica of the Philtower—legend has it that whoever tears the building down will be haunted by the gargoyle. You'll have to stand way back to see the colorful, glazed tile roof—an art deco topper to this otherwise traditional building.

Across the street to the south is another Waite Phillips building, the **Philcade Building.** Look at the exterior details—the terra-cotta pilasters and panels feature popular art deco themes. The interior is a monument to elegant art deco. You'll find geometric elements—a hallmark of

zigzag—floral themes and lots of gold leaf.

Walk 2 blocks west on East and West 5th Sts. to South Boulder Avenue. On the northwest corner is a three-story building that screams zigzag. Built in 1931, the **Pythian Building** was planned as a 13-story building but the Depression changed the plans. Inside is a riot of colored tiles and geometric patterns. Be sure and check the accordion-pleated ceiling fixtures.

Back at your car, you'll want to go north on either South Detroit Avenue or Elgin Avenue to East 1st St. Turn west until you see the **Union Depot** (now the Jazz Depot) on the north side of the street. You can either park in front of it on the South Boston Avenue side or across South Boston Avenue in the parking garage. The solid style of the building is Public Works Administration (PWA) art deco. While the style retains zigzag elements, it's certainly less frivolous—designed to project a feeling of stability in uncertain financial times. The Depot was built in 1931, designed by architect Frederick Kershner. You'll find information about the Jazz Depot elsewhere in this chapter. Since you've stopped, you might want to look at it now. This is also the ideal time to visit the Center of the Universe—see the Insiders' Tip.

Because of the one-way streets, when you leave the Depot, you'll go west to South Cheyenne Avenue and turn south to West 6th St., where you'll turn back east, continue on East 6th St., and leave the downtown area. Cross under the highway and go to South Peoria Avenue. Turn south, going 2 blocks to East 8th St., where you'll turn back to the west (toward downtown). On the south side of the street, just before it dead-ends, you'll see another PWA building, the **Fire Alarm Building.** This is another Kershner creation. Take time to examine the low-relief carvings—a fanciful combination of the heroic and the mythical. Built in 1934, this was the location where all fire alarms from across the city were received. If you have time, walk around to the back and check out the gargoyles.

Heading back to South Peoria Avenue, you're going to go south to East 11th St. and turn west. Continue past the Warehouse to South Boston Avenue and go south. You can't miss **Boston**

Avenue United Methodist Church. This is the brightest star in Tulsa's architectural panoply and you may want to make a special tour at another time—it deserves a trip of its own. See more details both about the building and its amazing designer elsewhere in this chapter. Here are some basics as you drive by. It was designed by a woman, Adah Robinson, and completed in 1929. The geometrics put it in the zigzag category but it is pure Adah. A Quaker, she seriously studied Methodism and infused the design with symbolism. There are 62 pairs of praying hands around the building, and the glass structure on top echoes the theme. Note that the hands are not clasped, but open, to receive God's blessings. The large figures over the main north entrance are John, Charles, and Susanna Wesley. The eastern entrance on the north side was originally a porte cochere. This was this first church in Tulsa in which the use of the automobile was a factor in the design.

Continue south on South Boston Avenue and turn west onto East 15th St. Continue on West 15th St. to South Riverside Drive and turn north. Facing Riverside Drive at South Houston Avenue, you'll see a white stucco building—the **Riverside Studio,** at 1381 S. Riverside Dr. Built in 1929 and designed by Bruce Goff, it was originally the home and studio of pianist Patti Adams Shriner. Note the narrow windows and black tiles—a piano-key theme perhaps. This is now the home of the Spotlight Theatre and the second-longest-running play in America, *The Drunkard.* (See the Arts chapter.)

Double back to West 15th St. and continue east on East 15th St. again to South Peoria Avenue, where you'll head south for three examples of the last art deco period—streamline. You have to look carefully to avoid missing the **City Veterinary Hospital** at 3550 S. Peoria Ave. Built in 1942, it was designed by Joseph Koberling, who, like Goff, was a former student of Adah Robinson. The horizontal bands, rounded corners, and glass block windows are classic streamline. The building was built in 1942 as a veterinary clinic and has never been anything else.

The last two examples of streamline are private residences. Go south on South Peoria Avenue to East 41st St. and turn east to South Utica Avenue. Go north to East 37th St. and turn east. You'll see the **Ungerman Residence** at 1718 E. 37th St. Built in 1941, it has some of the same elements as the veterinary hospital, with a little more angularity. Still, note the horizontal banks, the curved glass bay, and the glass blocks.

Back on South Utica, you'll pass the **Davis Residence** at 3231 S. Utica Ave. Built it 1936, it was designed by Mrs. Frances Davis, another former student of Adah Robinson.

You've now seen several examples of each of the art deco periods. Before you leave the area, this is a good time to look, practically across the street, at the Perryman Cemetery, at East 32nd St. and South Utica Avenue. It is described elsewhere in this chapter.

BIG SPLASH WATER PARK $$$$
4707 E. 21st St.
(918) 749-7385
www.bigsplashwaterpark.com
Located next to the Tulsa Fairgrounds, here's a really cool place to spend a summer afternoon. In addition to the wave pool and activity pool, the 10 slides include both tube and body slides with ultra-experiences like the Master Blaster—a sort of water roller coaster where the water pulls and pushes you through the tubes—and the Silver Bullet or Slick Shooter—seven-plus-stories-tall slides that bring new meaning to the term *wedgie.*

There are lots of ways to get wet at Big Splash. Try water basketball or rock climbing in the activity pool. This is a family-friendly facility—no smoking—and both the activity pool and wave pool are wheelchair accessible. For drier activities, how about horseshoes, volleyball, or basketball? And there are occasional special events like live entertainment, bingo, or giveaways.

Food vendors offer everything from salads and sandwiches to funnel cakes and Dippin' Dots. Bring cash; except for the front gate and the gift shop, you'll need cash for all other transactions.

Prices, while typical for this kind of activity, can add up fast for larger families, so check the

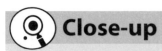

Close-up

Art Deco in Tulsa

Art deco grew out of many influences fomenting and fermenting after World War I. Artists were experimenting with modernism, cubism, and surrealism, and the world seemed ready to shed Victorian shackles and move in new directions. Art deco was one of those directions. Many of the ideas were showcased in the 1925 Exposition Internationale des Arts Décoratifs et Industriels Modernes, held in Paris.

Tulsa, too, was on the move. Oil was flowing and so was money. Eastern speculators and investors brought new ideas, and local movers and shakers could afford to see other parts of the world. They were ready to push Tulsa into the forefront of modern metropolises, and bold architecture was one way to express this feeling.

The earliest designs utilized parallel lines, chevrons, and zigzag motifs and often included elements of Egyptian or Aztec styles. Terra-cotta ornamentation was popular—often in brilliant colors. Intricate grillwork was another widely used element. Geometric figures were incorporated with more-fanciful motifs.

The second phase of the period came with the Depression and government programs like the Public Works Administration (PWA). A "prime the pump" program, it poured money into large federal projects from dams to aircraft carriers and local efforts like airports and hospitals. Over 70 percent of the new schools constructed during this period were a result of the PWA program. The architecture was less frivolous than the riotous colors of the zigzag era. Reliefs on buildings glorified labor and the common man. The buildings themselves were solid and sturdy-looking—good psychology for a society whose self-confidence had been shaken.

With recovery from the Depression, art deco moved into the streamline mode. Glass blocks and sleek curves were hallmarks. Designs recalled mighty ocean liners, diesel train engines, and low-slung automobiles with sensuous curves. From the extravagant ornamentation of early art deco, the style represented a nation moving forward.

Tulsa is fortunate to have examples of all three segments of the art deco heyday.

An abbreviated tour is suggested in this chapter. For more details, go to www.tulsapreservation commission.org.

Web site for special offers—like discounts for soda cans, etc. Children's discounts are determined by height rather than by age—under 48 inches saves several dollars.

The park is open seven days a week during swimming season.

BOK CENTER
200 S. Denver Ave.
(918) 894-4200
www.bokcenter.com
Tulsans are justifiably proud of their new area and events center. Designed by architect Cesar Pelli—who designed the Petronas Twin Towers in Kuala Lumpur, at one time the world's tallest buildings—the massive structure is clad

with 25,000 individual stainless-steel panels. The worlds' largest unsupported overhanging roof looms over the main entrance. With its sleek finish and curved silhouette, it provides a 21st-century counterpart to Tulsa's collection of streamline art deco structures.

Above the main lobby is one of the pieces of the $1.35 million art collection. Kendall Buster's *Stratum, 2008* looks like a feather-light cloud floating about the floor. Made of steel framing and translucent cloth, it actually weighs more than 5,000 pounds. Other artwork in the building includes four terrazzo medallions with American Indian designs by Bill and Demos Glass of Locust Grove; a series of paintings of the Tallgrass Prairie Reserve by Tulsan Mark Lewis; and a 24-foot painting made up of three panels and depicting rearing horses by Joe Andoe, formerly of Tulsa.

From the main ramp, you'll get a grand view of downtown Tulsa. The nearly 600 feet of glass required 1,100 individual glass panes. The glass is tempered to withstand winds of up to 100 mph. This glass wall cost approximately $7 million.

The BOK was designed to be the premier venue for sports and entertainment. There are over 16,000 fixed seats in the area plus removable seats at the ends of the arena. The BOK is home to the Central Hockey League Tulsa Oilers and the Tulsa Talons arena football team. The scoreboard is 30 feet high and 33 feet wide and weighs 50,000 pounds. For basketball and hockey games, it hangs 25 feet above the arena floor but can be raised to 80 feet for concerts.

Visitors have a number of food options, from snacks to sushi. Other amenities in the facility include club seats, box and suite options, three ATMs on property, and ample restrooms.

The best way to see the inside is by attending an event. To see about arranging a tour, check the Web site. Under "Guest Services" you'll find a drop-down box that includes an "A to Z Guide." Click on that and then scroll through the search box for "Tours of the BOK."

The BOK Center, which opened in August 2008, raced to the top of the ticket sales list during the first quarter of 2009. *Poolstar* **magazine listed the BOK number two in the United States and number nine in the world, with 149,302 tickets sold during that three-month period.**

BOSTON AVENUE UNITED METHODIST CHURCH
1301 S. Boston Ave.
(918) 583-5181
www.bostonavenue.org
Possibly the premier example of art deco architecture in Tulsa and one of the finest examples of vertical-style art deco anywhere, the Boston Avenue Methodist Church draws visitors from all over the world.

And this architectural icon was designed by a woman—Dr. Adah Robinson—who was the founder of the art program at Tulsa University. The building committee had chosen an architectural firm, but the chairman's wife objected so vociferously to their design that her husband, exasperated, told her to come up with something she liked.

She contacted Dr. Robinson, who, days later, came to her with a most unusual design. Because she was an artist, not an engineer, she proposed that one of her former students, Bruce Goff, a draftsman at a local architectural firm, help with technical details. He later became one of Oklahoma's most celebrated architects and is sometimes credited with Boston Avenue Methodist Church. The church's records belie that and give Dr. Robinson full credit.

Every feature of the building is full of symbolism, from the heaven-aspiring, 255-foot tower to the 62 praying hands around the parapets. Dr. Robinson considered light to be the most important symbol in the structure and used 11,500 square feet of transparent leaded and stained glass in her design. Other elements found throughout the building include the coreopsis and tritoma. Both Oklahoma wildflowers, the coreopsis represents the hardiness of the faith, and the tritoma, or torch lily, represents generosity. More than just a historical building, Boston Avenue Methodist Church is designated by the National Park Service a National Historic Landmark.

Guided tours of the building are available after the 11 a.m. service on Sunday or by appointment by calling the church office.

CAIN'S BALLROOM
423 N. Main St.
(918) 584-2306
www.cainsballroom.com
To an older generation, the names Cain's, Bob Wills, and western swing are inextricably linked. If this history is important to you, you may want to drive by the building just for a look. Inside, the ballroom looks like a cross between an airplane hangar and a high school gym. The building was

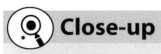# Close-up

Adah Robinson

One of Oklahoma's most iconic buildings was designed by a small, unassuming Quaker woman of gigantic talent. Adah Robinson was born in 1882 in Richmond, Indiana, a town with a rich cultural life. One of Adah's first art teachers had studied with William Merritt Chase and Cecilia Beaux. After her first teacher's death, she studied with several local painters and became the youngest member of the artists known as the Richmond Group. She subsequently studied at the Academy of Fine Arts and the Arts Institute in Chicago.

Adah had been close to her grandparents and her father and brother, but her relationship with her mother was not good and became worse over the years. Neither Adah nor her brother enjoyed robust health, and in 1905 the family moved to Oklahoma, hoping the climate would be beneficial to Homer, her brother. In 1908 both Adah and Homer contracted typhoid fever. Homer died and Adah's recovery was long and difficult. After her recovery, Adah got a job teaching art at Epworth University (a school that eventually became Oklahoma City University). When the decision was made to move the campus to Guthrie, Adah reluctantly decided not to move—she wanted to remain in Oklahoma City, near her father. She gave private art lessons, taught at the local high school, helped establish the Oklahoma Art League, and became an effective public speaker on the importance of art in life. One of the most popular and innovative courses she developed for her students was a course in city planning. Among the features of the course was a tour of Oklahoma City's architectural landscape. Adah thoroughly enjoyed working with the students, even turning down an attractive offer from the University of Oklahoma, because she felt what she was doing was more important.

Adah's relationship with her mother had deteriorated seriously after Homer's death. (In later years it became obvious that her mother suffered from mental illness.) Because things became so unpleasant, when she received an offer of employment from the superintendent of Tulsa Public Schools in 1917, she accepted.

She not only threw herself into her new job, she established an art club that was enthusiastically supported by the community. Adah enjoyed organizing exhibitions, and her ambitions weren't small. When she arranged an exhibition of old masters on loan from a New York gallery, including works by Rembrandt, Sir Joshua Reynolds, and Thomas Gainsborough, it was a highlight of the year. She also encouraged her students to prepare works for exhibitions. She was a popular teacher, and again she organized a city planning course. This time, instead of just looking at the buildings, the students evaluated them on the basis of their utility and how they fit with neighboring structures.

All her activities wore on her, and in 1925 she decided that the classes had gotten too large and the workload too great. She was ready to retire from teaching. She and a friend opened a small gallery called The Little Art Shop in downtown Tulsa. She didn't retire from other activities, and her next project was another art exhibition—this time of major art works in private Tulsa collections. The art world took notice and the show enhanced Tulsa's reputation as a cultured city.

It was right around this time that the members of the Boston Avenue Methodist Church decided that their facilities at East 5th St. and South Boston Avenue were too small, and they organized a building committee. Audrey Cole, the wife of the committee chairman, had attended some of Adah's lectures, and when the committee was at an impasse, she asked Adah's advice. The result was Adah's appearing at her house several days later with drawings. The design was radically different from anything the committee had seen. After discussion, the design was adopted.

Though Adah prepared detailed drawings, she needed an architectural firm to prepare blueprints. One of her former students, Bruce Goff (Class of '22) was working as a draftsman for a local firm, Rush, Endacott & Rush. Contracts were prepared specifying that Adah was in charge of all artistic decisions both inside and out.

Raised a Quaker, Adah wasn't familiar with Methodist history and practice, so she undertook an intensive study. What she learned was incorporated into the details of her design. Statues of John and Charles Wesley and their mother, Susanna, were featured above one entrance, and figures over the south entrance honor Francis Asbury, father of American Methodism; the middle figure represents an unknown circuit rider; the third figure is of William McKendrie, the first American-born bishop. The figures were molded in terra-cotta by another of Adah's former students, Robert Garrison, who had studied sculpture with Gutzon Borglum, sculptor of Mt. Rushmore.

Adah was everywhere and involved in everything. She made trips to Chicago to check on the sculptures and to St. Louis to sort out problems with the art glass. And she overworked herself until she had to be hospitalized for exhaustion. While she was gone, Bruce Goff changed one of her design elements. When she returned and saw what he had done, she insisted that he change it back. Details like these are important because in later years, Goff and the architectural firm tried to take credit for the design.

The building was finally complete. It had been much more expensive than the estimates—$1.3 million for the land and the building. The church caused a great stir in both the national and international press. As the accolades rolled in, Goff began inflating his role in the project. He even threatened to sue *National Geographic* magazine for citing Robinson as the designer. His lawsuit went nowhere. The *Geographic* writer had done his homework—and the Tulsa Chamber of Commerce verified Robinson's role.

The brouhaha caused a rift between the teacher and student. During the construction of the church, Adah had also designed her own house, and Goff and another former student were working on it. That ended Goff's participation in the project. The house still stands at East 12th St. and South Owasso Avenue.

When the church was almost finished, Adah was approached by the chancellor of the University of Tulsa (TU) with an offer to teach there—back to the classroom once more—and Adah established the TU art department.

Though the Boston Avenue Methodist Church is Adah's most impressive work, she built a foundation in the arts for her students through her teaching and for men and women all over the country with her public speaking. In 1939 the *Daily Oklahoman* called her "the woman who has done more to encourage art in Oklahoma than any other person...."

Adah was happy and productive at Tulsa University until an unfortunate conversation with the man who had replaced the chancellor who hired her. He stated that he didn't believe she had designed the church, even though she had the drawings to prove it. Her determination to leave TU was followed by a timely offer to go to Trinity University in San Antonio—an offer she accepted. She lived and worked in San Antonio until her retirement at the age of 76.

Adah had never married and all her family was gone, but she had many dear friends. One of her former students and his wife invited her to come live with them in Tulsa. They enlarged a small apartment attached to their home. Adah lived there comfortably, surrounded by friends and mementos of her long career, until her death in 1962. In 1999 the Boston Avenue Methodist Church was named a National Historic Landmark. People still make pilgrimages to see the structure and pay homage to the little lady who designed the great building.

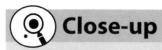 **Close-up**

Bob Wills

Probably no musical name is more closely associated with Tulsa than Bob Wills (1905–1975). Born in Texas, Wills learned to play the mandolin, guitar, and fiddle from his father and grandfather. As a teen he played local dances, and in his 20s formed a band that became popular both with live and radio audiences in the Fort Worth area.

The band's first big break was landing their own radio show, sponsored by a local grain elevator and mill. The show's host, manager of the flour mill, was something of a tyrant and refused to let the musicians play other gigs. When the band quit the show, the manager tried to keep them off other Texas stations. The band, called the Playboys, found a new job at KVOO, the voice of Oklahoma, in Tulsa.

The band, building a big fan base, cut their first record in 1935, the same year they began playing regularly at Cain's Ballroom. Their unique sound was a blend of jazz, boogie, blues, country, and the big band swing sound—it became known as Texas swing.

The Playboys played Cain's regularly until 1942, with World War II making big changes in the group. Wills reconstituted the group after the war, changing the personnel and sound. For the next few years, the group was riding high and turning out hit records.

Things were less than rosy with the group, however. Bob Wills's drinking and the public's changing musical tastes created problems for the group, though they still managed an occasional Top 10 hit.

Bob Wills suffered a heart attack in 1962 and a second attack in 1964. He disbanded the Playboys and continued to record and play concerts as a solo act. The Country Music Hall of Fame inducted Wills in 1968, and the Texas Legislature honored him the next year.

The day after the Texas honor, Wills had a major stroke. He recovered well enough to make several more public appearances before suffering another, more severe stroke. Although he lived for more than a year and a half, he never recovered consciousness and died in May 1975 in a nursing home. He is buried in Tulsa's Memorial Park Cemetery. The inscription on his headstone reads, "Deep Within My Heart Lies A Melody."

originally a car garage but became a ballroom in 1924. It was purchased by Madison Cain in 1930 and became Cain's Dance Academy. Closed during the '60s, it was reopened in the '70s as Cain's Ballroom.

The old spring-loaded maple dance floor from the original Cain's finally gave out, but the new one, with its distinctive concentric square pattern, looks and feels the same. Around the walls, pictures of stars of the past—Spade Cooley, Roy Rogers, Gene Autry, Hank Williams, Tex Ritter—look down on the scene of early triumphs. Up in the rafters is a '50s drum set used by the Playboys—post Bob Wills.

Though country stars still appear here in the birthplace of Texas swing—many genres are represented in the concert lineup. That the punk rock band, the Sex Pistols, once played Cain's is still the stuff of contemporary legend. For more information see Nightlife.

CREEK COUNCIL OAK
1750 S. Cheyenne Ave.

On the northwest corner of the intersection, you'll see a metal fence surrounding a large tree. This burr oak must have been a sapling in 1836 when the Lochapoka Creeks chose this spot to build a council fire with the ashes and charred remains of the last fires they lit in their Alabama home.

The Creeks had built their first Oklahoma homes nearby—homes that were destroyed during the Civil War. The Indians were scattered at that time, and when they returned they built homes elsewhere. The site was still used for Indian gatherings until the turn of the last century.

By the 1920s, the city had grown out to the area. Oil magnates were building palatial homes in the Maple Ridge subdivision. The Council Oak actually stood in Harry Sinclair's yard. The property was later owned by the Oral Roberts Evangelistic Association, which tore down the house but saved the tree.

A later owner planned to use the land for commercial purposes. Citizens, fearing that the tree would be cut down, petitioned the city. The city was able to obtain the property and created Creek Council Oak Park. The tree was put on the National Register of Historic Places in 1976.

While you're here, be sure and walk across the street to the Stickball Park, where you'll find more explanatory materials about the Creeks.

DISCOVERYLAND! $$$-$$$$
19501 W. 41st St., Sand Springs
(918) 245-OKLA
www.discoverylandusa.com

This is a summertime must for any visitor to the area. Discoveryland! is the official "National Home" of Rodgers and Hammerstein's *Oklahoma!* With the original book written by Lynn Riggs of nearby Claremore, and set in the Osage hills, the venue couldn't be more natural. And to see the play outdoors, with real horses pulling that surrey with the fringe on top, is a treat. The cast includes some of the best young voices in the country, and the dancing's exuberant and exciting.

Dress cool—Oklahoma summer evenings are often warm—and come early to enjoy a pre-show cowboy dinner, Indian dancing, and entertainment. There are package prices that include both the dinner and show along with program and intermission snacks, and children under a certain age are admitted to the show free of charge. An Indian Trading Post carries souvenirs, and there are free pony rides for little ones. And everyone enjoys the high-kicking cancan dancers in the western show that precedes the featured performance.

Presentations start in early June and run through mid-Aug. You'll definitely need reservations for the dinner. Tickets for the play only are often available at the door, but why take a chance? There are no shows on Sundays. Discoveryland! is located 5 miles west of OK 97 on West 41st St.

ELSING MUSEUM
105 C Learning Resource Center
Oral Roberts University
7777 S. Lewis Ave.
(918) 495-6262
www.elsing.oru.edu

The Elsing Museum is primarily a collection of geological specimens but includes other things that Willard Elsing was interested in as well. As a boy growing up in southeast Kansas, Elsing was fascinated with Indian artifacts, rocks, and, particularly, minerals.

As an adult, he opened a rock shop near Joplin, Missouri, in an important lead-mining area. Miners brought him specimens of galena, sphalerite, calcite, and other minerals, which he kept, traded, or sold. He continued to collect and buy other samples on his own—a particular favorite being amethyst.

After a meeting with Evelyn Roberts, the wife of Oral Roberts, Elsing agreed to bring his collection to Oral Roberts University, where it was displayed in half of a duplex he occupied on campus. After his death in 2005, at the age of 93, the collection was moved to the lower level of the Learning Resource Center.

Elsing was more interested in the beauty of his collection than scientific organization, so the collection has a bit of a random feel—Egyptian scarabs in one case, a display of malachite in another, some of his own artwork in a third. That's the charm and the frustration of the assemblage. That said, you'll find an exceptional collection of crystals and other rocks and minerals, geodes, and artwork made of, or incorporating, jade, ivory, and mother-of-pearl.

Call before you go to confirm that the museum will be open and to get specific information about parking. The museum is generally open afternoons, Wed through Sat. In addition to being closed Sun through Tues, the museum is also closed July 4th, Thanksgiving, and the week between Christmas and New Year's Day. There is no admission charge.

GILCREASE MUSEUM $
1400 N. Gilcrease Museum Rd.
(918) 596-2700
www.gilcrease.org

Oilman/art collector William Thomas Gilcrease, son of a Creek mother and non-Indian father, was a millionaire by the time he was out of his teens. The land allotment he received from the Dawes Commission in 1899 sat on land that concealed one of the nation's richest oil deposits.

He began collecting art at an early age and was particularly interested in Native American materials. His collection included not only art but artifacts and rare books. In spite of his wealth, Gilcrease found himself in a financial bind by the early 1950s. His new private museum had been open only a short time. Upon learning that the collection was to be put up for sale, the mayor rallied the citizens of Tulsa to pass a bond issue that enabled the museum and collection to remain in Tulsa—where it remains one of the city's greatest points of pride.

Artists depicting western subjects are an important part of the museum's collection—artists like Albert Bierstadt, George Catlin, Thomas Moran, Frederic Remington, and Charles Russell. Other artists' works include those of Thomas Eakins, Charles Willson Peale, James McNeill Whistler, John Singer Sargent, Winslow Homer, John James Audubon, and N. C. Wyeth.

Rare documents include the oldest existing letter from the New World, a 1512 missive from Diego Columbus, and a letter from Thomas Jefferson dated July 1 and 2, 1776. Other treasures include the only known existing handwritten copy of the Declaration of Independence, with the signatures of Silas Deane and Benjamin Franklin., and a first edition of John Smith's *The Generall Historie of Virginia, New-England and the Summer Isles*, printed in 1624. Due to their fragile nature, these documents spend most of their time in light- and temperature-controlled storage; however, they are put on display occasionally for special exhibits.

The design of the original portion of the museum—where the main entrance is—was based on an Indian longhouse. The signature sculpture on the grounds stands in front of the main doors—*Sacred Rain Arrow*—a bronze work by Allan Houser.

Today, the museum's holdings comprise Meso-American and pre-Columbian art, American and Indian art, and anthropological materials from North, Central, and South America. The archival collection, including many rare and precious documents and artifacts, is extensive. The museum is managed by the University of Tulsa for the city.

Of the museum's 440-acres, 23 have been made into historic theme gardens:

- Victorian Garden—In front of Thomas Gilcrease's surprisingly modest home, adjacent to the museum, you'll find a charming garden planted in the style popular between 1837 and 1901. Climbing roses embrace the wrought-iron gateway, and fragrant wisteria and showy hydrangeas present a romantic spring and summer show.
- Colonial Garden—The parterre style, so prevalent in Europe, was also popular in colonial America. Along the brick walkways, garden herbs are tucked in among the colorful annuals.
- Other gardens include the Rock Garden, Vista Garden, Pioneer Garden, and Pre-Columbian Garden.

The museum also boasts one of the best views in Tulsa from their Osage Restaurant, open for lunch Tues through Sat and on Sun for brunch. Be sure and stop in the well-stocked gift store for everything from inexpensive souvenirs to fine art.

The museum is closed on Mondays and Christmas Day. The museum and most of the grounds are wheelchair accessible. Loaner wheelchairs are available on a first-come, first-served basis.

When looking at information about an attraction's open days, keep in mind that this is Oklahoma—a firmly Bible-Belt state. Most attractions that are open on Sunday will open later than on other days of the week. If you're planning a visit on Sunday, be sure and check hours.

GOLDEN DRILLER
Tulsa Fairgrounds
4145 E. 21st St.

Tulsans either love or hate the *Golden Driller*. A work of art it is not. Big, it is. At one time it was the world's largest freestanding statue. At 76 feet, it doesn't even make the top ten today. Still, it is a monument to a time when oil was king and Tulsa was the throne.

Erected in 1953 for the International Petroleum Exposition, it was taken down, then put up again for the 1959 event. By this time GD had a fan club, and when he was put up again in 1966, he stayed up.

He's survived tornadoes, vandals, souvenir seekers and was even shot in the back with an arrow. He's made of angle iron, concrete, and plaster. His right arm rests on an old oil derrick taken from an oil field near Seminole, Oklahoma.

MARY K. OXLEY NATURE CENTER
6700 Mohawk Blvd., Mohawk Park
(918) 669-6644
www.oxleynaturecenter.org

The 800 acres in the nature center feature 11 miles of well-marked trails inviting exploration of a variety of habitats from forest to prairie to wetlands. The place to start is the Interpretive Center—to enjoy the educational exhibits and to pick up a trail map. There are also frequent interpretative programs and classes scheduled—occasionally with a minimal charge. There is no charge at the nature center, but if you come on the weekend you'll have to pay a small fee to enter Mohawk Park.

Exhibits include a number of hands-on items—buttons to push, specimens to feel, recordings to listen to. If you're here when school classes are visiting, you'll hear a nonstop serenade to birdcalls, frog songs, and squirrel scoldings. A busy beehive provides another item of interest. The interpretive center overlooks a small pond that hosts a variety of waterfowl and resident turtles.

Trails vary in length from less than a quarter of a mile to just over a mile and can be linked together to provide as long a walk as you want. Several trails of particular interest include the Red Fox Trail, a wooded path designed for a sensory awareness experience, and the Blue Heron Loop Trail, where you'll find two bird blinds overlooking Sherry Lake. Most of the trails are wheelchair accessible.

MUSEUM OF THE ROAD
Route 66 Harley-Davidson/Buell
3637 S. Memorial Dr.
(918) 622-1340
www.route66hd.com

Even if you don't suffer from motorcycle mania, if you're interested in the Mother Road—Route 66—make a stop here to see the little museum between the Route 66 Harley-Davidson dealership and the 5 & Diner.

Cases of artifacts are arranged in order of the states that the highway passed through—from Illinois to California. Full of souvenirs from the road's glory days, the cases hold old postcards, maps, matchbooks, doodads, and tchotchkes, all related to Route 66. The Oklahoma case even has a ceramic replica of Tulsa's *Golden Driller*.

If you know Route 66, you know the name Michael Wallis. Wallis, who's written a number of books on the Mother Road and even served as a consultant to Walt Disney and Pixar, also did the voice-over for the Sheriff of Radiator Springs in the movie *Cars*. The '97 Heritage Softail Classic, the robin's-egg-blue Harley Wallis rode while exploring the highway, is a focal point of the collection.

The small collection is located upstairs and is open whenever the Harley dealership is open—unless there's an event going on in the room—and it's free. Route 66 Harley-Davidson is closed on Mondays.

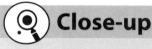

Close-up

Greenwood District

If you read the History chapter, you know why this district is important to Tulsa. If not, the quick version is: This was the site, in 1921, of one of America's worst race riots. Racism was well entrenched in the community, and a combination of misunderstanding and irresponsible rumors and reports triggered one of the uglier incidents in U.S. history. The result was the destruction of the Greenwood District, the heart of the black community. That area, which was dubbed the "Black Wall Street" for the success and prosperity of businesses in the community, was completely burned, along with a good portion of the nearby residential area. Many people were injured or killed, their homes looted, and the community torched.

Here are some suggestions for exploring the area and learning more about its history:

Greenwood Cultural Center
322 N. Greenwood Ave.
(918) 596-1020,

Start here for the background you'll need to appreciate what you are seeing. In the Good-win-Chapelle Gallery, you'll find an extensive display of photographs and documents related to the riot. Before you leave the room, look around at the African art collection. If you don't already have one, be sure and pick up a brochure for the walking tour. The cultural center is actually listed as the sixth stop on the tour. Just start here and catch up as you go.

The bookstore has a number of African-American items and a good selection of

books, including several by Dr. John Hope Franklin, noted historian, whose father was a survivor of the riot.

Mabel B. Little Heritage House
322 N. Greenwood Ave.
(918) 596-1007, (918) 596-1006

Although this house was built after the riot (1926), it was moved here from its original location. It is important because it is the only Greenwood neighborhood home built in the 1920s and it shows that members of the black community were able to survive, even thrive, in an atmosphere of racism. Called the Mabel B. Little House because Mrs. Little was

---

Plan your visit around a meal at the 5 & Diner. If it turns out that the museum is inaccessible, you'll still have a great time. Check the Restaurants chapter for more information.

OKLAHOMA AQUARIUM   **$$**
300 Aquarium Dr., Jenks
(918) 296-FISH
www.okaquarium.org

The Oklahoma Aquarium, on the banks of the Arkansas River, will open your eyes to underwater wonders. Exhibits range from the simplest of sea creatures—sponges, coral, and anemones—to complex animals with intricate behaviors like the electric eels, the archer fish, and the octopus.

In addition to impressive exhibits like the walk-through Shark Adventure, where giant bull sharks, the largest in captivity, and lemon, sand

tiger, and nurse sharks glide right over your head, smaller tanks, like the one displaying the jellyfish, hold visitors captive watching the watery ballet. The Coral Reef exhibit features a whole wall-window into the habitat of brightly colored fish. Over 200 exhibits house thousands of animals from at least 350 species.

In addition to the exotic fish, Oklahoma natives are on exhibit. You may not spend much time looking at bass or sunfish, but linger at the paddlefish tank. When one of these prehistoric-looking fish feeds, its mouth opens like a two-car garage. They swim through the water, mouth gaping, sifting out minute plankton for food. And don't miss the ancient snapping turtle (more than 120 years old) or the giant blue catfish.

Other Oklahoma natives are on exhibit in the Hayes Family Ozark Stream area. Beavers, otters, instrumental in the moving and preserving of the structure, it was the home of Sam and Lucy Mackey. Their frame home was burned down during the riot. Even though the insurance companies refused to pay off on policies, citing a "riot clause," the Mackeys were determined to rebuild.

The Mackeys worked for prosperous white Tulsans, providing housekeeping and yard services. They saved their money and were able to build this spacious and substantial home. Most of the furnishings in the house are not original. The courting sofa, the organ, and family portraits are among the few remnants of the Mackeys' personal property. It is a fascinating period piece from that time in Tulsa's history.

The house is open Mon through Fri. Admission is free but donations are suggested and appreciated.

Oklahoma State University–Tulsa
700 N. Greenwood Ave.
(918) 594-8000

The University sits on the site of the original Booker T. Washington School, and a monument to the institution is to be found on campus. During school hours, visit the B. S. Roberts Room, 151 North Hall. A permanent exhibit of photographs entitled "Black Settlers: The Search for the Promised Land in Tulsa" hangs here. The exhibition is the result of collaboration between author/historian Eddie Faye Gates and Tulsa photographer Don Thompson. Consider calling ahead as the room is often used for other purposes and the collection may be unavailable for viewing.

John Hope Franklin Reconciliation Park

Scheduled for completion by 2010, the park will provide an important focal point for the area. The centerpiece will be a three-and-a-half-story, towering sculpture by America's first African-American astronaut, Ed Dwight of Denver, Colorado.

Other sites in the district include the 1921 Black Wall Street Memorial, Vernon Chapel AME Church, Mt. Zion Baptist Church, and the 3 blocks of Greenwood Avenue north of Archer, the original heart of the commercial area.

and raccoons are the stars here. There's also a den cam in case the beavers are having a bit of a snooze when you visit.

Check the Web site for feeding schedules and times when the shark and ray touch pool and the turtle feeding pools are attended. Whether it's big doin's like the shark feeding or a smaller-scale activity—like putting krill on the side of the tank for the archerfish to shoot down—there are a number of things going on each day.

Don't forget to stop in the Karl and Beverly White National Fishing Tackle Museum, with its displays of antique tackle. From rods, reels, and lures to boats and motors, this is the largest, most complete collection of fishing tackle in the world. A Tulsa company, Zebco, produced the world's first backlash-proof casting reel. See it and its snarly predecessors here.

Grab a soda and a sandwich and enjoy a lunch on the deck overlooking the river. And be sure to make your last stop the gift shop, where you'll find all sorts of fishy items, from stuffed animals to art.

The museum is open every day except Christmas.

OKLAHOMA CENTENNIAL BOTANICAL GARDEN
3916 N. 57th West Ave.
(918) 289-0330
www.ocbg.org

The Oklahoma Centennial Botanical Garden's 160 acres will feature 60 acres of landscaped planting areas, including a children's garden, and 100 acres of native prairie and the ancient Cross Timbers, a belt of tangled trees that runs from

Kansas through Oklahoma and into Texas. That's the good news. But this project is in its infancy and, as of press time, only a tiny portion of the planned garden has actually been opened. Still, with every month, new features appear and older features become more refined and mature. And you can get in on the ground floor—watching the growth of this major project.

The concept of the garden has been growing for years—beginning with a small group of interested garden lovers. As the idea blossomed, the group was given acreage by Gentner Drummond and Tom Atherton, principals of Persimmon Ridge, LLC, along with the opportunity to choose the spot from the company's 1200-acre parcel.

And this is a prime spot—both from a topographic and a botanical point of view. So far, botanists from the University of Oklahoma have identified and cataloged approximately 400 plant species. What you can see now are drawings of a dream, the seven-acre lake that is rapidly filling, a small, temporary visitor center, and a walking trail that runs from the visitor center through ancient Indian hunting grounds to a grove of century-old persimmon trees. When finished, the facility will feature 15 major gardens and 60 specialty gardens, a 3,000-seat amphitheater, a permanent visitor center, an education center, a conservatory, an orangery, and an interfaith chapel. For now, you'll have to use a lot of imagination.

The facility is open on a limited basis so check the Web site. Classes, lectures, and demonstrations with titles like "Serpents of Summer," "Wildlife Rescuers," and "Global 'Worming'" are scheduled regularly.

OKLAHOMA JAZZ HALL OF FAME
111 E. 1st St.
(918) 281-8600
www.okjazz.org
The Jazz Hall of Fame is housed in the art deco Union Depot, which was built in 1931 and served Tulsa rail passengers until 1967. The spacious building provides room for exhibits and performances. (See Arts for more information.)

Posters and artifacts from famous jazz musicians are scattered throughout the space. One poster worth particular attention is a jazz family tree. Down one hall is a display on Oklahoma jazz history and the Wall of Fame—the greatest names in music—including Jay McShann, Patti Page, Kay Starr, Barney Kessel, Charlie Christian, and Jimmy Rushing. For music lovers and students, there's an extensive research library.

The facility is open Mon through Fri; Sat; by appointment. Admission is free. There is a charge for the Sunday afternoon concerts.

ORAL ROBERTS UNIVERSITY PRAYER TOWER
Oral Roberts University
7700 S. Lewis Ave.
(918) 495-7910
www.prayertower.oru.edu/
For a panoramic view of the ORU campus, the observation deck in the space-age-looking Prayer Tower is the place to go. A self-guided tour brochure will let you know what you're looking at for your 110-foot view. The 200-foot-tall tower, symbolically representing a contemporary cross, also houses a visitor center. Take a moment for silent reflection in the prayer room or view a 10-minute film called *A Man Like No Other* about founder Oral Roberts. There is no charge for admission.

PERRYMAN CEMETERY
East 32nd St. and South Utica Avenue
It's easy to miss this green, quiet spot tucked into one of Tulsa's most upscale neighborhoods. About the size of a corner lot, it's Tulsa's oldest cemetery. If you read the History chapter, you'll remember that the Perryman family once held most of the land that comprises present-day Tulsa. In 1849 the patriarch, Lewis, built a ranch complex close to this spot. Later, ranch headquarters, a few blocks south, became the first post office in what was called, officially, Tulsa. The earliest marked burial spot in the cemetery dates back to 1879. It's probable that there are older, but unmarked, graves. The last interment took place in 1941. You'll notice that some of the graves have what look like small huts built on top of them. This was a custom with several Native American tribes. The Perrymans were Creek. The

cemetery was deeded to the Tulsa Historical Society in 1987 by descendants Mary and Newton Perryman.

The cemetery wasn't exactly forgotten, but it needed some TLC, and in 2009, Tulsa Boy Scout Matt Heinrichs chose the cemetery for his Eagle Scout project—cleaning, trimming, and replanting to make the spot a more attractive memorial to one of Tulsa's most important families.

i It may be a slight exaggeration, but there's a spot in downtown Tulsa designated "The Center of the Universe." Where South Boston Avenue dead-ends—by the old Union Depot, now Jazz Depot—there's a pedestrian bridge with a large circle of dark stone squares set in the pavement. Stand in the center and shout or sing and listen to the echo. Don't worry about feeling silly. Everybody either does it or wishes they had.

PHILBROOK MUSEUM OF ART $-$$
2727 S. Rockford Rd.
(918) 749-7941, (800) 324-7941
www.philbrook.org

Philbrook was the home of Waite Phillips, one of three brothers who came to Oklahoma and made their fortunes in oil. Frank and L. E. stayed in Bartlesville—their company was Phillips Petroleum. Waite moved to Tulsa and started his own company. Shortly after his move, he bought a large acreage on the prairie south of town. On 23 of those acres, he built Villa Philbrook, an Oklahoma incarnation of an Italian Renaissance country estate.

The finest materials were used in the home's construction. Floors, fireplaces, and fountains were made of travertine and a variety of fine marbles. Other floors featured teak, walnut, and oak. The building was constructed with a steel frame and reinforced concrete walls and floors, all factors that made it good for use as a museum later.

In 1938, having lived in the mansion only 11 years, Waite and his wife gave the home to the citizens of Tulsa for use as an art museum. Philbrook opened in this capacity in 1939.

One of the great stories of Philbrook is that this was a home. People actually lived in these elegant rooms and the children roller-skated in the halls. The great majority of the collection you see today came from donations by philanthropists in the community. This created tremendous diversity in the holdings—from Native American, African, and Asian components to 14th-century Italian paintings and contemporary American works.

Another of Philbrook's strengths is that it combines three artistic expressions—not only the usual paintings and sculpture, but the architecture and ornamentation of the building itself and the beautiful landscaped gardens. The property is listed on the National Register of Historic Places.

In 1991 a 150,000-square-foot addition to the original building was completed—adding space for special exhibits, an extensive gift shop, and la Villa restaurant (open for lunch Tues through Sat and brunch on Sun—see the Restaurants chapter for details), classrooms, and the administrative offices.

In 2004 the gardens were given a thorough renovation. Each rock was labeled before it was removed. Aging pipes and plumbing were replaced, and then the gardens were reassembled. The original Hare & Hare design was preserved.

Both Herbert Hare, landscape architect, and Edward Delk, architect, were inspired by the Villa Lante, a 1566 estate north of Rome. A cascading water feature begins on the east terrace of the house and flows through formal gardens to pools below. At the bottom of the garden, a picturesque tempietto is reflected in the water.

Philbrook provides several items to help children enjoy their visit, including backpacks with drawing materials and clues for an art-inspired scavenger hunt. Check the Kidstuff chapter for more details.

At any given time, only about 10 percent of the museum's collection is on display. The museum also hosts three traveling exhibits each year, so almost anytime you go, you'll see different items on exhibit. Philbrook is closed on Mondays and major holidays. The second Saturday of each month, the museum admission is free.

RICHARDSON ASIAN ART MUSEUM
4770 S. Harvard Ave.
(918) 747-9393
www.richardsonart.org

Founder Dr. J. L. Richardson fell in love with Asian art while he was stationed in the Pacific during World War II. Through his lifetime he collected more than 1,000 pieces of artwork—most three-dimensional. Many of the pieces are on display in this museum.

The entry to the museum is through an elaborate Chinese entrance with red columns and yellow tile roof and guarded by two large, carved-marble Foo dogs. Foo dogs have traditionally been considered guardians and often flank the doors of buildings in China.

Inside is a spacious room with a high ceiling and an impressive crystal chandelier. Most of the displays are around the perimeter of the room, behind glass. The objects are beautiful but lacking explanatory material—frustrating for anyone who wants to learn about them, including where they came from, their use, and their symbolism.

Most of the pieces were made after World War II. There are many jade items, some pieces of amethyst, rose and clear quartz, and Peking glass. The 6-foot-tall vases are eye-catchers, as are the cloisonné temple incense jars. It's hard to miss the large jade ship, and a bronze sculpture of a dragon and phoenix may be the most popular exhibit.

There are actually a couple of pieces that children can touch—a pristine Kwan Yin, a small statue of Ho-Tei (a happy Buddha), and the dragon statue.

The museum is open Thurs through Sun. Be on the safe side and call before you go. There is no admission charge but donations are appreciated.

SHERWIN MILLER MUSEUM OF
JEWISH ART $
2021 E. 71st St.
(918) 492-1818
www.jewishmuseum.net

Though the Jewish community in Tulsa is not large, its contribution to the quality of life in the city has been tremendous. The Sherwin Miller Museum is an effort by some families in the community to preserve their heritage and to share it with others. Originally called the Gershon and Rebecca Fenster Museum of Jewish Art, it was renamed after its first curator, Sherwin Miller, who, with the purchase of a major collection, helped make this the "largest collection of Judaica in the American Southwest."

The main exhibits are divided into five areas covering archaeology, ritual objects, life cycle, ethnology, and fine art. A trip through the museum is a trip through the Old Testament. On display is pottery from two to three thousand years B.C.—from the land of Canaan before the time of Abraham. Ancient artifacts correspond with the march of peoples and history—a bronze Persian goblet, a Roman bottle. These simple items of everyday life bring Bible times to life.

Another section highlights the importance of the Torah, and ritual objects reflect the honor given to the sacred writings. Rich fabrics demonstrate skill and craftsmanship, and beautifully wrought metals reveal the reverence with which they were made.

For Christians, this place is Sunday school come to life. The traditions, festivals, and solemnities observed by Jesus are explained here. For everyone it is a lesson in history, with exhibits on events such as the destruction of the Second Temple A.D. 73), when the Jewish community was scattered (the Diaspora). And wherever they went, they took their faith and their traditions.

While these exhibits occupy most of the second floor, there is a small gallery for rotating items from the permanent collection or hosting visiting exhibitions.

On the first floor of the building is the Herman and Kate Kaiser Holocaust Collection. In addition to telling the sad story of the Holocaust, this section of the museum seeks to point out the dangers of discrimination and to encourage all to learn from tragedies of the past.

The museum is open Sun through Fri. It is closed on Sat, New Year's Day, Passover, Shavuot,

Memorial Day, the 4th of July, Labor Day, Rosh Hashanah, Yom Kippur, Shemini Atzeret and Simchat Torah, Thanksgiving, Christmas, and Sukkot.

SWAN LAKE PARK
1573 Swan Lake Dr.
(918) 596-7275
www.swanlaketulsa.org
It's hard to believe, but this idyllic little lake was once a spring-fed watering hole on the prairie—on the ranch of Colonel A. D. Orcutt, one of Oklahoma's first legislators. His son, and other developers, bought 25 acres to build a park. It was popular in those days to put an amusement area at the end of a trolley line—and that's where this was. Orcutt Lake Park, on the north side of the lake, boasted a roller coaster, a covered swimming pool, rowboat rentals, and a dance pavilion. In 1910 a small portion of the area was deeded to the city. By 1917 the area was becoming residential and the land was platted as a subdivision called Swan Lake. The park was then renamed.

With the area listed on the National Register of Historic Places, the homes around the picturesque park are highly desirable, and many incorporate swan motifs into their decor. Neighbors have been raising money to have the 1920s fountain in the lake rebuilt, hopefully in time for the park's centennial in 2010. Residents and visitors alike enjoy the attractively landscaped walking path around the lake—less than half a mile—and enjoy watching the swans and other waterfowl that come to this urban green space.

TULSA AIR AND SPACE MUSEUM AND PLANETARIUM $$
3624 N. 74th East Ave.
(918) 834-9900
www.tulsaairandspacemuseum.com
The museum focuses on Tulsa aviation history in particular but it's a history that embraces some of America's greatest aviation pioneers. Tulsa's first air event was a balloon ascension in 1897, commemorated here with a figure of a little girl looking up at a man and balloon. Six years later, the Wright brothers made their historic flight and things took off from there.

In 1911 Leonard Bonney came to the Tulsa Fair with his two-seater Wright Model B airplane. Local news reporters drew straws to see who would be the first Tulsan to fly in an airplane. Eugene Lorton, editor of the *Tulsa World*, won the opportunity and took with him special edition copies of the newspaper, which he released over the crowd—making it the first newspaper delivered by air!

The museum's full of interesting tidbits and actual aircraft—some of which visitors can actually climb into. Try your hand at flying in the F-16 Viper wind tunnel or operating the Space Shuttle robotic arm.

Tulsa's first "real" airport was built in 1928 and, in keeping with the downtown architecture, was a great example of the art deco style. The building's gone, but there's a re-creation of the facade and a few pieces that were salvaged from the original building on display here.

During World War II, Douglas Aircraft Company operated an air force plant producing B-24s, A-24s, and A-26s. Follow the story of the last B-24 built in Tulsa, the *Tulsamerican*. Watch a video of Oklahoma City resident Val Miller, the only remaining survivor (7 of the 10 crewmen survived when the plane crashed in the Adriatic Sea), as he tells of the *Tulsamerican's* last mission.

Or enjoy the story of the 42 Israelis sent to Tulsa to learn to work on airplane engines and airframes after the state of Israel was created in 1948. Adopted and hosted by the local Jewish community, the men went back to Haifa, where the Spartan School of Aeronautics facility, founded by Tulsa oilman W. G. Skelly, was replicated.

More hands-on exhibits are found in the "Eureka!" area. These exhibits come from museums that partner with the Tulsa Air and Space Museum—the Jasmine Moran Museum (Seminole), the Museum of the Great Plains (Lawton), Leonardo's Discovery Warehouse (Enid), and the Science Museum of Oklahoma (Oklahoma City)—and change several times a year.

The James E. Bertelsmeyer Planetarium features a 50-foot-diameter dome onto which a variety of programs are projected. It might be a star show or a voyage from an outer-space perspective.

The museum and planetarium are open Tues through Sat; closed Mon and major holidays. Tickets for the museum and planetarium can be purchased separately or as a combined discount ticket.

TULSA GARDEN CENTER/WOODWARD PARK
2435 S. Peoria Ave.
(918) 746-5125
www.tulsagardencenter.com

The Garden Center is an omnibus of activities. The main building, an Italianate Revival mansion, was completed in 1921 and cost over $100,000—more than a fortune at that time. Built for David Travis (whose family name was Rabinowitz), it sits next to the house of his brother, Samuel. The 13-acre estate comprised the main house, two greenhouses and a solarium, a swimming pool, two cottages, and a barn. Services for the local Jewish community were held in the ballroom before a temple was built.

Unless there is a special event going on, visitors are encouraged to visit the house. The entry hall features a black and white marble floor and a sweeping staircase with a lacy wrought-iron banister. Sunshine, filtered through an elegant stained-glass skylight, illuminates the stairs. The hall overlooks the front lawn. Painted panels and mirrors, framed with swirled gold molding, flank French doors. The only room that retains a semblance of a home is the library, wood-paneled and featuring a gold-leafed ceiling.

The whole complex is called Woodward Park. The Garden Center is actually just the mansion. In 1954 the city purchased the Travis mansion and grounds from oilman W. G. Skelly, who had purchased the home but never lived there. The property was added to Woodward Park, which the city had owned since 1909. Originally part of a 160-acre Creek allotment, it was purchased at a cost of $100 an acre. Citizens were scandalized at the expenditure—the park was far from the center of town and only accessible by wagon trails. Today, in the heart of one of Tulsa's most beautiful neighborhoods, its 45 acres are priceless.

One of the major features of the park is an azalea garden with over 15,000 plants. Obviously, spring is the best time to visit—the gardens are full of photographers and you'll even see an occasional artist with easel among the blooms. The park is also shaded by tall oaks and hickory trees, many older than the city itself.

The Municipal Rose Garden has been an attraction since it was built by the Works Progress Administration (WPA) in the '30s. The multi-terraced garden boasts nearly 5,000 plants representing nearly 250 varieties—from floribundas to grandifloras. Special favorites are the English garden roses. May through late June and Oct are the prime blossom seasons.

The formal sunken garden, built in 1924, is popular for weddings and features lots of color. The Anne Hathaway Herb Garden was started in 1939 and named in honor of William Shakespeare's wife, Anne, who was noted for her love of gardening and her cultivation of herbs like thyme, basil, mint, and rosemary.

While lovely anytime, the conservatory offers a touch of summer in the midst of winter. Its three sections feature orchids, mixed tropical plants, and cacti and bromeliads. The collections are housed in a Victorian Lord and Burnham greenhouse—the company responsible for the conservatory on Jay Gould's estate, Lyndhurst, and the famous Conservatory of Flowers in Golden Gate Park, San Francisco.

The newest additions to the Center are the Linnaeus Teaching Gardens. These areas are designed to encourage the home gardener, to show the latest and most appropriate plants for the area, and to demonstrate gardening techniques. The Linnaeus Teaching Gardens are reached by way of a long brick walk shaded with wisteria-draped pergolas. Azaleas, crape myrtles, and other shrubs and flowers line the walkway. The entry and gardens are a labor of lots of love—no tax dollars were used to create this attractive and useful facility—all the planting was done by 200 volunteers. Donated funds purchased plants and construction materials.

The area is compact but covers a wide variety of situations, demonstrating what can be done in a small space. Mini-waterfalls cascade into a pond; rocks and boulders are incorporated into the slopes. One area is reserved for a vegetable garden, another for herbs, while yet another is decorated more formally with a central fountain. Lots of volunteers are always on hand to answer gardening questions. There are green thumbs everywhere—as evinced by the healthy plants, which include a stunning clematis with blooms measuring 8 inches in diameter.

TULSA HISTORICAL SOCIETY
2445 S. Peoria Ave.
(918) 712-9484
www.tulsahistory.org
At the Tulsa Historical Society, even the building is an exhibit. The Italianate Revival mansion was built in 1919 for Samuel Travis, right next door to the mansion built for his brother David. The men, with two other family members, arrived in Tulsa in 1914 to seek their fortunes in the oil business—and five years later built their side-by-side palaces in the country south of town.

The historical society bought the Travis house (which had been occupied by several subsequent families and was on the verge of being demolished for a housing addition) in 1997. Renovation and expansion took a number of years, and the first exhibits were put on display in 2003. All work was finished in 2008, giving the society room to mount several exhibits simultaneously.

Exhibits change several times a year, making return visits more fun. The only permanent exhibit is a series of photographs and displays about the house. Changing exhibits have included everything from Tulsa's art deco treasures to the Skelly Oil Company and Oklahoma's five Native American ballerinas—Moscelyne Larkin, Yvonne Chouteau, Rosella Hightower, and Maria and Marjorie Tallchief.

Be sure and take time to walk through the gardens on the west side of the museum. Architectural artifacts, like a mounting block belonging to George Perryman and the cupola from the 1931 East Second Library, are scattered throughout the plantings.

The pièce de résistance is the sculpture, *The*

Five Moons, honoring Oklahoma's famous five Indian ballerinas mentioned above. The sculpture, visualized and begun by Tulsa artist Monte England, was completed by Native American artist and Oklahoman Gary Henson after England's death.

The museum is closed Sun, Mon, and holidays, and is free to the public. Check the Web site for information on current events, exhibits, and walking tours.

TULSA PORT OF CATOOSA/ARKANSAS RIVER HISTORICAL SOCIETY MUSEUM
5350 Cimarron Rd.
(918) 266-2291
www.arkansasriver.org
Who would have thought landlocked Oklahoma would have port access to the Gulf of Mexico? It's true, thanks to the McClellan-Kerr Arkansas River Navigation System. The port's a busy place with grain, chemicals, and heavy equipment being shipped in and out on barges that load and unload at the Port of Catoosa.

Start your tour at the Arkansas River Historical Society Museum in the Port Authority administration building. Watch a 10-minute video about the port and waterway, then check out the exhibits. Panels show the history of inland water traffic in the United States and the benefits of the waterway. You'll also see a variety of early Indian artifacts that were uncovered during the construction.

The waterway itself is an engineering marvel with 18 locks and dams along the 445-mile route to the Mississippi. There's a small, motorized model showing a boat going through a lock. There are no locks at the port—the nearest lock is about 7 miles south of Inola. You can get up close and personal with a tugboat, though. On display outside the museum is the M/V *Charley Border,* the first towboat at the port. You can walk around the main deck, and then check out the propellers and rudders. This 50-foot boat is considered a small towboat, handy for moving around in port. Large towboats on the Mississippi can move as many as 65 barges at once. One jumbo barge can carry as much cargo as 60 semitrailer trucks.

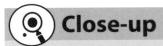 **Close-up**

Oklahoma's Indian Ballerinas

Visitors to the State Capitol in Oklahoma City are always impressed with a painting by Chickasaw artist Mike Larsen. *Flight of Spirit* depicts five graceful dancers in frothy white dresses. In the background, figures represent the Trail of Tears. The dancers—all born in the 1920s, all with Oklahoma ties, and all of Native American heritage—conquered the world's stages with their grace and beauty.

Rosella Hightower (1920–2008), of Choctaw descent, was born in Oklahoma but moved to Kansas City as a child. As an adult, she performed with the Ballet Russe de Monte Carlo, Ballet Theatre, Original Ballet Russe, the Grand Ballet du Marquis de Cuevas, and the American Ballet Theatre. She founded the Center for Classical Dance in Cannes, France, and directed several French ballet companies. She was the first American director of the famous Ballet of Paris Opera and was awarded France's highest honor, the Legion of Honor.

Moscelyne Larkin (1925–), of Shawnee-Peoria lineage, was born in Miami, Oklahoma. At 15, she joined the Original Ballet Russe. She later married Roman Jasinski, premier danseur of the company. Moscelyne also danced with the Ballet Russe de Monte Carlo and appeared as prima ballerina at Radio City Music Hall in New York City. Retiring from the stage, the couple moved to Tulsa, opened a ballet school, and founded the Tulsa Ballet.

Maria Tallchief (1925–) and her sister Marjorie (1926–), of Osage descent, moved to California from Oklahoma. Maria danced with the Ballet Russe de Monte Carlo, eventually marrying choreographer George Balanchine, who choreographed her most famous role as the firebird in Stravinsky's *The Firebird*.

Marjorie Tallchief danced with the American Ballet Russe de Monte Carlo, the Grand Ballet du Marquis de Cuevas, the Chicago Opera Ballet, and the Harkness Ballet. She also directed several American dance companies.

Cherokee Yvonne Chouteau (1920–) is the only one of the ballerinas not born in the state, but her heritage is distinguished as a direct descendant of Jean Pierre Chouteau, who established Oklahoma's first white settlement in 1796. She joined the Ballet Russe de Monte Carlo at age 14 and, though she didn't dance with Rosella Hightower at the time, remembers the older dancer comforting her when homesickness overcame her. With her husband, Miguel Terekhov, also with the Ballet Russe, Chouteau came back to Oklahoma as artists-in-residence at the University of Oklahoma (OU). In addition to providing the foundation for OU's dance degree program, they founded the Oklahoma City Civic Ballet, now Ballet Oklahoma.

Though they were depicted together in the painting, the five famous dancers never appeared as a group. The closest they came was when the Tulsa Ballet Theatre hosted a festival in 1967. Chouteau, Larkin, Hightower, and Marjorie Tallchief danced *The Four Moons*, a piece created for them. Only Maria Tallchief was absent. The entire group is honored in a sculpture, *The Five Moons*, on the grounds of the Tulsa Historical Society.

When you're in the museum, pick up a driving tour map. After you tour the museum and the towboat, you're ready to check out the port. As you drive through the industrial complex, you'll see companies that ship pipe, packaging, lumber, grain, petroleum products, even chemicals for night-vision binoculars. You'll also see the navigation channel, which ends right here. If you're lucky, you may get to see barges being loaded or unloaded.

The Port of Catoosa is the 15th largest port in the United States and ships over two million tons of goods a year. It takes a commercial tow (towboat plus barges) about five days to travel from Catoosa to the Mississippi River and about five more to reach New Orleans.

The museum is closed on weekends, New Year's Day, Good Friday, Memorial Day, July 4th, Labor Day, the four-day Thanksgiving weekend, Christmas Eve, and Christmas Day. There is no charge for the museum, but there is a small selection of souvenirs if you must spend money. If you want to take a picnic, there's a nice little gazebo and picnic tables at the museum—a good place to have a snack before or after your tour.

To get to the Port from I-44 or I-244, take OK 169 north to the Tulsa Port of Catoosa/46th St. North exit. Continue east on East 46th St. North (OK 266) to the intersection with OK 167. Continue straight ahead (crossing OK 167) into the port area. Follow the signs approximately 1 mile to Cimarron Road and turn right to the Port Authority Building.

TULSA ZOO AND LIVING MUSEUM $
6421 E. 36th St. North
(918) 669-6600
www.tulsazoo.org

Covering 84 acres in Tulsa's massive north-side Mohawk Park, the Tulsa Zoo's collection consists of approximately 500 species and 2,800 animals. Though not officially a botanical garden, the landscaping is both attractive and functional—the zoo grows a portion of the animals' food right on the grounds.

It's hard to pick a favorite exhibit area. The Elephant Encounter, in a building with exotically shaped portals reminiscent of Indian architecture, is a likely candidate. Besides housing the zoo's pachyderms, including a couple of females from the Oklahoma City Zoo who are visiting during reconstruction of their home (and there's the possibility of some large-scale romances), exhibits give guests both biological information and history. A life-size diorama, complete with wind, thunder, and lightning, shows early humans hunting a Columbian mammoth.

Another exhibit shows the use of elephants in warfare. And sculptures of elephants in art and culture—Asian images and even the contemporary Babar—add interest to the exhibit.

A major attraction, particularly in the winter months, is the Tropical American Rainforest—a 17,000-square-foot building with a circular route that gives guests glimpses from the floor of a flooded forest to the tip-top of the tree canopy, 50 feet above. Inhabitants in the temperature-controlled building include caimans, piranhas, howler monkeys, fruit bats, poison dart frogs, golden-headed lion tamarins, and jaguars. Outside, a giant Olmec head greets you, and inside, a replica of an Aztec bench, featuring the Prince of Flowers, helps set the mood for your journey. Other examples of Aztec, Mayan, and Incan art create an exotic ambience. More than 250 different species of plants—more than 3,500 specimens, from allspice and avocado to kapok and palms—thrive in the tropical environment.

One of the largest display areas is the North American Living Museum, which takes visitors on a tour of the Arctic tundra, southern Lowlands, eastern forest, and desert. Other popular exhibits include the polar bear pool, the black-footed South African penguins (also called jackass penguins for their loud, braying noises) and the Children's Zoo.

Keeper chats and animal demonstrations are scheduled regularly. The Children's Zoo has special events of its own—like the spring-break craftsmen demonstrations—sheep shearing, weaving, spinning, and wood carving—in addition to lots of animals to pet. The Children's Zoo is open from March through Oct, weather permitting.

Food and drink are available at the zoo and, while patronizing these services is encouraged, there are also picnic facilities for those who want to bring their own food. Zoo admission covers all exhibits. Train rides, the carousel, and camel rides cost extra.

The zoo is open 363 days a year—closed Christmas Day and the third Friday in June when they prepare for their annual WALTZ on the Wild Side. In Jan and Feb, if the overnight temperature is forecast to be below freezing, Polar Bear Days are declared and admission is half-price. See the Kidstuff chapter for more information.

SHOPPING

There are studies that indicate that the number one activity of travelers is shopping. If you're one of those travelers who takes an extra suitcase—empty—there are plenty of places to fill it up in Tulsa. There are a number of malls with the stores you'll find from coast to coast; these are handy when you know just what you want and who carries it. Many travelers, however, prefer to explore—always looking for that unique little boutique around the corner. You'll find plenty of shops to suit both kinds of shoppers.

If your shopping time is short, head for Utica Square. Yes, you'll find chain stores here—but they're really high-end ones. And there are a lot of shops carrying a lot of different merchandise. It doesn't hurt that there are also nice places to rest your feet or get a bite to eat.

For more adventuresome shopping, stroll down Cherry Street or South Peoria Avenue in Brookside. The shops listed here are just a starter. And if you fill up that suitcase, look under "Luggage" and you can buy another one.

MALLS AND SHOPPING CENTERS

THE FARM SHOPPING CENTER
East 51st St. and South Sheridan Road
www.farmshoppingcenter.com
Lots of shady trees and a restored rustic barn bring a country flavor to the city in this outdoor collection of shops and restaurants. From fast food (Ron's Hamburgers & Chili and Subway), cafeteria-style (Furr's), international specialties (Villa Ravenna and Margaret's German Restaurant & Deli) to all-American faves (Billy Sims Barbecue), you're sure to find something tasty here. And you'll find something different in the unique shops, which carry everything from dog collars to jewelry, herbal concoctions, and fine art. Or pick up sports souvenirs at Sports Fan-Attic. This is a fun place for strolling and window-shopping, and you'll probably find something you didn't know you needed!

JUSTICE TULSA HILLS SHOPPING CENTER
Hwy. 75 and West 71st St.
You'll find a lot of variety in this shopping center—not a mall, more like a bunch of strips and stand-alones. Look for names like Belk, Best Buy, Chili's, Lowe's, PetSmart, Ross Dress for Less, Mar-shalls, Books-A-Million, Target, Subway, McDonald's, Dress Barn, Michaels, and several places to buy moderately priced shoes.

PROMENADE MALL
East 41st St. and South Yale Avenue
www.tulsapromenade.com
Opened in 1965 as Southland, an outdoor mall, this shopping area was reinvented in the late '80s into Promenade, an enclosed mall. More than 100 stores call this shopping area home, with Dillard's, Macy's, and JCPenney as anchors. Other favorite stores include Victoria's Secret, American Eagle, Gap, and Bath & Body Works. In addition to a food court, you'll find Camille's Sidewalk Café and El Chico. The Promenade Palace movie theater has 12 screens. The Promenade Pacers walking club get its miles in here, and Momtopia, a club for moms and kids, has an interactive event the second Saturday of each month.

RIVERWALK CROSSING
Riverwalk Terrace and North Riverfront Drive, Jenks
www.riverwalkcrossing.com
Two blocks north of Jenks's East Main St. (Tulsa's East 96th St.), on the west bank of the Arkansas

River, is Riverwalk Crossing. You'll see a rather old-fashioned-looking, black metal archway leading to the shopping area. While there are not a great number of shops, the ones here are unique and interesting—and there are a lot of good restaurants plus a movie theater. Shops you'll find here include Island Nation, Azur Couture, and Cigar Box.

The attractive development is laid out along the riverbank, with lots of room for sidewalk dining, an amphitheater for entertainment, attractive sculptures, and a water feature. The summer concert series is hugely popular, and there are often several bands entertaining in different areas of the shopping center. Also in summer, the Jenks Farmers' Market is held every Saturday morning in the south parking lot and there are outdoor movies scheduled regularly.

UTICA SQUARE
East 21st St. and South Utica Avenue
www.uticasquare.com
This outdoor mall is so Tulsa—attractive, elegant, and just a bit pretentious. Built in 1952, it was the town's first suburban shopping center. Building requirements were stringent and styles range from Georgian and Williamsburg colonial to French country and contemporary. The many trees that were planted have grown large and their shade is most appreciated on sunny summer afternoons.

Utica Square is laid out in small blocks, like a little town. You'll find a number of the names you see in contemporary malls—Pottery Barn, Williams-Sonoma, Ann Taylor—plus Saks Fifth Avenue and Miss Jackson's, a Tulsa original. Lots of restaurants make their homes here, too. Going to the average mall may be a shopping trip; going to Utica Square is an experience.

On Thursday nights in summer, the area is packed with blankets and chairs and people enjoying the free concerts.

WOODLAND HILLS MALL
East 71st and South Memorial Drive
www.shopsimon.com
Tulsa's largest mall is located on the northeast

corner of this busy intersection. Major anchors include Dillard's, Sears, JCPenney, and Macy's. The multilevel mall is attractive and well lighted with lots of skylights. You'll find all the usual mall suspects here—plus a number of upscale stores like Ann Taylor Loft, Coldwater Creek, Coach, and Sephora. Kids love the large play area. The Cheesecake Factory is a favorite eatery, and the food court offers a wide variety of fast selections.

ANTIQUES

AMERICAN HERITAGE ANTIQUES
101 E. Main St., Jenks
(918) 298-9408
American Heritage sits in a prime spot on the northeast corner of East Main and North 1st Sts. Like most antique stores, the inventory changes and you can never be certain what you'll find, but the selection here is diverse and can range from scrimshaw and Native American items to kitchenware and art glass. Among the items they have carried in the past are art glass mushroom light shades, die-cast toy tractors, and salt-glazed rolling pins.

THE ANTIQUARY, LTD.
1325 E. 15th St.
(918) 582-2897
These aren't just your granny's things—though you'll find a little of that here—like Jewel Tea bowls and Fiestaware. But the Antiquarian also carries a lot of items from the 1800s. Look here for fine furniture, silver, china, architectural pieces, jewelry, and pottery from companies like Van Briggle and Roseville. And if you need a Victorian beer puller, check here first. The Antiquary also buys and consigns and conducts estate sales.

MILYNDA'S MEMORIES
102 S. 1st St., Jenks
(918) 298-5962
Milynda's, which used to be called Rebecca's Memories, houses booths of 54 vendors. In addition to antiques, you'll find some handcrafted items. Quality and stock vary from booth to booth, but one booth, near the front door, stands

out for its display of glass. Well lit with rope light, the glass and crystal is shown to maximum advantage. In particular, a Northwood coin spot cranberry pitcher grabbed attention with its colorful sparkle.

MISS MCGILLICUTTY'S
106 E. Main St., Jenks
(918) 298-7997
www.missmcgillicuttys.com
This store is huge—the rooms just keep on rambling. With over 30 dealers, Miss McGillicutty's carries a bit of everything. They have a number of pieces of furniture, both antique and reproduction—armoires, dining sets, even pianos. You'll find the usual dishes, books and toys, jewelry—and the unusual, perhaps antique fishing lures or tackle.

ART

JOSEPH GIEREK FINE ART
1512 E. 15th St.
(918) 592-5432
www.gierek.com
Large, light, and open, the Gierek gallery selectively displays only a small portion of the works for sale. Each piece is given plenty of room to be the center of your attention. Whether it's a large, colorful, abstract canvas or one of James Andrew Smith's stunning still lifes, all genres are represented here. With 27 years of experience, Joseph Gierek is respected by veteran art collectors and quickly wins the hearts of beginning collectors with his knowledge and advice.

LOVETTS GALLERY
6528 E. 51st St. (The Farm)
(918) 664-4732
www.lovettsgallery.com
This third-generation establishment has been serving Tulsa since 1978. They've been in their present location in The Farm shopping center about a year. The gallery is bursting with exciting art works from over 70 artists. About 15 percent of the artists are native Oklahomans. Antique Native American items complement contempo-

rary creations. Discreet lighting keeps the gallery from seeming crowded.

Although you'll find all sorts of subjects represented, art appealing to westerners is particularly prevalent here. Beautiful woods and ceramics, glass, jewelry, paintings, sculpture, photography—the materials and treatments show the tremendous diversity of the artists' works.

Fine framing is a hallmark of the gallery, and their selection rivals any in the surrounding states.

M. A. DORAN GALLERY
3509 South Peoria Ave.
(918) 748-8700
www.madorangallery.com
If you can keep from touching the sensuous curves of Ron Fleming's wood carvings, you deserve a prize. Fleming is just one of a diverse group of artists represented by the M. A. Doran Gallery. Another Oklahoman in the collection is glass artist Kreg Kallenberger. His pieces are on display in art museums around the world. Otto Duecker's floating fruits catch the eye, and his paintings of snapshots are sure to cause comment. The selection in here is always intriguing, and the Brookside location is ideal for browsers and window shoppers.

ZIEGLER'S ART AND FRAME
6 North Lewis Ave.
(918) 584-217
www.zieglerart.com
On the northwest corner of North Lewis Avenue and East Admiral Place, this double-decade-old emporium takes up almost the whole block. They carry a small number of original paintings and photographs but mostly carry prints, giclées, and posters. You'll find a huge selection of ready-made frames, and they are masters at custom framing. Be sure and check out the Tulsa room for photos, prints, books about Tulsa, and memorabilia from T-Town. Elsewhere in the store, areas feature artificial flowers, cards, decorator items, and oddities like "Ladies Only" screwdrivers with elegant handles and sink stoppers with pewter decorative pulls. Don't miss the Bargain Room—it's like a really cool

garage sale—everything from a framed reproduction of an antique Pacific Coast Trolley poster to plastic glasses with attached gorilla nose.

BABY BOUTIQUES/CHILDREN'S ITEMS

DINGBATS
1602 E. 15th St.
(918) 398-6422
www.ding-bats.com

Need a baby item? Classy baby's mommas shop at Dingbats. Owner Nicole Randolph can do everything from designing a nursery to assembling a baby carriage. Or she'll sell you a shower gift that literally takes the cake—disposable baby diapers fashioned into a replica of a multiple-layer cake decorated with ribbons and flowers.

Baby slings, baby clothing, diaper bags, baby carriers and car seats, cribs, baby-food cookers, you name it. If it's for baby, it's at Dingbats. And there's full service and maintenance on all gear.

KATHLEEN'S KIDS
8212 S. Harvard Ave.
(918) 742-2697
www.kathleenskids.com

Kathleen's has Tulsa's largest selection of clothing, shoes, accessories, and gift items for babies and children. She carries lines like Oopsy Daisy Baby, Haven Girl, Lelli Kelly, Rachel on the Flower, Juicy Couture, and Uggs. She also has cute big brother/big sister T-shirts. You'll find rows and rows of bows and, even better, you can choose ribbon for a custom-made bow—great if you want to match a particular outfit. The store has a wonderful play area for children—even snacks and videos—so you and your child can both enjoy the shopping experience.

BICYCLES

TOM'S BICYCLES
1506 E. 15th St.
(918) 592-2453
www.tomsbicycles.com

Tom's carries Giant, Kona, Felt, and KHS bicycles and all cycling accessories, including shoes, helmets, and clothing. And they service all kinds of bikes, so if you're traveling with your bike and have an emergency, here's help.

Tom's also carries disc golf equipment. With 14 courses in Tulsa, this is a growing sport.

BOOKS/SUNDRIES

STEVE'S SUNDRY, BOOKS & MAGAZINES
2612 S. Harvard Ave.
(918)743-3544, (888) 743-0989
www.stevessundrybooksmags.com

They advertise themselves as "Tulsa's own bookstore and more" and they've been in business since 1947. With over 50,000 book titles and 3,000 to 4,000 magazine titles, Joanie Stephenson and her crew have the map covered. This is a great place to look for books on Tulsa, too. As for sundries—defined as miscellaneous items—you'll just have to come see. That could include anything from salad dressing and toe separators to Route 66 memorabilia and Frankoma pottery.

Locals drop in for a read and a drink at the old-fashioned soda fountain. Joanie's father-in-law, the original Steve, bought it in 1947 from a downtown drugstore that was going out of business. Sodas and shakes are specialties and all the food is homemade except for the bread the sandwiches come on.

CIGARS/TOBACCO

ARCHER'S TOBACCO POUCH
5976 S. Yale Ave., Kingspointe Village
(918) 742-1660
www.thetobaccopouch.com

Everything for the cigar and pipe smoker—Archer's carries 10,000 varieties of cigars, 75 blends of pipe tobacco including 4 house blends, and pipes from a $6 corncob to a $150 Nørding, hand carved by the Danish master himself.

The Boardroom, a smoking lounge, is the site of cigar tastings and for viewing sporting events on a 72-inch TV. There's plenty of seating, a cooler of beer, chess, backgammon, and even WiFi if you brought your laptop.

CIGAR BOX
500 RiverWalk Terrace, Jenks
(918) 299-7110

409 Stone Wood Dr., Broken Arrow
(918) 355-0008
www.cigarboxtulsa.com
Proud of its specialty tobacco products and its premium cigar bar, the Cigar Box hosts a number of special events from wine or chocolate tastings and cigar events to sports broadcasts.

The full-service cigar bar offers wine, 30 different beers, and 15 Scotch whiskeys. The climate-controlled humidor stores cigars by Ashton, Padron, Arturo Fuente, and more.

You'll also find Meerschaum pipes, cigar clippers, and all your other tobacco needs here or in the Broken Arrow store in The Village at Stone Wood Hills.

CLOTHING AND ACCESSORIES

ABERSONS
3509 South Peoria Ave.
(918) 742-7335
www.abersonstyle.com
You don't have to go to Rodeo Drive to find fashion's first names. Abersons carries men's and women's clothing and shoes from designers like Lanvin, Armani, Stella McCartney, and Jil Sander. The store is sleek and elegant and so is the merchandise. Off-street parking is located behind the building.

AZUR COUTURE
500 Riverwalk Terrace Suite 115, Jenks
(918) 299-2350
www.azurcouture.com
You'll be met at the door by Poshcious, owner Dara Dupler's fashionably wrinkled shar-pei. Dara combs the markets on both coasts for fun, funky, and the trendiest fashions. This boutique is for the young, sharp and definitely hip shopper (sizes 0 to 12) looking for designer jeans and T-shirts or a one-of-a-kind dress. Trendy babies (newborn to 6 T) can get outfitted here, too.

DÉJÀ VU
6929 South Lewis Ave.
(918) 477-7700
www.dejavu-inc.com
Check this shop out if you would like to find a lightly worn designer dress at a great price. There are both designer items and new knockoffs in Déjà Vu. Prom dresses are also popular items. And then there's the story of the one-of-a-kind outfit that went to Mardi Gras three times with three different owners. Not only will you find dresses, pants, and shirts, you can accessorize with purses and jewelry.

ISABELLA'S DESIGN ORIGINALS
1311 E. 35th St.
(918) 744-9100
Catering to an upscale clientele, Isabella's is owned by mother and daughter Patricia Lambert and Kim Abdo. They custom-design clothing and jewelry, provide personal fashion consulting and personal shopping. In addition to their own designs, they carry shoes, other high-fashion clothing, and one-of-a-kind items in their boutique.

ISLAND NATION
500 Riverwalk Terrace, Suite 110, Jenks
(918) 296-9801
www.myislandnation.com
It's summer here even in the winter. With bamboo ceiling and walls, beachwear, and seashore-related decor items, you expect to hear the waves hitting the sand. This shop carries Tommy Bahama, Tori Richards, Life Is Good T-shirts and caps, Reef flip-flops, and much more. For a whimsical touch for your bath (or cabana, you lucky dog), pick up a couple of Happy Hooks—clothing hooks decorated with flamingos, palm trees, or mermaids. Or, if your bathroom is as close as you get to a watery getaway, try some of the wonderful Aromafloria bath and body products.

MARY-RUBY APPAREL
6034 South Yale Ave. (KingsPointe Village)
(918) 491-0808
www.maryruby.com
Mary-Ruby is a destination shop for lots of Okla-

homa women. In business since 1941, the store caters to the moderate to upscale woman who doesn't want to dress like a teenager. Mary-Ruby carries evening, everyday, casual, and cruise wear, as well as formal wear for the mother of the bride or groom. Service is a hallmark, and Mary Ruby's staff will special order. There's also a full-time alterations department. Connie Richter has owned the store for over a decade and a half and attributes the store's long history of success to the extraordinary level of service customers find here. The jewelry section is extensive and carries a number of styles of clip-on earrings.

A comfortable sitting area, complete with coffee, cookies, and magazines, makes accompanying a shopper here a pleasure. This is where the guys congregate when their wives are trying on clothes—but it's so congenial that sometimes the wives and staff join them.

MISS JACKSON'S
1974 Utica Square
(918) 747-8671, (866) 688-9702
www.missjacksons.com

Miss Jackson's is a Tulsa icon—generations of Tulsa women have shopped there, and the lucky ones have been "Miss Jackson brides." The store was founded in 1910—Miss Nelle Jackson had come to Oklahoma from the East with her mother in 1907. She had worked in retail in Pittsburgh and had built a reputation for her millinery skills and her excellent taste. It was her dream to have a shop of her own. From a tiny lingerie shop on the balcony of a jewelry store to larger emporia in downtown Tulsa, until its owner's retirement at 80-plus, Miss Jackson's was a byword for taste and elegance.

The store has changed hands several times and moved to Utica Square in 1962, but it remains the place where sophistication and style still reign supreme.

In addition to clothing, jewelry, shoes, and cosmetics, Miss Jackson's also carries gifts and fine crystal (Baccarat and Lalique) and china. Don't look for the latest fad here; look instead for items of enduring fashion and beauty.

SAXON JUDD AMBIENTE
3509 S. Peoria Ave., Suite 162,
The Consortium
(918) 743-6100

This store features men's clothing by Italian designer Ermenegildo Zegna. The Zegna Group, founded in 1910 in Treviro, Italy, by Ermenegildo Zegna, is still run by members of the family. From its start as a manufacturer of fine fabrics, Zegna moved into the ready-to-wear market, now carrying everything from shoes, suits, and ties to pajamas and underwear. Saxon Judd specializes in these definitely pricey but oh-so-elegant items.

DESIGN AND DECOR

CHARLES FAUDREE ANTIQUES AND INTERIORS
1345 E. 15th St.
(918) 747-9706
www.charlesfaudree.com

Charles Faudree is *the* name in interior design in Tulsa—his fans have elevated him almost to cult status. His shop is crammed with true designer pieces—elegant, unusual, one of a kind. His designs have appeared in all the top magazines and he's authored two books, *Charles Faudree's French Country Signature* and *Charles Faudree's Country French Living*. While you'll certainly find French pieces here, you'll also find items from all over the world.

GARBE'S
4137 S. 72nd East St.
(918) 627-0284, (800) 735-2241
www.garbes.com

People come from all over the region to shop at Garbe's, which has been in business since 1970. Their selection of light fixtures and lamps can't be beat, but they have so much more. From fans to faucets and sinks to sundials, water fountains to weather vanes, the variety of items for the home and decor is outstanding.

GARDEN DEVA
317 S. Trenton Ave.
(918) 592-3382
www.gardendeva.com

Lisa Regan's metalwork figures pop up in fine homes and elegant gardens everywhere—anywhere there's an owner with an appreciation of the fanciful. Her pieces range in size from tabletop figures to trellises, giant lanterns, and tall, decorated poles. Check the Arts chapter for more information about this creative artist and her fun gallery.

T. A. LORTON
1343 E. 15th St.
(918) 743-1600
www.talorton.com
Look for upscale decorative items and gifts here. Lorton's carries pillows, candles, coffee-table books, unusual light fixtures, china, and fine linens. It's always good to stop here because owner Tracy Lorton Salisbury has many interests and you never know what unique items have caught her eye, whether it's a cuddly baby blanket, silk plaid table napkins, or even a contemporary, steel canopy bed.

ZOLLER DESIGNS AND ANTIQUES, INC.
1603 E. 15th St.
(918) 583-1966
www.zollerdesigns.com
Debbie Zoller carries a mix of European antiques, reproductions, designer pieces, and decorative items. In business for 20 years, she's been in this location for the last 15. One of the more interesting pieces was a lamp with a high-heeled shoe on the base, an umbrella for the stand, and a shade fashioned like a lady's hat. And Debbie has the style to pull unusual items together into a stylish look.

FARMERS' MARKETS

Farmers' markets are becoming more and more popular, and there are several scattered throughout the metropolitan area. Opening and closing dates vary—some open as early as mid-April, others not until late May or early June. Closing dates range from September to November. Most of the markets have banners up during their open season. Obviously, the stock depends on the season. Most markets also carry homemade items like jams, jellies, bread, soap, etc. The locations listed here can change, so be aware. Here are some of the Tulsa area markets:

- Broken Arrow Farmers' Market
  418 S. Main St., Broken Arrow
  Thurs, late afternoon through early evening, and Sat until noon
  www.brokenarrowok.gov
- Brookside Farmers' Market
  Westlake Ace Hardware parking lot, East 41st St. and South Peoria Avenue
  Wed until noon
  www.cherrystreetfarmersmarket.com
- Cherry Street Farmers' Market
  East 15th St. and South Peoria Avenue
  Sat until 11 a.m.
  www.cherrystreetfarmersmarket.com
- Downtown Tulsa Farmers' Market
  Williams Green at 3rd St. and South Boston Avenue
  Tues, mid-morning to early afternoon
  www.localharvest.org
- Jenks Farmers' Market
  Parking lot of RiverWalk Crossing, Jenks
  Sat until noon
  www.jenkschamber.com

GIFTS

DWELLING SPACES
119 S. Detroit Ave.
(918) 582-1033

511 S. Boston at Philcade
www.dwellingspaces.net
Get your "I heart Tulsa" or "Okie Grown" T-shirts here, or Oklahoma postcards, books, CDs, DVDs—Mary Beth Babcock carries a lot of cool Oklahoma items. And she represents over 85 local artists, including Felix and Jayne, who have produced some cool clutches and accessories like vintage button rings.

This cool, hip shop is the place to find unusual decorative pieces, china, and even a $75 Alessi dog bowl with a bone handle. Mary Beth has an optimistic spirit and a quirky sense of humor. If you're stuffy, stay away.

THE GIFT GALLERY
4107 S. Yale Ave., Ste. 114, Tulsa
Promenade
(918) 622-0474

Little bit of this, little bit of that—Brighton items, candles, Oklahoma souvenirs, garden flags and banners, Leanin' Tree and Blue Mountain cards. The Gift Gallery also carries a number of items with Oklahoma University, Oklahoma State University, and Tulsa U. themes. There are a number of baby items, including the Mud Pie line.

LAMBRUSCO'Z CATERING MARKET AND DELICATESSEN
1344 E. 41st St.
(918) 496-1246
www.lambruscoz.com

People come here to shop for food—to eat here, take home for an immediate meal or to plan ahead. But while you're here, you may find some surprising items that you either can't live without or are perfect for that hard-to-buy-for sister-in-law. In addition to casual dinnerware, it could be a clever patio candle, a funky set of refrigerator magnets, or wooden salad tongs that look like garden tools. There are even some clever kiddy items like a fork made like an airplane for coaxing a reluctant toddler to open his mouth for a zoomful of peas.

MADE IN OKLAHOMA
4107 S. Yale Ave., Ste. 134, Tulsa
Promenade
(918) 664-0543

Vendors rent space here and sell everything from commercially produced products to homemade crafts. You'll find at least five different brands of barbecue sauce (an Oklahoma aphrodisiac), artwork, gift baskets, emu oil rubs, even wine bottle lamps and microwaveable pork rinds. This is a fun place to look for something different.

MRS. DEHAVEN'S FLOWER SHOP
106 E. 15th St.
(918) 583-0118, (866) 583-0118
www.mrsdehavens.com

With only three owners in over a century, Mrs. DeHaven's has been a constant in the com-

munity. It's been in its present location since the '50s, occupying a space originally built as a flower shop—in Spanish style with stucco walls, arched niches, and the original pressed tin ceiling. Don't miss the central chandelier—sometimes obscured by elaborate displays—with its arms like drooping palm fronds dripping with long crystals. There's only one other like it—in a jewelry store in Beverly Hills. Each store owner has tried to purchase the matching chandelier from the other—but no one wants to give one up.

The store teems with beautiful decorator pieces from pillows to a swan bowl with a red glass body and clear glass neck and head. All arrangements are custom-created, but this is a full-service shop and you can get everything from a couple of stems wrapped in paper to arrangements and bouquets for the most elaborate weddings.

Be sure and pay homage to the queen of the store—Willow—a gray tabby with her own pearl tiara. And, if you're extra lucky, the ruling King Charles spaniel may deign to let you pet him. As for the staff, they're talented, friendly, and helpful and will make you feel like royalty.

THE PERFECT TOUCH
4932 E. 91st St. (91st St. and South Yale Avenue)
(918) 496-8118, (800) 951-6759
www.perfecttouchgiftstore.com

One of Tulsa's largest gift stores, the Perfect Touch carries many popular gift lines, including Brighton, Vera Bradley, Lampe Berger, Webkinz, and more. Gobs of gifts and seasonal items give the shopper a wide choice. Jewelry, sandals, initialed items, pottery, picture frames, ornaments, scents—you're sure to find something you need—or just want.

GOURMET GROCERIES/ GOODIES AND BAKERIES

BLUE JACKALOPE GROCERIES & COFFEE
306 S. Phoenix Ave.
(918) 582-5344
www.bluejackalope.com

You have to be looking for this one—it's hidden away in one of Tulsa's oldest neighborhoods, the century-plus-old Crosbie Heights. Owner Scott Smith identified the need for a lost amenity—the corner grocery—for people in this close-to-downtown area. You won't find a lot of products here but it's perfect for picking up the bare necessities. And he carries fresh, local produce in season. Best of all, this is a center for the community—there's a coffee-table discussion group every Sunday afternoon from 3 to 6. Everybody's welcome. Topics? What's on your mind? And Scott makes a mean avocado, hummus, and Muenster cheese sandwich on whole wheat bread. Stop by to see this one-man effort to help rebuild and reclaim what was once a bustling, working-class neighborhood

CFC CHOCOLATIER
15 E. Brady St.
(918) 576-6000
www.cfcchocolatier.com
Patrick Aldred, a veteran chocolatier, opened this small showroom/kitchen where he produces gourmet truffles primarily for the wholesale market. But drop-ins can pick up some goodies or special order. Among his coolest products are Quartz Crystal Chocolates—chocolates with ingredients chosen to correspond to the holistic benefits of the particular stones for which they are named. Sounds a little do-do-do-do (think *Twilight Zone* theme)—but they taste oh-so-good.

GREAT HARVEST
5203 S. Sheridan Rd.
(918) 622-1115
www.tulsagreatharvest.com
Though there are Great Harvest shops all over the country, each one is different. The only requirements are that the owner buy wheat berries from the parent company—and this is the finest Montana wheat—and that the store feature Great Harvest signage. Wheat is milled on-site and bread baked daily—it's not possible to get fresher bread. And it's really tasty. This store makes a number of varieties. And if you call in advance, on Tues, Wed, or Thurs, you can tour the bakery.

Pick up a loaf or choose your fillings and get a sandwich to eat there or take out. Soup and salads are also available. Great Harvest is closed Sun and Mon.

THE GROCER AND THE GOURMET
East 61st St. and South Yale Avenue
KingsPointe Village
(918) 794-3032
Here is gourmet shopping with a capital G. The store carries over 100 artisan cheeses, olives, olive oils, game, imported Spanish ham—pata negra Jamón ibérico—hard-to-find brands of ice cream, fresh produce; the list just goes on and on. The artisan chocolates and desserts by Ghyslain are a treat for the eyes and the palate. The market also features breakfast and deli grab-and-go and a catering menu.

KOKOA
1722 Utica Sq.
(918) 742-7944
www.kokoachocolatier.com
Steven Howard handcrafts fantastic truffles—no commercial molds here—and sometimes trims them with real gold. You can't actually taste it, but, my, it feels decadent. You'll also find chocolate-dipped fruits and nuts. Buy one to savor or splurge and get one of the attractive gift assortments. Steven uses fresh dairy cream, pure fruit purees, fine liqueurs, vanilla beans, and Belgian chocolate in his creations.

LADONNA'S FANCY FOODS
1615 E. 15th St.
(918) 582-1523
www.ladonnasonline.com
Look on the big board behind one of the cheese coolers for the list of cheeses LaDonna's has on hand—it reads like an atlas of the world. You'll find special brands of familiar names and intriguing unfamiliar ones. Who could resist a cheese called Barely Buzzed, a Utah cheddar rubbed with espresso and lavender? These, and many of the others, are artisanal cheeses that you won't find at the grocery store. And the community has responded. LaDonna's been here for six years.

In addition to cheese, the store carries gourmet chocolate bars from Spain, France, Italy, and other destinations. There's a good supply of Oklahoma products here, too. LaDonna loves to support local efforts but she's strict: "These products have to be just as good as everything else we have on the shelves." Pick up gourmet foods from the Rockin' L-H Asparagus Farm; Ben Jack Laredo mustards; Scott Farms mixes; Sweet Spirit Foods barbecue sauces; Land Run Seasoning; and Pepper Creek Farms products, among others.

Browse through the wide variety of teas, ogle the olive oils, buy a butter bell, or grab a jalapeño griller (plain or with University of Oklahoma or Oklahoma State U. themes).

NOUVEAU ATELIER DE CHOCOLAT
205 S. Main St., Broken Arrow
(918) 258-2877 (800) 354-1830
www.nouveauchocolates.com
The shop has a decided art nouveau theme in its decor, and Mme. Joseph's accent adds to the ambience. Using fine Callebaut chocolate and traditional Belgian techniques, she crafts beautiful artisan truffles and other goodies including delicate raspberry Turkish delights topped with crystallized violets and crisp, double-dipped, chocolate caramel apples.

PARE
1441-A S. Quaker Ave.
(918) 582-PARE
www.parefoods.com
Want a nice home-cooked meal—without having to do it yourself? Let Paige Martin and Susan Simmons do it for you. Just north of the corner of East 15th St. (Cherry Street) and South Quaker Avenue, Pare is tucked into a tiny shop—just space for a cooler/counter and the kitchen—but packs in a lot of goodies for your perusal.

HOBBY SHOPS

THE HUSSAR
6029 S. Sheridan Rd.
(918) 492-3559
www.thehussar.com

This is the headquarters for any hobbyist interested in military history. Owner Mike Davidson has packed his store with toy soldiers for grown-ups—pre-painted figures and kits representing military units from many eras and countries. He also carries brushes, glues, paints, diorama supplies—anything you can think of to enhance your hobby. In addition, there are books on all phases of the hobby and military history. Military artwork, both in limited and open editions are also available. Mike even has some actual uniforms and accessories—including an authentic Scots Guards bearskin hat and a bobby's helmet. And Mike has written a number of books on painting military miniatures, so he's a great resource for his customers.

JEWELRY

PEARL DIVER
101 W. Main St., Jenks
(918) 299-3427
www.pearldiverok.com
What an appropriate shop for the town that hosts the Oklahoma Aquarium! Pearl Diver carries pearls from many parts of the world—strung into necklaces, set in rings, and used in other pieces of jewelry. But the fun thing to do is "pearl dive." Maybe that's over-describing it—you won't even get wet. Pearl Diver has an aquarium full of saltwater oysters from Hawaii. Each of them has been X-rayed and is guaranteed to contain a pearl at least 7 millimeters in diameter (pea-sized). If you're lucky, the oyster you pick out with a pair of tongs (that's the diving part) could have two or even three pearls—and they can be white, cream, pink, or black. Pearl Diver carries jewelry pieces to mount your pearl—the most popular being a tiny starfish/cage to snap the pearl into. And if you want an unusual gift, you can get a gift package containing an oyster in a can and a cage pendant to put it in. You have to open the oyster with a knife, but these aren't the heavy-shelled oysters that are served in oyster bars, so it's not a big deal. Open Wed through Sat.

LUGGAGE

HOBO JOE'S DISCOUNT LUGGAGE
6915 E. 71st St.
(918) 584-4243
Discount may be a misnomer—the luggage here is still expensive. But this store carries high-end brands. In addition to luggage, you'll find all sorts of necessities for travel. This is the place to buy converters for your electric appliances, money belts, travel bottles, and small hair dryers. One of the handiest items, with airline baggage regulations being what they are today, is a luggage scale. Whether you are traveling or not, this is a great place to fantasize about it.

MISCELLANEOUS

THE GADGET STORE
104 E. 15th St.
(918) 749-9963
www.thegadgetcompany.com
Here's where you look for those things you didn't know you needed—a pickle pincher perhaps, or brown recluse spider traps. The stock leans heavily towards the out of doors—axes, pocket knives, fly-fishing equipment. Think Orvis—this is an authorized dealer. You'll find a wide range of travel books, fishing guides, travel items (like a waist safe), and atlases. Caps, hats, watches, flashlights, wine bottle openers—those, too. You just have to stop by to see what else is on hand.

IDA RED–A CAIN'S BALLROOM ROCK AND ROLL BOUTIQUE
3346 S. Peoria Ave.
(918) 949-6950
www.idaredboutique.com
Here's a funky, fun place for fans of Cain's and rock. You can buy a variety of Ballroom memorabilia but the stock is heavy in the T-shirt department. They also carry CDs of local groups and even some videos on Tulsa. For collectors, there are miniature guitars from Guitarmania, and you'll find outré jewelry, posters, and Tom's shoes. Ida Red, named for a Bob Wills song, also carries a huge selection of old-fashioned candies like Necco Wafers. This is one of the very few places where you can buy Dublin Dr. Pepper—aficionados know that this is made with the original Dr. Pepper formula, which called for pure cane sugar, not corn syrup. You can also purchase Cain's (and several other venues) concert tickets here, and on Thurs, Fri, and Sat, there are live bands or special events in the back.

MUSEUM STORES

GILCREASE MUSEUM
1400 N. Gilcrease Museum Rd.
(918) 596-2700
www.gilcrease.org
The museum store here is chock-full of items for lovers of the West—prints, Native American art, jewelry, Pendleton clothing, scarves, and hats. You'll find a large selection of books relating to western history and culture, Native peoples, Tulsa, and Thomas Gilcrease—even cookbooks. Children will find a number of things to interest them, too. A postcard of their favorite painting is a good, and inexpensive, choice, but there are books, puzzles, and toys, too. Or perhaps you'd like your own Remington bronze—you'll find several here.

PHILBROOK MUSEUM OF ART
2727 S. Rockford Rd.
(918) 749-7941, (800) 324-7941
www.philbrook.org
This shop glitters with glass—wonderful, hand-blown pieces—and attracts visitors to cases of interesting jewelry. There are usually items that relate to a current exhibition as well as postcards and prints of favorites from the permanent collection. You'll find whimsical and unusual gift items—like their wildly patterned lunch totes. There are plenty of children's games, gifts, and books here, too.

TULSA AIR AND SPACE MUSEUM
3624 N. 74th East Ave.
(918) 834-9900
www.tulsaairandspacemuseum.com

What a great place to shop for items for the intellectually curious. There are model airplanes and science project kits, astronomy charts, gyroscopes, magnets, books and videos on aviation and space, toys, hat pins, T-shirts, and aviator glasses. And for the person who has everything—how about a Climbatron—a wall-walking robot that climbs up, down, and even upside down?

NATIVE AMERICAN/ SOUTHWESTERN CLOTHING, DECOR, GIFTS

LYON'S INDIAN STORE
401 E. 11th St.
(918) 582-6372
Larry Lyon's family has a long tradition of trading with Native Americans. His grandfather grew up near the Sioux in Nebraska in the early part of the last century. He became friends with many of the Indians, trading with them, and later recruiting them as performers for Wild West shows. Larry has a letter that shows that his grandfather was shipping goods to be traded at the Indian Store in Tulsa in 1928. In the '30s his grandfather moved to Oklahoma to work more closely with Pawnee Bill at his trading post.

Years later, when Larry's dad, Frank, was facing a job transfer, he made the momentous decision to buy the old store that his father had once helped supply. The store was renamed "Lyon's." When Frank retired, Larry and his wife took over the business. In 1996 the store moved to its present location in the historic Public Market building.

From the days when it was located by the train station, the Indian Store was a super stop for souvenirs—and it still is. But the real reason to visit is to see the works by Indian artists—Navajo and Zuni jewelry, native-made baskets, beadwork, and pottery and Pendleton items. Not only do they carry Pendleton blankets, but Pendleton jackets, purses, even gloves. Or you might pick out a handcrafted Indian flute. And when you leave, be sure to admire the terra-cotta work on the classic art deco building.

WEST SOUTHWEST TERRITORY
807 E. A St., Jenks
(918) 296-0957
www.wswterritory.com
Billed as "Tulsa's only Native American owned and operated Southwest store," West Southwest Territory carries an extensive collection of Native American–made jewelry, rugs, artwork, and pottery. Owner Vicki Holliday, of Cherokee descent, has made it her goal to represent as many tribes as possible and to promote Oklahoma-made and U.S.-made items. Pottery comes from many tribes and pueblos, including Navajo, Zuni, Acoma, Cherokee, and Sioux. Vicki also has delightful, handmade Cherokee dolls by Cherokee artist Margaret Flannagan. The assortment of jewelry, particularly turquoise, is impressive, and if you need a buffalo head to hang over your fireplace, you can get a beautiful one here for only $2,750.

PET NECESSITIES OR NOT

DOG DISH
6502 E. 51st St. (The Farm)
(918) 624-2600
www.dogdish.com
From mutt to mastiff, all your dog's needs can be met here. Run out of food? Forget the leash or dog dish? Or are you looking for a more fashionable collar or sweater for Fido? Or how about some doggy accessories for you—like the popular "Sleeps with dogs" T-shirt? Owner Shelli Holland-Handy carries all sorts of doggy-themed accessories for the home, books about dogs and dog training, and dog beds. You name it, she's got it. And the very special doggy bakery carries pupcakes and Yappy Birthday Bones. Whether you really need something or just want to check out a fun shop, do drop into the Dog Dish.

SPORTING GOODS

BASS PRO SHOPS
101 Bass Pro Dr., Broken Arrow
(918) 355-7600
www.basspro.com
If you haven't been in a Bass Pro Shop, go. In addi-

tion to equipment for any sport you can think of, the store is also a natural history museum and aquarium for the low, low price of—nothing! This multilevel structure features a cliff and waterfall right in the middle of the store. Mounted animal specimens, mostly native to Oklahoma, are displayed in life-like dioramas and 3-D settings. The pond below the waterfall and aquariums are full of native fish. And, in the restaurant, there's a huge saltwater tank with colorful sea creatures.

The store has a laser shooting gallery and an archery range for trying out bows and arrows, and outside, the pond is used for special events like casting, trying out kayaks, and catch-and-release fishing (at specific times). Customer service is the place to go for a fishing license.

NIGHTLIFE AND CASINOS

Remember, you're in Oklahoma. This is not noted as being a swingin' state. That said, you should be able to find enough after-dark excitement to keep you from watching reruns of *I Love Lucy* in your hotel room. If you're just looking for an after-dinner drink, most of the big hotels have nice bars. Below you'll find a list of the nightspots we've checked out. You'll find a variety of music, dancing, and drinking venues. What's hot this week may be gone next week, so check online or with your concierge (if your accommodation has one).

The main concentrations of night activities are in Brookside, on Cherry (East 15th) Street, and the Brady District. Almost all these places have minimum age limits that conform to the state liquor laws—21 and over, and picture ID, please.

When it's operating—usually Thursday through Saturday nights from 6 p.m. until the wee hours—the free T-Town Trolley runs a loop around the main entertainment areas. Saves the parking hassle, helps keep you safe on the road, and is pretty much a party all its own. And it's free. Check www.ttowntrolley.wordpress.com or call (918) 794-2485 for more information.

CASINOS

Gaming is big business in the state, with 35 tribes and 100 tribal casinos. They vary in size from small convenience stores with a few machines to glitzy mega-casinos with big-name entertainment and lots of amenities. Tulsa has three large casinos.

HARD ROCK CASINO
777 W. Cherokee St., Catoosa
(918) 384-7800 (800) 760-6700
www.hardrockcasino.com
This complex is huge. If you walk from the piano bar in the Cherokee Tower to the farthest corner of the gaming area, it's a quarter of a mile. This is the best way to get your exercise here since they took the arms off the one-armed bandits.

There are plenty of slot machines but, like most other casinos, there's no clinking of coins falling in the tray—it's all electronic. There are actually about 2,300 electronic games. In addition to the more traditional slots, you'll find video poker, bingo, Wheel of Fortune Super Spin, and lots and lots of others. Table games include poker—in many variations—blackjack, and bonus roulette and bonus craps (with cards).

The casino hosts three major poker tournaments each year, plus a number of smaller ones. The poker room is a big favorite with players. Unlike many casinos, there's plenty of room between tables and the chairs are top quality—a comfort in a tough game.

The hotel and casino, originally the Cherokee Casino Resort, has undergone a re-branding—now as the Hard Rock Hotel and Casino, Tulsa. It's still owned by the Cherokee Nation, but the change brings in the cachet of Hard Rock history and exciting decor and memorabilia.

In addition to the gaming, look for more entertainment. There's live music in the casino most nights—sometimes in several venues—from jazz in the C Note Piano Lounge to boot-scootin' at the Cabin Creek stage.

When your whistle needs wettin', you don't have to go far to find complimentary coffee and soft drinks or stronger libations. Literally the coolest spot is the Center Bar, with one of the largest frozen bar tops in the country.

Dining choices abound with not only the Wild Potato Buffet and McGill's on Nineteen, a fine dining venue, but a number of other choices including Toby Keith's I Love This Bar & Grill.

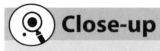

Close-up

Million Dollar Elm

The Osage casino takes its name from a historic tree called the "Million Dollar Elm." The Osages, unlike many other Indians, were able to retain mineral rights to their original land. In order to drill a well, an oil company had to purchase the right to drill. Colonel Ellsworth Walters served as auctioneer and held court under an elm tree. Osage land sat atop a rich oil field, and competition to drill was fierce. The record bid for drilling rights on a single 160-acre tract was $1,990,000. Thus, the tree got its name. The tree stood tall and proud near the Osage Nation Tribal Museum in Pawhuska until it died of Dutch elm disease and was cut down in the early 1980s. There is a monument there commemorating the site.

Lighter meals or snacks are also readily available.

For more details check the Accommodations chapter.

OSAGE MILLION DOLLAR ELM CASINO
951 W. 36th St. North
(918) 699-7777
www.milliondollarelm.com

The closest to downtown Tulsa, the Osage Million Dollar Elm is the smallest of the big three Tulsa casinos. You'll still find plenty of ways to play—there are over 1,300 state-of-the-art electronic gaming devices, and they change machines out regularly to add the newest machines. Machines take every amount from one penny to 25 dollars. One of the newest games is Vegas Star video roulette. There are also a number of poker and blackjack tables.

Be sure and sign up for a Players Club card—it registers you for drawings and gives you points for play. They have some great giveaways, including an annual One Million Dollar drawing. There's also a deli restaurant and the Nine18 Bar. Live local entertainment is featured in the Lounge on weekends.

The Events Center hosts major entertainers like Lee Ann Womack, B. B. King, Bonnie Raitt, Styx, and Ron White. For information on coming events, ticket prices, and to order tickets, call the Events Center at (918) 699-7667.

RIVER SPIRIT CASINO
8330 Riverside Parkway
(918) 299-8518
www.creeknationcasino.com

Oklahoma's newest casino, owned by the Muscogee (Creek) Nation, would be at home on the Strip in Las Vegas. Walking into the $195 million facility, you'll get into the spirit with the blues and greens of the carpet, the teal-colored ceiling, and the waterfall of beads surrounding the Mystic River Lounge.

Even the lighting is entertaining—the lights in the irregularly geometric overhead fixtures change colors and patterns. Casino-goers are often smokers. If you're not, you'll appreciate the $3 million air-filtration system that completely changes the air in the entire casino every seven minutes.

River Spirit features 2,745 gaming machines, including a number of "progressive" games where several casinos are linked for bigger jackpots. There are 24 blackjack tables and 15 poker tables. High-rolling regulars can use a private VIP lounge, where they can enjoy breakfast, lunch, and dinner or a quiet place to unwind between games.

All the artwork in the facility is by Creek artists and ranges from paintings and photographs to relief murals. A great deal of attention to detail has gone into designing River Spirit—even the bathrooms are extraordinarily nice.

The main bar is the Mystic River Lounge, a huge, circular space. This is also where free live entertainment is presented six nights a week. Some of the groups who have played here include Blues Traveler, the Bellamy Brothers, and the Four Tops.

The Scoreboard Sports Bar is the venue of choice for promotions associated with athletic teams and events. Enjoy sporting events on the 14 plasma-screen TVs while you imbibe or snack on Indian tacos, buffalo wings, or a Sooner Red chili dog.

Most people head for the 800-seat Visions Buffet. Its five stations offer American, Asian, barbecue, Italian, and international favorites. In addition, there's an amazing dessert bar with a chocolate fountain. Special features include a seafood buffet every Thursday evening and a Sunday champagne brunch. For a quick bite 24 hours a day, head for the Rain Bay Cafe.

River Spirit's fine dining venue is Elements Steakhouse and Grill (closed Mon and Tues). The decor emphasis is on natural tones and subtle, elegant style. As the name implies, their forte is steaks. Check the Restaurant chapter for more details.

COMEDY CLUB

LOONY BIN
6808 S. Memorial Dr., #234
(918) 392-5653
www.loonybincomedy.com

Be entertained by pros or maybe even get brave enough to sign up for an open-mic night. Munch on snacks and order a drink from the full bar. There are nonalcoholic beverages, too. Shows are Wednesday nights through Saturday nights. Check the Web site to see what's coming up.

CLUBS AND BARS

ARNIE'S BAR
318 E. 2nd St.
(918) 583-0797
www.arniesbar.com

Right next door to the Blue Dome building, Arnie's has been a fixture on the street for a long time. Small inside, it has a great little patio, it's noted as Tulsa's Irish pub. They serve not just Guinness but Southwick, Harp, and Killian's Irish Red. There's live music most Fridays and Saturdays and sometimes on Thursdays. Arnie's has a very faithful following but folks are always friendly to new faces. Arnie's opens at 2 p.m. daily.

THE BRU HOUSE BAR AND GRILL
3421 S. Peoria Ave.
(918) 743-7200
www.bruhouse.com

Open seven days a week for lunch and dinner, Bru House hosts happy hour every afternoon and all day Sunday. Its patio is particularly popular— maybe because that's the smoking area. There's live music Wed through Sat and an occasional DJ. Just a fun place to gather.

CLUB 209
209 N. Boulder Ave.
(918) 584-9944
www.club209tulsa.com

Club 209 is a sophisticated coffee and martini bar that describes itself as "a relaxed, non-smoking, diverse atmosphere promoting local arts." The club, just east of the historic Brady Theatre, is open evenings Thurs through Sun. Live entertainment is offered on Sat evenings—jazz, acoustic, bluegrass, light rock—no heavy bands. The former '40s-vintage garage now sports a stylish decor with both bar seating and a lounge area that includes double lounge chairs. Local art is displayed on the walls and around the room, and guests can drink martinis from glasses hand-blown at the nearby glass factory.

Friday nights are Wii or Xbox nights; karaoke is on Sundays. On Thursdays there's sometimes a live artist painting. And if you want to know anything about what's going on in the Brady District, ask for Greg.

The full bar carries wine and 25 different beers. The house signature drink is a Bananas Foster Martini. Food is served only for special events.

CROW CREEK TAVERN

3534 S. Peoria Ave.

(918) 749-9100

www.crowcreektavern.com

In the popular Brookside area, Crow Creek offers live music seven nights a week with cover bands on Friday and Saturday nights. The clientele is a mix of professionals and bikers—and sometimes they're both. There's always dancing on the weekends, and the two big screen TVs keep up with sports action. They offer daily lunch specials and their full bar keeps happy hour happy.

DIRTY'S TAVERN

325 E. 2nd St.

Loud and popular with the college crowd who love the Dirty's in Stillwater, Tulsa's Dirty's Tavern is located in the Blue Dome District. The music leans heavily toward red dirt and country with some rock thrown in. The building's brick walls, bare floor, and wood ceiling fit in fine with the casual, country emphasis. Picnic tables provide lots of the seating, so if you're not in a group when you come in, you soon will be. Pool tables, games, and darts are available, and there's live music and a cover charge on Fri and Sat nights.

F.B. OSCAR'S GASTRO PUB

1738 S. Boston Ave.

(918) 938-6960

www.oscarsgastropub.com

A restaurant and pub by day, Oscar's turns into a club Thursday through Saturday nights. Entertainment includes live bands and DJs. Music ranges from '80s, rock, and blues to Latin music and jazz. The decor is attractive with wood floors, furniture with clean, contemporary lines, and a tin ceiling. The full bar includes about 40 beers, with half of them on tap. The noise level is conversational through dinnertime but gets loud later. Closed Sundays.

GRAY SNAIL

1334 E. 15th St.

Lincoln Plaza Shopping Center

(918) 587-SLUG

www.myspace.com/graysnailsaloon

One of Tulsa's current faves, dance-oriented Gray Snail serves up live music or DJs seven nights a week. Music here is mostly rock. You can order drinks on the huge patio when the weather's nice. This is a popular place to get on the dance floor or simply people-watch.

JAMES E. MCNELLIE'S

409 E. 1st St.

(918) 382-PINT (7468)

www.mcnellies.com

Noted as a good place for a meal in the Restaurants chapter, McNellie's stays open late seven nights a week and is a great stop for a brew. There's live music upstairs several times a week. This is a fun family place to eat, but starting at 9 p.m. it's for adults age 21 and over. Check the Web site for specifics.

JEWEL

3340 S. Peoria Ave.

(918) 743-0600

www.jeweltulsa.com

Advertised as an upscale dance club, the decor doesn't disappoint. A chandelier hangs over the dance floor and laser and LED intelligent lighting offer special effects. There are reserved VIP areas and small, curtained lounges. Small plates and sushi from In the Raw are available. Live bands appear occasionally and there's a DJ every night. Open seven nights a week, Jewel allows smoking on the patio only, and there is a cover charge.

LEON'S

3301 S. Peoria Ave.

(918) 933-5366

www.leonstulsa.com

This is a no-smoking sports bar with entrees named after sports stars. Open for lunch and dinner, there's a special offer or entertainment for every night. Thurs and Sun, it's live music. Happy hour is Mon through Fri. On nights when there's no live music, recorded music or sports on TV keep things going. All the bands here are local and not cover bands. After 10 p.m. it's strictly for adults age 21 and up. Fri and Sat, Leon's is open until the wee hours, with pizza available after 10.

The crowd is eclectic. There are 18 televisions and a pool table. Smoking is allowed on the patio.

LOLA'S AT THE BOWERY
5 E. Brady
(918) 592-7995
www.lolasatthebowery.com
Talk about mixed messages—between the Bowery name and the skeleton on the door, you may wonder about going in here. Here's the scoop—the place was once called the Bowery Bar and the skeleton actually represents the Mexican Dia de los Muertos—remembrances of Lola's days in New Mexico. Lola herself is an attractive blond whose breads and pastries are killer good.

More of a restaurant than a club, it's still a great place for nightlife—perhaps before or after a local concert. Or just enjoy the live music and a drink—you'll find the schedule in the free *Urban Tulsa* that you can pick up around town. There's often music with dinner. On the upscale side, Lola's is nonsmoking and closed on Sunday. Check the Restaurants chapter for more information.

MAJESTIC
124 N. Boston Ave.
(918) 584-9494
www.majestictulsa.com
This is a large dance club catering to the GLBT community—but everyone's welcome. With state-of-the-art sound and lighting and multiple bars, this is a busy place. There are drag shows on Thursday and Sunday nights, and on Friday nights it's the "Hoe, You Think You Can Dance Contest." Ages allowed are 18 and up, Thurs, Fri, and Sun, and 21 and over on Wed and Sat. There's a small cover charge.

Obviously, this club attracts a younger crowd. Some people dance, while most just stand to listen to the music, watch the shows, etc.

MERCURY LOUNGE
1747 S. Boston Ave.
www.mercury-lounge.com
Open seven days a week, Mercury is noted for its cool music. Live entertainment is on Friday, Saturday, and Sunday nights—no cover bands.

Music covers a wide variety of genres from punk rock to country. If the band is right, there'll be boot-scootin' even though the place is packed. Other nights, the music comes from the jukebox. You won't find any of today's Top 40—but you might find yesterday's. Content ranges from Dean Martin to Red Dirt. About a quarter of the artists represented on the jukebox are local. The bar has a large group of regulars from all walks of life but everyone's welcome. There are no TVs—part of the attraction of this place is people actually talk to one another. Even if you come in knowing no one, you'll know people by the time you leave. If you're hungry, you'll have to settle for beef jerky—that's it. But there's plenty to drink.

NEW AGE RENEGADE
1649 S. Main St.
(918) 585-3405
www.club-renegade.com
This combination bar and show club is open from 4 p.m. until early a.m. nightly. They feature drag shows every Tues, Fri, and Sat, with a boxer-shorts contest the first Fri of the month and the Red Ribbon Review in the Rainbow Room the first Sat of each month. There's a small cover charge for some special events. Karaoke nights are Thurs and Sun; Mon is reserved for their pool tournament. Wed, everybody just hangs out. The third Fri and Sat of the month, look for Twisted Theatre—a drag show built around a movie theme. Some past greats have included *Mommy Dearest, the Musical* and *The Exorcist, the Musical.*

PINK
112 E. 18th St.
(918) 574-2729
This place is huge and includes four comfy lounges in the VIP area. Open Thurs through Sat, the dance floor's roomy and there are two dance poles. The music is edgier than that at most of the clubs. Feel like dancing on the bar or doing body shots? Go ahead. There's no live music here but no one seems to mind. They do have DJs. Pink is getting a reputation as the bar of choice for visiting celebs, including groups from Nickelback to the Pussycat Dolls.

POUR HOUSE

118 E. 18th St.

(918) 551-7600

During the school year, this midtown spot is popular with Tulsa University students, but the crowd is pretty eclectic. There's live music on Thurs, Fri, and Sat; the rest of the week, it's the jukebox. The two pool tables, the Megatouch, and video bowling are popular. Open seven nights a week, the bar stays busy—no food served.

SHARKY'S ON BROOKSIDE

3415 S. Peoria Ave.

(918) 742-9500

www.sharkworld.com

Large, fairly loud, and with a younger crowd, Sharky's offers billiards, shuffleboard, real dartboards, free Buzztime Trivia, and pinball. Thursday night is karaoke—called Sharkaoke here—and DJs get the music going on Friday and Saturday nights. Other nights, they fill in with a digital jukebox. With two full bars, you won't go thirsty. There are plenty of TVs, including a big screen, for viewing all the major sporting events.

VINTAGE 1740 WINE BAR

1740 S. Boston Ave.

(918) 582-0700

www.vintage1740.com

If you're looking for a sophisticated after-hours spot, this may suit you to a T. Open late afternoons and evenings seven days a week, Vintage 1740 has an extensive wine list—with frequent updates—imported beers, and a full selection of other alcoholic beverages. Choose from a variety of seating areas—bar seats, tall cocktail tables, or vintage furniture in little living room settings. The music is mostly light jazz and doesn't drown out conversation. The crowd covers a wide range of ages—getting younger the later it gets. Smoking is only allowed on the patio.

While the emphasis is on wine, there are a couple of specialties—a Pom Cosmo, featuring pomegranate juice in place of the cranberry juice; a Porch Swing, a combination of cucumber gin, Pimms, and homemade lemonade; and a mojito, made with mint grown right outside in the flower boxes.

Bar food is prepared by Oscar's next door and includes smoked salmon terrine, Mediterranean antipasti, Sonoma crab dip, and an artisan cheese plate with assorted cheese, dressed olives, seasoned flatbreads, and savory nuts. KoKoa chocolate truffles make a nice accompaniment to spicy red wine or dessert vintages.

OTHER NIGHTSPOTS

CAIN'S BALLROOM

423 N. Main St.

(918) 584-2306

www.cainsballroom.com

Cain's is so unique it deserves a category of its own. You can drink here, but the music's the thing. Cain's has hosted a lot of musical groups in its over-75-year history, and it has had its ups and downs. These days, it's ups. Cain's offers a full calendar of concerts, from bluegrass to hip-hop, rock to heavy metal. Concertgoers don't usually bother with chairs—they stand and rock to the music. Groups range from new talent and local favorites to national headliners. Ticket prices vary with the group.

Cain's has a full bar and plenty of parking, both in the lot across the street and on the street. This is a no-smoking venue.

Tickets can be purchased at the Cain's box office. For most concerts, you'll be able to buy tickets online or at any of several outlets around town. Check the Web site for particulars. For more information about Cain's, see the Attractions chapter.

JOE MOMMA'S

112 S. Elgin Ave.

(918) 794-6563

www.joemommastulsa.com

Owner Blake Ewing already owned a Joe Momma's in south Tulsa but always wanted a kitchen with a brick oven. Now he has it in this downtown location just around the corner from the Blue Dome. Open lunch, dinner, and late night, this is a great spot for pizza lovers, families, and members of the young crowd who want to skip the smoky bar scene but still hear good music. Joe Momma's presents live local bands on Friday and Saturday nights. On those nights, the late crowd can order pizza by the slice. Trivia night is on Thurs, karaoke on Tues, and there are arcade games, pinball, checkers, and board games available. Wine and beer are available, including Marshalls, a local brew. For more information see the Restaurants chapter.

KIDSTUFF

Tulsa's a great place for families and a great place for children. With lots of days of sunshine and not too many that are too cold—or hot—to go outside, the list of parks and outdoor activities is a long one. Be sure you check the Outdoors chapter. A number of activities and places are cross-referenced, but you know your child better than anyone else and you'll probably find things throughout the book that aren't mentioned here. These are just some of the very obvious choices.

Price Code

Admission prices are subject to change and some attractions vary depending on how much time you spend—and how much money you're willing to spend.

$	$1 to $10
$$	$11 to $15
$$$	$16 to $20
$$$$	$21 and up

ALL STAR SPORTS COMPLEX $
10309 E. 61st St.
(918) 459-0399
www.allstarsportscomplex.com

A mecca for team sports with seven ball fields, and sports camps, All Star is also fun for the visitor just passing through. Test your skill in the indoor batting cages with pitch speeds from 40 to 70 mph. One token gets you 15 pitches. There are also arcade games—air hockey, skeeball, billiards, and video games. Outside is a nicely landscaped miniature golf course (even though some of the rocks and flowers are decidedly fake). Called Gilligan's Island, it has tricky greens, waterfalls, and lots of water around the holes. The water is dyed a surreal teal, but it beats Oklahoma red. The course is nicely laid out with variations in elevations so you can't see all the holes in one glance. There's a Joe Momma's Pizza next door, good and handy. The facility is open seven days a week, except holidays.

AMERICA'S INCREDIBLE PIZZA COMPANY $-$$
8314 E. 71st St.
(918) 294-8671
www.incrediblepizza.com/tulsa

You know the minute you see the bright-blue facade with blue and white checked trim—this is a fun place. And it's huge—68,000 square feet—and has a capacity of over 2,000 with seating for 850. Basically, it's an indoor amusement park with food.

The amusement area has over 100 games—video games of all kinds, skeeball, air hockey, you name it. Some of the games are redemption games—kids can win tickets or prizes. But that's not all. Go for regular bowling, glow bowling, or for mini-bowling with smaller lanes and lighter balls. Or play the nine-hole miniature golf course—holes are Route 66–themed, and the scorecard has fun facts about the Mother Road on it. You can golf and learn a little geography and history at the same time. Bumper cars are popular and there's even an indoor go-cart track. For the littlest family members, there's a nice playground area. And IPC has the only XD Theater in the area. The Incredible Pizza Company prides itself on being a full-family experience.

That goes for the food, too—all-you-can-eat buffet with pizza, pasta, salad, and desserts plus changing items like lasagna, burgers, hot dogs, tacos, beef stew, meat loaf. Almost everything is made from scratch, including the pizza dough.

Then you have a choice of four different eating areas. The overall theme is the '50s. You can choose from The Diner, black and white tile floor, glass blocks, red and black Naugahyde upholstery on booths, chrome tube chairs, and pictures of classic drive-ins and classic cars. One whole wall is devoted to Route 66. Fifties music plays over the speakers. The Starlite Theater re-creates a drive-in movie and features family hits from the '50s and '60s. The gymnasium looks like—well, you get the idea—complete with folding tables like you'd find in a school cafeteria. The Disney channel plays on a giant screen here—unless there's a special sporting event like an OU-OSU game—in that case, well, it is a gym! The quietest of the rooms is the Living Room, with decor that would have been comfortable in Beaver Cleaver's house. The pictures around the wall look like they came from the Dick and Jane readers—or a Sunday school teacher's poster packet. And the TV plays oldies like *Leave It to Beaver, Bewitched,* and *The Andy Griffith Show.*

The buffet is surprisingly inexpensive—a good deal even if you don't play the games. You can buy game cards in any amount—games range in price from less than a dollar to several dollars. You know, of course, that you are going to leave a bunch of bucks here—but your kids will have a great time. Check the Web site for specials—they'll save you some dough.

BASS PRO SHOPS
101 Bass Pro Dr., Broken Arrow
(918) 355-7600
www.basspro.com
Yes, it's a store but it's also fun to visit. Throughout the store, you'll find dioramas and displays of animals. Yes, they're dead and stuffed, but try not to dwell on that—they could have just been really old. It's a challenge to see who can find the first squirrel or skunk. You won't have much trouble spotting the larger specimens.

And there are huge tanks of native fish and a big saltwater aquarium in the restaurant. The two-story cliff and waterfall are big attractions. The laser shooting range is also popular.

Check the Web site for special events. In summer there's something almost every weekend, including "camp" sessions where kids can

learn to build a campfire, identify birds, set up a rod and reel and bait a hook, and read a compass. On special days, there's kid's catch-and-release fishing in the pond by the store. There's even a cute kids' section on the store Web site. This is smart marketing—building tomorrow's customer base—but it's also a lot of fun for kids, so take advantage of these opportunities.

BIG SPLASH WATER PARK $$$$
4707 E. 21st St.
(918) 749-7385
www.bigsplashwaterpark.com
Oklahoma summers can be sweltering, so what's better than a refreshing dip to cool off? This venue, on the corner of East 21st St. and South Yale Avenue at the Fairgrounds, provides all sorts of water fun, from the gentle wave pool to wet, wild slide rides.

You can use a credit card at the gate and in the gift shop, but it's cash only for everything else. And there are several elses—food, tube rental, locker rental. Changing facilities and showers are available and life vests are provided free of charge for young guests.

Food is available in the park. No outside food or beverages are allowed in Big Splash, but if you want to bring a picnic, there are tables just outside the gate. You can have your hand stamped for reentry.

This is a popular place for birthday parties. You'll have reserved tables and the overall price includes food—though you'll have to BYOC (cake).

For more information check the Attractions chapter.

BLUE BELL CREAMERY $
8201 E. Hwy. 51, Broken Arrow
(918) 258-5100
www.bluebell.com
For a cool tour, call for reservations to see Blue Bell ice cream being made and packaged.

The tour starts with a short film about the company followed by a plant walk-through. And, like a cherry on a sundae, it's topped off with complimentary ice cream in the cute Country Store. Tours are given Mon through Fri in the

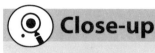 **Close-up**

Seeking Sitters

Mom Adrienne Kallweit wanted to make sure her child's day care was safe. With her background as a licensed private investigator, she turned her talent to the task and was astonished by what she found. She pulled her son out of the day care and started screening sitters for him. Soon friends were asking her to do the same thing for them. And Seeking Sitters was born—right here in Tulsa. This idea turned out to be so popular that Adrienne and her husband, David, founded the business in 2004. There are now franchises in a number of states. And Adrienne received the Mayor's Entrepreneurial Spirit Award in 2007.

Whether it's a one-time event, a regular appointment or date night, or full-time day care, Seeking Sitters provides prescreened sitters. There's an initial membership fee, then several pricing options depending on the number of times you think you'll use the service.

With Seeking Sitters, you can count on professional, reliable child care. And, by the way, you will be screened too, for the safety of the sitters. Check out the Web site at www.seeking sitterstulsa.com or call (918) 749-3588.

summer, two or three days a week during the school year. Call for reservations.

BOUNCEU $
8922 S. Memorial Dr.
(918) 249-0090
www.bounceu.com/cities/tulsa.ok
From big inflatable bounce houses and giant slides to an obstacle course and spider maze, BounceU offers lots of opportunities for physical activity. In addition to open bounce sessions, the facility offers classes like Create and Bounce—a blend of playtime and creative time—and Bounce and Learn—games and exercises to build motor skills and improve social interaction.

Summer series include camps with themes from "Circus Science" and "Jurassic Giants" to "Knights and Princesses" and "Dogs, Cats & Pets." Birthday parties are a big deal here, too. Be sure you make a reservation, even for the open bounce sessions, because the number of children playing at one time is limited for both fun and safety reasons. And be sure and bring socks.

FUN HOUSE $
500 RiverWalk Terrace, Ste. 100, Jenks
(918) 254-1646
www.riverwalkfunhouse.com

The Fun House features all sorts of video games, arcade games like whack-a-gator and ice ball, skeeball, air hockey, and coin-operated pool tables. This is a good spot for working off some energy on a rainy day.

GILCREASE MUSEUM $
(18 AND UNDER, FREE)
1400 N. Gilcrease Museum Rd.
(918) 596-2700
www.gilcrease.org
Gilcrease's children's programming is as exciting as their collection—and that's saying something. Whether you're a family traveling through or living locally, there are things your children will be interested in. Ask for a Trailblazer Bag at the front entrance (no additional charge). Inside you'll find a variety of items to enjoy in the museum or at home—a booklet about some of the art treasures in the museum, touch objects from the Gilcrease Education Collection, and sketch paper and artist's materials. Also request a SmART card—better than baseball cards—with clues and fun facts about something in the museum's collection. You can get a new one each week—52 in all.

Several of the galleries have printed guides that help make the experience more enjoyable for youngsters. For example, the guide for "The

American West" area shows a picture of a George Catlin buffalo painting. First, of course, you'll want to find the real painting. The guide gives more information about bison and buffaloes and even has an easy drawing lesson on bison. There are lots of questions in the guide to help children think more about what they are seeing and why or how the artist painted the subject. It will probably make you think, too. In addition to word games and puzzles, there are even instructions on how to make your own mountain shirt. Kudos to Gilcrease for their thoughtfulness and thoroughness.

Be sure to visit the Kid's Site—an interactive area designed to coordinate with the current exhibition. If you're here after school or on the weekend, check out the Creative Learning Center. This is a place for children to try different art materials, read books, or make a take-home project. The Kravis Discovery Center, manned by museum volunteers, offers up-close looks at more than 5,000 artifacts. Computer terminals provide information and history for each of the items.

For those of you who are able to plan ahead, check the calendar of events on the Web site for special programming. There are often family activities planned on Saturday afternoons. And spring break and summer are perfect times to sign up for special classes on everything from life in the Old West to art with recyclables.

While there is an admission charge for adults, youngsters 18 and under are admitted free, making this a really family-friendly place. The museum is closed on Mondays and Christmas Day. For more information see the Attractions and Arts chapters.

i The Gilcrease Museum owns a number of paintings by Thomas Moran. As his works became popular, a number of copies of his paintings were produced. In order to fight forgery, he began adding his thumbprint to his signature. See if you can find one.

KALEIDOSCOPE $
6202 S. Sheridan Rd.
(918) 340-5252, (866) 587-5173
www.kaleidoscopecm.com
Aimed at children from ages 2 to 12, this museum offers a wide variety of hands-on experiences, including a large area, Kids' City, for role-play. Put on an apron, grab a note pad, and kids are ready to take orders in a pint-size restaurant; try a new hairstyle in the beauty shop, or sort and weigh mail in the mini–post office. Other areas include art activities, a crime lab where children can solve mysteries, take fingerprints, and hunt for jewels (hidden throughout the museum), and even a jail for miscreants. Or kids can watch their shirts and shoelaces glow in the black-light room—technically a Snoezelen multisensory environment

For more-active play, there's a two-story playhouse, a fireman's pole, two climbing walls—one is 23 feet high—and crawl-through play spaces. For creative activities, an art room with paints and other materials provides for quieter moments.

All activities are included in admission, with the exception of the giant climbing wall and snacks. There's a little snack bar that features pizza, chicken strips, and other kid favorites. The facility is closed on Mondays.

LASER QUEST $-$$
2909 S. Sheridan Rd.
(918) 663-5551
www.laserquest.com
Not your grandmother's hide and seek, Laser Quest is a combination of tag and hide-and-seek in the dark. Lit only by black lights or strobe lights, accompanied by music and made mysterious by fog machines, it's zap or get zapped. Players wear special vests with sensors. Each session lasts 20 to 25 minutes, and players get points by lasering other players.

The atmosphere is stimulating, so it may be too intense for younger children. Laser Quest suggests five as a minimum age.

School year hours and summer hours are different, so check the Web site. Reservations are suggested during summer—probably not a bad idea anytime. Since the sessions are short, you'll probably wind up paying for more than one—and that adds up. They do occasionally offer special deals, so, again, check the Web site.

MARY K. OXLEY NATURE CENTER
6700 Mohawk Blvd., Mohawk Park
(918) 669-6644
www.oxleynaturecenter.org
The Oxley Nature Center, in addition to being a great place to take a family walk, offers a number of special programs for kids. Most of the programs are on Saturdays. Examples of past offerings include Discovery Club for 3- to 5-year-olds, Adventure Club for ages 6 through 8, and Junior Naturalists for kids from 9 to 11. Topics range from how birds build nests to what clouds tell us about the weather. Astronomy programs are popular, and several moon walks have been offered. Some programs require registration; others are drop-in friendly. Check the Web site for programs and special events. More information about the center can be found in the Attractions and Outdoors chapters.

MEADOWLAKE RANCH $$$$
3450 S. 137th West Ave., Sand Springs
(918) 494-6000 (800) 256-5323
www.meadowlakeranch.com
Looking for something different to do? How about Dude for a Day or Ranch Hand for a Day (or half day)? Enjoy a variety of activities, including horseback riding, tomahawk throwing, calf-roping, and having a picnic lunch. If you're doing the whole day, you can add other activities, which might include pistol or rifle shooting, canoeing, swimming, hiking, mountain biking, or just enjoying a bit of a snooze in a hammock under the trees.

This is also one of the few places in the area where you can take a two-hour trail ride. There are also shooting sessions available by the hour. Check out the Web site for all the offerings.

OKLAHOMA AQUARIUM
300 Aquarium Dr., Jenks
(918) 296-3474
www.okaquarium.org

This place is fun for the whole family. With regular demonstrations, fish and turtle feeding, and touch pools, the experience is enhanced. And there are lots of special activities aimed at children and youths. Seacamps, offered during summer and winter breaks and on school holidays, give youngsters a chance to learn more about the environment and the oceans, and the creatures that live in them. Special days are offered for scout groups and homeschoolers. The Discovery Channel's popular shark week is celebrated at the aquarium with extra demonstrations and activities. How about sleeping with the sharks? The museum has several sleepovers each year. College students interested in related careers can apply for internships at the aquarium.

PHILBROOK MUSEUM OF ART $-$$
(18 AND UNDER, FREE)
2727 S. Rockford Rd.
(918) 749-7941 (800) 324-7941
www.philbrook.org
Don't be fooled by the elegant exterior of this great museum. It is elegant—but family-friendly. Little guests can check out backpacks with art materials and sketch pads for budding artists. There are also family fun guides, turning a tour into a giant treasure hunt. It's hard to think about Philbrook as a house where a family lived and children played, so there's material that talks about that time—with fun details like the children roller-skating down the halls of the third floor. There are always special activities for families on Saturdays—and drop-ins are fine. And if you go on the second Saturday of the month, admission is free. You can see the museum and gardens, do a make-and-take project, and your wallet is no lighter.

For regular visitors, the museum has a program called MyMuseum designed for children 4 to 12. Upon signing up, and that's free, your child will receive a MyMuseum art kit and membership card. Visit the museum each month and have your child bring the membership card. He or she will receive a new art supply for the kit. In addition, there's a new Art Card with fun facts and activities.

PURPLE GLAZE STUDIO $$-$$$
3303 S. Peoria Ave.
(918) 592-6900

6528 E. 91st St.
(918) 491-6900
www.purpleglazestudio.com

This place is fun for both grown-ups and kids—paint your own pottery piece or try a mosaic. Jeff and Jim Stunkard—the father-son duo who own the two studios—have hundreds of unfinished ceramic items to choose from. Whether it's a mug or bowl or even a pair of hands to hold a roll of toilet paper, you'll find something fun to paint. They'll help with the design or you can create your own. A child's original artwork on a cup or plate makes a great grandparent gift.

If you plan to use the item, like a plate or mug, you'll do the design in an underglaze, then pick up the piece in a few days after it has been glazed and fired. Decorative pieces, especially appropriate for children, can be painted with an acrylic stain, sprayed with a sealer, and taken home immediately. This is a neat family or group activity.

The studio fee per person is $6 plus the cost of the pottery piece—from about $5 up. Take advantage of special prices—no studio fees on Mon and Wed; children's fees are only $2. Usually you won't have a problem just dropping in, but it does get crowded around holidays. To be safe, call ahead and reserve a table.

QUIKTRIP PLAZA
East 41st St. and South Riverside Drive
River Parks

Though this park space is used year-round, it's especially great in hot weather when the water features make for cool fun. There are several different water play areas—jets of water that shoot in a random sequence, a bubbler table, a raised canal play area with cascading steps, and more.

The "dry" play area features a variety of colorful active play structures installed on foam matting for safety. The playground was designed by a Danish company, Kompan, which was started a number of years ago by a young artist, Tom Lindhardt, who discovered that children were much more interested in his large sculptures for climbing on than for looking at. This inspired him to combine his artistic sense with a study of children and play—and he came up with Kompan, which comes from the Danish word *kumpan,* or "companion." The children won't know the difference, but it's good to know that there's a lot of study behind the design.

SAGE CULINARY STUDIO $$$$
3746 S. Peoria Ave.
(918) 933-5005
www.sageculinarystudio.com

Sage teaches kids cooking classes to preschoolers through teenagers. Recipes are adapted and preparation is kid-friendly, but you'll be amazed at what these kids are making—everything from spaghetti pie to sushi. And they're eating it, too.

One Saturday a month, there's a Brunch Bunch class in which a parent and child cook together. In summer, Sage offers cooking camps. And this is a unique spot for a birthday party.

Classes are kept small and preregistration is a must.

TULSA AIR AND SPACE MUSEUM AND PLANETARIUM $$
3624 N. 74th East Ave.
(918) 834-9900
www.tulsaairandspacemuseum.com

There's a lot of history here but enough hands-on exhibits to interest even the young visitor. From climbing stairs to peek into an airplane or trying your hand at flying in a simulator, there are many things to do and learn. Changing exhibits from other museums in the Oklahoma Museum Network (Tulsa Air and Space Museum, Jasmine Moran, Museum of the Great Plains, Leonardo's Discovery Warehouse, and Science Museum Oklahoma) provide added interest.

The museum plans special classes for home schooling, and public and private school groups. During summer months, Aerospace Camps are scheduled for youngsters from first through ninth grades. This is also a cool place for a birthday party.

TULSA CHILDREN'S MUSEUM

www.tulsachildrensmuseum.org

This is a strange one. It's a museum without walls—a museum that's in the process of becoming. In the meantime, they sponsor family concerts and outreach programs at a variety of venues throughout town. Check the Web site for the latest information.

i The free publication *TulsaKids* is a gold mine of information on what's going on in Tulsa—special events, school information, entertainment, health, you name it. You can pick it up off of conveniently placed racks or sign up for an e-newsletter online at www.tulsakids.com.

TULSA COMMUNITY COLLEGE

(918) 595-7566

www.tulsacc.edu/ce

While TCC offers some academic, family, and youth enrichment classes during the school year, in summer the schedule really shines. The school lists over a dozen short-term classes for youngsters ages 5 to 18. Here's a chance to try on some careers like journalism or medicine—with a simulated patient that screams and yells—or learn the ins and outs of indie film making. There are several campuses in the area.

TULSA ZOO AND LIVING MUSEUM $

6421 E. 36th St. North

(918) 669-6600

www.tulsazoo.org

Everybody loves the zoo, and the Tulsa Zoo loves all its guests, especially the young ones. In addition to the excellent exhibits—the Elephant Encounter, Chimpanzee Connection, Conservation Center, Tropical American Rain Forest, North American Living Museum complex, and more—there are special demonstrations and classes available.

In addition to daily keeper chats and animal demonstrations, the zoo offers a number of special classes. Summer and school breaks are ideal times for camps and classes, with shorter sessions offered through the year. Some of the events are targeted at specific ages but others, like the Night Prowl or After Dark in the Rain Forest, are for families. Check the Web site because advance registration is required.

A special feature at the Tulsa Zoo is the Nature Exchange. Children are encouraged to bring collected items, like shells, fossils, rocks, and leaves, to share. They can earn points in several ways: the uniqueness of the item; how much they know about it already; what condition it's in. There are some specific exceptions to things that may be brought, and all collecting must be done in a responsible manner—again, check the Web site for specifics. The children can exchange their items for others or keep their points banked for future use.

All zoo exhibits are included in the price of admission. The carousel, camel rides, and the train are extra. The zoo added a new train in 2009—the ONEOK Safari train. That's the official name, but the name Tiger Train is catching on. The train features orange and tan tiger stripes. It makes two stops—one near the entrance, the other on the far side of the zoo. A ride is a good way to get a feel for the layout of the zoo, and, besides, it's always fun to ride the train.

Zoo birthday parties are also a lot of fun. Just be sure to book well in advance.

The zoo is open every day except Christmas Day and the third Friday in June (to prepare for their major fund-raiser, WALTZ on the Wild Side.) The Children's Zoo Contact Yard is open from Mar 1 to Oct 31, weather permitting. See the Attractions chapter for more information.

THE ARTS

Tulsa may not be the political capital of Oklahoma, but few would argue with the statement that it is the state's culture capital. Having two stunning art museums is a great selling point, but Tulsa doesn't stop there. It also boasts a symphony, ballet and opera companies, a variety of theater groups, and an art cinema.

Whether you like classical music or contemporary, pop art or pop culture, there are lots of opportunities to explore the visual and aural arts. The architecturally avant-garde BOK Center hosts major concerts—everything from Elton John and Fleetwood Mac to the Jonas Brothers and Keith Urban. The Performing Arts Center is the venue of choice for everything from intimate theater productions to Broadway extravaganzas. And both of those places feature impressive art collections.

As a matter of fact, you'll find art all over town. The assortment of art deco buildings in Tulsa illustrates the full range of that architectural style. Public sculptures like David Lee Brown's untitled spiraling stainless-steel work in front of the Performing Arts Center catch the imagination, while Jay O'Meilia's *Oklahoma Indian Ballerina* in Williams Center Green at East 3rd and South Main Streets catches the heart.

Probably the most popular works are the NatureWorks installations in the River Parks. This organization, involved in wildlife conservation, gives a new sculpture each year to honor a local conservation hero. Not surprisingly, the sculptures feature animals—from a family of bears cavorting in a waterfall to Black Mesa mule deer.

Performing arts are well represented in Tulsa—the symphony, opera, and ballet are key players. But there are many other organizations providing cultural opportunities to the community. The Tulsa Oratorio Society presents masterworks of choral music. The University of Tulsa and Oral Roberts University add to the mix with musical and theater presentations, lectures, and special events.

The Oklahoma Center for the Book focuses on promoting reading and writers, sponsors the Oklahoma Book Awards, and brings readers and writers together for special events. The Tulsa Town Hall lecture series has been sponsoring appearances by prominent figures since the mid-1930s.

From low comedy to lofty intellectual pursuits, there's no excuse for being bored in Tulsa. If you can't find something to do—you're not looking.

ART GALLERIES

GARDEN DEVA
317 S. Trenton Ave.
(918) 592-3382
www.gardendeva.com
No, that's not spelled wrong—it really is *deva.* That's a Sanskrit word meaning "Happy Spirit."

And that spirit comes through Lisa Regan's metal sculptures. They're mostly two-dimensional—playful representations of women, mermaids, flowers, and fish, some with cutout texts. Lisa works in steel, copper, and aluminum, cutting it with a plasma torch. Whether they are garden decorations, trellises, gates, or tabletop art, Lisa's creations add joy to life. She's been featured in

Better Homes and Gardens and *Southern Living* magazines and has appeared on HGTV.

You won't be able to miss her building. It's painted purple with bull's eyes of blue, magenta, and buttercup. One of her fanciful sculptures—in shades of turquoise, chartreuse, and purple—is mounted by the door.

The gallery also provides a showcase for several other artists, painters, and jewelry makers. Garden Deva is closed on the weekends.

JOSEPH GIEREK FINE ART
1512 E. 15th St.
(918) 592-5432
www.gierek.com
In Gierek's spacious gallery, he displays only a small percent of the art he has for sale—changing exhibits and featuring different artists. Representing about 45 different artists, he carries paintings, sculpture, and glasswork. Styles range from abstract to representational, and artists come from all parts of the country. About a third of them are from Oklahoma. Gierek represents Allan Houser's estate, and you'll find some beautiful Houser work here.

LOVETTS GALLERY
6528 E. 51st St. (The Farm)
(918) 664-4732
www.lovettsgallery.com
This gallery has instant appeal, there's such a variety of artwork that greets you as you walk in. Dark gray walls provide a neutral background for the art, and strategically placed lighting highlights each piece.

Lovetts has been in business for 31 years and represents about 70 artists in all kinds of media from glass and pottery to paintings, sculpture, and jewelry. All genres are represented. There are also some magnificent antique Indian pieces—a set of Lakota "possible" bags, made in the 1870s or '80s from buffalo hide and decorated with glass beads and tin cones with horsehair, was one of the recent pieces on display.

Lovetts also does fine art and archival framing and carries the largest selection of moldings in a five-state area.

A third-generation family business, Lovetts also has a foundation that awards an annual scholarship to a college-level art student and sponsors occasional lectures on subjects of artistic interest.

The business is located in The Farm shopping center.

M. A. DORAN GALLERY
3509 S. Peoria Ave.
(918) 748-8700
www.madorangallery.com
The M. A. Doran Gallery represents an eclectic assortment of artists, regionally, nationally, and internationally known. And their media range from paintings, sculpture, and photography to glass, jewelry, and fine crafts. Look for pieces by Oklahoman Kreg Kallenberger, whose works are to be found in collections from the Los Angeles County Museum of Art to the Victoria and Albert Museum in London. Other internationally exhibited Oklahoma artists represented here include Otto Duecker, Ron Fleming, and Tom Palmore.

TULSA PERFORMING ARTS CENTER GALLERY AND PERMANENT COLLECTION
110 East 2nd St.
(918) 596-7122
www.tulsapac.com
Thanks to a city ordinance that mandates that 1 percent of construction costs for public buildings be dedicated to the purchase of art for the building, the $18 million Performing Arts Center (PAC) was able to purchase an impressive array of art for the facility. The collection encompasses a variety of styles, from romantically representational to enigmatically abstract. In the latter category is a massive assemblage of shiny chrome and smoked glass suspended over the East 3rd St. lobby. The piece is unnamed but the artist, Stanley Landsman was inspired by the Apollo-Soyuz space program and the Apollo moon landing.

It's a pleasure to see Alexandre Hogue's *Hondo Canyon Cliffs*—especially if you were disappointed by not finding any of his work in the gallery that bears his name. The hues of an extraordinarily large watercolor, *Dusk at Kodai*

🔍 Close-up

Tulsa Performing Arts Center

Tulsa's Performing Arts Center (PAC) was built in 1977 by architect Minoru Yamasaki, who designed the World Trade Center towers and who also built the BOK Tower, which is across the street from the PAC. John Williams, CEO of Williams Companies, had purchased property in downtown and planned to build two 30-story towers connected by a bridge over Boston Avenue. Convinced that one taller tower would be more efficient, he was left with a large, empty piece of property. Williams offered to raise half the money needed to build a performing arts center, and the city voted to match the funds. The result is a venue that hosts a wide variety of productions and serves numerous arts entities. The facilities are used regularly by 14 community organizations, including the Tulsa Ballet, Tulsa Opera, and Tulsa Symphony.

The building, which from the outside looks like a big beige box, houses four theaters, studio space, and a large reception hall. Two of the theaters are "black box" facilities—the Liddy Doenges Theatre and the Charles E. Norman Theatre. These spaces are flexible and affordable and often are used for the Summer Stage Festival, cabaret concerts, and smaller events. The John H. Williams Theatre is a traditional theater with fixed seating. Broadway shows and big events take place in the 2,365-seat Chapman Music Hall. The audio engineers who designed the acoustics for Lincoln Center in New York City also designed the acoustic elements for this theater. Seating is continental, with no center aisle and ample space between rows.

The PAC Gallery hosts art exhibits that change monthly and is open to the public Monday through Friday and during performances in the Chapman Music Hall. The PAC also has an impressive art collection that comprises 72 pieces by international, American, and regional artists. Pieces range from an impressive work by British sculptor Barbara Hepworth to paintings and silk tapestry. Outside the building is the PAC's signature piece—a 10-foot-tall untitled sculpture of spiraling bars of stainless steel. It was the inspiration for the winged PAC logo. The permanent art collection can be seen during PAC events or on group tours arranged by appointment.

by Joseph Raffael, are reminiscent of Monet's palette. Barbara Hepworth's solid but sensuous *Seaform* is one of the highlights of the collection. Part of the collection features Native American artists like Woody Crumbo, Doc Tate Nevaquaya, and Joan Hill. Lovers of Wilson Hurley's sweeping landscapes and amazing clouds will enjoy his *Summer Storm Building over Mt. Taylor.* The whole collection is exciting, as much for the variety of genres represented as for the variety of media chosen by the artists. There are 76 pieces in the collection, which is scattered throughout the building. The works can be viewed during events or, if you have a group, by appointment.

The PAC also has a small gallery for exhibits that change monthly. Often the artists are local. Most of the works are available for purchase. Access to the gallery is through the East 3rd St.

entrance. It is open to the public during business hours Mon through Fri or when events are taking place in the Chapman Theatre. There is no admission charge.

ART MUSEUMS

GILCREASE MUSEUM
1400 N. Gilcrease Museum Rd.
(918) 596-2700
www.gilcrease.org

Atop a rise in the Osage Hills on the northwest side of Tulsa is the Gilcrease Museum, one of the nation's most comprehensive collections of art of the American West. But don't go expecting a cowboys-and-Indians kind of a museum. Oh, yes, those things are here—drawings, paintings, and sculpture by Charles M. Russell and Frederic Remington, and plenty of Native American artifacts—but there's so much more. Glorious, romantic visions of the West by artists like Albert Bierstadt and Thomas Moran are not surprising, but you'll also find classic American master-pieces like Charles Willson Peale's portraits of George Washington and James Madison and James McNeill Whistler's mysterious *Nocturne, the Solent.*

A section of the museum is dedicated to the arts of Meso-America. The gold artifacts are par-ticularly eye-catching. This part of the collection focuses on the cultural history of North, Central, and South America from earliest inhabitants to contemporary times.

Many of the archaeological artifacts can be found in the Kravis Discovery Center. In this area there are shelves and shelves and drawers and drawers of items. Find an item that intrigues you, and you can go to a nearby computer terminal and call up details about the item.

In addition to fine visiting exhibits, a high-light of the museum year is the annual Rendez-vous, which takes place between mid-April and mid-June. Here's an opportunity to see (and purchase) works by the finest contemporary western artists.

The museum property comprises 460 acres, with 23 acres having been turned into historic themed gardens that correspond to portions of the museum's art collection. The pre-Columbian Garden relates to the oldest items in the col-lection and features plants grown or gathered by the early Osage Indians. Contrast the formal Colonial Garden and its symmetrical parterre design with the sprawling Stuart Park, where native plants like blazing star, Mexican hat, and Shumard and chinkapin oaks run rampant. The Gilcrease home, used for classrooms but not open to the general public, is also on the site. The Victorian Garden beside the house complements the 1914 structure.

Bronze sculptures grace the museum grounds and throughout Stuart Park visitors will find chainsaw-carved creatures like raccoons, owls, and other woodland animals. Spring is a particularly beautiful season at the Gilcrease, with azaleas, redbuds, and dogwoods painting the landscape with their pastel palettes.

The museum is open Tues through Sun, closed Mon and Christmas Day. Check the Web site for scheduled tours, which are free with museum admission. Adult admission is $8. Visi-tors 18 and under are admitted free. Don't miss the well-stocked gift shop and the Osage Restau-rant, which is open for lunch Tues through Sat and for Sunday Brunch.

i **Check out the WaterWorks Art Center in Newblock Park. Part of the Tulsa Parks program, this is a great place for classes from painting to metalsmithing, and they host regular art exhibits. Call (918) 596-2440 or click on Tulsa Parks under Cul-ture and Recreation on the city Web site at www.cityoftulsa.org.**

PHILBROOK MUSEUM OF ART
2727 S. Rockford Rd.
(918) 749-7941 (800) 324-7941
www.philbrook.org

Philbrook is a triple-treat museum combining fine art, interesting architecture, and stunning gardens. The original part of the building was the home of Waite and Genevieve Phillips. The impressive Italian Renaissance Revival–style mansion was designed by Kansas City architect Edward Buehler Delk, the designer of Kansas City's elegant Country Club Plaza.

Though the Phillips donated their house to the city for an art museum, little art came with the gift. Philbrook's extensive collection was made possible by gifts from many of Tulsa's generous philanthro-pists. Thirty-five Renaissance paintings and sculp-tures came from the Samuel H. Kress Collection.

Laura Clubb was an Oklahoma teacher and rancher's wife. After oil was discovered on their property, she was able to pursue her interest in art. Her collection filled a hotel in Kaw City. Upon her death, Philbrook received 87 19th-century American and European paintings, including Thomas Moran's *Grand Canyon,* William Bou-guereau's *The Shepherdess,* and William Merritt Chase's *The Blue Kimono.*

On the lower floor of the museum you'll find examples of its extensive Native American collection. Waite Phillips was a passionate student of the West and is quoted on one of the panels, saying, "Oil fortunes were made out of Indian lands. I have a deep feeling of gratitude to the American Indian and I want to see his culture preserved." Incongruous as it may seem in the ornate Italian structure, Phillips had one of the rooms on this floor designated and designed as his "Santa Fe room."

A highlight of the collection is an extensive display of southwestern Pueblo pottery—San Ildefonso, Santa Clara, Acoma—they're all here—well displayed and easy to compare. Part of this collection comes from the collections of Clark Field—pottery, basketry, and art from the first half of the 20th century. The collection in this section of the museum contains traditional and contemporary Native American art as well as Anglo artists' interpretations of Native American culture.

The rooms on the main floor feature European works, including a charming painting by Bouguereau, *The Little Shepherdess,* and Italian painting and sculpture. This floor was the main living area for the Phillips family, and the architecture and decor are an important part of the museum experience. The great hall, with its turned columns, heavy furniture, and entry onto the large deck leading to the gardens, is a highlight. In the library, with its globe light fixture, you'll find a history of the house and family. As you walk to the west, you'll come to the original sunroom. The frosted tile floor once served as a lighted dance floor—copied, it is said, from one that Genevieve Phillips saw in a Paris nightclub.

The rooms beyond were added on after the house was given to the city. Don't miss the small blue and white *Madonna and Child* in glazed terra-cotta, a sculpture from the workshop of 15th-century sculptor Luca Della Robbia.

Upstairs are American paintings. There's a particularly lovely painting by *Moran of the Grand Canyon*—in a grand gold frame and visible through an arched doorway. In another room your eye will be caught by sensuously curved, sere hills. Upon closer inspection you'll see the

form of a woman. This is Alexandre Hogue's *Erosion No. 2–Mother Earth Laid Bare,* painted in 1936. Hogue, who headed the University of Tulsa School of Art for a number of years, featured erosion in many of his landscapes. Compare his pared-down panorama with the hills and valleys of James Valerio's *Bed* several rooms away.

A major building project in the '90s added 75,000 square feet to the museum's space. The Kravis wing houses special exhibition galleries, an art reference library, classroom and studio space, and an auditorium, gift shop, and restaurant.

Be sure to take time to enjoy the gardens. From the east terrace, formal plantings zigzag down the slope to a rocky outcropping and pool surrounded by flowers. At the base of the garden is a small, white tempietto—a perfect photo op. The gardens were carefully renovated a few years ago, retaining the elegant original design but replacing worn plumbing and giving the grounds a refreshing redo.

Philbrook is closed Mondays and major holidays. Admission is $7.50, with guests age 18 and under admitted free. Lunch is served between 11 a.m. and 2 p.m. in the restaurant, la Villa. Reservations are recommended, and absolutely necessary for the popular Sunday buffets. See the Restaurants chapter for more details.

i **Tulsa was one of the first cities in the nation to establish a 1 percent for public art program (1969). One percent of the cost of construction of any municipal project must be set aside for public art. The construction of the BOK Center resulted in a $1.4 million budget for art for the space.**

RICHARDSON ASIAN ART MUSEUM
4770 S. Harvard Ave.
(918) 747-9393
www.richardsonart.org

The red columns, yellow tile roof, and ferocious Foo dogs are a dead giveaway. This isn't Kansas—but it could be a typical temple in China. This is the entrance to the Richardson Asian Art Museum, founded by Dr. Jack L. and Joni Richardson.

Dr. Richardson, an orthopedic surgeon and former chief of staff at Tulsa's St. John's Hospital, developed a passion for Asian art while on his tour of duty during World War II. He collected pieces for over 50 years—sculpture, furniture, glassware, temple items—over 1,000 pieces in all. Many of these are on display here, including a number of jade items in various shades and colors, including a rare red jade figure There are some fine examples of cloisonné and a striking statue of Kwan Yin. A Japanese wedding gown is one of the few pieces from that country.

You have to look closely for the driveway to the museum. The temple entrance is not obvious from the road. The museum is open Thurs through Sun, with no admission charge. Check the hours on the Web site and consider calling ahead.

DANCE

TULSA BALLET
1212 E. 45th Place South
(918) 749-6030
www.tulsaballet.org
Moscelyn Larkin, an internationally famous ballerina, was born in Miami, Oklahoma. Married to Roman Jasinski, a premier danseur, the couple danced together with the famous Ballet Russe. Upon their retirement in 1954, they returned to Larkin's home state to establish a dance school— and wound up founding the Tulsa Civic Ballet.

Though the name has changed a couple of times, the institution owes its existence to the couple who helped build it into a world-respected company.

In 1995, Naples native Marcello Angelini was named artistic director. While retaining traditional favorites, like the annual production of The Nutcracker, the company, under Angelini's direction, has added more than 60 new works to the repertory. These productions were all premiers, either for Oklahoma, America, or the world.

The season consists of six productions plus touring appearances. Major productions are presented at the Performing Arts Center. More-intimate works are performed in the company's

Studio K–Kivisto Hall, a modern, five-million-dollar theater that seats 295.

FILM

CIRCLE CINEMA
12 South Lewis Ave.
(918) 592-FILM
www.circlecinema.com
Circle Cinema is a mecca for true film fans, and its roots were in cofounder Clark Wiens's childhood. During World War II, Clark's father showed war footage to California farmers to motivate them to grow more crops for the war effort. Clark says his dad told him the farmers would get so fired up they practically took flashlights into the field to start plowing sooner. "That's the power of film," he said. Clark grew up and started his own business, but he never forgot his father's words.

Realizing the importance of appreciating diversity in culture and points of view, he began working with Tulsa schools to rent theaters that were empty during the day and showing movies that reflected other times, other ways of life, and that broadened the horizons of the students who saw them. A friend suggested that they buy a theater together.

Located in Tulsa's first suburban shopping center, the 1928 Circle Theater had lived out its life as a first-run theater and finished as a shabby, "adult" movie house. It stood empty for some time until the men purchased it. In 2003 the Circle Cinema Foundation was established, and the first theater, a 110-seat house, opened in October 2004. The second auditorium, with 50 seats, opened later. The stated purpose of Circle Cinema is "community consciousness through film."

The theater is open every day and shows independent, foreign, and documentary films. The foundation has partnered with over 100 community organizations, bringing in special films to relate to their missions. Six different ethnic film clubs, started at the Circle, get together to view films in their own languages. Circle Cinema has also premiered almost every Oklahoma-made film since their opening. Two new spaces are in the works, and equipment here can be utilized both by local film students and by major studios working in the state. So it not only promotes film but supports making films.

Between the power of film and the power of Clark Wiens, Circle Cinema is making a significant contribution to the cultural calendar of the city. The movies cost about what you'd pay at a theater in the mall, but the experience is priceless.

i Here's a blast from the past—remember piling in the car to go to the drive-in movie? You can still do that in Tulsa—and have a choice. The Admiral Twin Drive-In has been showing first-run films and classics since 1951. Open only in the summer, the theater runs double features and takes cash only. It's at 7355 East Easton St.—just north of I-244, between North Sheridan Road and North Memorial Drive. Check www.selectcinemas.com for shows and times.

INTERDISCIPLINARY ARTS

LIVING ARTS
307 E. Brady St.
(918) 585-1234
www.livingarts.org
Interdisciplinary is just another word for "this organization covers so many bases, it doesn't have a category." Whether it's deconstructing, synthesizing, fusing, melding, morphing, or just plain defying definition, this organization takes traditional arts and combines them in new and interesting ways. It could be poetry, painting, or performance art—whatever, you'll find this an exciting venue. Living Arts presents creative workshops, performances, exhibitions, films/videos, demonstrations, and lectures.

In supporting and promoting local artists and bringing acclaimed artists into Tulsa, Living Arts is operating on the creative cutting edge.

MUSIC

CHAMBER MUSIC TULSA
2210 S. Main St., Ste. A
(918) 587-3802
www.chambermusictulsa.org
Founded in 1954, Chamber Music Tulsa sponsors a six-concert series that brings to Tulsa not only the finest young American musicians, but world famous groups. The elegant, intimate Saturday night performances, which include wine and a light dinner, are available only to season subscribers, but the Sunday afternoon concerts are open to the public. They are held in the Performing Arts Center.

COUNCIL OAK MEN'S CHORALE
(918) 748-3888
www.counciloak.org
The Council Oak Men's Chorale was unintentionally started by a group of singers who banded together to sing for a World AIDS Day observance in 1997. Like the Indian Council Tree that they chose for a name, they started small but have grown strong. The group rehearses weekly and gives three scheduled concerts each year, in addition to a number of private performances. The group consists of both gay and gay-affirming men and is conducted by Elizabeth Smith Curtis.

i Looking for something unusual? Check www.choregus.org. In ancient Greece, the choregus was the person in charge of getting the chorus and overseeing productions. In Tulsa, it's Ken Taylor and his company, Choregus. The Web site will give you a schedule of events he's bringing to town—could be a major dance company, an opera star in concert, or a theatrical ensemble.

DFEST
www.dfest.com
Dfest, originally DiversaFest, is only a two-day event, but its purpose and scope is so impressive that it's included here. It didn't start that way. Tom and Angie Green were in a rock band and

they wanted to compete in a national festival but needed some buzz to help them get in. So they organized their own small festival just for the exposure. They invited a dozen other bands to participate. Tom says, "We didn't put a lot of thought into it—just asked the other bands to vote for us." As it turned out, the weather turned uncooperative and only about 150 people came out to hear them. But it was enough.

They were accepted in the 2002 Jim Beam Rolling Stone Band of the Year competition—and they won. It was a big shot in the arm for their band, but people back in Tulsa kept asking about another festival. It happened, and it grew and became so big that Tom and Angie stopped touring with the band and took on the festival as their contribution to the music world.

But it's more than just the bands and the music. The Greens learned a lot about the music business from their experience, and they're passing that knowledge on. Now the festival has an extensive lineup of workshops and seminars presented by professionals from all facets of the business. Topics range from band agreements and budgets to sponsorships and investors, marketing, licensing, and clinics by top musicians. Dfest is designed to take participants from the naïve, "let's start a band" mindset to the nitty-gritty knowledge it takes to survive in a big, big business that eats talent for breakfast.

And then, of course, there are the bands. In 2009 the festival invited over 150 of them—from well-known acts like the Black Crowes to unknowns who sent in audition tapes.

"When we started," says Tom, "we had to beg industry people to come. Now they've seen that we're doing their screening for them, and they're flocking to Tulsa to look for tomorrow's stars."

LIGHT OPERA OKLAHOMA
2210 S. Main St.
(918) 583-4267
www.lightoperaok.org
Light Opera Oklahoma (LOOK) was founded in 1983 to preserve and promote classical musical comedies and operettas. Productions take place during summer and are presented in repertory

style. Performances take place in the Performing Arts Center.

The company includes both professional musicians and apprentice actor/singers and technicians. They are accompanied by a professional orchestra. Productions have ranged from the *The Merry Widow* to *The Music Man*.

OKLAHOMA JAZZ HALL OF FAME
"The Jazz Depot"
111 E. 1st St.
(918) 281-8600
www.okjazz.org
The Jazz Hall of Fame not only salutes jazz greats of the past, it offers lots of opportunities to hear contemporary jazz greats and the up-and-comers. There's a year-round schedule of concerts, but, like any good band, there are breaks, so check the Web site to see what's going on. Most of the concerts are held on Sunday afternoons.

The Hall also sponsors an annual June JazzFest, which features local talent and a major headliner.

TULSA OPERA
1610 S. Boulder Ave.
(918) 582-4034
www.tulsaopera.com
The roots of Tulsa Opera go back to 1948 when a group of Tulsans formed the Tulsa Opera Club. Productions included opera, light opera, and operettas, and the popularity of the performances grew rapidly. In 1951, in keeping with the names of significant organizations around the country, the name was changed simply to Tulsa Opera.

The 1955 season opened with *Madama Butterfly*, and signaled an intention to make grand opera the main focus. There was an eager audience for these weightier works, and the move advanced the organization toward national prominence.

Productions are well attended and receive excellent reviews. Professional principals are brought in for major roles, with up-and-coming artists from around the region filling out the cast. Tulsa Opera draws enthusiasts from not only Oklahoma but Texas, Kansas, Arkansas, and

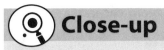 **Close-up**

Summer Music

When the weather turns warm, outdoor concerts sprout like weeds across Tulsa. Be sure and bring lawn chairs; even the places that have seats fill up fast. The schedule changes a bit from year to year, but you can probably count on these. Check the Web sites to be sure.

First Fridays at LaFortune Park
Gardens of LaFortune
5323 S. Yale Ave.
www.parks.tulsacounty.org/lafortune.aspx

From rock 'n' roll to pop and blues, once a month from May to Sept, folks gather in LaFortune Park for these free concerts. They start at 7 p.m. and last two hours.

Outdoor Summer Concerts
KingsPointe Village
East 61st St. and South Yale Avenue
www.kpvtulsa.com/events/events.htm

Once a month, concerts take place on Friday nights from May to Sept. The stage is set up between Pei Wei and the Bank of Oklahoma. The concerts start at 7 p.m.

Starlight Band Concerts
River West Festival Park
www.starlightbands.net

Held at the amphitheater on the river in River West Festival Park, these free summer concerts are popular events. The Starlight Band has been entertaining Tulsans since

1947. Check the Web site for the schedule and bring your blanket or folding chairs and enjoy the music. The concerts start at 8 p.m.

Summer at RiverWalk
300 Riverwalk Terrace, Jenks
www.riverwalkcrossing.com/events.html

RiverWalk Crossing offers lots of events during the year. Among the most popular are the summer concerts. They're free, from 8 to 10 p.m., Friday nights in May, Friday and Saturday during June through Aug, and Saturday evenings in Sept.

Summer's Fifth Night
Utica Square
East 21st St. and South Utica Avenue
www.uticasquare.com

These Thursday night concerts have become a Tulsa tradition mid-May through Aug. Music hits all the genres from bluegrass to smooth jazz. Look for favorite groups like the Red Dirt Rangers—but whoever's playing, they'll be good. Music starts at 7 p.m.

Missouri and was named by *Opera News* one of America's ten top regional operas.

Tulsa Opera is noted for showcasing future stars in the opera world. Talented singers like Stephanie Blythe, Sarah Coburn, and Alfred Walker have appeared in Tulsa Opera productions, as have legends like Jussi Björling, Anna Moffo, Beverly Sills, and Roberta Peters. Artistic director Kostis Protopapas served as assistant conductor of the Los Angeles Opera, Santa Fe Opera, and Lyric Opera of Chicago before taking

the position of assistant conductor in Tulsa. He was named artistic director in 2008.

Tulsa Opera stages three productions each season, with three performances each. All performances take place in the Chapman Music Hall at the Performing Arts Center.

TULSA ORATORIO CHORUS
www.toconline.org
The Tulsa Oratorio Chorus, founded in 1992, is a nonprofit choral group made up of 100 vol-

unteer singers. Participation is determined by auditions that are held before the beginning of each season. The group rehearses in the Boston Avenue Methodist Church; performances are traditionally given in the Performing Arts Center, though occasional concerts are performed in other venues.

The group is dedicated to performing major choral works. Their repertoire is extensive and includes Bach's *Mass in B minor,* Brahms' *Requiem,* and works by Norman Dello Joio, John Rutter, George Handel, Joseph Haydn, and Gustav Holst.

The director is Dr. Tim Sharp, formerly conductor of the Master Singers Chorale in Memphis, where he was dean of fine arts and director of choral activities at Rhodes College. He is also the Executive Director of the American Choral Directors' Association.

TULSA SIGNATURE SYMPHONY AT TULSA COMMUNITY COLLEGE
10300 E. 81st St.
(918) 595-7786
www.signaturesymphonyattcc.org
The symphony situation in Tulsa gets a bit confusing. You'll hear people talk about "when we didn't have a symphony." What that means is a full-time orchestra. Signature Symphony has been around since 1978, beginning as a small, professional (that means "paid") chamber orchestra called the Tulsa Little Symphony. They changed their name in the '80s to the Oklahoma Sinfonia and played both a classical and pops series at the Brady Theatre for over 10 years.

In 1997 they were invited to become the orchestra in residence at the VanTrease Performing Arts Center at Tulsa Community College (TCC). Another name change went with the move—now they're the Signature Symphony at TCC—but it's the same professional group it's always been. They still do both a classics and pops series plus a series called Performance Plus, a combination of lecture and small ensemble or solo concert. They also support college productions and the Tulsa Ballet and do outreach programs in the Tulsa schools and surrounding communities.

TULSA SYMPHONY ORCHESTRA
111 E. 1st St.
(918) 584-3645
www.tulsasymphony.org
The Tulsa Symphony Orchestra is fairly new on the scene, having been organized in 2005. Tulsa had been without a major orchestra for several years following the demise of the Tulsa Philharmonic, which had served as the premier orchestral ensemble since 1948.

The reorganized orchestra followed a new pattern, with musicians taking a major role in orchestra management. The whole thing works like synchronized swimming—lots of things are happening under the water to make the surface appearance seem effortless. And what the public sees—or in this case, hears—is a solid orchestral sound, with programming that is appealing without being condescending.

Not only does the orchestra present a full season of concerts, but the musicians support a number of other performances by arts associations.

THEATER

AMERICAN THEATRE COMPANY
3003 E. 56th St.
(918) 747-9494
www.americantheatrecompany.org
Over 40 years ago, a group of students and former students from the University of Tulsa (TU), under the direction of Kitty Roberts—also a TU grad and working as program director at a local radio station—banded together to form the American Theatre Company. Their goal was to form a resident professional company to bring a variety of high-quality theater performances to the community. Their first home was an abandoned furniture store.

Their perseverance has paid off, both for the company and for the community. They have presented a constant stream of productions—both straight plays and musicals—which keeps the community coming back for more. Presenting classics like *Hamlet* and *Hedda Gabler* to comedies like *Tartuffe* and *Greater Tuna*, the American Theatre Company has become an important

Close-up

Old Lady on Brady

Constructed between 1912 and 1914, this building was designed to be Tulsa's original munici-pal auditorium and convention center. Over the years, many famous people have appeared in the Brady Theater—George M. Cohan, Tony Bennett, Buddy Holly, Bill Cosby, Helen Hayes, Will Rogers, and Jerry Seinfeld, to name a few. Enrico Caruso sang here in 1920. Local legend says that it was here that Caruso caught a cold, which led nine months later to his death. It's said that his ghost haunts the theater. Contemporary entertainers like comedian Robin Williams and the band Chickenfoot prove there's life in the old girl yet.

part of the Tulsa arts community. The annual production of a musical *Christmas Carol* is must-see holiday fare for many Tulsans. The company has also produced David Sedaris's *The Santaland Diaries* for mature audiences who wanted a little more nog in their holiday drink. The theater is also actively involved in education, building audiences for the future.

Be sure and check the Web site for current and upcoming productions. Like most independent arts organizations, their advertising budget is bare bones, and it's easy to miss what's happening by looking only at the newspaper.

CLARK THEATRE
11440 E. Admiral Place
(918) 669-6455
www.clarktheatre.com

Founded in 1978 and sponsored by the Tulsa Parks and Recreation Department, the Clark The-atre is dedicated to producing theater by and for young people. All shows are performed by young actors ages 10 to 18. Auditions for shows are open to any youngster in that age range. Through the school year, the theater staff holds classes for youth in acting, sound, and lighting techniques. In summer there are camps in visual and performing arts culminating with student performances.

Through the year, the theater mounts productions ranging from Shakespeare to Broadway musicals. In 2009 the company won a TATE (Tulsa Awards for Theatre Excellence) for the best youth production and shared a TATE with Theatre

Tulsa for their joint production of *Up the Down Staircase.*

DISCOVERYLAND!
19501 W. 41st St., Sand Springs
(918) 245-OKLA
www.discoverylandusa.com

From the first notes of "Oh What a Beautiful Morning," sit back, relax, and enjoy one of America's best-loved musicals performed in the setting that inspired it. Rodgers and Hammerstein's *Oklahoma!*, based on Oklahoman Lynn Riggs's book *Green Grow the Lilacs,* tells the story of Oklahomans and their "brand-new state."

Discoveryland!, founded in 1976 by the Jeffers family, has been showcasing *Oklahoma!* every summer since 1977. In 1993, at a performance for the nation's governors during the National Governors' Conference, Mary Rodgers, daughter of composer Richard Rodgers, and William Hammerstein, son of lyricist Oscar Hammerstein, announced the designation of Discoveryland! as the "National Home" of their fathers' musical *Oklahoma!*

In addition to many other honors, Discoveryland! was named one of the "Top Fifty-one National Treasures" by *InStyle* magazine and, in 2009, was named "Best Family Entertainment in Oklahoma" by the Oklahoma City CBS-affiliate station, KWTV.

The large outdoor theater seats 1,500 guests, and the enormous stage makes possible the use of a half dozen live horses. Performers are selected through national auditions and include some of the most talented young singers and dancers in the country.

And the play's just part of the package. Make reservations and come early for a western dinner and lots of preshow activities. An evening at Discoveryland! is an essential Oklahoma experience—good entertainment for good people having a good time.

From early June through mid-Aug, there are performances every night except Sunday. The theater is located 5 miles west of OK 97 on West 41st St. See the Attractions chapter for more information.

GRACE-ANN PRODUCTIONS
(918) 491-3410
www.grace-ann.com

With impressive credits from New York City, E. Kirby Jr. came to Tulsa and wanted to start a performing arts program. Grace-Ann Productions now produces three to five shows a year, drawing from talent in the community. Past productions have included *The Wiz, Into the Woods, Altar Boyz,* and *Six Degrees of Separation.* Most productions take place in the Performing Arts Center, but other venues around Tulsa are used occasionally.

In addition to the productions, the organization sponsors training and workshops in American Sign Language, dance, drama, fitness, pageant coaching, piano, visual arts, and voice.

HELLER THEATRE
4825 S. Quaker Ave.
(918) 746-5065
www.hellertheatre.com

Managed by the same staff that runs the Clark Theatre, this, too, is an entity of Tulsa Parks and Recreation. Clark Theatre is the youth program; Heller is for adults. Classes in improvisation and writing are held during the theater's season. The theater produces contemporary comedy and drama. All auditions are open to the community.

Theater camps for youngsters are available here during the summer.

NIGHTINGALE THEATER
1416 E. 4th St.
(918) 633-8666
www.nightingaletheater.com

This small space in a semi-industrial district just east of Peoria hosts and presents some of Tulsa's edgiest theater. It's truly a labor of love—literally started by a group of friends who met in high school and grew up to do the Mickey Rooney-Judy Garland "Let's put on a show" thing. The first production was a play by cofounder John Cruncleton, who wrote his first full-length play at the age of 16. At 21, deciding he wanted to produce a play he had written, he enlisted friends and family to help. They rented a space and presented the three-and-a-half hour, five-act extravaganza. And they were hooked.

The group was united in a desire to produce original works, and have been doing it since 1995. Their company is called Midwestern Theater Troupe, and they own the Nightingale Theater. Having moved from pillar to post the first few years, the group took a year off from performing and raised money to buy their own place. The pillars of the organization are John and Sara Cruncleton and Jeff and Amber Whitlatch. Between them, they are the brains, brawn, heart and soul, and cast and crew of the organization. John is the resident playwright. The company has mounted a dozen new works. They do occasionally present works by established authors like William Shakespeare and Jeff Goode, but 90 percent of their productions are premieres.

Nightingale Theater is one of the busiest venues in town. Several other companies use the theater for their productions. So you have the opportunity to see all sorts of productions from Edward Albee to Eve Ensler, contemporary and new genre dance by the Monica Huggins Dance Theatre, or something experimental by a completely new group.

The Nightingale has racked up several impressive firsts in its relatively short career. It hosted the region's first productions of *The Vagina Monologues* and *The Laramie Project.* And the last Saturday of the month is the time for *"Old Crow Confessions."* They call it "cringe theater," and it will make you wince, laugh, and maybe even cry. It's described as an AA meeting with booze and music. Audience members get on stage and "confess"—it has to be unscripted and spontaneous and true—with nothing but the speaker, a spotlight, and a glass of whiskey. Every nonperformance is different.

Nightingale is a place for taking risks, being honest, and participating in humanity. No other theater in Tulsa offers such continuously challenging productions. They're now a registered nonprofit corporation, with *nonprofit* being the operative word. No one gets paid—every dime goes back into the theater and productions. So check their site to see what's going on. Chances are it's something exciting. Bring cash; no credit cards accepted.

ORAL ROBERTS UNIVERSITY THEATRE DEPARTMENT
7777 S. Lewis Ave.
(918) 495-6861
The Oral Roberts University (ORU) theatre and dance departments put on several productions throughout the school year. Many of these productions take place on campus in ORU's 1,000-seat Howard Auditorium, but periodically the department will use one of the other great venues around town. There are also many concerts, featuring everything from choral music to jazz combos and wind ensembles. These concerts are usually held in the Timko-Barton Building on campus. For information on upcoming productions and concerts, call the ORU communications arts department.

PLAYHOUSE THEATRE
(918) 872-1245
www.playhousetheatretulsa.com
One of the newest kids on Tulsa's burgeoning theatrical block, Playhouse Theatre kicked off its first season in 2009. Artistic director Chris Crawford spent several years researching regional theater companies and gathering a coterie of actors, playwrights, and designers with the purpose in mind of building a significant regional theater company. In the first season, productions included the classic, tragic love story *Romeo and Juliet* and the contemporary scare fare *Boy Gets Girl.*

Both Crawford and managing director Courtneay Sanders are Oral Roberts graduates and received their master of fine arts degrees at the University of Arkansas, Fayetteville. The Playhouse is a professional theater and includes both local actors and out-of-state talent. Crawford and Sanders plan for the group to achieve Actors' Equity Association status within the next few years. Their principal goal, however, is to produce plays that they like and that Tulsans enjoy seeing, including classics, comedies, and new works.

The first production for children, *Lily's Purple Plastic Purse,* will be presented in May 2010. They plan to add regular fall and spring children's productions in the future.

SPOTLIGHT THEATRE
1381 Riverside Dr.
(918) 587-5030
www.spotlighttheater.org
The Drunkard has been playing at the Spotlight Theatre since 1953, making it the longest running play in America and second longest in the world—second only to London's *The Mousetrap* by Agatha Christie, which opened in 1951. What keeps people coming to the theater? The play is hokey by today's standards. It was actually written in the late 1800s and was taken seriously by the audiences of its day. It was a preachment against the evils of alcohol. This production plays it like an exaggerated melodrama—played for laughs. Little Mary's father, the drunkard, promises he won't go back to the bar until she recovers from an injury. Little Mary announces that she is not getting well but is, in fact, dying, thereby assuring that her father will never drink again. A sad scene, it's played with such broad humor that the audience feels little sadness at Little Mary's cheerful demise.

In between acts, the audience sings along with a superb piano player—belting out old, old favorites that are so long in the tooth that many of the younger members of the audience might be left silent while the seniors sing "Bill Bailey" and "Bicycle Built for Two" with gusto.

This is one of the entertainment bargains in Tulsa. And you get two shows for the price of one—the melodrama and the olio—a vaudeville-style variety show. Cast members rotate, as do olio performers. The play is always the same, but the olio differs from week to week.

The show is fun, funky, and clean. There'll be no Tonys awarded for it, but the delight and dedication of the troupe is obvious and contagious.

Another reason to go to the theater is to see the building. Designed by Bruce Goff for piano teacher Patti Adams Shriner, it's one of Tulsa's art deco classics. The white stucco exterior is accented with narrow vertical windows and black tiles—like piano keys. These shapes are echoed in the glass of the huge round window, center front. Inside are replicas of the original Olinka Hrdy murals that decorated the walls of the piano studio. Shriner and Hrdy went 'round and 'round—arguing about the colors in the murals and the execution of the design elements. The murals all had music themes but Shriner was adamant in her disdain and dislike of jazz. She refused to have any references included in the paintings. The murals were nonrepresentational with strong linear elements—abstract but with definite structure. It was Hrdy's "gotcha" that in the design of one of the paintings, she spelled out the word "jazz," hidden within the swirling and busy patterns of the picture. The word is almost impossible to detect—until the color is removed as a disguising element. In other words, if the mural is photographed in black-and-white, the "jazz" is revealed.

The show plays every Saturday night (unless a major holiday falls on Saturday). The Spotlight is also involved in children's theater and mounts regular performances throughout the year.

SUMMERSTAGE FESTIVAL
Performing Arts Center
110 E. 2nd St.
(918) 596-7111 (800) 364-7111
www.tulsapactrust.org
While there are always events happening at the Performing Arts Center (PAC) during the year, for eight weeks in the summer there's a virtual

hurricane of performance activities. Presenting groups range from major players to small entities. Most performances are in one of the three smaller theaters in the PAC. And the price for many of these events is more than reasonable. Past events have included comedies, musicals, improv performances, and concerts from chamber music to bluegrass gospel. There are very few dates in June and July when there is nothing going on, and lots of dates when you'll have multiple choices.

THEATRE TULSA
207 N. Main St.
(918) 587-8402
www.theatretulsa.org
For over 80 years Theatre Tulsa has served as the city's premier community theater. It started as Tulsa Little Theatre in 1922, putting on productions in various venues. Toward the end of the decade, the group bought property at East 15th St. and South Delaware Avenue. The first production at this site was performed in 1929 in a tent.

The first show in their own building took place in 1932. Tulsa Little Theatre was the first community theater in the country to produce Thornton Wilder's *Our Town* and Arthur Miller's *All My Sons*. In 1979 there was a name change from Tulsa Little Theatre to Theatre Tulsa. In 1989 the company moved into the Performing Arts Center, becoming a resident theater company there.

The company continues to produce works from Shakespeare and Wilde to musicals and contemporary comedies. In 2009 their production of *Up the Down Staircase* won first place in the TATE (Tulsa Awards for Theatre Excellence) competition.

UNIVERSITY OF TULSA THEATRE
(918) 631-2566 (department)
(918) 631-2567 (box office)
www.utulsa.edu/theatre
Watch during the school year for a schedule of student productions, which range from Shakespeare to contemporary drama and musical theater. Performances take place in Chapman Theatre, a 375-seat theater with a proscenium

thrust stage, or Theatre II, an experimental space adaptable to a variety of configurations. The theaters are located in Kendall Hall, which is just east of the towered library.

Productions are announced on the Web site, on the University's classical radio station, KWTU (88.7 FM), and in the *Tulsa World, Urban Tulsa Weekly,* and *TulsaPeople*.

i For a quick look at what's going on in art, theater, music, lectures, etc., check the Events page at the Web site of the University of Tulsa's classical radio station, KWGS. The address is www.publicbroadcasting.net/kwgs/events.eventsmain.

OUTDOORS

Tulsa's located in the area of Oklahoma designated "Green Country," and the rolling hills and trees in summer bear that out. It's also in an area with plenty of water available for water activities. Tulsans take full advantage of all these assets.

Several entities oversee a great deal of Tulsa's green space. There are over 125 city parks covering approximately 6,000 acres. All this space, part of Tulsa Parks, includes 2 nature centers, a garden center, 21 swimming pools, 197 sports fields, 83 playgrounds, the River Skate Park (with River Parks), 69 picnic shelters, 11 community centers, hiking and biking trails, fitness facilities, gymnasiums, and 2 dog parks.

Tulsa River Parks manages parks and trails along the Arkansas River. The Tulsa County Parks Department oversees about 1,700 acres in Tulsa County, including LaFortune Park within the city limits of Tulsa.

Within the parks systems alone, there are myriad ways to have fun out of doors. Add to that the number of golf facilities, neighborhood parks, lakes, and, of course, the river itself, and you'll find lots of places and ways to get fresh air, exercise, and have just plain fun.

BICYCLING

Cycling is big in Tulsa. Even though there are few marked bike lanes 8½ miles), Tulsa has been recognized as a "Bicycle-friendly Community" by the League of American Bicyclists in Washington, D.C. As of mid-2009, Tulsa has 41 miles of designated bike routes, with close to 200 miles in a bicycle master plan. In addition, there are 100 miles of paved trails and 40 miles of natural surface trails. Significant money, from private foundations and public funds, has been put into extending and improving Tulsa's trails system.

The eastern bank section of the River Parks trails is one of the most popular venues thanks to the increasing length of dual trails. For those interested in long rides, still primarily on multiuse trails, it's possible to ride from the campus of Northeastern State University in Broken Arrow all the way to River City Park in Sand Springs, a total of over 30 miles. The Osage Prairie Trail stretches from Oklahoma State University–Tulsa to Skiatook, about 14 miles.

One of the most popular projects is the River Parks bicycle-sharing program, Tulsa Townies.

Thanks to the Warren Medical Research Foundation, a number of 35-pound, single-gear comfort bikes are available for the program. Painted pink, to honor the St. Francis Health System (and to discourage theft), the bikes can be checked out free from four different locations—West 21st, East 41st, and East 96th Sts. and Riverside, and River City Park in Sand Springs.

A credit card is necessary to check out a bike. If the bike is not returned to one of the cycle stations within 24 hours, the cardholder is charged $100. You don't have to check it in at the same location where you checked it out. The bikes receive weekly maintenance.

There are dozens of cycling teams in the Tulsa area and two major cycling organizations. The Tulsa Wheelmen is made up primarily of racing cyclists, while the Tulsa Bicycle Club offers both individual and family memberships and sponsors rides ranging from leisurely to lengthy.

Cycling events are big in Tulsa, with the biggest being the Tulsa Tough Race and Ride. This annual event draws over a thousand participants from all over the world, including cyclists who have also competed in the Tour de France. You can find more information on this May event in the Annual Events chapter. One of the coolest events in conjunction with the Tulsa Tough is the Children's Hospital Tough Kids Challenge. Up to 300 bicycles are given to youngsters of third-, fourth-, and fifth-grade age. To be eligible for a bike, the children must complete several courses, complete a worksheet on bicycle safety, and participate in a ride during the Tulsa Tough event.

Tulsans are serious about bicycle fun. Whether you just want to ride around the block or join in the Oklahoma Freewheel, a weeklong, cross-state ride, you'll find lots of people in Tulsa who share your interest.

i **Popular on the West Coast, bike polo has finally made it to Tulsa. At press time the group of enthusiasts was still looking for a permanent home. Drop-ins are welcome. Check www.tulsabikepolo.com for updates on locations.**

BOATING—ROWING, KAYAKING, CANOEING

The portion of the Arkansas River known as Zink Lake—between West 11th and the Zink Dam at East 29th St.—is popular for nonmotorized boating. The Tulsa Rowing Club regularly practices and competes on the river, and kayakers revel in the white water created by a rock jetty just below the PSO plant. There's a public boat ramp at 2100 S. Jackson Ave.

CIRCUS SKILLS

CIRCUSOUL
310 Riverwalk Crossing, Jenks
(918) 381-TRAP
www.circusoul.com
If you ever dreamed of being that "daring young man on the flying trapeze," you can do it just across the river from Tulsa in Jenks. Just south of the Riverwalk shops, close to the pedestrian bridge, you'll see the 30-foot trapeze rig that Kerry and Allie Valdes use for their classes. Kerry says, "Most of the people who come here have

never tried trapeze before. If you can climb a ladder and hold the bar, you can do this." Classes are one and a half hours long and include demonstration, education, and the experience. The Valdes have a full trapeze rig supported by four large A-frame structures, a fly bar, catch bar, safety lines, and net. The first challenge is climbing the 23-foot ladder.

The facility is outdoors, so it's totally weather dependent. They're closed from about mid-Oct until it warms up in the spring. Walk-ins can sometimes be accommodated, but it's best to call ahead. They will also be giving classes in aerial silk—that's the thing that looks like a long scarf that the Cirque de Soleil performers do such amazing things with. A basic session runs approximately $35.

DISC GOLF

Several of the city parks—Hunter McClure, Mohawk, and Reed—have disc golf courses, as does Haikey Creek in Broken Arrow. River Parks has just installed a new 18-hole course on the east side of the river near East 41st St. The tee boxes are concrete, and informational signs on each hole show a map and par for that hole.

FISHING

There are some great lakes around Tulsa. Look under Lakes for more details about the larger ones. These include Keystone and Oologah. Closer in, fishing is permitted at Mohawk Pond, which is small, just under one and a half acres in Mohawk Park. The pond has bluegill, largemouth bass, and channel cats. You can also fish at Lake Yahola, right next to Mohawk Park. This large reservoir covers 431 surface acres. There's bank fishing only, but there are two fishing docks and picnic tables and shelters. You'll catch crappie, channel catfish, and white bass here.

Leake Park, at East 74th Place and South Memorial Drive, is a great place to take little people fishing. There are lots of bluegill and green sunfish, and park facilities are handy. Owen Park has two wheelchair accessible fishing docks on its eight-plus acres. Bank fish for channel cats and bluegill. Remember, wherever you fish, you need an Oklahoma license. In typical Oklahoma legal fashion, there's a caveat to that. For nonresidents, no youngster under the age of 14 needs a license. Residents and nonresidents of certain states who are under age 16 are exempt. If you're from out of state and have children between ages 14 and 16 wanting to fish, you'll have to check the regulations to see whether or not they'll need a license.

For more suggestions for urban fishing holes, see www.wildlifedepartment.com/tulsaurban fisheries.htm.

GOLF

Price Code

$.................. Less than $15
$$ .... $16 to $24
$$$ .... $25 to $43
$$$$.................. $44 to $52
$$$$$.............. $53 and over

Golf courses have a variety of prices—with cart, without cart, senior, twilight. The price code will reflect the weekend (highest) price. If a course has two sets of dollar signs, the first refers to the price without a cart, the second with a cart. Those with only one code marking include the cart in the price. Some allow you to walk, but you pay the same price. Rates change frequently, so check the Web site, or even better, call for confirmation.

BAILEY RANCH GOLF CLUB $$$
10105 Larkin Bailey Blvd.
(East 89th St. North), Owasso
(918) 274-4653
www.baileyranchgolf.com
Owned by the City of Owasso, Bailey Ranch offers 18 holes of links-style golf. The layout wanders through and around trees, creeks, lakes, and grassland, making it one of Oklahoma's most scenic layouts. Water plays a big role on this course, with either ponds or creeks on over half the

holes. The signature hole is the 17th—requiring a tee shot over water. This hole was named one of the "Five Great Holes You Should Play" in the *Tulsa World*'s 2007 golf guide. Designed by Bland Pittman, the 6,260-yard (from the men's tees), par 72 course opened in 1993. PGA pro Corey Burd is the director of golf.

You're not required to use a cart on this course. Soft spikes and shirts with sleeves are required. You can reserve a tee time eight days in advance, and this is recommended for weekend play. The course is occasionally closed for tournament play, so check before you go if you don't have a tee time reserved.

A driving range and full practice facilities are available. The clubhouse has a well-stocked pro shop and Bailey's Grille, which prepares breakfast items, burgers, hot dogs, and sandwiches.

BATTLE CREEK GOLF CLUB $$$
3200 N. Battle Creek Dr., Broken Arrow
(918) 355-4850
www.battlecreekgolf.net
Owned by City of Broken Arrow, this links-style, 18-hole course features more than 80 bunkers and eight ponds. The course is 6,114 yards long, measured from the men's tees, and is a par 72.

The layout makes for an interesting course, and challenging greens are a standard. The 11th hole offers its own challenges. Don't let the short yardage (100 yards from the front tees, 140 from the back) make you complacent. You'll be hitting into a prevailing south wind, and the two-tiered green is surrounded by water on the front and sides. Your par three can go up fast here.

The course has practice facilities, a pro shop, and a grill that serves up burgers and beer, among other items, to hungry or thirsty golfers. You can walk the course if you want, but a cart is strongly recommended. Tee times can be reserved a week in advance and are necessary for Saturday morning play. Collared shirts are required, both on the course and the practice facilities. If you wear golf shoes, they need to have soft spikes. The course is closed occasionally for tournament play.

CHEROKEE HILLS GOLF CLUB $$$$$
Hard Rock Casino
777 W. Cherokee St., Catoosa
(918) 384-7600
www.hardrockcasino.com

This is a fun course to play if for no other reason than it was designed by the legendary Perry Maxwell in 1924. A recent redesign by Tripp Davis tweaked some of the holes but the course is essentially as Maxwell made it. A par 70 course, it's 6,635 yards from the men's tees. The course features contoured fairways, rolling greens, and challenging bunkers and is just a pretty place to play. In 2008 *Golf Week* magazine named it one of the top five public-access courses in the state of Oklahoma. In 2007 PGA contender John Daly chose to play his pretournament rounds here rather than on the PGA course.

Expect to see water, rocks, wetlands, and brushy roughs. The sixth hole is one of the best—or worst—a par five, laid out amongst rocks with an undulating, unforgiving green. Golfers should observe proper dress on the course. The facility has a pro shop and a grill. Price code includes cart and range.

CLARY FIELDS GOLF COURSE $$$$
9999 S. 49th W. Ave.
(918) 248-4080
www.claryfields.com

This course is as interesting for its owner as for its golf. D. W. Kang is the only combination PGA member/Tae Kwon Do grandmaster in the world. A natural athlete, he took up golf at age 38. And now he owns Clary Fields. If it weren't such a cliché, this course could be called one of Oklahoma's best-kept secrets.

In a quiet, secluded area of Tulsa—north of the Creek Turnpike and west of US 75, this 5,527-yard, par 71 course provides a peaceful place to enjoy the game. Designed by Trip Davis, the course opened in 1999. The landscape features rolling fairways, undulating greens, mature trees, large bunkers, and water on over half of the holes.

Probably the most talked-about hole is the par five No. 4.—the "barn hole." More than one golfer has left his mark on the red metal barn off the fairway. Hole No. 1 is popular for its sweeping approach.

There's a good pro shop, a grill for sandwiches and snacks, a bar, and a practice facility for driving, pitching, chipping, and putting. Soft spikes and collared shirts are required. Tee times can be reserved a week in advance and are recommended for the weekends. The course closes for tournaments.

EMERALD FALLS GOLF COURSE $$$$$
7501 E. Kenosha St., Broken Arrow
(918) 266-2600
www.emeraldfalls.com/golfcourse.html

The heart of a new residential development, the Emerald Falls Golf Course was named No. 6 out of America's ten "Best New Public Golf Courses of 2008" by *Golf Digest* magazine. Designed by Jerry Slack, the 5,916-yard, par 72 course features Zorro Zoysia fairways, Meyer Zoysia roughs, and A1/A4 bent-grass greens. Native grasses and rock have been utilized in the landscaping and ponds, and streams and waterfalls provide challenges on 12 of the 18 holes. Holes No. 7 and No. 8 are challenging due to the length of the holes and the size of the greens. Large trees, native plants, and rolling terrain make this course attractive.

Practice before you play on the five-acre driving range, which features multiple tee areas and big target greens with bunkers. PGA member Billy Neal is the director of golf operations.

The clubhouse houses a pro shop and Bernie's, a restaurant open for lunch and dinner several days a week.

No denim is allowed on the course, and collared shirts with sleeves are required. There are some other dress rules, too, so if you have a question, call first. You can walk after 3:30 p.m. if you want, but the cart is included in the greens fee. The course closes for tournaments. If you buy a membership, you can reserve your tee time a week in advance; otherwise it's four days. It's not necessary to reserve for the weekend, but it's a good idea.

LAFORTUNE PARK GOLF COURSE $$$
5501 S. Yale Ave.
(918) 496-6200
www.lafortunegolfclub.com

Continuously voted Tulsa's favorite public golf course, LaFortune features two 18-hole courses—a championship course with four sets of tees and a lighted, par three course. Designed by Floyd Farley in the early '60s, the course has recently been renovated by course designer Randy Heckenkemper.

The 6,416-yard, par 72 championship course features Bermuda fairways and bent-grass greens. Incorporating water hazards, sand bunkers, and undulating greens, the course offers plenty of challenges to players. The signature hole is No. 6, a 190-yard, par three, uphill hole with a two-tiered green and a pond and waterfall on the left of the green. One of the toughest holes is No. 18, a well-bunkered, well-treed par five, with the last 100 yards straight uphill.

The staff here is first rate, with Patrick McCrate, director of golf, and Chris Jarrett, head golf professional, both PGA members, plus five PGA affiliate assistants. The club has been recognized by the PGA for its teaching program. This is the first public course in Oklahoma to offer the five-day "Get Golf Ready" program.

The par three course is ideal for quicker play or working on your short game. The lights extend playing time and offer a bit of evening relief on hot days.

Practice facilities are extensive, with a lighted driving range with 200 yards of grass teeing area. There are also two putting practice greens and a professional short-game complex.

Tuesday and Thursday nights are reserved for league play. Tee times can be reserved a week in advance and are a good idea.

A brand-new clubhouse was scheduled for completion in late 2009. The new facility will house not only the pro shop but a restaurant and tournament room. The pro shop at LaFortune is noted for its extensive selection of equipment.

MOHAWK PARK GOLF COURSE $$-$$$
5223 E. 41st St. North
(918) 425-6871
www.tulsagolf.org

Mohawk Park is the grand old man of Tulsa public links. It comprises two 18-hole courses, Woodbine and Pecan Valley. Woodbine was built in the '20s and then renovated by Floyd Farley in the '30s. The 6,482-yard, par 72 course features Bermuda grass fairways and bent-grass greens. There are three par three holes and three par fives on the course. This parklike course features tall trees, generous fairways, and large greens.

The newer Pecan Valley course is shorter, tighter, and has more par three holes than Woodbine. Pecan Valley is 5,288 yards long with a par of 68. The first nine holes have been redeveloped with only par threes and par fours. This front nine is used for the First Tee program for young golfers.

Mohawk Park has a large driving range with a grass hitting surface, practice bunkers, and practice greens. There is a snack bar that serves burgers, hot dogs, and other sandwiches, and breakfast on weekends. The pro shop is well stocked to meet any needs.

PAGE BELCHER GOLF COURSE $$-$$$
6666 S. Union Ave.
(918) 446-1529
www.tulsagolf.org

The two courses here, Olde Page and Stone Creek, are fairly straightforward and flat. The par 71, 6,338-yard Olde Page opened in 1977. The most scenic hole is probably No. 11, with an undulating fairway and water to the right and a sand trap to the left of the slightly elevated green. Hole No. 4 is most difficult for long hitters. There's water at about 280 yards, so you need to hold back on your drive.

Both courses are nicely treed with parklike fairways. Stone Creek has a bit more water, with eight holes featuring some involvement. Hole No. 18 is a good, strong finishing hole. A long par four, it demands a good second shot. Falling short means a shot to an elevated green and will probably add a stroke or two extra. Stone Creek was named one of America's "Top Fifty New Public Courses" when it opened in 1987.

The facilities include practice areas, a pro shop, and a snack bar. Tee times can be reserved two weeks ahead, and proper dress and soft spikes are requested.

You can walk the courses if you like.

HIKING, JOGGING, WALKING

The path along the Arkansas River is perhaps Tulsa's most popular place for cycling, jogging, and walking. The combination of the river, the trees, the art, and periodic places to rest makes this unbeatable. Mohawk Park has 9 miles of trails, and LaFortune Park has a 5-kilometer jogging/walking trail. Other city parks with trails of a mile or more include: Leake, Lubell, McClure, Redbud Valley, Sequoyah, Summerglen Plaza, and Whiteside. Also part of the city parks system is the Midland Valley Trail, a 3-mile trail that stretches from Maple Park to the River Parks. Serious hikers like Turkey Mountain for the challenges it presents—but they have to share the trails with mountain bikers and equestrians.

HORSEBACK RIDING

MEADOWLAKE RANCH
3450 S. 137th West Ave., Sand Springs
(918) 494-6000
(800) 256-5323

Tom and Sue Lynn Warren have plenty of room for trail riding on their 1,000-acre ranch. You'll roam over open prairie, through shady forests, along ranch roads, and by clear, spring-fed lakes. Trail rides last about an hour and a half plus time for saddling, etc. The rates are $69 for an adult, $49 for children 12 and under. Smaller children may be required to ride with a parent or wrangler. The charge is the same for either single or double riding. For more experienced or advanced riders, ask about the romantic, moonlight rides. Reservations are a must. There is a weight limit per horse, so ask if you're in doubt.

LAKES

KEYSTONE LAKE
(918) 865-2621

Like most of Oklahoma's lakes, this 26,000-acre flood-control lake is a U.S. Army Corps of Engineers lake. That means that shoreline building is severely restricted. The lake is noted for its wooded shoreline, sandy beaches, rolling hills, and rocky bluffs. There are 16 recreation areas around the lake, 11 boat ramps, 3 marinas, 2 off-road vehicle areas, 5 short-distance trails, and camping facilities ranging from primitive to full hookups. Boats can be rented at the Keyport Marina and Pier 51. Fish in the lake include striped bass, sand bass, black bass, lake-strain smallmouth bass, crappie, and catfish. There are two state parks on the lake. Lake activities include fishing, boating, swimming, and waterskiing. Keystone is about 15 miles west of Tulsa.

KEYSTONE STATE PARK
1926 State Hwy. 151, Sand Springs
(918) 865-4991 (800) 654-8240
www.touroklahoma.com

Pier 51 is located in the park—with boat rental, fuel, boat ramps, and Pier 51 Café (seasonal). The park has both tent and RV camping, and 22 cabins with fireplaces. Two of the cabins have Jacuzzi tubs and all the cabins have DirecTV. There are playgrounds, a children's fishing pond, a hiking trail, and a fitness trail in the park. Necessities are available in the cabin office.

OOLOGAH LAKE
(918) 443-2250

This is one of Oklahoma's premier sailing lakes, but activities also include fishing, picnicking, camping, and waterskiing. The lake covers 29,500 acres and has 14 boat ramps and 11 public-use areas. Five of the areas have full hookups, and three of these have dump stations. Boat rentals are available at Redbud Bay. Fisherfolk go after largemouth bass, white crappie, white bass, channel, flathead and blue catfish, bluegills, sandbass, walleye, and striped bass hybrids. The lake is about 30 minutes northeast of Tulsa.

WALNUT CREEK STATE PARK
North 209th West Avenue, Prue
(918) 865-4991
www.touroklahoma.com
This park has swimming beaches, boat ramps (both lighted and unlighted), a softball field, playground areas, picnic areas, and RV and tent camping. A 15-mile trail, the Sand Plum Trail, provides a variety of terrains and beautiful views of the lake. The trail is enjoyed by hikers, mountain bikers, and equestrians. The equestrian campground has electrical hookups, water, picnic areas, grills, picket posts, and a comfort station.

NATURE CENTERS

MARY K. OXLEY NATURE CENTER
6700 Mohawk Blvd., Mohawk Park
(918) 669-6644
www.oxleynaturecenter.org
This is the perfect place to stretch your legs any time of year. On a crisp fall day, enjoy the autumn color; in spring look for shy violets, wild blue phlox, and other early-blooming wildflowers. Even in winter the stark landscape offers its own beauty—and ducks, geese, and other waterbirds can be seen in the wetlands areas. Summer flourishes with butterflies, birds, and lots of green.

The Center is the hub of a number of connecting trails—good for short walks or, by joining paths, longer hikes. Maps are available at the visitor center, which is open every day (with the exception of major holidays). Check the Web site for a schedule of nature talks, walks, and other events. The visitor center was renovated in 2009 and now has exhibit space, a gift shop, and classroom space. Displays and exhibits in the visitor center include a life-size tree with buttons that can be pushed to activate the calls of several different birds. There's also a computer terminal where visitors can find ways to help the environment around their own homes.

Most of the trails are wheelchair accessible. Walks in the North Woods Unit are a little more rugged. The longest trail in this area, the North Woods Loop (1.2 miles), goes through the Nature Center's "wilderness" area. Admission is free.

For more information see the Attractions and Kidstuff chapters.

REDBUD VALLEY NATURE PRESERVE
16150 Redbud Dr., Catoosa
(918) 669-6460
www.oxleynaturecenter.org
The Redbud Valley Nature Preserve is a special treasure for those who are willing to make the effort to explore it. A tiny bit of Ozark wonderland being pinched off by commercial development, it was saved by the efforts of a determined Tulsa University professor, Dr. Harriet Barclay, the Nature Conservancy, and the people of Tulsa.

Although the property comprises 200 acres, visitors are restricted to about a mile of rough trails. From those trails, however, the visitor goes from the cool shade of limestone bluffs to the hot, dry cliff top—passing unusual and endangered plants and even fossils. In protected areas, sugar maples and blue ash grow, and columbine, walking fern, and Dutchmen's breeches thrive in the shade. Higher up, yucca, smoke trees, and prickly pear seek sustenance from the shallow soil atop the limestone bluffs.

The preserve is open Wed through Sun, closed on city holidays. There is a small nature center with exhibits and a naturalist to answer questions. Picnic tables, restrooms, and drinking water are available in a nearby shelter. No admission charge.

PARKS

There are three main park entities in the area: Tulsa Parks, County Parks, and River Parks. Tulsans make little distinction among the three. Of all the groups, Tulsa Parks covers the most territory and offers the most extensive list of activities and programs. Tulsa County and the city cooperate in producing a *Recreation and Activity Guide*. You can download this publication, but you'll need lots of paper if you want to print it. It's much easier to stop by one of the park centers and pick one up, or call (918) 596-PARK or e-mail tulsaparks@cityoftulsa.org with a request for a copy.

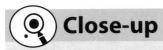 **Close-up**

Keystone Ancient Forest Preserve

Once, a band of forest, thick and impenetrable, stretched from Kansas, across Oklahoma, into Texas, covering about 30,000 square miles. This area was known as the "Cross Timbers." Washington Irving wrote about trying to ride through the area in 1835 and commented, "It was like struggling through forests of cast iron." Most of that area is gone today, but a small portion near Keystone Lake has been identified as the Keystone Ancient Forest Preserve.

Covered in post oaks and red cedars, the terrain was so difficult that the area was ignored by settlers—too rocky for farming, too many trees for grazing, and tough, scraggy wood not deemed fit for cutting. Some of these trees are 300 to 500 years old. Undisturbed, they remain a monument to a landscape that was.

The preserve is now owned by the City of Sand Springs. It is not yet open to the general public, though this is a goal that is being pursued. Trails are primitive and not easy to follow and are not wheelchair accessible. The only way to visit right now is in a group with a minimum of 10 people. This is probably not appropriate yet for children under the age of 10, but you can always ask. To visit this historic area, call (918) 246-2561 or e-mail visitancientforest@sandspringok.org, including the date, time, and duration of your planned visit, the number in your group, and your telephone and e-mail contact information.

Looking to legally slip the leash? Tulsa has two dog parks open with two more planned. Try Joe Station Bark Park in Newblock Park, 2279 Charles Page Blvd., or Biscuit Acres Bark Park, Hunter Park, 5804 E. 91st St.

City Parks

CITY HALL
175 E. 2nd St.
(918) 596 PARK
www.tulsaparks.org

Since the city manages over 125 parks, they won't all be named here! Below, you'll find a couple of historically interesting parks, but city parks are referenced throughout this chapter according to activities they provide. And you'll find a complete list of parks at the above Web site.

CENTENNIAL PARK
1028 E. 6th St.

At just over 11½ acres, this small park packs a lot of enjoyment into a small space. The landscaping, with an attractive pond, is stunning and there's a short walking trail (about a half a mile). The com-munity center here houses a seniors' program and meeting rooms for community activities.

CREEK COUNCIL OAK PARK
1750 S. Cheyenne Ave.

This spot is mentioned both in the History chapter and the Attractions chapter, so this may sound redundant. But it's important. This is where a small band of Creek Indians, fresh from their Trail of Tears from Alabama, rekindled their tribal fire. There's an ethno-botanical display with plants used by the Creeks for food, fiber, medicinal, and ceremonial purposes.

MOHAWK PARK
5701 E. 36th St. North

At 3170 acres, Mohawk is the city's largest park. It is the home of the Tulsa Zoo, two golf courses, and a nature center. In addition, there is a spray-ground, playground, playing fields, 9 miles of trails, and a disc golf course. The park has several picnic shelters and over 100 picnic tables. Bank fishing for bluegill, catfish, and bass is popular in Mohawk pond. Admission to the park is usually free, however, at certain peak times, a small admission fee is charged.

OWEN PARK
560 N. Maybelle St.

Owen Park accidentally became Tulsa's first park. On this site in 1904, a storage facility for explosives used at oil wells accidentally detonated, destroying the property and creating a giant crater. This eventually became Owen Lake, and townspeople gathered there regularly. The city purchased the property in 1909, creating Tulsa's first official city park.

Today there are play facilities for youngsters, basketball and tennis courts, and a recreation center. The oldest existing house in Tulsa was moved to the park property—a small 1880s cabin that was built at 400 North Cheyenne Ave. and belonged to a Methodist minister.

The lake is still there—a nice piece of Tulsa history surrounded by huge trees, which makes a pleasant place to walk.

WOODWARD PARK
2101 S. Peoria Ave.

Another of Tulsa's oldest parks, Woodward is a great place for strolling. In spring the azaleas paint a rocky hillside with color; in summer the roses in the Municipal Rose Garden attract many visitors, and fall brings attractive foliage. There is a playground and picnic shelter.

County Parks

(918) 596-5990
www.parks.tulsacounty.org

HAIKEY CREEK PARK
East 113th St. and South Garnett Road, Broken Arrow/Bixby
(918) 369-5998
www.parks.tulsacounty.org/HaikeyCreek
.aspx

This 151-acre county park straddles the city limits of Broken Arrow and Bixby. It features playground equipment accessible to children with disabilities, a jogging path and fitness court, softball fields, soccer fields, disc golf, and four lighted tennis courts. There are also picnic tables, grills, and picnic shelters.

LAFORTUNE PARK
5323 S. Yale Ave.
(918) 496-6220
www.parks.tulsacounty.org/LaFortune.aspx

The only one of the county parks located in the City of Tulsa, LaFortune is home to one of Tulsa's most popular golf courses, which boasts both an 18-hole championship course and an 18-hole, lighted, par three course. In addition, there are 21 lighted tennis courts, a 5-kilometer lighted walking and jogging trail, a swimming pool, and croquet lawn. Plenty of parking is available at the park, and there are lots of spots for picnics.

The park is also home to a community center, which offers classes in everything from smocking to quilting, painting to Pilates, and bridge to Zumba. A branch of the City-County Libraries occupies a portion of the complex. Summer evenings, folks bring blankets or lawn chairs for the popular—and free—First Friday Concert Series.

River Parks

(918) 595-2001
www.riverparks.org

River Parks is a combination of trails and park areas that stretch from Sand Springs to 101st St. On the east side of the Arkansas River, the most-used part of the parks, the main areas of activity are between 11th and 101st Sts. The river here is lined with magnificent cottonwood trees and features a dual trail system for runners, walkers, and cyclists. Gathering areas with benches and tables provide resting spots along the trails.

At 16th St., there's a river overlook with picnic tables and, close by, a shady spot to sit. At 19th St., you can check out a Tulsa Townie bike at one of River Parks' four cycle stations.

The 29th St. Pedestrian Bridge is a center of activity. This 1,400-foot-long structure was once a bridge for the Midland Valley Railroad. Reconfigured into a pedestrian walkway, it offers a great view of the Zink low-water dam and Zink Lake to the north. On the west bank of the river is the home of the Tulsa Rowing Club, and you'll often see sculls on the water. To the south, again on the west side of the bridge, just below the Public

Service Oklahoma (PSO) power plant, is the Tulsa Wave, a stretch of rapids popular with kayakers. PSO graded and stabilized the bank and built a path and dock so that kayakers can have easy access to the white water. South of the bridge is a rugby field and a disc golf course. Another disc golf course is south of 41st St.

Almost all the amenities in the River Parks are thanks to donors and volunteers. One of the outstanding contributions is the 41st St. Plaza, which was funded by QuikTrip Corporation, whose home is in Tulsa. This nearly $3 million project includes a playground, shelter, restrooms, and plaza area. The playground has a number of interesting water features for summer play and a unique piece of play equipment designed in Denmark. Friday nights during the summer, musicians perform in the plaza.

South of I-44, there's a parcourse and restroom at about 56th St., and trail improvements continue from here to 101st St. All along the parkway, visitors enjoy beautiful bronze wildlife statues donated in honor of individuals or groups who have been great supporters of wildlife and conservation efforts. Each year NatureWorks has added a new statue to the collection, which now stands at over a dozen. Everyone has a favorite—it could be sculptor Robert Ball's playful river otters at 70th St., Kim Kori's giant frog, *Dreaming of the Kiss,* at 43rd St., or the impressive rocks and waterfall that serve as a base for Jim Gilmore's *Bruins Riverpark Picnic* at 71st St.

The other parks in the River Parks system include several sites on the west bank of the Arkansas, including Turkey Mountain, River West Festival Park, and a trail from the 11th St. Bridge south to 71st St. On the east bank, a trail runs north from 11th St. and Riverside Drive to connect with the KATY trail, which continues west to Sand Springs.

TURKEY MOUNTAIN URBAN WILDERNESS AREA

Another River Parks area, this one consists of over 300 acres of wilderness along the west bank of the Arkansas River. From the 300-foot top of

Turkey Mountain, visitors have a great view of Tulsa. A number of dirt trails traverse the heavily wooded property. The trails are used by hikers, bikers, and horseback riders. Mountain bikers give the trails thumbs-up for the challenge—rocky ups and downs and tight turns. There are three well-marked trails with a total trail mileage of about 15 miles. A sign at the trailhead provides information about markings and trail lengths.

An enlarged, paved parking lot with areas for horse trailers was being constructed in the summer of 2009. When improvements are finished, a man-made rock-climbing area and improved lighting and restroom facilities will be in place.

i Mayor Kathy Taylor, in an effort to improve the health and fitness of Tulsa's citizens, began a program called "Tulsa's Million Miles." Tulsans are encouraged to walk, run, swim, or bicycle and log their distances at the program's Web site, www.tulsamillionmiles.com.

SKATEBOARDING

RIVER SKATE PARK
474 W. 23rd St.
(918) 596-2527 or (918) 596-7275
www.riverparks.org

On the west bank of the Arkansas River, this park is not large but has many elements—24 in all. Skaters will find half- and quarter-pipes, grind rails, ledges, jump boxes, and pyramids. The area is fenced and lighted and has seating for spectators. For lessons, exhibitions, and operations, call Tulsa Parks.

SWIMMING POOLS

For cool summer fun, check with Tulsa City Parks—(918) 596-PARK—to find out which pools will be open. The pool at LaFortune Park, a county park, is located at 5500 S. Yale Ave. Call (918) 496-6220 for hours. The fees at these pools are minimal—less than $5. The city also has 23 spray-pools, and four water playgrounds.

TENNIS

Fifty of the city parks have tennis courts; the courts are lighted at 22 of the parks. There's a total of 71 courts in all. LaFortune Park has 21 lighted courts, and Haikey Creek Park in Broken Arrow has 4 lighted courts.

SPECTATOR SPORTS

Tulsa certainly has its share of spectator sports, but to be honest, Tulsans are more doers than watchers. Yes, there are professional and college teams and they have their followers, but probably the biggest event of the sports year is when Union High School plays Jenks in football. It's such an intense rivalry that it's dubbed the "Backyard Bowl."

The sentimental favorite sport has got to be baseball because of the town's long history with the game. The first official Tulsa baseball team was the Oilers, founded in 1905. During the years of their affiliation with the St. Louis Cardinals, later-greats like Dizzy Dean and Nellie Briles played in Tulsa. Another baseball great, Warren Spahn, coached the Oilers from 1967 to 1971. Tulsa's had a baseball team off and on ever since.

Other professional sports haven't fared as well. Tulsa had a professional football team, the Oilers (do we detect a theme here?), who played in the Texas Professional Football League in 1966. In 1967 they played as the Thunderbirds, then moved to Bartlesville and folded. The city had brief flutters with the American Football Association, first as the Mustangs, later as the Thunder. Then in 1983 a United States Football League team from San Diego played in Tulsa as the Oklahoma Outlaws, with Doug Williams as quarterback. A year later the team was off to Arizona.

Professional soccer with the Roughnecks of the North American Soccer League lasted from 1978 until 1984. They may just have been ahead of their time—soccer's one of the fastest growing sports and lots of Tulsans are playing it. In the mid-'80s about 6,000 people (youths and adults) were playing soccer in Tulsa. In 2009 there were 21,000 participants.

The Fast Breakers were Tulsa's first professional basketball team. In their first year in Tulsa, 1988, they won the Continental Basketball League championship. They left Tulsa in 1992. Both the University of Tulsa and Oral Roberts University have had some great basketball teams, and they both have faithful followings. For the last couple of years, pro fans have cheered the 66ers. They are now owned and operated by, and directly affiliated with, the NBA Oklahoma City Thunder.

One of the sports highlights of the year is the annual Henry P. Iba Award Dinner, sponsored by the Rotary Club of Tulsa. This event salutes a male and female athlete of the year, chosen on the basis of community involvement, drawing major sports figures from across the country. Past winners have included Drew Brees, Shannon Miller, Karl Malone, and Ozzie Smith, and keynote speakers for the event have included Tommy Lasorda, Archie Manning, and Lou Holtz.

Hockey has a long history in Tulsa. The first minor league team, named—are you ready for it?—the Oilers, joined the American Hockey Association. They won the AHA championship in 1929 and 1931. They played the next season in Minnesota but came back to Tulsa mid-season. The team lasted until World War II.

After the war, the Oilers were back—this time part of the United States Hockey League. This stint lasted five seasons before the league disbanded. The Central Hockey League (CHL) had the same up-and-down history, and for a few more years the team came and went. The current CHL started in 1992, and the Oilers have played in Tulsa ever since.

So much for the past. What's going on today?

OVERVIEW

Today Tulsa baseball fans cheer for the Drillers, a Double-A affiliate of the Colorado Rockies, and the home team since 1976. Since 1932, Tulsa's teams have played in the stadium at the Fairgrounds. In 2010 they are scheduled to move into a new state-of-the-art ballpark, ONEOK Field, in the historic Greenwood District in downtown Tulsa.

The 66ers, the development team for the Oklahoma City Thunder, cover the court for basketball fans. And the Golden Hurricanes (University of Tulsa) and the Golden Eagles (Oral Roberts University) are perennial fixtures on the local sports scene.

The Central Hockey League Oilers are still here, and fans love them. The rivalry between Tulsa and the Oklahoma City Blazers has always been a fierce one. The Oklahoma City franchise closed up shop in the summer of '09. Sad for Oklahoma City, but sad, too, for Tulsa fans who enjoyed the intense competition.

Tulsa's other pro team is the Talons, a minor league arena football team. The team's been very successful—appearing in the play-offs every season since the team started.

Oklahoma is horse country and there are many equine events for spectators. Check the schedule at the Fairgrounds—all the big horse events are there. Throughout the year, you'll be able to see almost any breed, from Arabians to Welsh ponies. All the shows will have action classes—depending on the breed, it could be jumping, cutting, reining, trail, or dressage. And there's a short horse-racing season at the Fairgrounds, too.

For a different kind of horsepower, try the drag strip of raceways. And if you get tired of watching, consider taking a course. Over the years, golf fans have been able to watch their favorite players at PGA events hosted by Tulsa's Southern Hills Country Club. Tulsa University hosted the NCAA Women's Golf Championship in 1999.

Fans hope there will be more events like this in the future.

PROFESSIONAL SPORTS

TULSA DRILLERS BASEBALL
(918) 744-5998
www.tulsadrillers.com

The Drillers are scheduled to move into their new home, ONEOK Field, in time for Opening Day, 2010. Fans are excited about the new venue—a $60-million project—and its design. With three colors of brick and two shades of zinc, the architecture is contemporary but features art deco touches—terra-cotta medallions and rounded corners that pay tribute to Tulsa's great art deco heritage. Due to the shape of the site, the ballpark faces southeast, about 90 degrees off the usual orientation, but builders hope this will take advantage of summer southerly breezes and counteract the short distance to the right field fence.

The Drillers have been affiliated with the Colorado Rockies since 1976. In 2004 they were recognized as the Texas League Organization of the year, the fourth time they've won the award.

The Drillers, part of the Texas League, play teams from Little Rock, Frisco, Texas, Springdale, Arkansas, San Antonio, Springfield, Missouri, Corpus Christi, and Midland, Texas. They've won the league championship three times and have appeared in the playoffs seven times since 1998. They're the only team in Texas League history to draw over 300,000 fans for ten consecutive years.

TULSA 66ERS
(918) 585-8444
www.tulsa66ers.com

The Tulsa 66ers professional basketball club, named after the famous highway running through downtown Tulsa, is owned and operated by, and directly affiliated with, their NBA parent club, the Oklahoma City Thunder. Players Shaun Livingston, D. J. White, and Kyle Weaver have all been Tulsa favorites before being called up to the Thunder.

The 66ers are members of the NBA Development League, founded in 2001. The annual D-League Draft, held in November, allows the

66ers to select the top prospects from a pool of college, former NBA, and top international players. Almost 20 percent of the end-of-season (2009) rosters of NBA teams were former NBA Development League players.

Since the 2005–2006 season, the 66ers have provided an affordable, family-friendly experience to hundreds of thousands of fans from Tulsa and the surrounding region. Tickets have ranged from $10 to $90 depending on seat location. The 66ers play downtown at the Tulsa Convention Center.

TULSA OILERS
(918) 632-7825
www.tulsaoilers.com

The Oilers are the longest-tenured team in the reorganized (1992) Central Hockey League. They won the CHL Championship that year. Their longest streak of winning seasons came between 1999 and 2006—seven straight—the longest since professional hockey came to Tulsa in 1928.

The Oilers have endeared themselves to fans, not only with their exciting play but through their record of community involvement, both as individuals and as a team. Team members made approximately 200 appearances in the community in 2009 and donated many dollars to local charities. They also encourage education through their Grades for Blades program—children in participating schools who earn a B average or better can qualify for free tickets to the games. They've also had a promotional partnership with the Tulsa Rampage of the Western States Hockey League. The Rampage is a Junior A team, the only one in the state of Oklahoma. The Rampage builds support for the sport at grassroots level—developing both young players and adding fans.

Tulsa fans have repaid the team with 18 sellouts in their old home, the Tulsa Convention Center. It's going to be a lot harder in their new venue—the gigantic BOK Center.

TULSA TALONS
(918) 294-1000
www.tulsatalons.com

For those folks who can't get enough football—who weep when the last Super Bowl commercial fades from the screen—there's arena football. Other than a smaller field, no punts, and fans who aren't freezing or sweating, it's pretty much like regular football. The season runs from late March through July. The Talons have done well with consecutive winning seasons and trips to the playoffs each year. They won the Arena Cup IV in 2003 and won the National Conference Championship in 2007.

Their head coach, Mitch Allner is the only person in af2 history to win a championship both as a player and as a coach. The Talons' home field is in the BOK Center.

COLLEGIATE SPORTS

ORAL ROBERTS UNIVERSITY GOLDEN EAGLES
7777 S. Lewis Ave.
(918) 495-6000
www.orugoldeneagles.com

ORU's head baseball coach Rob Walton was named 2008 Coach of the Year by USA Baseball. The basketball teams usually do well also. Check the Web site for sporting events on the campus.

TULSA UNIVERSITY GOLDEN HURRICANES
(918) 631-2381
www.tulsahurricane.com

The Golden Hurricanes have chalked up some pretty impressive stats during their history. They've won six national championships, four in women's golf (NCAA: 1982, 1988; AIAW: 1980, 1982) and two in men's basketball (NIT: 1981, 2001). The Tulsa basketball team also won the College Basketball Invitational Championship in 2008. All in all, the Tulsa basketball team has made 19 postseason tournament appearances since the 1980–1981 season. In the NCAA finals they've made it to the Sweet Sixteen three times and the Elite Eight once. Its football teams have appeared in 15 bowl games, including the Liberty Bowl in 2005, Armed Forces Bowl in 2006, and the GMAC Bowl in 2008.

Tennis is a fast-rising sport at TU, with student-athlete Arnau Brugues being named All-American in 2006, 2007, and 2008. The school hosted the 2008 NCAA Men's and Women's Tennis Championships at their outstanding facility, the Michael D. Case Center.

OTHER OPPORTUNITIES

For horse racing, check the schedules at:

FAIR MEADOWS RACE TRACK
3901 E. 21st St.
(918) 743-7223
www.fairmeadows.com
The season is short—just about a month. During racing season, the restaurant on-site is open; though you can't see the track from there, there are screens broadcasting the races. In the off-season, the nearby Fair Meadows Racing and Sports Bar features simulcasts from other tracks. It's open seven days a week.

For auto, motorcycle, or BMX racing, look at the Web sites for:

HALLETT MOTOR RACING CIRCUIT
59901 E. 55th Rd., Jennings
(918) 356-4814
www.hallettracing.net
Hallett's 1.8-mile, 10-turn road-racing course has over 80 feet of elevation change and is rated technically difficult. Since it opened in 1976, Hallett has hosted auto racing, motorcycles, and high-speed go-carts. Organizations like the Sports Car Club of America and local clubs like those of Porsche and Ferrari owners like to use the facilities.

Spectator facilities are great—from three grandstands or infield hillsides. And if you get tired of being a spectator, consider Hallett's School of High Performance Driving.

TULSA RACEWAY PARK
3101 N. Garnett Rd.
(918) 437-7223
www.tulsaracewaypark.com
This is the place to see dragsters, hot rods, and super stocks. They also host motorcycle races. Check out the souvenir stand for Tulsa Raceway Park and International Hot Rod Association merchandise.

ANNUAL EVENTS

Tulsa's a great place to party, and there are lots of community events to choose from. Whether it's art or exercise, you can usually count of some good food, too. Or just pick a food festival—how about barbecue or fresh corn on the cob? Oktoberfest combines the best of food and heritage.

With living green a watchword, look for festivals that help with the environment—herb festivals are big in the spring. Or celebrate harvest at a wine festival.

In addition to big annual events, arts and charitable organizations schedule fund—and fun—raisers. The best way to keep track is by picking up a copy of *TulsaPeople*. If you're out of town, check it out online.

Spring and fall are big festival seasons, because they're the best weather—not too hot, not too cold. Whatever you do, do find a festival and join the fun. It's an excellent way to feel part of the community. If you like visiting with people, check out some of the smaller events with pancake breakfasts. That's an ideal place to talk to the locals. And they'll enjoy visiting with you.

JANUARY

CHILI BOWL NATIONALS
Fairgrounds
www.chilibowl.com
Before you get your mouth set for a bowl of spicy chili, this event is about midget racers, not cooking. The four-night event began in 1987 and is billed as "racing's winter answer to football's Super Bowl." The indoor track, a quarter-mile clay oval, is groomed for best performances. Qualifying races lead up to the Saturday night finals with an always-exciting 50-lap finish.

FEBRUARY

NEW GENRE FESTIVAL
Various venues
(918) 585-1234
www.livingarts.org
The New Genre Festival is hard to pin down—even putting it on this calendar is a challenge because it happens in late February–early March and runs for five or six days. Every year is different, with artists responding to the call for proposals in new and unusual ways. And that's what makes this festival so exciting. It's a chance to see what local and international working artists—whether in performance, music, video, visual arts, or multimedia—are doing. Thanks to a partnership with the National Performance Network, there is also a Community Residency, making it possible not only to see or hear the artist's works but to interact with creative minds.

Festival passes are available for purchase or you can buy individual tickets to events. A number of elements are free. So unbutton your mind, get flexible with your schedule, and enjoy the festival.

MARCH

NEW GENRE FESTIVAL
(see February)

EARTH FEST
Tulsa Zoo
6421 E. 36th St. North
(918) 669-6600
Celebrating Earth Day, the zoo plans all sorts of activities to get its guests thinking green. There are lots of crafts and green-themed things for kids to do; educational demonstrations, and recycling

opportunities. Live music, face painting, and earth-friendly vendors add to the festivities.

APRIL

HERB AND PLANT FESTIVAL
Downtown Jenks
(918) 277-1528
www.jenksgardenclub.com

The Herb and Plant Festival stretches several blocks down Main Street and spills over onto several side streets. One of Oklahoma's largest herb festivals, this one showcases over 150 booths with vendors showing herbs, fruits, vegetables, succulents, perennials and annuals, bushes, shrubs—even trees. And there are spots selling home decor, garden accessories, and garden necessities.

Festivities start early with the annual Kiwanis Club pancake breakfast. Food booths assure you won't go hungry, and you can enjoy entertainment and activities for children. Approximately 15,000 folks show up for this event, and the whole town pitches in to make it fun. The Jenks Garden Club sponsors the festival and provides most of the man- (or woman-) power, but local police, firefighters, city employees, and the high school ROTC and Future Farmers of America do yeoman duty. This is small-town America at its best.

HERBAL AFFAIR AND FESTIVAL
Downtown Sand Springs
www.herbalaffairandfestival.com

Just as herbs and spices make food interesting, herbs and food make this festival interesting. More than 100 vendors feature herbs for cooking, for medicinal purposes, and for pure decoration. Internationally recognized herbalists will be speaking about uses of herbs, cultivation of herbs—pretty much everything you need to know about herbs. Food vendors offer choices from Cajun shrimp and Polish sausage to fajitas and roasted peanuts. Cooks from local Amish and Mennonite communities—and the ladies from the Methodist Church—will be serving homemade breads, noodles, cinnamon rolls, and pies.

Entertainment goes on through the day on two stages—the main stage and the children's stage, where local dance groups perform. Other activities are also available for children, and nearby in the school gym is an art show of student work.

Sand Springs doesn't have a town square—it has a town triangle, and the festival is set up around the little park in the center. Admission is free.

MAY

BBQ'N MUSIC FESTIVAL
Washington Irving Park
South Memorial Drive (US 64), south of East 131st St.
(918) 365-8550
www.bixbybbqfestival.com

Formerly the BBQ'n Blues Festival, the event has branched out and now includes musical acts of all stripes—from blues to bluegrass and jazz to jammin'. Always the Friday evening and Saturday before Mother's Day, the festival features nonstop entertainment and lots and lots of barbecue. The only admission charge is a per-vehicle one, but there are several ways to spend your money here. You can buy barbecue—and other festival-type foods—from vendors, and you can buy Taster Kits for the barbecue competition. The music's all free.

The barbecue contenders—over four or five dozen teams—take their 'cue seriously. The competition is sanctioned by the Kansas City Barbecue Society. If you want to taste, check the schedule and arrive before competition starts. And you can vote for your favorite for the "People's Choice" award.

Other activities include a children's play space with inflatables, face painting, clowns, and activities. You must purchase wristbands for this area.

There's an attended and secure parking area for cyclists and special events, and promotions are aimed at the motorcycle contingent. The area was originally called "The Hog Pen," but since "hog" usually refers to Harleys, riders of other kinds of motorcycles felt slighted. In spite of the obvious barbecue connection, nobody wanted it to be called "The Pig Pen," so it's just called "The Pen."

BLUE DOME FESTIVAL
Blue Dome District
www.bluedomeartsfestival.com

This is the people's party. Held on the same weekend as Mayfest, this festival has more of a hometown feel—maybe not as slick, a little bohemian—but a great gathering of local artists and musicians. This festival gets you in on the ground floor with a number of new and emerging artists who will be making names for themselves in the future. Plus, there are lots of established creators who have a special fondness for the festival. Some artists have booths at both Mayfest and Blue Dome. Both events take place downtown, making it the best place in Tulsa to be on this weekend. Having two festivals isn't a matter of competition; it just gives visitors twice as much to see, and hear—there's plenty of musical entertainment, and you won't have to go far to find food.

ROOSTER DAYS
Broken Arrow
www.roosterdaysfestival.com

What do you do when you're overrun with roosters? Back in 1931, that was a problem for local farmers who needed infertile eggs to sell and barter. So a special market day was set to bring extra roosters to town. Well, any gathering worth crowing about features entertainment, food, and fun, and it wasn't long before these elements were added. Now the day has morphed into a four-day festival with everything—but the roosters. The town has changed—few farmers around now—but the festival is still going. Featuring a carnival, parade, live entertainment, and, of course, food, it's a favorite event that takes place from Thursday through Sunday, Mother's Day weekend. And, leading up to the official events, a rooster egg hunt keeps both grown-ups and kids guessing. They follow published clues until someone finds the hand-painted egg—then collects great prizes. The festival's free; food and carnival rides aren't.

TULSA ARTCAR WEEKEND
Living Art Space and Blue Dome Festival
(918)-585-1234
www.livingarts.org

In case you wonder what an artcar is, you'll have to come to the festival to find out. It can be anything—but there's an actual car in there somewhere. It can be painted or covered with who knows what or transformed into something completely different, say a telephone. It all depends on the vision of the artist.

Many of the participants are from out of town—they travel to a number of artcar festivals or shows during the year—but locals are welcome to enter, also. There is an entry fee charged. It costs nothing to just watch, whether it's the Friday night static display at the Admiral Twin Drive-In, the Saturday morning drive-around through midtown and Brookside, or the afternoon parade downtown between the Blue Dome Festival and Mayfest. After the grown-up parade, there's a kids' boxcar parade with prizes. The weekend ends with an artcar party with live music and adult beverages—and, yes, there's a charge for that.

TULSA INTERNATIONAL MAYFEST
(918) 582-6435
www.tulsamayfest.org

This is Tulsa's major art party, and it's been going on for over 35 years. With more than 100 artists, a multitude of musicians, and a plethora of performers, it stretches from West 3rd to West 6th Sts. on South Main Street and spills out onto the side streets. The KidZone offers a variety of activities for youngsters of all ages.

Several of the venues are indoors, including the Invitational Gallery, where works by some of Tulsa's finest artists will be on display. Artists displaying works in the outdoor areas have been selected through a jury process—so you probably won't find Elvis on velvet here. But you will find fine paintings, photography, sculpture, jewelry, folk art, leather goods, and more.

The festival is free—the only expenses are for food and any art you can't resist. Parking is wherever you can find it downtown—and, yes, that will probably cost something. But there will be shuttles scooting through the downtown area to pick up festivalgoers. Festival attendance runs between 350,000 and 375,000 for the four-day event—so you'll be in good company, and plenty of it!

TULSA TOUGH
www.tulsatough.com
A three-day cycling fest, the Tulsa Tough has something for everyone, including professional-level races, tour rides, kids and youth activities, live music, and vendors. This USA Cycling event is nationally recognized and attracts over 1,500 participants annually from all over the world. The prize list is the third largest of any race on the USA Cycling National Racing Calendar—$150,000 in 2008.

One of the fun events is the 8-mile Townie ride—not a race, just a nice scenic ride—advertised as a Spandex-free event.

ZOOFARI
Tulsa Zoo
6421 E. 36th St. North
(918) 669-6603
www.tulsazoo.org
Usually held the first Friday evening in May, this fun, family event includes eats, animals, and entertainment. Ticket prices cover everything. A number of Tulsa's favorite restaurants have food booths; there are arts and crafts, keeper chats, and docents with animals. From inflatables for the younger kids to laser tag and a rock wall for older ones, there really is something for all ages. But you don't need to have children to enjoy a lovely spring evening at the zoo—and the chance for a backstage peek at some of the zoo's most popular exhibits.

JUNE

GREEN CORN FESTIVAL
Downtown Bixby
(918) 366-1408
www.bixbyoptimist.org

Held on the fourth Thursday, Friday, and Saturday of June, the Green Corn Festival is a trip to an earlier time of family picnics, parades, and local talent contests. Activities include carnival rides, bingo, games, arts and crafts, music, a parade, and food. The favorite food is, of course, roasted corn. The cooks peel back the husks, remove the silks, put the husks back on, and roast the corn until it's done. Then they pull back the husks and dip the hot corn in butter—yum. They go through over 100 bushels of fresh corn. Funnel cakes, Indian tacos, root beer, turkey legs—all the fair favorites are here, too.

There's no admission charge for the festival; you just pay for what you want to eat or buy. There is a charge for the youth talent show. Everything is based on kids and family—no alcohol. Sponsored by the Bixby Optimist Club, the proceeds go to scholarships and to buy shoes and eyeglasses for needy kids in the community. This is an event for all ages—a lot like a family reunion. Older folks sit in the shade and visit while the "young-uns" run around and play games or enjoy contests like the frog and turtle races.

ROUTE 66 BLOWOUT
Downtown Sapulpa
(918) 224-5709
www.sapulpamainstreet.com
Classic cars, trucks, and motorcycles come rolling in early on the first Saturday in June, and the party's on. The approximately 300 vehicles will be parked downtown for inspection and judging. Meanwhile, the Rotary Club has a salsa-making contest; there's a juried fine-arts show; and between 75 and 80 vendors sell everything from foods to crafts.

SKIATOOK BLUEGRASS FESTIVAL
Sports Complex, Skiatook
(918) 261-3443
www.skiatookbluegrass.com
This annual June event, which began in 2004, is small but growing, and features both nationally and regionally recognized talent. The first event starts on Thursday night with gospel music. In addition to the bluegrass groups, fans look for-

ward to bluegrass karaoke and the junior fiddle contest, plus arts and crafts exhibitors. You won't get hungry—there are plenty of food vendors.

Bring blankets or lawn chairs, and, for daytime concerts, hats and sunscreen. There are some shaded spots, but there's no guarantee you'll get one. Tent campers and RVers are welcome, and hookups are available. Festival grounds are behind the Sports Complex. See the Web site for a map, schedule of events, and ticket prices.

STONE BLUFF LAVENDER FESTIVAL
Lavender Hill Farm
24474 E. 191 St. South, Haskell
(918) 482-2338
www.lavenderhillfarm.net
It's not Provence, but close your eyes and let the scent of two acres of lavender wash over you and it's the next best thing. The festival's a good time to visit the fields, the gift shop, and the winery. Plus, over 40 other vendors are there, carrying everything from gardening items to crafts and bath and body products. Stop in the lemonade tent for some lavender lemonade. Food is available—usually barbecue, wraps, funnel cakes, etc. And there are tastings at the winery on the property. Other features include carriage rides and lavender sales (both plants and cut), and the Tulsa Humane Society brings adoptable dogs. Come for a cookie—go home with a puppy.

There's a $5 charge for the festival—children under 12 are admitted free. Parking is free, and professional parking crews make sure it's easy to get in and out. Check the Web site or call for driving directions.

TULSA PRIDE AND DIVERSITY
Centennial Park
1028 E. 6th St.
www.tulsapride.org
Since 1980, Tulsa's LGBT community has been united in support of diversity. The Pride Festival is a two-day event featuring the Open Arms Youth Project talent show, theater presentations, music and other live entertainment, a pancake breakfast, an interfaith worship service, vendors, and

even a dog show. The highlight is the evening Pride Parade, which starts in the Brady Arts District and winds through downtown to the park.

In 2009, over 23,000 people joined in the festivities.

ZEBCO "TAKE ME FISHING" DAY
Various venues
(800) 494-3224
Held during Oklahoma's Free Fishing Days, Zebco sponsors this great family event. They buy thousands of "eating-size" catfish and bluegill and release them in specified park ponds. Six hundred of the fish are tagged and can be turned in for prizes before noon, when the event ends. The average-size catfish is about a pound and a half. The event is for children with accompanying adult(s). Bring your own tackle; a cooler and ice for transporting fish, drinks, and snacks (no concessions available); lawn chairs; insect repellent; and sunscreen.

JULY

DFEST MUSIC CONFERENCE AND FESTIVAL
Downtown
www.dfest.com
Dfest is an oak that grew from a tiny acorn. Tom Green and Angie DeVore-Green came up with the idea in 2002 to help promote their band, Ultrafix. They organized a small festival with other local bands, and even though the weather was uncooperative, the fans weren't; in fact, the fans encouraged them to make it an annual event.

Like Topsy, it grew and is now one of the city's major events. There's an educational component to the festival, with seminars for musicians ranging from performance clinics to business basics and beyond. For the general public the biggest interest is in the concerts, which start late in the afternoon. A large section of the Blue Dome District is fenced off—you'll need to purchase wristbands—and about 150 bands play at over 14 venues in the area—some indoors, some out. Bands range from local, unsigned bands to headliners.

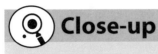 **Close-up**

Zebco

Zebco sponsors a wonderful local event, "Take Me Fishing" Day. Most fishermen (and women) know the name Zebco for its top-quality fishing tackle, but most don't know how the company got started.

Once there was a Tulsa company named Zero Hour Bomb Company. They manufactured time-detonated explosives that were used in the oil fields. They were facing expiring patents and changing technology and were looking for ways to diversify their manufacturing operation.

R. D. Hull was a Texas watchmaker—and an inveterate tinkerer. He'd come up with a way to make a fishing reel that wouldn't backlash. He had a model he'd made out of plywood and a coffee can lid. He showed company officials how his stationary spool was an improvement over traditional revolving spool reels. He explained that he'd gotten the idea from watching a grocer pull string to wrap a package of meat.

It was a marriage made in heaven. In June 1949, the first 25 handmade Zebco Standards rolled off the production line. The earliest models were branded with the name of Zero Hour Bomb Company, but by 1956 the name had been shortened to Zebco. The company dropped its other products and concentrated on fishing equipment.

Vendors hawk everything from T-shirts to tacos, and food is available at many of the concert locations.

TULSA FREEDOMFEST
River West Festival Park
Veterans' Park
1924 Riverside Dr.
www.tulsasalutesfreedom.com

Tulsa's biggest blowout—or blowup—is Freedom-Fest. There are usually concerts leading up to July 4th, but the big party is on Independence Day. There are three main locations for gathering. River West Festival Park has the most activities, with inflatables, face painting, food, and lots of music. Veteran's Park is headquarters for an old-fashioned family picnic and music. This site also features live entertainment, inflatables, and concessions. The River Park area at West 19th St. and South Riverside Drive will also have concessions and live music. The highlight of the festival is, of course, the fireworks display. Beginning at about 9:30 p.m. and lasting approximately 30 minutes, this is the city's premier pyrotechnic event. Schedules for music, etc., change from year to year, so watch the *Tulsa*

World and check the Web site for what's happening where and when.

SEPTEMBER

OKLAHOMA SCOTTISH FESTIVAL
River West Festival Park
717 S. Houston Ave.
www.oklahomscottishfestival.com

Grab your sporran and *sgian dubh* and head for the hills—of west Tulsa—to celebrate Scottish traditions. Games galore, including caber tossing and the Braemar stone toss, a parade of Scottish-breed dogs, whiskey tasting, music, and more are featured. The Kids' Glen has mini-games along with make-and-take crafts, races, and storytelling. And there are interesting animals like Dexter cattle and Clydesdale and gypsy horses. This is fun for the whole family—except maybe the whiskey part. The admission fee is slight, so come watch or even participate. How about the Farmer's Walk—women carry 75 pounds in each hand, men 175 pounds, and participants who walk the farthest win.

The festival runs from Friday evening through Sunday.

OCTOBER

ART ON MAIN
Downtown Jenks
(918) 299-5005
www.jenkschamber.com

This popular outdoor street festival attracts more than 8,000 people annually. Over 115 of the state's best artists—painters, sculptors, potters, jewelry makers, and photographers—display their works. Local wineries set up tasting booths and food vendors provide a variety of goodies. And you can count on some great music—from jazz to salsa.

GREEN COUNTRY WINE FESTIVAL
Stone Bluff Cellars
24145 E. 191st St. South
(918) 482-5655
www.stonebluffcellars.com

Wine tasting, winery tours, food, music, arts and crafts, entertainment, and a children's area are featured at the Wine Festival. Admission is charged but parking is free.

OKTOBERFEST
River West Festival Park
2100 S. Jackson Ave.
www.tulsaoktoberfest.org

You will love this festival—everybody does. It's been named "Best Festival in Oklahoma" at the Governor's Conference on Tourism, "Best Festival" by *Urban Tulsa Weekly* readers, one of the "Top Ten Oktoberfests in the U.S.A." by *USA Today* and "Best German Food Festival" by *Bon Appetit* magazine. If you're beggin' for bratwurst or pleading for potato pancakes, you're in luck. There are lots of other choices, too. Get ready for lots of music, including bands from Germany, polka dancing, and the chicken dance. The list of arts and crafts vendors is lengthy. Add to that carnival rides—this is one whopper of a festival.

It runs from Thursday evening through Sunday. There is an admission fee and a parking fee. Save a little and use the shuttle service or the trolley. Come for the *gemütlichkeit* and enjoy the bier, brats, and bands.

TULSA RUN
www.tulsarun.com

The largest and oldest of Oklahoma's runs—if you don't count the Land Runs—the Tulsa Run features 15K, 5K, and 2K events. In 5K, there's also a wheelchair race. The 2K is a fun run. Over 10,000 runners participated in 2008's event. The race-course is a classic urban course, laid out through some of Tulsa's most scenic areas. Preceding the races is a Fitness Fair, and on race day bands play along the route. There's a party at the finish line, with inflatables for kids and medical and massage tents for runners.

TULSA STATE FAIR
Fairgrounds
East 21st St. between South Harvard and South Yale Avenues
(918) 744-1113
www.tulsastatefair.com

Dating back to 1903, the Tulsa State Fair has been a staple on the city's calendar, running from the fourth Thursday following Labor Day through the second Sunday of Oct. It features all the standard fair fare—animal exhibits and competitions, music, entertainment, rides, rodeo, big-name acts—everything from racing pigs to roses.

One of the most spectacular contests is the Oklahoma State Sugar Arts Show, the largest judged sugar arts show in the United States. Stroll by elaborate wedding cakes and clever cupcakes. Many of these creations look too good to eat!

While there is a gate charge to enter the fair, most events are free—even the big name musical entertainers. There is a charge for rodeo or ice show tickets, but that includes admission to the fair.

NOVEMBER

DIA DE LOS MUERTOS (DAY OF THE DEAD) ARTS FESTIVAL
Living Art Space
307 E. Brady St.
(918) 585-1234
www.livingarts.org

There's a nominal fee for this festival, which features live music, dancing, and Mexican food. Family altars are displayed in the gallery, and there's a kids' area where youngsters can create their own altars and make sugar skulls. After dark, there are fire dancers and a skeleton parade.

DECEMBER

CHRISTMAS IN THE PARK
Rhema Bible Church
1025 W. Kenosha St., Broken Arrow
(918) 258-1588
www.rhemabiblechurch.com
About 200,000 people drive through or park and walk through the campus, which is covered with nearly two million lights—over 100,000 of them are synchronized to music, and some are ani-

mated. The display is open from the day before Thanksgiving through New Year's Day. There's no admission fee but any donations are used in community service. Check the schedule for carriage rides. Concession stands sell hot chocolate, coffee, and funnel cakes.

PSO HOLIDAY PARADE OF LIGHTS
Downtown Tulsa
(918) 583-2617
www.tulsadowntown.org
This wonderful nighttime parade is a long-standing holiday tradition. It features marching bands, dance teams, entertainment, floats, and giant helium balloons—the Macy's Thanksgiving Parade kind. Always the second Saturday evening in Dec, it's a season highlight. And, of course, it's free.

DAY TRIPS

While you'll find plenty to keep you busy in Tulsa, there are a number of interesting spots to visit in the area. Visiting some of these places will help you appreciate the history of this part of the state.

Tulsa wasn't the only city affected by the discovery of oil. So, too, was Bartlesville. From the early part of the last century, Phillips Petroleum has been an important part of the community. Even though the company's presence has been reduced by defections to Texas, the years of company generosity have written indelibly on the town. Ponca City has its own oil legacy with the story of E. W. Marland and Conoco.

To the east, Muskogee and Tahlequah are good places to learn more about the Native Americans in the area. And the Illinois River draws huge crowds of people who want to float downstream in its cool, clear waters.

And you can't forget Route 66. Jaunt north to Miami—there are some highlights in this chapter. Or head toward Oklahoma City. You don't have to stop at Arcadia, where the route in this section ends. There's a lot to explore in Oklahoma City. So much that we recommend you buy *Insiders' Guide Oklahoma City*. Yes, that's a shameless plug, but it really will be helpful.

This chapter is arranged alphabetically by city except for the two Route 66 Road Trips, where towns and attractions are listed in the order in which you'll come to them.

Attractions Price Code

The following code will be used to indicate the cost of one adult admission. Keep in mind that children's tickets will probably be less and young children may be admitted free. Most places offer senior discounts and many offer military discounts. Always ask.

$	$1 to $5
$$	$6 to $10
$$$	$11 to $15

Restaurant Price Code

The dollar signs represent the cost of entrees for two, excluding appetizers, beverages, etc.

$	$15 or less
$$	$16 to $25
$$$	$26 to $35

BARTLESVILLE

The settlement that would become Bartlesville started in 1873 with a gristmill on the Caney River.

The mill was already there when Jacob Bartles and his family moved to the area. It was still Indian Territory then, but because his wife was a Delaware Indian, he was entitled to buy property. He ran the flour mill and added a general store. Bartles had two men working for him—William Johnstone and George Keeler. They decided to open their own business, another general store south of the river. When the railroad came through, it bypassed Bartles's business, so he put his store on rollers and moved it north to what is now Dewey, deserting the community named after him. It took 145 days to change locations, and the store stayed open the entire time.

Bartlesville, Indian Territory, was officially incorporated on January 15, 1897. It was just a few months later that oil was discovered in Bartlesville and the town's destiny was changed forever. In 1904, two Iowa farm boys came to the territory looking for oil. They found it and in 1917 founded the Phillips Petroleum Company. Thanks to the Phillipses and other entrepreneurs, the town grew and like its southern neighbor, Tulsa, prospered and added amenities that other towns could only envy.

Though the oil business has undergone drastic changes—with corporate headquarters moving away from the state—Bartlesville still retains a significant Phillips presence. Phillips was extremely generous to the town and many benefits remain. One of the newest attractions is the Phillips Petroleum Museum. Other tourist attractions include Frank Phillips's Bartlesville home and his country getaway, Woolaroc. The city also benefited from the largesse of individuals and corporations based here and can boast a magnificent auditorium, an architectural icon, and an outstanding annual music festival—OK Mozart.

Every year since 2000, the National Trust for Historic Preservation names America's "Dozen Distinctive Destinations." Bartlesville made that list in 2006. Come find out why. For more information on Bartlesville, contact the Convention and Visitors Bureau at (877) 273-2007 or on the Web at www.visitbartlesville.com.

BARTLESVILLE AREA HISTORY MUSEUM
401 S. Johnstone Ave.
(918) 338-4290
www.bartlesvillehistory.com

Most area history museums are of interest only to people from the area. This one is a cut above the rest. Yes, it's all about area history, but that history is also the history of the beginnings of the oil industry in Oklahoma. You'll be welcomed to the museum, which is on the fifth floor of the City Center Building, by an animated mannequin of early area photographer Frank Griggs. Griggs documented the life and people of Bartlesville for 70 years. The museum staff is still going through the photos—they have thousands of them in their database. You'll learn about the three major tribes in the area—Delaware, Osage, and Cherokee—and early residents like Jake Bartles, William and Stella Johnstone, and George Keeler. Admission to the museum is free but donations are welcome. The museum is open Tues through Sat and is closed on holidays.

DEWEY HOTEL MUSEUM $
801 N. Delaware St., Dewey
(918) 534-0215

Dewey is just spittin' distance from Bartlesville—and it's where Jacob Bartles moved when he left town. The store he built is gone—it was located where the Tom Mix Museum is today. But the hotel he built—and where he and his family lived—still stands proudly on the opposite corner. Built in 1899, it was named in honor of Admiral George Dewey and his triumph in the Spanish-American War. Everyone from outlaws to oilmen dined in the spacious dining room, and Mrs. Bartles served tea in the front parlor. Although it's called a museum, the exhibits are minimal—the hotel is the exhibit. It's open daily, except holidays, between May 1 and Dec 20.

FRANK PHILLIPS HOME $
1107 S. Cherokee Ave.
(918) 336-2491
www.frankphillipshome.org

This imposing neoclassical home was built for Jane and Frank Phillips in 1908. The couple lived there until their deaths—hers in 1948, his in 1950. Their daughter Elizabeth and her family lived in the house until 1973, when she donated the home and its contents to the State of Oklahoma. This is the only oil baron home in Oklahoma that retains original furniture on the original site. The house was remodeled in the 1930s and the decor hasn't been changed since then. Notice the silk damask wall coverings and the Waterford chandeliers in the music room and dining room.

In what was once the garage, behind the home, is a small museum that features the lives of the Phillips family. Having drilled many wells on Osage lands, ventures profitable to both Phillips and the tribe, Frank was selected by the Osages as the first white man to be made an honorary member of the tribe. Replicas of the elaborate headdress and clothing presented to both Frank and Jane Phillips are on display in the museum.

The home is open Wed through Sat and the second Sun of every month. Check ahead for tour times.

INN AT PRICE TOWER
510 S. Dewey Ave.
(918) 336-1000, (877) 424-2424
www.pricetower.org/innatpricetower

For the ultimate experience of Wrightiana, "stay the night with Frank Lloyd Wright." That's the catch phrase for the Inn at Price Tower. Nineteen rooms in the 19-story structure have been turned into a modified bed and breakfast. New York architect Wendy Evans Joseph designed the rooms and must have been channeling FLW—she's retained his style with integrity. The colors are just Wright—celery greens with accents of his favorite Cherokee red. The furnishings are pure period, but the fixtures are total 21st century. One word of caution—if you're short, look up high for the temperature control. If you try to regulate the room temperature with the most convenient thermostat, you'll only be heating the bathroom tile floor.

Breakfast is continental—not fancy, but you won't starve. The Copper Bar in the Tower is open Tuesday nights through Saturday nights for drinks and light dinner. Staying in the Tower is a unique experience, so if you day trip lasts overnight, take advantage of the opportunity.

Rates for 2009 were $145 for a standard room and $245 for a two-story suite.

KEEPSAKE CANDLES
263 County Rd. 3022
(918) 336-0351, (888) 636-0351
www.keepsakecandles.com

This business is a real acorn to oaks story. Ed Ririe's mother had an antique glass collection. Looking for a project for a church bazaar, she suggested that Ed might make candles, using the glass to make molds. It took him a little while, but he figured out how to do it and the business was born. Ed didn't stop there. He also figured out how to make the candles in two parts. The wax in the colored outer shells has a higher melting point than the scented wax in the center. So when the candle burns down, you can take it back to Keepsake and get it refilled or you can drop a votive candle inside the shell. So the name Keepsake has a double meaning. The first candles

were made from Mrs. Ririe's keepsake glass, and the sturdy wax shell makes the candles themselves keepsakes.

A visit to the factory/store will reveal an amazing variety of candles. There are candles that look like bowls of oatmeal, candles that look like pumpkins, and candles that look like pottery pots.

Most of the candles in the store were made right there in the factory. You'll also find gift items. If you want to see candles being made, visit between 10 a.m. and 3 p.m., Mon through Fri. They're not always making candles, but you'll still get an explanation of how they do it. Keepsake is closed on Sundays and holidays. During the Christmas season, they sometimes post extended hours.

KIDDIE PARK $
200 N. Cherokee Ave., Johnstone Park
(918) 336-5337
www.kiddiepark.net

If it's summer and you're traveling with little ones, this stop is a must. Since 1947 this little amusement park has been a highlight of summer fun for children 12 and under. The rides are tiny and tame and so inexpensive. Your child will have a great time and your wallet will not be much lighter. Most rides are just a quarter or two. And the little carousel is sporting spruced-up horses thanks to a local Boy Scout's Eagle project. If you yearn for simpler times, visit Kiddie Park. The Kiddie Park opens the first weekend in May and is open Fri and Sat only until the last weekend in May. In June, July, and Aug, the park is open Tues through Sat evenings. It's closed on the Fourth of July.

NELLIE JOHNSTONE NO. 1
200 N. Cherokee Ave., Johnstone Park

Oil slicks were noticed on the surface of small streams in the Bartlesville area as early as 1875. In 1897, George Keeler and William Johnstone began drilling a well near their store on the west bank of the Caney River. Cherokee Indians in the area immediately protested. In 1898 the U.S. Congress passed a law that cleared the way for the men to take legal title to the land. The site was named for Johnstone's daughter Nellie, who was a granddaughter of Delaware chief Journeycake. The derrick was rebuilt and the well began producing—Oklahoma's first commercial oil well.

Over the years, several replicas of the original derrick have been erected on the site. The current incarnation is part of a more extensive plan for a plaza honoring the Nellie Johnstone. There's a large sign that describes each part of the derrick and how it works.

You won't need to spend much time here, but it's worthwhile to swing by this historic site.

OK MOZART
(918) 336-9900
www.okmozart.com
This is an event, not a place, but such a big event that it qualifies as one of Bartlesville's great attractions. Founded in 1985, this nine-day festival takes place all over town. Large formal concerts are presented in Bartlesville's striking community center. Designed by Wesley Peters, chief architect of Taliesin West (the Frank Lloyd Wright Foundation), the concert hall seats over 1,700 people. The acoustics are outstanding. Other events take place in other areas of the center and in local churches, businesses, and historic sites. One of the highlights is an outdoors pop concert on the grounds of Woolaroc, capped off with a spectacular musical fireworks finale.

Don't let the Mozart in OK Mozart fool you. You can hear plenty of classical music. But if Bach doesn't rock your boat, never fear, there's everything from bluegrass and boogie to zydeco. And not all presentations are musical. Past events have included jewelry making, storytelling, art exhibits, and even a mother-daughter princess tea complete with crumpets and crowns.

And the musicians run the gamut, too. In previous seasons concertgoers have been entertained by big names like Ben Vereen, Kristin Chenoweth, the Canadian Brass, Frederica Von Stade, Itzhak Perlman, and P.D.Q. Bach. It would not be an exaggeration to say that this festival is the number one musical event in the state.

PHILLIPS PETROLEUM COMPANY MUSEUM
410 S. Keeler Ave.
(918) 661-8687
www.phillips66museum.com
Billy Parker's 1914 pusher plane soars over exhibits that cover the company's history and accomplishments. If you thought that Phillips just made gas for your car, think again. One of the displays is a huge bank vault with stacks and stacks of paper—all patents held by the company, including one that resulted in, among lots of other things, the hula hoop. Find out why the company has 66 in the name. Here's a hint—it involves a famous highway and a speedometer. There's a lot to see here, and the Phillips people have done a great job. The museum is open daily, except holidays.

PRICE TOWER AND PRICE TOWER ARTS CENTER $-$$
510 S. Dewey Ave.
(918) 336-4949
www.pricetower.org
Famed architect Frank Lloyd Wright designed a number of skyscrapers—only two were ever built. And locals will discount the 14-story Johnson Tower, touting the Price Tower as Wright's "only realized skyscraper." It was so revolutionary in its design that it does deserve to stand alone. Wright described it as "the tree that escaped from the forest." At 19 stories, each of its floors is cantilevered from a central support—the tree trunk of the structure. The tower is as quirky as its creator—walls meet at odd angles, and the spaces are compact. Wright controlled every detail of the construction—designing the built-in furniture, choosing colors, and even designing fabric.

It was planned as a combination office, living, and retail facility. Designed for inventor and manufacturer H. C. Price, it served as company headquarters. Price and Wright didn't always see eye to eye. Wright envisioned a taller building; Price wanted only a couple of floors. The Price Tower is a compromise—something Wright did seldom and reluctantly. The only conflict that Price won was to have a large globe installed in his office. Wright didn't want anything with curved lines.

The globe is still there. Guided tours, which include the top-floor executive office, the H. C. Price corporate apartment, and the temporary and permanent gallery collections, are scheduled on Tues and Thurs at 11 a.m. and 2 p.m., Fri and Sat at 11 a.m., and Sun at 2 p.m. Even if you're not there for a tour, do visit the galleries—you'll get more of a feel for the building, and exhibits on the second floor include a number of Wright-designed items, material relating to Bruce Goff, and other architects.

TOM MIX MUSEUM $
721 N. Delaware Ave., Dewey
(918) 534-1555
www.tommixmuseum.com
Although born in Pennsylvania, Tom Mix found his way to Oklahoma in the early years of the 20th century. He worked at several different jobs—tending bar in Guthrie, as town marshal in Dewey, and working on the famous 101 Ranch. It was his skill with horses that landed him a job with a movie company that was filming nearby. He headed for Hollywood, where he made over 300 movies, most of them silent. In his heyday, he was truly king of the western genre, doing all his own stunts, rescuing damsels in distress, capturing villains, and, all the while, looking stylish and cool.

The Tom Mix Museum isn't large and it won't take you long to see all the exhibits, but plan a little extra time to watch one of the Tom Mix movies playing in the little theater. The museum is open Mar through Dec, Tues through Sun. It's closed in Jan and open weekends only in Feb.

WOOLAROC MUSEUM AND WILDLIFE PRESERVE $$
1925 Woolaroc Ranch Rd.
(918) 336-0307 (800) 636-0307
www.woolaroc.org
Everybody needs a place to get away, and this was Frank Phillips's. Though only about 12 miles from his Bartlesville mansion, it was a completely different world. Of the 17,000 acres he owned in the area, he chose the most ruggedly scenic ones to locate Woolaroc, named for the woods, lakes, and rocky terrain of the site. Here the Phillipses

entertained presidents and performers, businessmen, and badmen.

Today Woolaroc encompasses the Phillips lodge, Woolaroc Museum, the Heritage Center with a multimedia presentation on the property, the wildlife preserve, a petting barn, and a snack and sandwich concession. This is one of Oklahoma's best bang-for-the-buck opportunities.

Start by checking out the large Arkansas pine lodge. The great room was influenced by the style of the El Tovar Hotel at the Grand Canyon. Mounted on the balcony railing is an impressive longhorn head, a gift from Fort Worth's Amon Carter. It used to snort smoke but now is strictly nonsmoking. Docents on the property will assure you that the array of mounted animal trophies were from animals that died of natural causes—mostly. The elephant head was a gift from John Ringling, of circus fame. Seems he lost his entire circus to Frank during a high-stakes poker game. Ringling won the circus back the next day, but when one of the circus elephants died, he had the head mounted and sent to Phillips as a memento of the night he owned the circus.

The Navajo rugs scattered around the room are part of Phillips's valuable and historic collection. The Steinway grand piano is covered with Arkansas pine bark—a material used to frame many of the paintings in the museum collection. The antler chandeliers came from the Waldorf Astoria Hotel in New York City.

Next, visit the museum, which houses one of the finest collections of western and Indian art in the country. At the entrance, glass mosaic tiles depict large figures representing Native American cultural groups, with smaller designs replicating actual Indian designs found on pottery and paintings. The doors themselves are of stainless steel and bronze, with eight circular inserts decorated with onyx plaques engraved with designs found on shell gorgets from the Spiro Mounds.

Museum exhibits are organized by broad chunks of time beginning with "The Dawn of History." Concerned mainly with the archaeology of the New World, it emphasizes the richness of Oklahoma's heritage, particularly the Spiro and Mississippian culture.

Other areas bring the cultures of the South-west into focus—pueblo pottery, blankets, arti-facts, and paintings. A number of the Taos School of artists are represented here—Bert Phillips, Oscar Berninghaus, and Joseph Henry Sharp—as well as Charles Russell, Frederic Remington, George Catlin, and Thomas Moran.

Downstairs you'll find everything from guns to a gas station. Be sure to give yourself enough time to explore all the exhibits—and don't forget a stop in the gift shop.

If you're traveling with children, you'll have to stop in the petting barn. If you're there at the right time of year, you might get to pat a baby buffalo. And as you drive around the property, you will see more bison.

The Woolaroc bison herd was started in 1926 when Phillips had 90 of the animals shipped from South Dakota. In addition to buffalo, look for elk, longhorn cattle, deer, donkeys, aoudads, ostriches, and more.

Woolaroc's an amazing place. Frank Phillips once said, "If I can get a man here, I can make a deal." It's certainly a good deal for visitors.

MUSKOGEE

Muskogee has long been important because of its position at the confluence of three rivers—the Grand, Verdigris, and Arkansas. For thousands of years, native peoples lived in the area. After the Louisiana Purchase, trappers and traders came to the region. As eastern Indians were pushed westward, they encroached on the lands of the Osage people.

The government built a fort here in 1824. As the Indian Removals began, more tribes came into the area—Cherokees, then Creeks. A pivotal Civil War battle was also fought near here.

To learn more about the history of the area, visit these sites:

CONOCO MUSEUM
501 W. South Ave.
(580) 765-8687
www.conocomuseum.com

Here's a great little museum with lots of informa-tion about how the oil industry works. It would be easier to enjoy if you could forget that its start was so disastrous to E. W. Marland. You'll learn that story at the Marland Mansion; it's very lightly touched on in the museum. Still, there are lots of interesting displays showing the evolution of technology and the advanced equipment and techniques for extracting oil, both on land and under the sea.

FIVE CIVILIZED TRIBES MUSEUM $
1101 Honor Heights Dr.
(918) 683-1701
www.fivetribes.org

Originally the home of the Bureau of Indian Affairs Agency, the museum's 1875 building is on the National Register of Historic Places. Displays on the lower level feature art and artifacts of the Cherokee, Chickasaw, Choctaw, Creek, and Seminole tribes. Photos, jewelry, pottery, baskets, clothing, and documents are among the exhibits. Upstairs is a gallery where Native American art is exhibited.

HONOR HEIGHTS PARK
641 Park Hill Dr.
(918) 684-6302
www.discoverourtown.com

Not so historic, but nonetheless an important local attraction, Honor Heights Park, dedicated in 1920, attracts thousands of visitors every spring with its amazing display of color. Over 35,000 aza-leas, tulips, daffodils, and redbud and dogwood trees put on a spring show that has cameras clicking all over the 113-acre park.

MARLAND MANSION $$
901 Monument Rd.
(580) 767-0420, (800) 422-8340
www.marlandmansion.com

Built between 1925 and 1928, this was the sec-ond Ponca City home built by Pennsylvania oil entrepreneur E. W. Marland. Marland rode a roller coaster of booms and busts, making and losing fortunes. He was on top of the world when he built the palace on the prairie—an Italianate palazzo with Waterford crystal chandeliers, hand-painted ceilings, and paneling of rare pollard oak from the English royal forests, cut with permission of the king.

Marland's personal life was as interesting as his home—and fodder for the tabloids of the time. The head of his own oil company, Marland Oil, he was snookered by the "wolves of Wall Street" and J. P. Morgan, who took over the company. Never one to stay down long, Marland later rose to the U.S. House of Representatives and became governor of Oklahoma.

The museum is open daily (except major holidays), with guided tours at 1:30 p.m. on weekdays and 1:30 and 3:00 p.m. on Sat and Sun.

PONCA CITY

Like a number of Oklahoma cities, Ponca City was founded as a result of a land run—this one, the Run of 1993, opened up the Cherokee Strip to development. The Strip was a skinny piece of land 58 miles wide and approximately 225 miles long. Originally called the Cherokee Outlet, the land had been assigned to the Cherokee Nation as an outlet to hunting grounds in the Rocky Mountains. The Cherokees leased some of the land to ranchers, and cattle drives came through regularly. The government eventually bought the land (at about $1.40 an acre) from the Indians and opened the Outlet plus some Pawnee and Tonkawa lands for settlement on September 16, 1993.

Oil has been the major influence in Ponca City's history, with E. W. Marland and Marland Oil kicking the action off. The company morphed into Continental Oil, then Conoco, and finally ConocoPhillips. Although the company is now headquartered in Houston, there's still a significant presence in town. Major attractions reflect Ponca's petroleum heritage.

STANDING BEAR PARK
2401 S. 7th St.
(580) 762-1514
www.standingbearpark.com
Standing Bear was a chief of the Ponca Indians when they were moved from Nebraska in the

1870s. This was, in essence, their Trail of Tears. Many Poncas died on the trip and, once in Oklahoma, did not thrive. Standing Bear's son was one of the people who became ill. Realizing that he was going to die, he made his father promise him that he would be buried in the land of his ancestors.

When Standing Bear and some of his tribe tried to take the boy's body north to Nebraska, they were arrested and imprisoned. Up until this time, the law had not recognized civil rights for Indians, who were not considered "persons." Standing Bear's eloquent plea at his trial, an echo of Shylock's speech in The Merchant of Venice, convinced the judge, who ruled that Standing Bear must be considered a person under the law, giving important recognition of the worth and dignity of Native Americans.

The museum and outdoor exhibits in Standing Bear Park salute the six tribes in the area—the Ponca, the Otoe-Missouria, the Kaw, the Tonkawa, the Pawnee, and the Osage. A statue of Standing Bear is a focal point of the landscape, and there's also a labyrinth on the grounds.

THREE RIVERS MUSEUM $
220 Elgin Ave.
(918) 686-6624
www.3riversmuseum.com
Just as three rivers watered the area, three groups—Native Americans, blacks, and Anglos—were part of building Muskogee and the surrounding area. Exhibits highlight early pioneers, including Miss Alice Robertson, Oklahoma's first congresswoman; early institutions; and transportation.

The museum is housed in the 1916 Midland Valley Railroad Depot. It is open Wed through Sat.

ROUTE 66 NORTHEAST FROM TULSA TO MIAMI

Route 66, the Mother Road, America's Main Street, the Will Rogers Highway—by whatever name it was known, it stretched 2,448 miles from Chicago to Santa Monica, California. Birthed from America's flowering affection for the automobile, it was midwifed by Tulsa's own Cyrus Avery in the '20s. Oklahoma has about 400 miles of Route 66 and more miles of original alignment than any of the other seven states it passes through. The highway was decertified in 1985, so it's not always easy to find. Oklahoma Official State Maps have portions of it marked as State Highway 66, but if you're really serious about following the old road—and want to stay off the interstate as much as possible —you'll need a detailed map like the ones produced by the Oklahoma Route 66 Association. Sometimes you can find them at state visitor centers, sometimes not. The best thing to do is order one from the association. Their Web site is www.oklahomaroute66.com (click on "Store").

A good starting place in Tulsa is the Warehouse Market Building at East 10th St. and South Elgin Avenue. If you haven't done the art deco driving tour, take time to look at this beauty— built in 1929 and a landmark on Route 66. From here, head east on East 11th St. This was Route 66. Stay on East 11th all the way to South 193rd East Avenue. (Remember, streets in Tulsa go east and west, avenues go north and south.) Turn north. This next part is tricky since road construction on I-44 is expected to continue for some time. There are two options: Get onto I-44 but watch closely for the exit to Catoosa, or continue north, under the highway, and quickly make a right turn on South Cherokee Street, which angles northeast. There may be signs pointing you to Route 66—if so, follow them. Otherwise, turn right on East Pine Street and you'll get there.

i To enjoy a classic Route 66 memory, drive on 11th St. Just east of Peoria, you'll see a 1930s-era neon MEADOW GOLD sign. It's about a mile west of its original spot, but it's the same height and facing the same direction as it did 70-plus years ago. It sits atop a commemorative plaza.

Catoosa

The Catoosa 66 icon is the **Blue Whale** on the west side of the road. There's a small parking lot,

and you should be able to get out and see the whale. This was actually built several years after the eclipse of the historic highway by the interstate. Hugh Davis built the structure for his wife as an anniversary present in 1972. She must have been the girl who had everything. In its heyday it was a popular spot for local kids who enjoyed diving and sliding into the water from the happy cerulean cetacean. Today it attracts photographers and nostalgia buffs, but its days as the hit of the old swimming hole are long gone.

Chelsea

As you go through Chelsea, detour long enough to drive by the **Hogue House** at 1001 S. Olive St. This is a Sears Roebuck home, ordered from Chicago and shipped, precut, by rail. It cost $1,600 in 1913. The Hogue House is a private home, so no touring—but you can snap all the photos you want.

On your way out of town, look for the Chelsea Motel sign. It's not particularly scenic, but it is a relic of the Mother Road.

Claremore

J.M. DAVIS ARMS AND HISTORICAL MUSEUM
333 N. Lynn Riggs Blvd. (Hwy. 66)
(918) 341-5707
www.thegunmuseum.com
The J.M. Davis Gun Museum is a thoroughly modern building with row after row of cases with well-presented items. The facility could be the envy of many other museums around the country. The fact that it contains over 20,000 guns and related items, plus 1,200 beer steins, makes this place Bubba heaven. There are also assorted musical instruments, Victorian statuary, music boxes, and knives and swords. You may find yourself singing a paraphrase of that old Paul Simon song, "Fifty Ways to Cleave Your Lover." The museum is open every day except Christmas and Thanksgiving. With all the items, you're sure to find something that catches your interest, even if you're not a firearms fan.

WILL ROGERS MEMORIAL
1720 W. Will Rogers Blvd.
(918) 341-0719
www.willrogers.com

You'll have to turn off Route 66 to make this stop. You'll see signs to the Memorial. If you thought Will Rogers was just the Jay Leno of his day, you have a lot to learn. And you'll learn it here at the Will Rogers Memorial.

As you enter the museum, you'll be greeted by a life-size portrait of Will Rogers by Charles Banks Wilson. Inside, you'll learn that Rogers was successful in every communications medium of his day—he wrote for newspapers, appeared on stage and in the movies, and was a hit on broadcast radio. He was one of the nation's most loved figures. Rogers's folksy common sense made people laugh and made people think. Take time to read some of his quotes. They're as timely today as they were in the early 1930s. He helped the nation survive the Great Depression, and his words again translate across the decades: "… every international banker ought to have printed on his office door, 'Alive today by the grace of a nation that has a sense of humor.'"

Exhibits include artifacts and photographs, his saddle collection, memorabilia from his days in vaudeville and the Ziegfeld Follies, and newspaper front pages announcing the deaths of Will Rogers and Wiley Post in a plane crash near Point Barrow, Alaska. Most poignant are items found in the plane's wreckage.

Another exhibit is related to Will's and Walt Disney's love of the game of polo. Walt was actually working on a Donald Duck cartoon featuring a polo game including Will Rogers, Laurel and Hardy, and Harpo Marx among the players. When he heard of Will's death, he removed his drawings of Will from the cartoon out of respect for him and his family.

There are several theater areas in the museum. A couple show Will's films, while another shows a film about Will himself. If you really take time to peruse all the materials available here, you'll spend several hours.

Be sure and rub the toe of Jo Davidson's heroic statue of Will, *Never Met a Man I Didn't Like.*

The statue was cast twice. The other one is in the National Hall of Statuary in the United States Capitol.

The museum overlooks Will Rogers's tomb, marked by the statue of Will on his favorite horse, Soapsuds. The statue was created by Electra Waggoner and is called *Riding into the Sunset.*

Will purchased this property, not far from his birthplace near Oologah, in 1911. He intended to retire here.

The Will Rogers Memorial is open every day. Admission is free but contributions are gratefully accepted.

While you're this close, you might be interested in detouring a bit farther and stopping by Will Rogers's birthplace, the Dog Iron Ranch, near Oologah. It's just about 15 minutes northwest of the Memorial.

Will Rogers was born in the southeast bedroom of this white, log-walled frame house on November 4, 1879. The house was built around 1870 and was originally located less than a mile from here. When Lake Oologah was under construction, the house, which would have been under water, was moved.

The family was comfortably situated, and Will's father, Clem Rogers, was highly respected. He served five terms in the Cherokee Senate and was a delegate to the Oklahoma Constitutional Convention. Rogers County was named for him. Will lived here until his mother died in 1890 and his father moved to Claremore.

The large barn is not original to the property but was erected by Amish craftsmen in 1993 as a structure typical of the period. You'll see goats, donkeys, horses, and longhorn cattle on the ranch. And you'll get a beautiful view of Lake Oologah from Will's front porch.

You may wonder about an orange windsock as you walk across the driveway. A weathered sign will tell you that this grass field is actually an airfield dedicated in July 1931 by Will Rogers, Wiley Post, and Harold Gatty. (Post had just completed his record-breaking flight around the world with Gatty as his navigator.)

For a reasonable rate, you can camp with an RV here for up to four nights. There's a bathroom and there are hookups for electricity.

Foyil

TOTEM POLE PARK
21250 E. Hwy. 28A
(918) 342-9149

About 4 miles east of Route 66 on OK 28A is Ed Galloway's Totem Pole Park. You can bet that Mother Roaders made this detour—it's just the kind of quirky place that made the traveling so appealing. Ed Galloway taught woodworking at a school for fatherless boys from 1911 to 1936. In the summer he and his wife, Villie, often invited students to come camping on 20 acres the Galloways owned near Foyil. In 1936 he began building a stone house on the property. Many of the rocks had been gathered by the boys on their summer excursions. Although Galloway wasn't a trained mason, he was good at figuring things out and finished the house within a year.

It was then that he began the work for which he would become noted. He wanted to create a tribute to the American Indian by building the tallest totem pole in the world.

Using a framework of steel and stones, he added concrete, one bucket at a time, carving as he went. When finished, the largest of the structures he built stood 90 feet tall. It took 11 years to complete, with 28 tons of cement, 6 tons of steel, and 100 tons of sand and rock. More than 200 carved pictures, including 9-foot-tall standing portraits of Geronimo, Sitting Bull, Chief Joseph, and an unnamed Comanche chief, cover the totem. And he didn't stop there.

In addition to his concrete creations, Galloway carved approximately 300 violins, each of a different kind of wood. If the Fiddle House is open, you'll be able to see them plus other carved pieces. There's a tiny gift shop in the Fiddle House. The hours are limited because the shop is dependent on volunteers, but even if it's closed you can enjoy a lot of Galloway's work. Call ahead to check on hours. Admission is free, but they'll really appreciate a purchase or donation.

Miami

COLEMAN THEATRE
103 N. Main St.
(918) 540-2425
www.colemantheatre.org

The do-not-miss attraction in Miami is the Coleman Theatre, a 1929 combination vaudeville theater and movie palace. Built by George Coleman, a local mining magnate, it featured a Spanish Mission Revival exterior with a Louis XV interior.

Though the theater never closed, it did go through a period of serious stagnation. The Coleman family gave it to the City of Miami in 1989. Hundreds of hours of work from a cadre of dedicated volunteers has restored the luster to the theater. Gold leaf, stained glass, and sparkling crystal kindle the imagination. And you may have a fleeting thought of the Phantom of the Opera when you see the elegant, 2,000-pound glass, brass, and crystal chandelier. It had been stored in a barn for years before being rediscovered, refurbished, and reinstalled in its original location.

The theater is open for tours Tues through Sat. Call for times. Or check the Web site for events—lots of plays and musical presentations happen here. And, if you're really lucky, you might get to hear the Mighty Wurlitzer. Tours are free but a donation is appropriate.

i Practice before you go. In Oklahoma, Miami is pronounced "my-am-uh" not "my-am-ee."

Vinita

SUMMERSIDE VINEYARDS AND WINERY $ (BISTRO)
441251 E. Historic Route 66
(888) 508-WINE
www.summersidevineyards.com

There's a charming little winery here with a tasting room, gift shop, and a bistro that is open for lunch Thursday through Sunday. They produce a number of varieties of wine, but their cream sherry has won so many awards it is usually wait-listed.

Try to plan your trip so you can have lunch here. The homemade soup is always good, the salads are wonderful, and the sandwiches are great, too. The ginger salad is quite popular—crisp greens, dried blueberries, mandarin oranges, toasted almonds, blue cheese, and Asian ginger dressing with shrimp.

If you've already eaten, at least have some of their artisan foccacia made with rosemary, olives, and almonds and served warm with olive oil and pesto dipping spices. And take time to look at the unusual gift items.

ROUTE 66 SOUTHWEST FROM TULSA TO ARCADIA

Arcadia

You can't miss the iconic **round barn**—stop and check it out. It was built in 1898, and the inside of the round roof is as beautiful as any woven basket. And just on the other side of town you'll see a giant pop bottle—a striking architectural structure that is 66 feet tall. Probably the fanciest filling station in Oklahoma, this is **Pop's.** Their claim to fame—aside from the amazing architecture—is that they carry over 500 kinds of soda pop. You'll find everything from Abbondio Pompelmo & Fragola to Zenmaster Blackberry Cream. And their hamburgers are great.

You're now approaching Edmond and Oklahoma City. And this Route 66 day trip stops here! There's way too much to do in that area—it's worthy of a several-day stay. We suggest you get *Insiders' Guide Oklahoma City* and do it right!

Bristow

Bristow boasts that it has more miles of brick streets than any other Oklahoma town. Notice the vintage brick buildings as you drive through.

Chandler

The **Route 66 Interpretive Center** is a must—unless you're here at the wrong time. As of press time, it was only open in the summer, Tuesday through Saturday. You might want to check this out ahead of time at www.route66interpretive-center.org, or call (405) 258-1300. The exhibits are neat, but perhaps the most interesting thing is

how the staff dealt with displaying things without using walls. It's in the old red rock armory.

As you drive through town, watch the west side of the street for the great little **Phillips 66 station**—the restoration was done carefully.

Davenport

If you didn't have a bite at the Rock Café, you might want to make a stop in Davenport. **Dan's Bar-B-Que Pit** isn't fancy, but it has great 'cue.

Sapulpa

Sapulpa was once home to two brick plants and four glass plants. It's also the home of **Frankoma Pottery,** which sits on an old alignment of Route 66, now called Frankoma Road. Though no longer owned by the Frank family, the company continues to make pottery from Oklahoma red clay. Stop by the plant, factory store, and museum.

Stroud

If it's close to lunch, stop at the 1939 **Rock Café.** This structure has been a fixture on the highway since 1939. The inside is not that old—it burned a year or so ago, but the walls are original. Just don't expect them to light a fire in the fireplace. If you've seen the movie *Cars,* the character Sally Carrera was based on owner Dawn Welch.

On your way out of town, stop at **Stable Ridge Winery,** 2016 Route 66 West. The tasting room is in a turn-of-the-last-century church. Stable Ridge has garnered a number of international medals for its wines.

Here's another option—detour north up OK 99 to **Territory Cellars,** another winery. In addition to wine, they serve lunch and dinner on Thurs and Fri. Ask about their grape ice cream—yum.

TAHLEQUAH

Tahlequah is the capital of the Cherokee Nation, and this is the place to come to learn about the Cherokees and their history. Even the street signs are in English and Cherokee.

Cherokees began coming to the area in the early 1800s—even before the infamous Trail of

Tears. To learn more about Cherokee history, you won't do better than a visit to the Cherokee Heritage Center and the Murrell home just south of town.

Other local attractions include a driving tour of the historic residential area, the Thompson House (a furnished Queen Anne Carpenter Gothic home that is listed on the National Register of Historic Places), and Seminary Hall at Northeastern State University. This building dates back to the late 1880s but traces its roots back to the original Cherokee National Female Seminary, which began in the mid-1800s. Pick up brochures at the Talequah Area Chamber of Commerce Visitor Center, 123 E. Delaware St.

During the summer, check for the schedule of weekend shows produced by the talented students at Northeastern State University. With two theaters going, you can have a little bit of country or perhaps some rock 'n' roll.

The town also has some interesting boutiques, antique shopping, and good places to eat. A large carved statue of Ganesha isn't easy to find in Oklahoma, but you'll find one at the Iguana Cafe, an eclectic eatery with great sandwiches. Patrons praise the pizza at Sam and Ella's—and, yes, if you say it fast, it was named after a bad bug! Don't let that stop you—the food's fine and perfectly safe.

CHEROKEE HERITAGE CENTER $$
21192 S. Keeler Dr., Park Hill
(888) 999-6007
www.cherokeeheritage.org

The Cherokee Heritage Center offers a broad-brush picture of Cherokee history from early days in their eastern homes through the Trail of Tears to Oklahoma. The Ancient Village, Tsa-La-Gi, is a living-history village depicting Cherokee life before European contact. Interpreters demonstrate basket making, pottery, stickball, bow and arrow making, and canoe building. During the summer, activity is at its height with the largest number of interpreters on site.

Another area of the grounds, Adams Corner, illustrates life in a late-1800s village. The buildings here include restored structures dating between 1875 and 1890 and have been brought here from a variety of locations in Indian Territory.

Inside the main building is a museum, gift shop, and small snack bar. The premier exhibit in the museum deals with the Trail of Tears. The displays tell the stories of pre-removal days and the first treacherous treaties, the vicious treatment of the Indians by many of the soldiers, and recorded stories from the removals of other tribes.

One of the most moving areas of the exhibition is the display of life-size figures on the trail. Across one side of the room is a large tapestry of 16,000 black, white, and red beads representing the Cherokees who were driven to Oklahoma on the Trail of Tears. Twelve-thousand white beads represent those who survived the trip. The black beads represent a conservative estimate of those who died, and the red beads represent the 2,000 additional victims as estimated by Elijah Butler, the physician for the first detachment on the trail.

Visitors in June, July, and the first half of Aug have the opportunity to see the presentation *Under the Cherokee Moon* on Friday and Saturday evenings. There's also an optional dinner preceding the show. Tickets to these events are not included in the general admission price.

ILLINOIS RIVER

The Illinois River is Oklahoma 's favorite place to float, kayak, or canoe. There are approximately a dozen outfitters who rent watercraft; most will help with drop-offs and pickups. Prices vary widely and depend on the type of watercraft you choose, which day you go, and how far you want to float. Two good choices include

MURRELL HOUSE "HUNTER'S HOME"
19479 Murrell Home Rd., Park Hill
(918) 456-2751
www.ok-history.mus.ok.us

The Murrell home comes as a real eye-opener to many visitors. It brings home the point that many of the Cherokees who were pushed out of their eastern homes were educated, well-to-do citizens. Built about 1845, "Hunter's Home," named for owner George Murrell's love of foxhunting, is Oklahoma 's only remaining antebellum mansion. The Greek Revival–style, three-story mansion is furnished with pieces from the period. As in the broader society, the Murrells, while not unusual, were not typical. For a look at a typical Cherokee house of the period, visit the log cabin on the property.

Mar through Oct, the house is open Tues through Sun. Nov through Feb, it is open Wed through Sun. Be sure and call ahead or check the Web site to make sure this information is up to date.

SPARROW HAWK CAMP
21985 N. Ben George Rd.
(918) 456-8371
www.sparrowhawkcamp.com

TALL GRASS PRAIRIE PRESERVE
10 miles north of Pawhuska
(918) 287-4803
www.nature.org/wherewework/northamer-ica/states/oklahoma/preserves/tallgrass.html
Once miles and miles of open prairie covered parts of 14 states. Today less than 10 percent of that prairie remains—too small an area to be considered a viable ecosystem. The Nature Conservancy has purchased almost 39,000 acres of the area in hopes of returning it to the functioning and complex combination of plants and animals that it once was.

Two key elements are considered necessary to make that happen—bison, commonly, though incorrectly, called buffalo, and fire. Beginning with a herd of 300 bison in 1989, a herd that now numbers 2,600, and, using prescribed burns, the conservancy replicates the natural incidents that remove dead vegetation, control invasive vegetation, and increase the hardiness and productivity of many of the native plants.

Visitors to the preserve take a looping route on county roads, some paved, some gravel, through waving grass and colorful wildflowers. It's not unusual to spot bison—you may even encounter some in the road—but even though there are a lot of animals, they have a lot of room to roam. There are five scenic turnouts on the route. Fall and spring are best for bird-watching, and wildflowers are prominent in May and June and again in late summer. Bison calving season is April through June, with a peak in May. Other prairie inhabitants include white-tailed deer, armadillos, beavers, woodchucks, badgers, coyotes, bobcats, opossums, and skunks.

A leisurely drive takes about two hours. There are picnic tables near the preserve headquarters and a couple of walking trails. The preserve is open every day from dawn to dusk. The visitor center is staffed by volunteers and is open regularly between mid-Mar and Nov. Other times it's catch as catch can. There is no admission charge to the preserve.

WAR EAGLE RESORT
13020 N. Hwy. 10
(918) 456-6272, (800) 722-3834
www.wareagleresort.com

RELOCATION

There's a lot of evidence that Tulsa is a great place to relocate—to live, to grow a business. In the first half of 2009 alone, Tulsa made a number of impressive lists. Forbes.com ranked the city as the fifth most livable in the nation. Relocate-America named it the number one place to live, and the Brookings Institute placed it second of the nation's 100 largest metropolitan areas on its listing of top-performing cities during the recession, through the first quarter.

Now that you've picked Tulsa, you'll need to decide where in Tulsa you want to live. And how you want to live. Are you an apartment person or do you want a lot of space? Do you like historic areas or are you set on something brand new? Are schools a factor in your decision? What about transportation—do you want to walk or ride to work, take public transportation, or are you sticking with your own vehicle? How close do you want to be to cultural activities, parks, work, or sports facilities?

Don't let the decisions put you into a tizzy. Pick your top two or three priorities. Tulsa's not so big that you're really going to have to sacrifice much anywhere you choose.

OVERVIEW

Tulsa has traditionally fanned out from downtown to the east and the south. Downtown is basically defined by the highways that surround it—I-444 on the south and east, I-244 on the west and the north.

Uptown is a small area just south of downtown and includes a burgeoning eating and entertainment area known as SoBo (South Boston). Boundaries are a bit blurred and often depend on whom you ask. Both south and east of uptown is midtown. Probably the broadest categorizations would be downtown, uptown, midtown, south Tulsa, north Tulsa, east Tulsa, and west Tulsa.

GETTING ESTABLISHED

Relocating involves lots of little details. This chapter attempts to organize the information you need to get settled quickly. It won't answer all your questions or solve all your problems, but, hopefully, it will be able to point you in the right direction. More detailed information on schools, hospitals, retirement, and churches will be found in individual chapters.

METRO GOVERNMENT

CITY OF TULSA
One Technology Center
175 East 2nd St.
(918) 596-2100 (Mayor's Action Line)
www.cityoftulsa.org

The City of Tulsa Web site has all sorts of information—city services, public safety, community programs, environmental programs, city departments, you name it. There's so much information on the Web site, it can get frustrating trying to find exactly what you want. You may be tempted to bypass the Web site and call. Lots of people do this, so expect to be put on hold. Be patient; you won't have to go through a series of choices. Your call will be answered by a real live person (who will probably tell you that the information is available on the Web site).

i Among all charitable foundations in the United States, the Tulsa Community Foundation ranks 16th—ahead of such notables as the Carnegie, Mott, Annenberg, Doris Duke, Walton Family, and Don Reynolds Foundations.

CHAMBERS OF COMMERCE AND VISITORS BUREAUS

Chambers of commerce can give you general information about living and doing business in Tulsa. They'll give you a relocation packet that has a lot of the information you'll find here plus a Convention & Visitors Bureau (CVB) visitor guide and calendar of events. Keep in mind that lots of times, listings are purchased and there's only one included in a category. Convention & Visitors Bureaus tell you what to do and where to eat and stay. Chambers and CVBs often work closely together, and some of the smaller communities only have chambers. The Tulsa Chamber of Commerce was named "2008 Chamber of the Year" by the American Chamber of Commerce Executives.

GREENWOOD CHAMBER OF COMMERCE
(918) 585-2084
www.greenwoodchambertulsa.com

OKLAHOMA BLACK CHAMBER OF COMMERCE
(918) 712-4181
www.oklahomablackchamber.org

TULSA CHAMBER OF COMMERCE
(918) 585-1201
www.tulsachamber.com

TULSA CONVENTION AND VISITORS BUREAU
(800) 558-3311
www.visittulsa.com

UTILITY CONNECTIONS

For service information about areas not listed here, contact the local chamber of commerce or check www.tulsa.com.

Cable and Satellite
COX COMMUNICATIONS
(918) 806-6000
www.cox.com

DIRECTV
(918) 280-2200
www.directv.com

Electricity
PUBLIC SERVICE COMPANY OF OKLAHOMA
(888) 216-3523
www.psoklahoma.com

Natural Gas
OKLAHOMA NATURAL GAS
(918) 834-8000
www.ong.com

Phone Service
AT&T supplies service to most of Tulsa's residents, but there are several other companies that offer telephone options.

AT&T
(800) 464-7928
www.att.com

COX COMMUNICATIONS
(918) 806-6000
www.cox.com

Water, Sewer, and Trash Services
CITY OF TULSA
(918) 596-9511
www.cityoftulsa.org/city-services/utilities.aspx

DRIVER'S LICENSE

For an initial license, a written test as well as a driving test administered by an examiner from the Department of Public Safety are required. Manuals are available at most Oklahoma Tag Agencies or online at www.dps.state.ok.us/dls/pub/ODM.pdf.

If you have a valid driver's license from another state, first make sure your vehicles are registered in Oklahoma. You can do that at any tag agency. After that, you can go to any Driver's License Exam Station (see locations below).

Often, written and driving tests are waived. You will probably have to take a vision test.

You should have two forms of identification with you. Your out-of-state driver's license will serve as one form. You definitely need proof of citizenship—a birth certificate, passport, naturalization papers—something that proves you are not here illegally.

Be prepared for a wait—this process can be harrowing. Go as early as you can. The last test is often administered well before closing time.

Tulsa Exam Stations include:

EASTGATE METROPLEX
14002 E. 21st St., Suite A, lower level
(918) 632-7700

3190 W. 21st St. South
(918) 428-4030

OAK CREST SHOPPING CENTER
Broken Arrow
1635 S. Main St.
(918) 259-0764

VOTER REGISTRATION

TULSA COUNTY ELECTION BOARD
555 N. Denver Ave.
(918) 596-5780
www.tulsacounty.org
You can register to vote if you are at least 18 years old, a U.S. citizen, and a resident of Oklahoma. There are some exceptions, so check the State Election Board Web site (www.ok.gov/-elections/voterreg.html) for details. Voter registration applications are available at the County Election Board, post offices, tag agencies, libraries, and other public locations. Or download an application form on the state board Web site.

You can register at any time, but no voter identification cards will be issued during the 24 days before an election. Oklahoma has a closed primary system. You can only vote in the primary and runoff elections for candidates in the party from which you are registered. Judicial offices and state questions are nonpartisan, and all voters are eligible.

NEIGHBORHOODS AND NEARBY COMMUNITIES

Downtown Tulsa

This is an area of oil boom elegance, of tall business buildings, the shiny BOK Center, and the Performing Arts Center (PAC). It also includes the Brady Arts District—an up-on-coming entertainment area with restaurants, clubs, and such classics as Cain's Ballroom and the Brady Theater. The Blue Dome District, another entertainment area, takes its name from a 1925 filling station with a distinctive blue dome. Greenwood, just north of the business district was once known as "The Black Wall Street," and East Village is the area bordered by the Katy Railway, East 7th St., South Detroit Avenue, and US 75. The Pearl is defined on the west by US 75, the east by South Utica Avenue, the south by East 11th St., and on the north by I-244. Within these areas are some emerging housing possibilities, including lofts and the beautiful Village at Central Park—described as Oklahoma's first "new urbanist" neighborhood, it was built for walkability and convenience and won the Sierra Club's Earthcare Award.

Odd One Out

Crosbie Heights, just west of downtown, south of West 2nd St., between Nogales and Newblock Park and ending at West 7th St., was developed in 1908. It is one of Tulsa's oldest neighborhoods. As a middle-class area, it hit the skids a number of years ago. But it's on the road to becoming fashionable for families looking for close-in houses at good prices. The area suffered from lack of access to convenient shopping—there was no place to stop for groceries that was handy. Now there's a neighborhood grocery store—the Blue Jackalope—and a place where neighbors can get together and discuss what's going on. It's becoming an involved and interesting community and an area worth giving a second look.

Uptown

This is a small area south of downtown where you'll find the Council Oak, the Ambassador

Hotel, and the SoBo entertainment area. There's some residential housing here but not as much as in midtown.

Midtown

Here's an area with cachet. Just east and south of downtown, the area is contained by the Arkansas River on the west and South Yale Avenue on the east. It starts just south of the ambiguous downtown border (with midtown squished in there somehow) and ends at approximately East 51st St. This includes some of the town's priciest real estate—with Utica Square and the Philbrook in the heart of it. It also encompasses funky Cherry Street and fashionable Brookside.

New lofts are springing up near Cherry Street. Most of the area is residential, though it's hard to tell because the main streets sport strings of businesses. But get off the biggies and you'll find some charming neighborhoods.

South Tulsa

This area includes pretty much all of Tulsa south of 51st St. New developments crowd up against older neighborhoods. You'll find a wide variety of housing prices in this part of town. In the southeast corner of this area, the Union School District overlaps Tulsa and Broken Arrow. The area is so large you can find almost anything here, including some of Tulsa's most exclusive housing. There are huge malls and several large medical complexes.

East Tulsa

This is a suburban area between East Admiral Place and East 21st St. and stretching to Mingo. It's characterized by smaller, middle-class homes and is bisected by a good-size portion of old Route 66. The Fairgrounds are on the western edge of the district, as is Whittier Square, Tulsa's first suburban shopping center.

West Tulsa

The northern part of this section of Tulsa holds lots of remnants of Tulsa's more active oil days, with refineries and industrial developments close

to the river. There is some nice real estate here—you just have to look a bit harder for it. Farther south you'll find The Oaks Country Club and a lot of development going on around West 71st and US 75.

North Tulsa

There are some very historic areas on this side of Tulsa. Greenwood hugs the border between downtown and North Tulsa. Just to the west of Greenwood is Brady Heights, developed just after the turn of the last century, an area once known as the "Silk Stocking District." A middle- and upper-class area, the houses range from Victorian to prairie style. West of the Tisdale Parkway is an interesting area with several large, impressive homes. This property once belonged to Dr. Samuel Kennedy, one of Tulsa's first physicians. The Kennedy Mansion Bed and Breakfast is here. The area was late in developing because Dr. Kennedy got into a fuss with the city and stipulated in his will that the property should not be developed until 20 years after his death. The Tulsa Country Club is in this area—on land they obtained from Dr. Kennedy. Farther to the west is the Gilcrease Museum and Gilcrease Heights. The area also encompasses Mohawk Park, the Tulsa Zoo, and Tulsa International Airport.

SURROUNDING COMMUNITIES

Bixby

Still retaining its rural roots, Bixby is noted for fresh, locally grown vegetables. Their Green Corn Festival celebrates one of their most popular crops. Real estate is good in Bixby and buyers have many choices—from large, rural lots to smaller, traditional houses in town, as well as homes in new housing areas. The schools have a good reputation, and there is a charming park along the Arkansas River.

Broken Arrow

Broken Arrow is the fourth largest city in Oklahoma—about 90,000 people. It still has a small-town downtown, but it's moving fast in adding

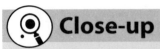 **Close-up**

Dennis R. Neill Equality Center

Oklahoma has some loud voices who've gotten a lot a publicity for their stances against gay rights. This has raised questions with companies who have LGBT employees and are considering moving them to Tulsa. The good news is, don't believe everything you hear. Tulsa, on the whole, is a welcoming and safe community. Its LGBT citizens participate fully in community activities, and there are few nonprofit organizations that don't benefit from their participation and talents. Eighteen churches, a synagogue, and even a Moslem organization have formally declared themselves "open and affirming."

Originally called Oklahomans for Human Rights, the group later changed its name to Tulsa Oklahomans for Human Rights, and now the organization is known as Oklahomans for Equality. Their name has changed but their goals haven't. Headquarters for the group is the Dennis R. Neill Equality Center, named for the center's top benefactor.

This is a primary resource for LGBT people considering a move to Tulsa. Their Web site provides a lot of community information. But this organization and this building are not just for the LGBT community. The facility hosts dances, movie nights, art shows, and more—and they're always open to the public.

restaurants, hotels, and upscale amenities. The school district has an excellent reputation, and there are many new housing developments in the area. For several consecutive years, the city has been named to *Money* magazine's list of "Top 100 Places to Live." Broken Arrow's also been rated the "safest city in Oklahoma." Broken Arrow is probably the fastest growing town in the Tulsa Metropolitan Statistical Area (MSA).

Jenks

Jenks is a really cool little community that has come to life with developments on the Arkansas River. And there's a big development designed to tie the River Walk Crossing to the historic downtown. With good schools and easy access to lots of activities and shopping, Jenks is a popular choice for newcomers. It's home to the Oklahoma Aquarium and is known as the "Antiques Capital of Oklahoma." Even with its proximity to big city amenities, the town retains small-town friendliness with events like the spring herb festival and an October festival of art, wine, and jazz.

Owasso

Owasso, north of Tulsa, has been slower to grow than some of the southern suburbs, but it's taken

off now. In 2009, BusinessWeek.com included Owasso on its list of "America's Biggest Boomtowns." The ranking reflected the city's growth, the quality of schools, infrastructure, accessibility, and retail growth. Owasso's also the home of Stone Canyon, Oklahoma's newest and largest Planned Unit Development. Planned as a community of 10,000 people, the area already has a new school. It also has a beautiful new private golf club with a Robert Trent Jones course. Owasso's also home to Garth Brooks and Trisha Yearwood who live on a ranch east of town.

REALTORS

There are hundreds of Realtors in the area and dozens of real-estate firms. The following names are just a few of many capable Realtors. Each Realtor listed is a certified residential specialist—that means advanced training in listing and selling and meeting rigorous production requirements. Less than 4 percent of all Realtors nationwide receive this certification. Each of the following individuals will be more than happy to help you find just the right home in Tulsa.

BONNIE GROSS CRS
Coldwell Banker Select
9455 N. Owasso Expressway, Suite M,
Owasso
(918) 272-9557 (office)
(918) 695-8487 (cell)
bgross@cbtulsa.com (e-mail)

CORRIE EGGE CRS, BROKER ASSOCIATE
Coldwell Banker Select
501 S. Aspen Ave., Broken Arrow
(918) 259-5242 (office)
(918) 230-8433 (cell)
cegge@cbtulsa.com (e-mail)

PAT HAMILTON CRS, BROKER ASSOCIATE
ERA John Hausam Realtors
6550 E. 71st St.
(918) 492-2000 (office)
(918) 230-9703 (cell)
pat.hamilton@era.com (e-mail)

PAT ROBERTSON CRS, BROKER ASSOCIATE
Keller-Williams Realty
2651 E. 21st St., Suite 100
(918) 712-2252 (office)
(918) 740-2436 (cell)
probertson@kw.com (e-mail)

RAY RICHARDSON CRS, GRI
RE/MAX Executives
7615 E. 63rd Place, Suite 105
(918) 254-0600 (office)
(918) 605-8952 (cell)
rayrichardson@cox.net (e-mail)

HEALTH CARE AND WELLNESS

Tulsans have many excellent options available for health care. With three major medical centers and several other hospitals, 1,800 doctors, 400 dentists, 'round-the-clock air and ground emergency medical transportation, and enhanced 911, citizens are well served.

The three biggest organizations are St. John Medical Center, Hillcrest Medical Center, and St. Francis Health System. From the latest technology to something as simple as the surgical checklist devised at the instigation of the World Health Organization, each of the hospitals strives to provide the best patient care.

Other hospitals include SouthCrest, the Orthopedic Hospital of Oklahoma, and Cancer Treatment Centers of America at Southwestern Regional Medical Center. A key provider in the health-care spectrum is the Oklahoma State University Medical Center, which provides health care for a large portion of the area's uninsured and Medicaid patients. It is also the teaching hospital for the Oklahoma State University College of Osteopathic Medicine. The University of Oklahoma School of Community Medicine is rapidly becoming a transforming force in the health of the Tulsa community.

There are a number of urgent-care clinics across town—good for travelers and after-hours medical problems. Physicians' referral numbers are given in the Insiders' Tip box.

Health care is no longer just about treating illness or injury. An important component is prevention. There are numerous entities in the area—from hospitals to city parks—that are working to provide opportunities for improving health and fitness.

And just the lifestyle being promoted through initiatives like the mayor's Million Miles challenge encourages Tulsans to take responsibility for their own health.

Hopefully, your stay in Tulsa will be both happy and healthy and you won't need the information in this chapter. But it's here—just in case.

OVERVIEW

The three largest hospitals are located just east of downtown (Hillcrest), in midtown (St. John), and in south Tulsa (St. Francis). In this section, you'll find addresses for both hospitals and urgent-care centers. You'll also learn a bit about Tulsa's hospitals and some of the programs they're known for. In reality, most people don't get to shop for hospitals; insurance often makes that choice for them—that and where their doctor has privileges.

Although they do not have a hospital in Tulsa, the University of Oklahoma's College of Medicine has a large campus and trains about 40 percent of Tulsa's physicians. The college has several clinics in the area and offers medical services in fields from family medicine to dermatology, geriatrics, and sports medicine.

The University of Oklahoma School of Community Medicine has facilities in several public schools and two low-income housing centers, providing affordable care to underserved populations in the Tulsa area. It has also entered into a partnership with IBM to develop an electronically centralized information base so doctors and other providers can access a number of sources of information about patients.

Most of the urgent-care clinics—the resort for most travelers with medical difficulties—are freestanding, often located close to a hospital. These are the places to go for minor emergencies and illnesses. Of course, if you have serious symptoms, get to one of the hospitals' emergency rooms. If you have chest pains or any other indication of a heart attack or stroke, call 911 immediately.

If your stay in Tulsa is lengthy, or if you are a new resident, you may be interested in some of the wellness programs in town. For short visits, most hotels have fitness facilities, and there's always that wonderful walk along the river for exercise. Curves fitness center locations are included because, with a travel pass, members can work out wherever they go.

Residents have a number of good options. You'll find health clubs and gyms in the phone book. Some hospital-affiliated programs are described here. They're sometimes overlooked—too bad, because you'll find some of the best trainers and fitness experts in these facilities.

URGENT-CARE FACILITIES

ERGENT CARE
9445-C Riverside Dr.
(918) 299-4333
www.ergentcare.com
Open Mon through Sat, 10 a.m. to 10 p.m., and Sun, 2 to 10 p.m. They accept most insurance, including Medicare. No appointment is necessary.

PEDIATRIC URGENT CARE CENTER
7723 E. 91st St.
(918) 895-7808
Open Mon through Fri from 4 to 11 p.m. and on Sat and Sun from 9:30 a.m. until 10 p.m., the facility is attractive and the decor designed to reassure young patients. Services range from treating earaches and sore throats to more serious needs like cuts, broken bones, and asthma attacks. Lab and X-ray services are available. No appointment is necessary. The center accepts most insurance policies and will provide a quick and full report to the child's own doctor.

ST. JOHN URGENT CARE
1717-A S. Utica Ave.
(918) 748-1300

8131 S. Memorial Dr.
(918) 872-6800

The hours are from 9 a.m. until 9 p.m. Mon through Fri and from 10 a.m. to 6 p.m. on Sat and Sun. No appointment is necessary and most insurance plans, including Medicare, are honored.

i When you travel, be sure you have a list of all your medications in your wallet or purse. That's the first thing you'll be asked if you need medical treatment on the road.

WARREN CLINIC URGENT CARE CLINIC
6160 S. Yale Ave., Springer Building
(918) 495-2600
www.warrenclinic.com/services/urgent.aspx
Associated with St. Francis Hospital, the clinic is open from 9 a.m. to 9 p.m. Mon through Sat and from 1 to 9 p.m. on Sun. No appointments are needed and most insurance, including Medicare, is accepted.

HOSPITALS

CANCER TREATMENT CENTERS OF AMERICA AT SOUTHWESTERN REGIONAL MEDICAL CENTER
10109 E. 79th St.
(800) 788-8484
www.cancercenter.com
This specialty hospital employs the latest technologies in surgery, radiation therapy, and chemotherapy and supplements these with nutrition therapy, naturopathic medicine, mind-body medicine, and spiritual support. They specialize in integrative and compassionate care in warm and welcoming facilities. And the facilities are beautiful—with light halls and open courtyards. They even have an RV parking area for patients who live or travel in their RVs.

HILLCREST MEDICAL CENTER
1120 S. Utica Ave.
(918) 574-1000
www.hillcrest.com
Hillcrest Medical Center began as Morningside Hospital and School of Nursing—founded by nurse Dolly Brown McNulty in 1918. The nursing

school, a three-year program, provided thousands of nurses in its 58-year career. Morningside was renamed Hillcrest in 1940.

In its distinguished history, Hillcrest has created a long list of "firsts." Among these accomplishments are Tulsa's first heart surgery program, the city's first family-centered childbirth program, Oklahoma's first burn-treatment center, the state's first hospital-sponsored helicopter ambulance, and Oklahoma's first hospital-based rural outreach program with comprehensive specialty clinics in surrounding communities.

The 691-bed hospital is one of Oklahoma's most respected medical facilities. Some particular points of pride include the Peggy V. Helmerich Women's Health Center, the Spine and Orthopedic Center, the Kaiser Rehabilitation Center, and the Hillcrest Center for Diabetes Management. The latest technology can be found in the Helmerich Cancer Center—the CyberKnife, a computer-controlled radiosurgery system that operates with sub-millimeter accuracy, is being successfully used to treat tumors that were formerly untreatable.

In March 2009 the Oklahoma Heart Institute at Hillcrest opened—the state's largest dedicated heart hospital for the prevention, diagnosis, and treatment of heart disease.

The same year, Hillcrest was designated a "Value Based Care Center," one of five regional centers and the only one in Oklahoma. This is a program from the Centers for Medicare and Medicaid Services designed to provide savings to the system through coordinated care. There are also monetary incentives to participating patients. The plan applies to cardiology care and orthopedic procedures.

OKLAHOMA STATE UNIVERSITY MEDICAL CENTER
744 W. 9th St.
(918) 599-1000
www.osu-medcenter.com
The OSU College of Osteopathic Medicine is recognized as one of the best schools in the nation for primary care. Its 235-bed, acute-care hospital is managed by St. John Health System.

It not only serves as a care-giving facility for the community but as a teaching hospital for the medical school.

The facility is the home of Hillcrest Medical Center's Children and Adolescent Behavioral Health Services and has been included in the National Pediatric Acquired Brain Injury Plan, which seeks to ensure that Oklahoma children with brain injuries receive not only appropriate medical treatment but continuing care and therapies.

This hospital provides health care for the bulk of Tulsa's uninsured and Medicaid patients. They also have a Sleep Lab where patients with sleep apnea, narcolepsy, restless leg syndrome, and other sleep-interrupting problems can be evaluated.

ORTHOPEDIC HOSPITAL OF OKLAHOMA
2408 E. 81st St., Ste. 900
(918) 447-5000
www.orthooklahoma.com
Founded by physicians, OHO is dedicated exclusively to orthopedic surgery and rehabilitative care. OHO is located in south Tulsa in the CityPlex Towers and contains 10 surgical suites for in- and outpatient care, 25 hospital rooms, an imaging center, and a therapy center. Procedures undertaken in the facility include reconstructive surgery, arthroscopy, total joint arthroplasty, treatment of spinal disorders, sports medicine, repair of complex fractures, treatment of hand injuries, microsurgery, and other orthopedic operations.

The physical therapy center focuses on a variety of rehabilitative strategies. An unusual component is the aquatherapy program. The facility includes a SwimEx 600T isokinetic therapy pool with variable depth workstations. Therapy is available at the OHO and three other locations in the area.

ST. JOHN MEDICAL CENTER
1923 S. Utica Ave.
(918) 744-2345
www.sjmc.org
St. John Medical Center, founded in 1926 by the Sisters of the Sorrowful Mother, is part of the Mar-

ian Health System. St. John is a nonprofit facility. Nearly 700 physicians and thousands of other health-care professionals work to bring the best care and latest technology to northeast Oklahoma. The hospital is nationally recognized for the excellence of its cardiovascular, orthopedic, and palliative-care programs.

Saint John's has a few guest rooms available for family members accompanying patients, and they have arrangements with several local hotels for hospital discounted rates.

ST. FRANCIS HEALTH SYSTEM
6161 S. Yale Ave.
(918) 494-2200
www.stfrancis.com

Founded in 1960 as a not-for-profit Catholic health-care organization, St. Francis has grown from a 275-bed building to a massive complex with more than 700 physicians.

The hospital was a gift to the Tulsa community from William K. Warren Sr. and his wife, Natalie Overall Warren.

Notable components of the health-care system include, in addition to the core facility, the Children's Hospital, Natalie Warren Bryant Cancer Center, the Saint Francis Heart Hospital, the Warren Clinic, and the Laureate Psychiatric Clinic and Hospital.

One of the newest additions is an eight-suite surgery center for outpatient procedures. The hospital has also set aside a special area for patients 70 and older. This is the first and only specialty unit designed to improve the hospital experience for senior patients.

SOUTHCREST HOSPITAL
8801 S. 101st East Ave.
(918) 294-4000
www.southcresthospital.com

SouthCrest was founded in 1999 and has 180 licensed beds in its facility. Some of the key services include a Cardiovascular Center, Women's Pavilion and Special Care Nursery, Orthopedics and Neurosciences, an emergency room, and an outpatient diagnostic center.

Tulsans revel in being tops of many lists—except this one. In 2007 Tulsa was rated the worst major city in the United States for spring allergies. The ranking is heavily weather-dependent, so with a colder, longer winter in 2009 the city moved down to number 22. Still, if you have allergies, be alert. For a daily assessment of tree, mold, weeds, and grass irritants, go to www.allergyclinicoftulsa.com.

FITNESS FACILITIES

CHARLES SCHUSTERMAN JEWISH COMMUNITY CENTER
2021 E. 71st St.
(918)495-1111
www.csjcc.org/health-wellness-recreation.htm

Open to the entire community, the facilities include a fitness center with cardio equipment and weight training, personal trainers, classes, squash and racquetball courts, steam rooms, saunas, whirlpools, and massage therapists. Outdoor facilities include a swimming pool, tennis courts, basketball court, a lighted walking track, a softball diamond, and a regulation-size soccer field. There is an annual membership fee and pool membership is separate.

CURVES
1314 E. 15th St.
(918) 585-1850

7282 S. Lewis Ave.
(918) 492-2292

11103 E. 41st St., Suite C
(918) 663-4500

8007 S. Sheridan Rd.
(918) 493-2639

3944 S. Hudson Ave.
(918) 270-2151
www.curves.com

Curves features a circuit of resistance machines designed to work the entire body in a 30-minute workout. Curves has a membership fee and monthly dues. Members who plan on traveling should ask for a travel card from their home Curves.

HEALTH ZONE AT ST. FRANCIS
5353 E. 68th St.
(918) 494-1671
www.healthzone.saintfrancis.com
This is a first-class facility with all the amenities—two pools, aerobics studio, free-weight area, cardiovascular equipment, a three-lane indoor track, basketball, volleyball, and racquetball courts, on-site child care, and a healthy snack bar. There are over 100 aerobic and water-aerobic classes offered, and personal trainers are available. Top that off with a spa whose services include massage therapy, facials, brow and lash tinting, waxing, and makeup application and consulting. It's not inexpensive, but if you'll use it, it's worth the price of the joining fee and monthly dues.

HILLCREST EXERCISE AND LIFESTYLE PROGRAM (HELP)
1265 S. Utica Ave., 2nd floor
(918) 579-4900
www.hillcrest.com/content/help.htm
The HELP regimen concentrates on wellness, aerobic, and strength training. When you join, you'll receive an evaluation by a certified fitness instructor and a training plan will be prescribed. Classes include several especially for seniors—flexibility and strength training—plus yoga and tai chi.

OWASSO FAMILY YMCA
8300 N. Owasso Expressway
(918) 272-9622
This Y has an indoor pool, fitness equipment, and classes. Child care is available while you work out. Check for specific times.

SOUTH NEIGHBORHOOD YMCA
10031 S. Yale Ave., Suite 105
(918) 518-5940
This is an "express" Y—no pool, but cardio equipment, weights, and classes. There is also child care while you work out.

THORNTON FAMILY YMCA
5002 S. Fulton Ave.
(918) 280-9622
Thornton has both an indoor and an outdoor pool, exercise equipment, basketball, racquetball, classes, and a full weight room. Child care during your workout is available.

TULSA COMMUNITY COLLEGE FITNESS AND WELLNESS CENTERS
Metro Campus
909 S. Boston Ave.
(918) 595-7348

Northeast Campus
3127 E. Apache St.
(918) 595-8496

Southeast Campus
10300 E. 81st St.
(918) 595-8640

West Campus
7505 W. 41st St.
(918) 595-8225
www.tulsacc.edu/page.12p?durkj=1382
This may be one of the biggest bargains in Tulsa. For a small fee you can join the Alumni and Friends Association and be eligible to use the fitness facilities. There is also a semester charge for use. All facilities have classes, cardio equipment, free weights, aerobics room, and an indoor walking and jogging track. The two newest centers—Southeast and West—also have climbing walls.

W. L. HUTCHERSON FAMILY YMCA
1120 E. Pine St.
(918) 382-9622
This is Tulsa's newest facility. Amenities include an indoor pool, fitness classes, exercise equipment and weights, aerobics, and child care while you exercise.

YWCA MULTICULTURAL CENTER
8145 E. 17th St.
(918) 628-1030
Facilities include an indoor pool, workout

machines, and aerobics and fitness classes. Child care is available during workouts at specific times. Check for current hours.

YMCA
www.ymcatulsa.org
There are several facilities around town. The Downtown Y is (as we go to press) in the process of relocating. There is a joining fee and you'll pay a monthly fee for membership.

YWCA PATTI JOHNSON WILSON CENTER
1910 S. Lewis Ave.
(918) 749-2519
This center has a fitness room with cardio and weights, fitness and aerobics classes. The pool is used for aquatics classes and lap swims. Limited child care is available during workouts—call 24 hours in advance.

OTHER RESOURCES

PLANNED PARENTHOOD
Midtown Health Center
1007 S. Peoria Ave.
(918) 587-1101
www.plannedparenthood.org
There are several other locations for this organization but the Midtown Center has the widest range of services. In addition to the expected pregnancy testing, birth control, emergency contraception, and abortion referral, the facility also offers men's and women's health programs, general health care, patient education, HIV testing, HPV and hepatitis vaccines, STD testing and treatment, and LGBT services.

TULSA HEALTH DEPARTMENT
James O. Goodwin Health Center
5051 S. 129th East Ave.
(918) 582-9355
www.tulsa-health.org
The Web site has pertinent information about current health concerns in the community. The center offers a number of services, including medical services for uninsured children. Many immunizations and vaccinations are available here, as are testing programs for tuberculosis, sexually transmitted diseases (STDs), and HIV/AIDS.

Looking for a physician? Try one of these referral lines:
Hillcrest Physician Referral
(918) 585-8000
St. Francis Physician Referral
(918) 494-5463
St. John Pulse Line
(918) 744-0123
OU Physicians
(918) 619-4400

EDUCATION AND CHILD CARE

Before white settlement in Indian Territory, there were schools. Some of them, like the Cherokee schools, were founded and administered by the Indians themselves. In Tahlequah in 1851, two boarding schools were established. The majority of the teachers were Cherokees who had been educated in eastern colleges. Among the courses offered were Greek, Latin, French, and German. Other nations also established schools. After the Civil War, missionaries from different religious denominations came to the territory to establish missions for the Indians.

When the railroad arrived and more white families moved in, these new residents wanted a school for their children. Because, by law, the white settlers were not permitted to collect taxes, they set up a subscription school. Each family paid a monthly sum toward paying the teacher. This first effort turned sour when the patrons discovered they'd hired a professional gambler.

The Presbyterian Board of Missions agreed to send a missionary to build Tulsa's first schoolhouse in 1884. By 1886 there were 75 students, both Indians and whites, attending the school, a one-room affair with two big stoves in opposite corners for heat.

In 1897 the Mission Board gave notice that they were closing the school but that the citizens could purchase it. J. M. Hall (who was prominent in settling Tulsa) and three other men borrowed money and became trustees of the property until Tulsa was incorporated in 1898 and tax money could be used to pay the debt. By 1906, bond moneys had been raised to build the city's first elementary school, Sequoyah, and the first high school.

In 1890 the first Catholic services were held in a private home. It wasn't until 1899 that Holy Family church had its own building. It was that same year that Sister Katherine Drexel founded the school associated with that church. Her mission was to aid Native American and African-American children. Today Holy Family School still serves a diverse population and holds a place of honor as Tulsa's oldest private school.

In 1907 an enterprising group of businessmen—and, yes, J. M. Hall was right in the middle of this effort, too—talked a small Presbyterian college in Muskogee into moving to Tulsa. The school kept the name Kendall College until 1926, when it became the University of Tulsa.

As Tulsa grew into a metropolitan city, citizens found it irksome that they had no public institution of higher learning. In 1965 another private school opened—Oral Roberts University—as a charismatic, interdenominational Christian college. Finally in 1970, Tulsa Junior College, now Tulsa Community College, was established. Today, in addition to these schools, Oklahoma State University, the University of Oklahoma, Langston University, and a number of regional schools, both public and private, maintain presences in Tulsa.

Today in Tulsa, approximately two-thirds of the population (25 and older) has had some college education, with about one-third holding bachelor's or advanced degrees. With a variety of opportunities, both traditional and contemporary, including online learning and technical schools, Tulsans and their families have access to education as never before.

OVERVIEW

This section looks at public schools in Tulsa and nearby communities, private schools, colleges and universities, and specialized learning opportunities. Frankly, educators speak a different language, and a lot of it sounds the same. They all want "positive outcomes" and offer to provide "optimum learning opportunities to meet every child's needs." If any of the schools do not state that they are inclusive of all races, genders, and religions (or non-religion), this will be mentioned in the write-ups. This book simply offers a listing and description of the main school districts and major private schools.

You'll need to do some research before making any decision. If you're relocating, talk to Realtors. Of course, it's best, but not always possible, to talk to other parents. Check online for the school's mission statement and philosophy. Is it consistent with your goals for your child? In the case of a religious school, make sure you are comfortable with what your child will be taught. Will it conflict with your beliefs or values? Obviously, you'll want to visit the school—and it's helpful to make at least one visit without your child and one visit with. Ask about class size, teacher qualifications, school accreditation. How many of the teachers have national certification? How many have advanced degrees? In the case of high school, what advanced classes are offered, what percentage of the graduates goes on to higher education? Depending on your child's grade level and situation, what does the school offer in the way of programs to meet special needs, including those for gifted students? What about arts, physical education, and extracurricular activities including athletics? What's the transportation situation? And how about campus safety, drugs, gangs, bullying, etc.? Did you feel welcome at the school? In the case of private schools, be sure and ask about extra fees that are not included in tuition figures.

Good luck choosing a school district or school. It's a big job and there are lots of options.

PUBLIC SCHOOLS

BIXBY PUBLIC SCHOOLS
109 N. Armstrong St., Bixby
(918) 366-2200
www.bixbyps.org
The Bixby Public School district, approximately 70 square miles, serves nearly 4,400 students in its six buildings. There are two elementary schools, two

fifth- and sixth-grade centers, a middle school, and high school.

Art and vocal music are part of the curriculum for all grades. Older students participate and compete in drama, speech, and debate. The school has an excellent band program with a marching band, concert band, jazz band, and winter guard. The high school choir was one of two high school choirs invited to sing at Carnegie Hall in 2009.

High school students have the opportunity to take any of six Pre-Advanced Placement classes and seven AP classes. Languages taught include Spanish, German, and French.

Bixby competes in Class 5A sports. Athletic activities include basketball, baseball, cheerleading and dance, golf, soccer, swimming, tennis, volleyball, cross-country, football, softball, track, and wrestling.

BROKEN ARROW PUBLIC SCHOOLS
701 S. Main St., Broken Arrow
(918) 259-4300
www.baschools.org
The Broken Arrow school system comprises 115 square miles in Tulsa and Wagoner Counties. The western part of the city of Broken Arrow is actually in the Union School District. Over 16,000 youngsters are served in 15 elementary schools, 5 middle schools (grades 6 through 8), 2 intermediate schools (grades 9 and 10), and one high school for juniors and seniors.

Music, visual arts, and physical education are important parts of the curriculum in addition to the traditional academic subjects. Before- and after-school care are available (at a fee) at various locations.

Students in middle school can take Pre-Advanced Placement courses, and upper-level students can choose from 45 AP classes. Visual arts, chorus, band, and physical education classes are offered as electives. Between middle school, intermediate, and high school, students can take a number of years of Spanish, French, German, or Latin. Teachers are prepared to teach students at every level, so students with higher levels of proficiency will be challenged.

EDUCATION AND CHILD CARE

Seventy-five percent of Broken Arrow High School graduates go on to college. The teacher/student ratio is 1 to 21 in the elementary grades, 1 to 23 in the middle grades, and 1 to 25 in the high school. .

Broken Arrow's competitive athletic program is highly successful and competes in football, basketball, track, volleyball, softball, wrestling, swimming, baseball, soccer, golf, and tennis.

In addition to the challenging academics available, parents are impressed with the extensive array of special education services.

JENKS PUBLIC SCHOOLS
205 E. B St., Jenks
(918) 299-4411
www.jenksps.org

The Jenks Public Schools district covers 39 square miles and includes some areas outside its city limits. At its nine schools, the district serves approximately 10,000 students. The system is divided into two elementary schools, two intermediate schools, a middle school, freshman academy, high school, and alternative center.

If you look at the success of Jenks High School graduates, you'll see why that ranking is so high. In the past decade, Jenks has produced a number of National Merit Scholars and two Presidential Scholars. More than 80 percent of Jenks graduates go on to college, many to some of the nation's most respected schools.

Jenks High School offers approximately 30 Advanced Placement courses each year, with Pre-AP classes offered for middle school and freshman academy. Languages offered include Spanish, French, German, and American Sign Language. Jenks has also begun a Chinese Initiative program designed to provide educational, cultural, and language opportunities for students. Among the features of the program are a principals' exchange, a guest teacher program for teachers from China, and student exchanges for both middle school and high school students.

Visual and performing arts opportunities include vocal music, band, orchestra, art, drama, speech and debate, and cinema. Athletics offered include baseball, basketball, cheer and pom,

cross-country, golf, soccer, fast- and slow-pitch softball, swimming, tennis, track, volleyball, and wrestling.

In 2005 the Jenks Public Schools received the prestigious Malcolm Balderige National Quality Award. The award, given to businesses, educational organizations, and nonprofit entities, is based on a number of criteria, including leadership, strategic planning, focus on market and workforce, and measurement, analysis, and results. The award puts Jenks alongside recipients like the City of Coral Springs, Richland College, IBM, and Xerox.

OWASSO PUBLIC SCHOOLS
1501 N. Ash St.
(918) 272-5367
www.owasso.k12.ok.us

The Owasso Public School District is the seventh largest in Oklahoma and covers approximately 72 square miles. The student population is growing at about 4 percent per year—with about 9,000 students now. Presently there are eight elementary schools, centers for grades six through eight, a mid-high school, high school, and RAM Academy, an alternative school. In addition to traditional classroom instructors, the district has a large Special Services division and seven full-time registered nurses.

The district has a superb performing arts center, with an auditorium seating 1,500 people, and brand-new tennis facilities. More classrooms have recently been added to the high school, along with a commons area, two state-of-the-art science labs, and two art studios. A new athletics facility and wellness center was scheduled to open in late 2009.

The high school offers 13 AP classes. Owasso students score above the national average on the ACT test, and over 80 percent of high school graduates pursue further education. In addition to core subjects, students participate in vocal music, speech and debate, theater, and band—the Pride of Owasso. (To hear the band, go to www.prideofowasso.com.) Sports offered at the schools include baseball, basketball, cross-country, football, golf, soccer, softball, swimming,

174

tennis, track, volleyball, wrestling, and Special Olympics.

TULSA PUBLIC SCHOOLS
(918) 746-6800
www.tulsaschools.org

The largest school system in Oklahoma, Tulsa Public Schools serves 41,000 students in 58 elementary schools, 15 middle schools, and 9 high schools. Other locations include seven alternative schools. Of Tulsa's 3,224 teachers, 1,165 hold master's degrees; 94 have doctorates. Ninety-three of Tulsa's teachers are National Board Certified. The overall teacher/student ration is just under 1 to 13.

There are two foreign-language immersion schools—Zarrow International Elementary School for Spanish and Eisenhower International Elementary School for both French and Spanish. Mayo Demonstration School of Science and Technology serves elementary students from all parts of the district who are selected from a random drawing,

Thoreau Demonstration Academy serves grades six through eight—its MicroSociety program provides real-world contexts for academic learning. Students, with the help of teachers, parents, and business volunteers, create a functioning society within the school context. By creating their own government, businesses, arts organizations, etc., they become immersed in the free-market economy and the realities of taxes, property issues, social concerns, and the political system.

Booker T. Washington is Tulsa's high school for Advanced Placement and the International Baccalaureate program. It was ranked number 74 in *Newsweek*'s list of the top 1,500 U.S. public high schools in June 2009.

Four of Tulsa's high schools are magnet schools. Hale High School explores wellness and global cultures through cuisine, tourism, and health and human performance. The school has a professional-level kitchen and a student-run bistro called Nathan's. It also boasts a state-of-the-art fitness facility where students can become involved in the dynamics of health and human performance.

Webster High School specializes in broadcasting and digital media. It has a state-of-the-art TV studio where students learn video, film, news production, and editing using the latest equipment and edit suites. Journalism, marketing, and graphic design are also components of the program.

Fine and performing arts take the stage at Central. Facilities include art and dance studios, a black box theater, and a vocal recording studio. Students learn not only the discipline of their choice but the business end of that discipline.

McLain specializes in scientific and technological utilization. Areas of study include environmental science, wave mechanics, atmospheric science, aeronautics and aviation technology, aerospace, avionics and robotics, and materials science. Its official title is McLain Magnet High School for Scientific Exploration and Technology Utilization. And yes, they do have a football team. Go MMHSFSEATU!

Beginning with the 2009–2010 school year, Tulsa Public Schools have partnered with the Teach for America program. About 50 of the nation's highest-ranking college graduates will be placed in high-needs classrooms. The results of this type of program in other cities has been profound. Administrators believe that they and their teachers will also learn from the program, and what they learn will influence the way teachers are trained and evaluated in the district. The district is also redesigning programs to improve the graduation rate and increase the number of students going on to higher education.

TULSA TECH
6111 E. Skelly Dr.
(918) 828-5000
www.tulsatech.edu

This school, with its multiple campuses, really needs a category of its own. Originally part of the Tulsa Public Schools, it became its own independent district and eventually changed its name from Tulsa Vo-Tech to Tulsa Tech. It serves high school students and adults—over 3,000 full-time students and almost 70,000 adult learners a year. In addition to college preparatory courses, programs include architecture and construction; arts, audio/visual technology, and communications; business, management and administration; education; health science; hospitality and tourism; human services; information technology; manufacturing; marketing, sales, and service; science technology and engineering; transportation, distribution and logistics; business services; and online courses.

i Tulsa-area schools are very competitive in athletics. In 2009, in Class 6A (the largest enrollment category), state champs included Owasso for baseball and volleyball; Jenks girls' golf and soccer, and both girls' and boys' swimming; Union boys' cross-country, track, and football; and Broken Arrow fast-pitch softball. Winners in 5A competition were Booker T. Washington girls' basketball and football; Bishop Kelley boys' cross-country, soccer, tennis, and volleyball; and Bixby boys' swimming. In 3A, Cascia Hall boys won state championship titles in baseball, golf, tennis, and football.

UNION PUBLIC SCHOOLS
8506 E. 61st St.
(918) 357-4321
www.unionps.org

The Union Public Schools Independent District is located about 8 miles southeast of downtown Tulsa and dates back to 1919 when it was literally out in the country. Four small communities—Alsum, Boles, Mayo, and McCollough—consolidated to form Union. The communities have disappeared but the spirit of community has not.

Union serves approximately 14,500 students at 19 facilities—13 elementary schools, a 6th/7th-grade center, an 8th-grade center, an intermediate high school (grades 9 and 10), a high school, and an alternative school. There is also an early childhood center

Special facilities serving the district include the 2,000-seat Performing Arts Center, located at the high school, and the Union Multipurpose

Activity Center, which houses a 6,000-seat arena, fine arts and athletic offices, classrooms, a wellness and sports medicine center, and a district spirit store carrying a variety of Union-logo clothing items and accessories. The Intermediate High School is the site of the baseball/softball complex and a challenging ropes course. The soccer complex is located at the eighth-grade center The sixth/seventh-grade center is home to the district's 3-meter swimming pool and has a seating capacity of 400.

The teacher-to-student ratio in the elementary schools is 1 to 22.6. Art, music, and physical education classes are a regular part of the elementary curriculum. Each school has specialists in remedial reading, speech therapy, and special education. In addition, each school has its own library/media specialist, nurse, and school counselor.

There are 23 Pre-AP courses and 21 AP courses offered to older students. There are currently four levels of Spanish, French, and German taught, and in the fall of 2009, Chinese was added to the curriculum. Also in the fall of 2009, a special program, the Union Collegiate Academy, was added for selected juniors and seniors. This five-point, one-hour class gives students an opportunity to look at college and career options, engage with professionals in the community, and be introduced to a number of academic disciplines. The program partners with the University of Oklahoma–Tulsa, Oklahoma State University–Tulsa, Tulsa Community College, Northeastern State University–Broken Arrow, the Tulsa Technology Center, and the University of Tulsa.

Union programs offer over 100 opportunities for students to be engaged in fine arts, speech and debate, clubs and organizations, and intramural and competitive sports. Team sports include football, cross-country, volleyball, fast- and slow-pitch softball, wrestling, swimming, basketball, golf, soccer, track, tennis, and baseball. Most of the Tulsa area schools, including Union, compete in pom and cheer. Union also has a competitive drill team, and many former High-steppers have gone on to join the famous Kilgore Rangerettes. Secondary student activities include band, chorus, drama, color guard, jazz, speech, debate, student leadership organizations, and subject- and interest-related clubs. Union's Air Force ROTC unit was Oklahoma's only representative in the 2009 Presidential Inaugural Parade.

Of Union's 1,041 teachers, 374 have advanced degrees and 69 are nationally certified. Approximately 93 percent of Union graduates continue their education beyond high school.

PRIVATE SCHOOLS

ALL SAINTS CATHOLIC SCHOOL
299 S. 9th St.
(918) 251-3000
www.allsaintsba.com
All Saints was founded in 1981 and is located next to St. Anne's Catholic Church in Broken Arrow. It serves families from a number of parishes in the greater metropolitan area. The student body is just over 300 pupils in prekindergarten through eighth grade. The staff consists of approximately 16 classroom teachers and 6 teachers of special subjects.

The curriculum is traditional, with emphasis on math, language arts, science, and social studies. The students also have a daily religion class and participate in weekly Mass. Additional subjects include Spanish, Latin, art, computers, music, and physical education.

All Saints is accredited and evaluated yearly by the Oklahoma Conference of Catholic Schools Accreditation Association, which is recognized by the Oklahoma Department of Education.

The tuition (2009–2010) is $3,600 for parishioners and $4,200 for others. Some financial aid is available. Uniforms are required.

AUGUSTINE CHRISTIAN ACADEMY
6310 E. 30th St.
(918) 832-4600
www.acatulsa.org
This independent, nondenominational Christian school uses curricula from a variety of sources, including published Christian curricula and staff-generated activities based on a classical model

of education. As a Christian school, they believe that students should learn to integrate their faith and values, based on rigorous Bible study, throughout all their studies. The school serves youngsters from prekindergarten through high school. Children attend one formal chapel service a week plus two student-led events. Learning is based on the classical triumvirate of grammar, dialectic, and rhetoric—a sequence designed to help the youngsters learn, reason, and persuade. Studies include traditional core courses. Instruction in Latin begins at the kindergarten level. High school students take a rigorous college-preparatory course and can elect to add studies in rhetoric, economics, Greek, and Hebrew. Art and music are an integral component of the curriculum. Additional opportunities exist for participation in journalism, choir, drama, and student leadership. Development of strong character is a major goal.

Ninety percent of the graduates go on to college, and some enter the military. There was one National Merit finalist in the 2009 graduating class. The school is a member of the Association of Classical Christian Schools. Tuition for grades 1 through 5 (2009–2010) was $4,450; for grades 9 through 12 it was $5,800. Scholarships are available. Uniforms are required.

BISHOP KELLEY HIGH SCHOOL
3905 S. Hudson Ave.
(918) 627-3390
www.bkelleyhs.org
Over 800 students attend this four-year private college-preparatory school, which has an attractive and spacious 40-acre campus. Though a good majority of the students come from Catholic middle schools, boys and girls of all religions, races, and economic backgrounds are welcome. The curriculum includes theology, English, mathematics, science, business, social studies, communications, foreign languages, computer science, fine arts, and physical education. The school offers a number of Advanced Placement courses and four years each of Latin, French, German, Spanish, and Chinese. Ninety-five percent of the graduates go on to college.

Over half of the faculty members have master's degrees, and the teacher/student ratio is 1 to 12. The school, which was founded in 1960, is accredited by the North Central Association and the State of Oklahoma.

Tuition for the 2009–2010 school year was $6,650 for Catholics (supporting a parish) and $8,775 for non-Catholics. Some financial aid is available. All students are required to perform 25 hours of Christian service for each school year. Students are required to wear uniforms.

CASCIA HALL PREPARATORY SCHOOL
2520 S. Yorktown Ave.
(918) 746-2600
www.casciahall.org

An attractive 40-acre campus with towering trees and buildings designed in neo–French Norman style helps Cascia Hall make a memorable first impression. The academic record of the 80-plus-year-old school is even more impressive. One hundred percent of the graduates go on to college, and in 2009 the school had three National Merit Scholars. The school consists of a middle school and upper school, for 6th through 12th grade, and the curriculum is college preparatory with an emphasis on liberal arts. Ten Advanced Placement courses are offered, as well as five years of German, three years of Chinese, six years of Spanish, four years of Latin, and six years of French.

The school has an outstanding college-counseling program, starting with help for freshmen in planning their educational futures. In addition to challenging academics, athletics are not neglected. Cascia Hall is ranked in the top five of all high school athletic programs in the state regardless of class. Other extracurricular activities include pep band, chorus, drama, academic bowl, bell choir, debate, a literary magazine, and a school newspaper, plus a number of special-interest clubs.

The school enrollment is just under 600 students. The faculty is under the direction of the Augustinian Friars—a teaching order associated with Villanova University, Merrimack College, and several other secondary schools. It is accredited by the North Central Association and the Oklahoma State Department of Education.

Students are required to take theology classes, and uniforms are mandatory. Sixty-seven percent of the teachers hold advanced degrees and two have received national certification. The 2009–2010 tuition was $10,875 for all grades.

CHRISTIAN MONTESSORI ACADEMY
3702 S. 90th East Ave.
(918) 628-6524
www.montessorilearning.org

Christian Montessori Academy serves children between the ages of 3 and 12, using the prescribed Montessori method—no traditional texts. The school is small—about 50 students with small classes.

The school is located in Aldersgate United Methodist Church. It includes religious values in the curriculum but is nondenominational. Options available to students include swimming, piano lessons, soccer, and computer skills. The year's tuition (2009–2010) is $5,100. Extended care is available for an extra charge.

EVANGELISTIC TEMPLE SCHOOL
1339 E. 55th St.
(918) 743-5597
www.etstulsa.com

Evangelistic Temple School is an interdenominational Christian school serving approximately 250 students from preschool through high school. Textbooks come from both Christian and secular publishing companies. The school was founded in 1984 by the Evangelistic Temple Church. The first class graduated in 2008. Eighteen out of 19 graduating seniors went on to college. The school offers Advanced Placement courses in calculus and physics. A number of the teachers have advanced degrees and all are trained in teaching an integrated Biblical worldview—helping students to see God revealed in every subject.

The large school building includes a computer lab, gym, library/conference room, areas for art and vocal music, and a cafeteria. There are two well-equipped playgrounds, but sports like football, golf, and track utilize other facilities in the community. Additional activities include basketball, volleyball, and cheerleading.

Class sizes vary by age—the largest classes are middle school. Overall, the classes average about 18 students. All teachers are state certified or licensed. The school is accredited by the Association of Christian Schools International.

The tuition (2009–2010) is $4,856 for grades 1 through 8 and $5,271 for grades 9 through 12. Extended care before school is offered at no extra charge; for after school care there is a fee. Financial aid is available. Uniforms are required.

HOLLAND HALL
5666 E. 81st St.
(918) 481-1111
www.hollandhall.org

The campus and facilities of this school could be the envy of a small college. The 162-acre campus houses the three levels of the school, an arts center, chapel, sports facilities, and nature areas. Emphasis is on broad knowledge of liberal arts and strong character development. There's also a community service component to the program. Students in middle and upper school can take advantage of overseas exchange programs that range from several weeks to a year. Typically, all graduating seniors attend college. The faculty is strong, with half the teachers holding advanced degrees.

Holland Hall is accredited by the Independent Schools Association of the Southwest, a member of the National Association of Independent Schools, the National Association of Episcopal Schools, the National Association for College Admission Counseling, and the College Board, and has been a member of Cum Laude Society since 1968. Holland Hall has been recognized by the Oklahoma State Regents for Higher Education for superior college preparation and is one of only three Oklahoma Educational institutions to belong to the Center for Academic Integrity.

Students wear uniforms. Tuition in 2009 ranged from $3,900 for two-day preschool to $15,400 for high school.

HOLY FAMILY CATHEDRAL SCHOOL
820 S. Boulder Ave.
(918) 582-0422
www.holyfamily-tulsa.org/school

An old-fashioned, beige brick building houses the Cathedral School for youngsters from preschool through eighth grade. The preschool uses a Montessori approach. Kindergarten and higher grades study a traditional curriculum with additional classes in religion, music, art, physical education, leadership and ethics, and technology. The school touts its small classes and experienced teachers. Students are required to wear uniforms and attend weekly Mass. The 2009 tuition is $3,525 for Catholic families and $4,435 for non-Catholics. Financial aid is available.

IMMANUEL CHRISTIAN ACADEMY
400 N. Aspen Ave., Broken Arrow
(918) 251-5422
www.icaba.org

Opened in 2002, Immanuel Christian Academy is sponsored by Immanuel Lutheran Church, a member of the Lutheran Church–Missouri Synod. It serves approximately 170 students, in preschool through ninth grade, on a 30-acre campus with facilities in the church, an annex, playgrounds, and sports fields. In addition to core subjects, students take art, music, physical education, and technology. Spanish is introduced in the classroom in kindergarten through third grade with formal instruction for fourth graders and up. Latin was added for the upper grades in 2009. The school is expanded a grade a year and by 2012 will have a full high school program. Currently, eighth- and ninth-graders can enroll in Pre-Advanced Placement classes in mathematics, English, science, and social studies. Average class size in the school is 12 students. Extracurricular activities include volleyball, basketball, track, cross-country, and football. Extended care is available.

Students attend chapel weekly and uniforms are required. Tuition for 2009–2010 ranged from $4,500 to $5,500.

LINCOLN CHRISTIAN SCHOOL
1003 N. 129th East Ave.
(918) 234-8150
www.lincolnchristianschool.com

On the campus of Tulsa's Church on the Move, and part of its ministry, Lincoln Christian School emphasizes "Godly character, academic excellence, and extracurricular activity." It is accredited by the International Christian Accreditation Association and the North Central Association and is recognized by the state of Oklahoma.

Currently serving approximately 750 students in kindergarten through 12th grade, Lincoln has separate buildings for the primary (kindergarten through 5th grade) and secondary (6th through 12th grades) schools. There are special facilities for art, music, science, and computer labs. The school offers five Advanced Placement courses.

Students have daily religion classes and attend weekly chapel services. Admission preference is given to church members; nonmembers will be considered if they agree with the school's philosophy. Students have daily religion classes and weekly chapel services. Church on the Move is a nondenominational charismatic church.

Tuition (2009–2010) ranges from $3,960 for kindergarten to $4,600 for middle and upper school for tithing members of Church on the Move. The cost is higher for nonmembers.

MARQUETTE SCHOOL
1519 S. Quincy Ave.
(918) 584-4631
www.marquetteschool.org

Marquette was founded in 1918 as Sacred Heart School by members of the Ursuline Sisters. Today it is administered by lay educators under the supervision of the pastor and administration of Christ the King Parish. It serves close to 400 students in kindergarten through eighth grades and also has an Early Childhood Development Center for children 18 months to kindergarten-ready. Its programs combine Catholic values and a comprehensive curriculum. Their RISE (Religious Inclusive Student Education) program accommodates children with special needs in regular classroom settings. The maximum class size is 22 students. After-school care is available, though the hours are not as extensive as those at some other schools.

Art, music, and physical education are important parts of the curriculum. Students also have daily religious studies and attend weekly Mass.

The school is accredited by several agencies, including the State of Oklahoma through the Oklahoma Conference of Catholic Schools Accreditation Association. Tuition (2009–2010) is $3,958 for parish members, $5,125 for nonmembers.

METRO CHRISTIAN ACADEMY
6363 S. Trenton Ave.
(918) 745-9868
www.metroca.com

Serving close to 1,000 students, in preschool through 12th grade, Metro was founded in 1983 as a college-preparatory, interdenominational Christian school with no church affiliation or government funding. Its Web site states: "Accredited education. Christian Principles. College Preparatory. Promising futures."

Visual arts and music are part of the core curriculum in the elementary grades and offered as electives in higher grades. The school offers band, orchestra, choir, and drama.

In addition to the regular classes, honors classes are offered at the middle school level and 15 Advanced Placement courses are offered in high school. Out of 94 teachers and administrators, 42 percent have master's degrees.

In 2009 the Metro boys' tennis team was runner-up for the state Class 4A finals, and the girls' volleyball team received the same ranking in their state competition.

The 2009 tuition rates ranged from $5,425 for kindergarten to $7,750 for grades 9 through 12. The school is accredited by the State of Oklahoma Department of Education and the North Central Association and participates in the Oklahoma Secondary School Activities Association (OSSAA).

MONTE CASSINO
2206 S. Lewis Ave.
(918) 746-4238
www.montecassino.org
Founded in 1926 by the Benedictine Sisters, Monte Cassino educates children from the preschool level through eighth grade. Spanish and French are introduced at the preschool level. The elementary curriculum includes traditional subjects, computers, art, music, and Spanish. Spanish, Latin, and French are available in middle school. Pre-AP classes offered in the middle school include English, social studies, pre-algebra, algebra, and geometry. The youngsters, who are required to wear uniforms, participate in daily prayers and weekly Mass.

The school has an extensive sports program, including golf and tennis teams. They're even more competitive academically, participating regularly in chess competitions, Academic Bowl, Mathcounts, the National Geographic Bee, and the National Spelling Bee.

The campus is beautiful, with many large trees. Buildings include the Early Childhood Learning Center, the elementary school, middle school, chapel, monastery, and Performing Arts Center.

The 2009–2010 tuition for a two-day preschool student was $3,020. For five-day students, the cost was $7,568. There are discounts for more than one student in a family, and some financial aid is available.

RIVERFIELD COUNTRY DAY SCHOOL
2433 W. 61st St.
(918) 446-3553
www.riverfield.org.
The 120-acre campus of this school, with its barnyard animals, hiking trails, and outdoor classrooms, is an inviting introduction to the array of learning opportunities the school offers its students. The challenging, personalized curriculum is presented as an integrated process, blending many subjects and activities.

The school currently serves 500-plus students from infancy through high school.

It was founded in 1984 and prides itself on enriching students through innovation, small class sizes, and positive, collaborative relationships. The school has grown over the years, with its first graduating class in 2007. All its graduates have gone on to further education.

The preschool philosophy is inspired by the Reggio Emilia approach—a student-centered, experiential, inquiry-based learning model. The school is known nationally as a benchmark for early-childhood education programs. This approach also filters into the primary school, which uses Reggio concepts in conjunction with Literacy First and everyday mathematics curricula.

German and Spanish are offered in middle school and high school, and in addition to required courses, students can participate in the arts, speech and debate, athletics, and a number of other activities. The school's rock band is a favorite choice. Sports offered include basketball, cheer, cross-country, football, golf, softball, tennis, baseball, and girls' volleyball.

Riverfield is a close community of students, faculty, and parents. Experienced faculty help develop the whole person and a confident and responsible student, building a foundation for a lifetime of learning. There is an abiding commitment to the outdoors through campouts for older students, community service projects, Roots and Shoots—an international environmental and humanitarian program founded by Dr. Jane Goodall—and other outdoor education experiences.

Riverfield is accredited by the Independent Schools Association of the Southwest and the National Association for the Education of Young Children. Tuition ranges from $7,310 to $9,320.

ST. PIUS X SCHOOL
1717 S. 75th East Ave.
(918) 627-5367
www.spxtulsa.org
Housed in several buildings, St. Pius X serves approximately 380 students from preschool and prekindergarten through eighth grade. Accredited by both the State of Oklahoma and the

Oklahoma Conference of Catholic Schools, St. Pius X was named a "Blue Ribbon School" by the U.S. Department of Education for its academically superior program.

A unique feature of the school is its Synergistic Lab for middle school students. Here lessons in earth and physical science are taken out of the textbook and put in real-life situations. It's a method that makes the learning immediately meaningful, and kids love it.

The general curriculum is supplemented with art and music and extras like the Academic Bowl, Mathcounts, Boy and Girl Scouts, speech and drama, and yearbook.

Students participate in daily prayers and weekly Mass. Uniforms are required. Tuition for 2009–2010 was $3,460 for Catholic families, $5,525 for nonparishoners.

TOWN AND COUNTRY SCHOOL
5150 E. 101st St.
(918) 296-3113
www.tandcschool.org

Town and Country, established in 1961, is Oklahoma's only accredited, nonpublic, full-day K–12 program specifically designed for the needs of children with learning disabilities. Over the years, the school has expanded its program to include students with attention deficit/hyperactivity disorder and Asperger's syndrome.

The average enrollment is 125, and classes—each with a teacher and assistant—are limited to 12 students. The curriculum covers language arts, math, social studies, and science. There are also programs in music, art, computers, and physical education. Drama, yearbook, architecture, and environmental science are offered to upper school students.

The school provides continuity, individual attention, family support, and curriculum modifications to meet individual needs. Curriculum is chosen to accommodate learning abilities and patterns. Speech therapy is available for students needing help in this area.

Student admission requirements state that a student must have a primary diagnosis of a learning disability, attention disorder, or Asperger's

syndrome, and have an average to above-average IQ. Tuition ranges from $8,670 to $9,680. Financial aid is available.

UNIVERSITY SCHOOL AT THE UNIVERSITY OF TULSA
800 S. Tucker Dr.
(918) 631-5060
www.uschool.utulsa.edu

This school has it together for gifted youngsters from preschool through eighth grade. Flexible grouping allows children to work at a comfortable level. The basics are all here plus a real awareness for the creative aspects of education. The administration and staff have the credentials and experience to work with kids who don't fit easily into an educational box. If you want specifics, check the Web site—it helps in reading it if you are also gifted.

The school is housed in a two-story building on the University of Tulsa campus. In addition to classrooms, the school has a large gymnasium and stage, library, indoor and outdoor play areas, five common areas, and a butterfly garden.

Admission to the school is based on testing, which covers verbal, quantitative, perceptual, and creative abilities. Students scoring in the 90th percentile and above are considered for admission. Other factors include professional recommendation, parent inventories, and interviews. Tuition for two-day preschool starts at $4,525 and rises to $8,760 for older students.

HIGHER EDUCATION

Tulsans have many opportunities to pursue higher education. Please keep in mind that these are thumbnail sketches of each organization. Probably the trickiest area is cost. Some schools give a blanket figure, others give tuition and fees. These entries try to give you a way to compare schools by giving basic tuition—average course load of 15 hours times the cost per credit hour. Again, some schools tuck fees into those figures, others don't, so you'll have to do some careful research when you get serious about enrolling. Some degree programs have higher per-credit-hour fees than others. And the list of extra charges seems pretty extensive. You have some good options, but be a careful consumer and look for hidden costs when you're calculating the education bang-for-buck ratio.

LANGSTON UNIVERSITY
914 N. Greenwood Ave.
(918) 877-8127
www.lunet.edu/tulsa

Part of the state system of higher education, Langston, historically a school for African Americans, now serves a diverse, multicultural population. Like its neighbor, Oklahoma State University–Tulsa, it teaches junior, senior, and graduate-level courses. Students take their first two years elsewhere, often at Tulsa Community College. Also like OSU, there is no student housing.

The school has a brand-new facility and serves a student population of between 500 and 550 students. All faculty members hold advanced degrees and classes are small. Situated just north of downtown, the university does not have a parking problem. That, plus the most affordable tuition in town, makes Langston a good choice.

Bachelor's degrees are granted in accounting, business administration, computer and information systems, corrections/criminal justice, elementary education, management information systems, management, liberal education, nursing, psychology, rehabilitation services, sociology, and special education. Master's programs include entrepreneurial studies, rehabilitation counseling, and urban education.

Langston is also one of nine public universities participating in the Regent's Reach Higher program, designed for adults who have completed some college but never finished a degree. Flexible class schedules and online learning will facilitate completion and result in a bachelor's degree in organizational leadership.

The large building housing the classrooms also features a student lounge, computer labs, and a learning resource center. There are numerous student clubs and associations. Tuition (minus fees) was $2,676 for the 2009–2010 school year.

NORTHEASTERN STATE UNIVERSITY
3100 E. New Orleans St., Broken Arrow
(918)-449-6000
www.nsuba.edu

A branch of Northeastern State at Tahlequah, NSU at Broken Arrow serves approximately 3,000 students on its 246-acre campus. Like other state schools in Tulsa, it teaches upper-division and graduate classes only. Bachelor's degrees are offered in 26 areas of study. There are 11 graduate programs plus certification in education, library media and information technology, financial planning, reading specialist, school counselor, and writing program administration.

In addition to traditional classroom settings, courses are offered through interactive TV (ITV) and online. Like the other public schools with branches here, NSU concentrates on upper-level classes. Students get their lower-level hours elsewhere. Here's where NSU has a real advantage. Tulsa Community College teaches a number of courses on the NSU Broken Arrow campus. The two schools are working to make that transition seamless.

There are at least 15 student organizations on campus, with more to be added. The average age of undergraduates is 26. Tuition for undergraduates is $3,210.

OKLAHOMA STATE UNIVERSITY–TULSA
700 N. Greenwood Ave.
(918) 594-8229
www.osu-tulsa.okstate.edu

The small but attractive campus is basically an extension of the large Stillwater campus. Students on the Tulsa campus earn the same degrees as those in Stillwater and, indeed, may take a number of classes on that main campus, facilitated by BOB—the big orange bus—that shuttles back and forth the 70 miles between the two campuses.

The median age of the students is 25, and the school concentrates on junior-, senior-, and graduate-level course work. The faculty includes local instructors and those who commute from Stillwater. More than 40 undergraduate degrees are offered, including aviation science, business, engineering, liberal arts, education, early-childhood development, journalism and broadcasting, and health and human performance. Master's degrees are offered in as many fields, and EdD and PhD degrees are offered in education, computer science, educational psychology, electrical engineering, and environmental science.

Classes have been taught in Tulsa since 1982; OSU-Tulsa was established in 1999. There are approximately 2,700 students—all commuters, with no resident housing (although this is being considered).

The campus is on the site where Booker T. Washington High School once stood. It was one of the few buildings to survive the fires during the 1921 Riot. The school changed locations in 1950 and the building was demolished. There is a marker on the campus telling about the school's history.

OSU-Tulsa is home to the Oklahoma Center for Poets and Writers founded by author Teresa Miller. The center houses the Oklahoma Writers Hall of Fame and sponsors, every even year, the Celebration of Books, one of the largest conferences for writers in the Southwest. Through the center's activities, Oklahomans have heard such important writers as Pat Conroy, Tony Hillerman, Maya Angelou, N. Scott Momaday, and Edward Albee. The center also houses archives of manuscripts by Oklahoma authors including Carolyn Hart, William Bernhardt, and Michael Wallis.

Just west of the campus is the Helmerich Advanced Technology Research Center, where members of the OSU engineering faculty, graduate students, and visiting scholars work on the development of new materials—ceramics, composites, aerospace materials, polymers, and metals—for future industries.

OKLAHOMA STATE UNIVERSITY CENTER FOR HEALTH SCIENCES
1111 W. 17th St.
(918) 582-1972
www.healthsciences.okstate.edu
OSU's Center for Health Sciences specializes in osteopathic medicine and offers degrees in medicine, the biomedical sciences, forensic sciences,

and health-care administration. Only 88 students are admitted to the College of Medicine each year. The school has been ranked 20th in the nation in rural health care and 45th in primary care. St. John's Hospital, Tulsa, manages the OSU Medical Center (hospital).

OKLAHOMA UNIVERSITY
OU-Tulsa Schusterman Center
4502 E. 41st St.
(918) 660-3000
http://tulsa.ou.edu
Located on what was formerly the Amoco Research Facility campus, the Schusterman Center consists of a number of buildings on a large, attractively landscaped site. This isn't a school where students start before going off to college. The average age of a student here is 38, typically working full time. The University has six bachelor's degree programs. Bachelor of science degrees are offered in medical imaging and radiation science radiography; radiation sciences sonography; early-childhood education; and nursing. There's a bachelor of arts program in liberal studies, and bachelor of arts or science degrees are offered in multidisciplinary studies. There are master's programs in architecture, arts and sciences, education, engineering, nursing, and public health, and doctoral programs in medicine, physical therapy, education, engineering, and pharmacy. There are 10 medical residency programs. In addition, the school offers certification in Kodály (an approach to music education).

The Oklahoma University School of Community Medicine combines both preventive and public-health education with health care of individuals. The school has just joined in partnership with IBM to develop an information-based, community health care model that will utilize digital health-information technology to provide coordinated, patient-centered care.

Student services include counseling, career services, computer labs, a writing lab, fitness center, lounges, and a cafe. There are several student organizations, including a student association, but campus life is not the focus of the school. All programs do, however, have a community service component, and students participate each year in the nationwide Big Event—again, involving community service.

Tuition can change and fees vary widely from one program to another. For 2009, based on a 15-hour semester load and per-credit-hour rate, tuition was $7,170 for a year.

OKLAHOMA WESLEYAN UNIVERSITY
10810 E. 45th St., Ste. 100
(918) 728-6143
www.collegeonmytime.com
www.okwu.edu
OWU has a strong presence in Tulsa, with a campus and academic programs specifically designed for working adults. The school is ideal for students who need flexibility in order to complete their degrees. Accelerated night classes, virtual classrooms, and online learning are among the methods available. Accredited at both the regional and national levels, OWU students can earn master's, bachelor's, and associate's degrees in education, business, nursing, ministry, psychology, and general studies. Upon enrollment, tuition is locked in—a real advantage. Tuition for undergraduate course work ranges from $310 to $375 per credit hour.

ORAL ROBERTS UNIVERSITY
7777 S. Lewis Ave.
(918) 495-6161
www.oru.edu
Oral Roberts University opened in 1965, a small liberal arts college with a decided religious foundation. It went through some tough times a couple of years ago, but the foundation was strong and the University has rebuilt trust and reputation with hard work, strong faculty, and a massive infusion of cash from a major donor.

The architecture, which reminds some of a *Jetsons* cartoon, definitely looks dated—but it's been out so long, it may be back in. The improved financial picture has helped add new facilities and update older ones. The center of the campus is the Prayer Tower, a 200-foot structure with visual references to the cross and crown of thorns. From the observation deck you can get a good view of the rest of the campus, including the gold, geodesic-domed Howard Auditorium. Most of the buildings are white with gold trim and part of the campus is on a hill—bringing to mind the Biblical reference to a "city upon a hill." Oral Roberts just added the "shiny" before Ronald Reagan's "shining city" became part of our national vocabulary.

While some of the rules have relaxed over the years—girls can wear jeans now—the student body is still expected to maintain high moral and ethical standards. You won't find coed dorms here, but there are common areas joining segregated facilities.

The school offers undergraduate degrees in various areas of arts and cultural studies, business, education, nursing, science and engineering, and theology and missions, and master's degrees in business, education, and theology and missions. In all, ORU offers 65 undergraduate majors, 14 master's programs, and 2 doctoral degrees. The largest majors are pastoral Christian ministry, mass media communications, business administration, psychology, biology, and nursing.

The school is competitive in a number of athletic endeavors—particularly men's basketball. Other sports offered are golf, soccer, tennis, cross-country, track and field for both men and women, baseball for men, and volleyball for women.

Average current enrollment is just over 3,000, with students coming from many states and countries. Tuition for 2009–2010 was $18,476.

PHILLIPS THEOLOGICAL SEMINARY
901 N. Mingo Rd.
(918) 610-8303
www.ptstulsa.edu
PTS has made an effort to provide the best in theological education and preparation for local church ministry, and its students currently represent more than 20 denominations. The school itself is affiliated with the Christian Church, Disciples of Christ. The school was founded in 1907 as part of Phillips University in Enid. While the school had a second campus in Tulsa for several years, in 1997 it consolidated both facilities, choosing Tulsa as the permanent location.

Academic programs offered include: a certificate in graduate theological studies; master of arts in ministry and culture, with emphases in congregational leadership, Christian education, history and practice of Christian spirituality, and theology, ethics, and culture; master of theological studies; master of divinity; and doctor of ministry. Directors of ministerial formation are provided for five groups besides Disciples of Christ. They are the Lutheran, United Methodist, Presbyterian, United Church of Christ, and Cooperative Baptist organizations. This makes it possible for students not only to receive a strong ecumenical background but also to be grounded in their own denomination's history and church government.

The seminary is located in a two buildings on a 7½-acre campus. Facilities are state of the art, and the Yetter Memorial Garden and Labyrinth is state of the heart. In addition to classrooms and offices, there is an academic/student center, chapel, and a 140,000-volume library and archives.

Knowing that a number of the students are working, the seminary schedules classes to accommodate them. Most classes meet once a week, and classes are offered on weekends and in concentrated course formats. A few courses are available through a distance learning program. Tuition is $485 per credit hour. Ninety-five percent of the students receive some sort of financial aid.

ROGERS STATE UNIVERSITY
1701 W. Will Rogers Blvd., Claremore
(918) 343-7777 (800) 256-7511
www.rsu.edu
This is the closest thing Tulsa has to a residential public university—and Claremore isn't that far away. Rogers State, a four-year regional college, served just over 4,000 students in 2008. It is the first public university in Oklahoma to offer bachelor's and associate's degrees completely on the Internet.

RSU was founded in 1909 as Eastern University Preparatory School; it closed in 1917. The facility reopened in 1919 as Oklahoma Military Academy and in 1971 became Claremore Junior College. In 1982 the name was changed to Rogers State College, and in 1998 it became Rogers State University. The campus, right across the street from the Will Rogers Memorial, is large and attractive. Almost all the buildings, with the exceptions of the historic, gold-domed Preparatory Hall and the decidedly art deco Auditorium, are red brick with white trim. A wildlife area abuts the campus, a good resource for the biological sciences department, but it also provides hiking and fishing spots for the community.

Associate's degrees are awarded in accounting, applied technology, business administration, biological science, computer science, criminal justice, elementary education, emergency medical services, legal assisting, liberal arts, nursing, physical science, secondary education, and social sciences. Undergraduate programs include applied technology, biology, business administration, business information technology, communications, community counseling, elementary education, game development, justice administration, liberal arts, social science, sport management, and visual arts.

Athletic programs include basketball, baseball, softball, rodeo, golf, soccer, and cheerleading. Several programs offer interesting off-campus study opportunities—the Washington Center Internship Program grants college credit for specific internship experiences in Washington, D.C., and international study.

Being a residential school, many extracurricular and student activities are offered. The Greek system is small—two sororities and one fraternity. Intramural sports give students a chance to play and compete, and student clubs and associations provide opportunities to join with others in common interests. Basic tuition for 2009 was $2,700.

SOUTHERN NAZARENE UNIVERSITY–TULSA
10159 E. 11th St., Ste. 200
(918) 664-4100
http://tulsa.snu.edu
Offerings are limited at this office/campus site, but there are some unique features of SNU that

you will want to consider. Affiliated with the Nazarene church, curriculum is presented with a Christian worldview. Two undergraduate degrees are offered: organizational leadership, and family studies and gerontology. This is a degree-completion program, so students enter with 60 hours of previous college credit. Graduate programs include master's degrees in business administration, management, educational leadership, marriage and family therapy, counseling psychology, nursing education, and nursing leadership.

Every student receives a wireless laptop—the entire campus is wireless. Classes are one night a week. Instruction takes place on the campus, but all syllabuses, assignments, etc., are available online.

Tuition, fees, books, and computer added up to $18,900 for the 2009–2010 school year.

SPARTAN COLLEGE OF AERONAUTICS AND TECHNOLOGY
8820 E. Pine St.
(918) 836-6886
www.spartan.edu

With a history going back to the early days of Tulsa aviation, Spartan was established in 1928. They offer associate's degrees in avionics, aviation maintenance, quality control and nondestructive testing, and pilot training. In addition, students can work toward—and earn—a bachelor of science degree in aviation technology management. While the primary focus is on a career in aviation, training can equip students for technical opportunities in other industries. The professional pilot program trains both commercial and private pilots. The flight program facilities include the school's own control tower, 50 airplanes, and three simulators.

Over the years, Spartan has prepared approximately 90,000 pilots, aviation mechanics, and technicians. The school offers career-placement services and student housing, Facilities include a cafeteria, library, student store where books or tools can be purchased, and student activity centers. Current student enrollment is about 1,000 students. Tuition for 2009–2010 was $14,570 for

technical programs and $18,313 for flight programs. Financial counseling services help with tuition.

TULSA COMMUNITY COLLEGE
6111 E. Skelly Dr.
(918) 595-7000
www.tulsacc.edu

TCC is a nonresident commuter school with four campuses in the Tulsa area. Many of its programs are designed to transfer to four-year institutions; other programs are geared toward career placement, either for initial entry into the job force, retraining, or upgrading skills. Classes are offered days, nights, and weekends, and online.

Programs leading to further study or to certifications include arts and communications; business; community services; health sciences; manufacturing; science, technology, engineering, and mathematics; and transportation, logistics, and distribution.

Each of the four campuses—Metro at 909 N. Boston Ave.; Northeast, 3727 E. Apache St.; Southeast, 10300 E. 81st St.; and West, 7505 W. 41st St.—has computer labs, many of which are open for all students and have staff to provide assistance. There are also campus cafes at each location.

While this is not a residential school, there are still opportunities for campus involvement. There are more than 65 campus organizations related to interests like foreign languages, art, and science, and groups associated with occupations like the Student Nurses' Association or the Journalism and Mass Communications Student Association. The Student Government Association works with the Student Activities office to plan events, represents the student body, and gives students an opportunity to make their voices heard. While the school does not participate in collegiate sports, it does support intramural sports like coed volleyball, flag football, softball, basketball, tennis, golf, and others.

In-state tuition was less than $2,000 for the school year 2008–2009. There are, of course, other fees and textbooks to be considered.

UNIVERSITY OF TULSA
800 S. Tucker Dr.
(918) 631-2000
www.utulsa.edu

The university's beginnings date back to 1882 when Presbyterian missionaries began a small boarding school for Indian girls in Muskogee. In 1894 it was upgraded to college status and renamed Henry Kendall College. The school moved to Tulsa in 1907. It became the University of Tulsa in 1920. The private school is nondenominational, though it maintains an affiliation with the Presbyterian Church (USA).

The campus comprises more than 200 acres with approximately 75 buildings. The heart of the campus is a large lawn known as "The U" where many campus-wide activities take place. On warm days it's a prime spot for sunbathing. The iconic building on the campus is probably the McFarlin Library with its sturdy tower, but old-timers might cite the H. A. Chapman Stadium (originally Skelly Stadium) for its location on historic Route 66.

Classes at TU are small—with an average size of 19 students—with a 10-to-1 student-faculty ratio for undergraduate classes. There are approximately 4,300 students—undergraduate, graduate, and law. The university grants 59 undergraduate degrees, 33 graduate degrees, 10 doctoral degrees, and a JD degree.

About half of the students are from Oklahoma; 13 percent of the students are international. Seventy percent of the students live on campus, either in student housing or fraternity or sorority houses. The size of the campus and student body provides a close-knit campus community, but the programs offered are comparable to a comprehensive state university. Students like the flexibility offered here, particularly the ability to create individualized, cross-discipline programs.

The university is strong in the fields of accounting; management information systems (MIS); petroleum, mechanical and chemical engineering; English; environmental law; and psychology. One of the emerging specialties is the field of computer science and information security. TU was one of the first six schools selected by the National Science Foundation for the Federal Cyber Service Initiative, which trains information-assurance professionals for service with the federal government. Most active in these efforts is Dr. Sujeet Shenoi, the F. P. Walter professor of math and computer science, who was named the 1998-1999 Carnegie Foundation Professor of the Year.

The University of Tulsa consistently makes *U.S. News and World Report*'s list of top universities. The 2009 *Princeton Review* included TU in the top fifty best values, citing quality of life, town/gown relations, and race/class relations as outstanding features.

CHILD CARE

This is a critical area and you'll have to do the legwork and make the choice that is best for your child. There are some resources that will make your job easier. Several are listed below. Many churches have day-care facilities, and a number of private schools, and some public schools, have extended care for an extra fee.

Oklahoma is one of a small number of states that have a rating system for child-care facilities. Centers are awarded one to three stars (three is the highest rating) depending on the facility's compliance with licensing regulations, the level of education of caregivers, parental involvement, learning environment, and participation in national accrediting programs. Look for accreditation by the National Association for the Education of Young Children when you are looking for a child-care center.

CHILDREN'S LEARNING LAB
Tulsa Tech
3850 N. Peoria Ave.
(918) 828-2052

CROSSTOWN LEARNING CENTER
2501 E. Archer St.
(918) 582-1457

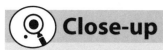 **Close-up**

Little Light House

Marcia Mitchell founded the Little Light House in 1972—a response to her daughter Missy's struggle with vision impairment. No services were available in Tulsa. Finally, a doctor in Oklahoma City told Marcia, "There's nothing available. If you want something, you're going to have to start it." And she did.

Today a beautiful and modern facility provides services for approximately 80 children, from birth to age six, with a wide variety of disabilities—and there are double that number on the waiting list. Children with difficulties including mental, sensory, learning, and physical impairments receive daily teaching from certified special-education teachers and licensed professionals in physical, occupational, speech, and low-vision therapy.

There is no tuition charge, and all operations are underwritten by donations—the organization is classified 501(c)(3). No government or United Way funds are accepted.

The Little Light House is a blessing and a beacon in the community. For parents whose children need the services, it is a blessing. For the entire community, it is an inspiration to see little ones succeed in difficult circumstances. The Little Light House is located at 5120 E. 36th St. The phone number is (918) 664-6746. The Web site is www.littlelighthouse.org.

And Missy? She's all grown up, a graduate in music education from Oklahoma Baptist University and a Christian recording artist. She also holds a master's degree in Christian counseling and marriage and family therapy.

HAPPY HEARTS ACADEMY
1010 N. Yale Ave.
(918) 835-2941

OKLAHOMA CHILD CARE RESOURCE AND REFERRAL ASSOCIATION
(918) 834-2273
www.oklahomachildcare.org
This Web site should be your first stop. This organization has done a lot of your work for you. They can point you in the right direction and save you time. You'll still have to visit centers you're interested in, but this group will make it easier. The number given is the Tulsa County resource number. The group's headquarters is in Oklahoma City, and their number is (888) 962-2772.

Listed below are two of the area's three-star facilities.

TRINITY EPISCOPAL DAY SCHOOL
501 S. Cincinnati Ave.
(918) 582-2556
www.trinitytulsa.org

TULSA COMMUNITY COLLEGE
Child Development Center
7505 W. 41st St.
(918) 595-8244
www.tulsacc.edu/page.asp?durki=39

MEDIA

From before Tulsa's incorporation, communication was important in the area. Of course, print was the first of the "modern" methods of spreading the news. Today, print is still important in Tulsa. Its daily paper, the *Tulsa World*, is holding its own in a changing market, and while about 75 percent of its readers come from the seven-county Tulsa Metropolitan Statistical area, it's popular with readers across the state for its breadth of editorial opinions.

Tulsa has a number of publications that can be picked up from racks located in libraries, stores, and businesses. Even some slick magazines are delivered this way. With all forms of communication, you have to stop and try to figure out how they are paying for "free" content. Advertising revenue is important and you'll have to determine how much of an effect that has on editorial material.

All the media are trying to figure out how traditional communication works in a digital age, and almost all the newspapers have online editions. Radio stations are adding Internet broadcasting, and the television stations all have Web sites.

People are beginning to realize that online sources of news may not be the ultimate answer—clicking from one site to another is surprisingly time consuming, and in scanning a newspaper, readers actually get more news on more topics than by looking down a list of selected headlines on a computer. Community papers are growing because they fill a niche—providing news about what's happening in "our" neighborhood.

Oklahomans are friendly people. And they're interested in what's going on. Tulsa has a number of ways to find out.

OVERVIEW

The first printing press in what is now Oklahoma arrived at Union Mission, Indian Territory, in 1835. It was used to print religious tracts and the first book printed in what would become Oklahoma, *The Child's Book*, or *Istutsi in naktsokv*, a Muskogee-language primer. The first newspaper in Oklahoma was the *Cherokee Advocate*, in 1844. By 1895, Indian Territory had 41 weekly papers and one daily.

Tulsa had several early newspapers. One of the earliest, perhaps the first, was the *Indian Chief*, in 1884. Tulsa businessmen, eager to put a better face on the town, started the *New* Era in 1895. It was succeeded by the *Tulsa Democrat*, which made its debut in September 1904. The first issue of the *Tulsa World* appeared a year later. The *World* was purchased by Eugene Lorton in 1917

and has been controlled by the Lorton family since that time. In 1919 a former editor of *Collier's* and *Cosmopolitan* magazines and the *Wisconsin State Journal* newspaper, Richard Lloyd Jones, purchased the *Tulsa Democrat*, renaming it the *Tulsa Tribune*. The paper remained in the Jones family until it closed in 1992.

Though the first radio broadcast in Oklahoma occurred just after World War I, it wasn't until the 1920s that things got really going. In May of 1922, a company organized by oilman William Skelly was broadcasting entertainment on its station, WEH. KFRU started up in Bristow in 1925 and showcased local talent like Otto Gray and his Oklahoma Cowboys. A year later, the station was given the call letters KVOO, and in 1927 it completed a move to Tulsa. In 1928 the station was purchased by William Skelly. The station became famous as the radio home of Bob Wills and His Texas Playboys. Both nationally famous commentator Paul Harvey and actor Tony Randall got their starts at the station, and in the late '20s a singing cowboy named Orvon Gene Autry performed on the station.

Tulsa's first television station, KOTV, Channel 6, began broadcasting in November 1949. Channel 2, originally KVOO-TV, now KJRH, signed on in December 1954.

DAILY NEWSPAPERS

BROKEN ARROW LEDGER
110 W. Kenosha St.
(918) 258-7171
www.baledger.com
Since 1903, locals have been keeping up with their neighbors and community events with the *Ledger*. The paper concentrates on local news, an events calendar, school activities and sports, and church and business news. The newspaper has an online edition and headlines by e-mail.

JOURNAL RECORD
Tulsa Bureau
401 S. Boston Ave., Ste. 105
(918) 295-0098
www.journalrecord.com
Published in Oklahoma City, this is the state's best source of business, legislative, legal, and real estate news. It's available in print, online, and with e-mail daily updates.

TULSA DAILY COMMERCE AND LEGAL NEWS
20 E. 5th St., Ste. 105
(918) 585-6655
www.tulsabusiness.com
The *Daily Commerce and Legal News* has served Tulsa's legal community since 1909. It is published Monday through Friday, except legal holidays. The paper lists all new cases in District Court, bankruptcy filings, deeds and mortgages, and more.

TULSA WORLD
315 S. Boulder Ave.
(918) 583-2161
www.tulsaworld.com

The *Tulsa World* has been around since 1905 and owned by members of the Lorton family since 1917. It is one of the few independent, family-owned newspapers in the United States. It has been the only daily paper in Tulsa since the closing of the afternoon *Tulsa Tribune* in 1992.

Every Thursday the newspaper includes a supplement called "Spot" featuring entertainment for the coming week—movies, concerts, live music, events, restaurants, wine, and more.

The news is available through the print edition, on the Web site, by e-mail, mobile phone, and RSS feeds. To subscribe, e-mail circulation@tulsaworld.com or call (918) 582-0921 or (800) 444-6552.

Weekly Newspapers and Magazines

BIXBY BULLETIN
103 N. Cabiness Ave.
(918) 366-4655
www.bixbybulletin.com
This paper was founded in 1903, making it the oldest business in Bixby. Published on Thursday, it is delivered to 2,000 homes in Bixby. An online edition is available, as are headlines by e-mail.

HISPANO DE TULSA
Zapata Multi-Media
4935 E. 22nd Place
(918) 622-8258
The oldest Spanish-language newspaper in northeast Oklahoma, this publication covers issues of interest and importance to the Hispanic community.

JENKS JOURNAL
116B E. Main St., Jenks
(918) 299-6451
www.jenksjournal.com
Published weekly, the newspaper focuses on community issues and stories. The paper is available in print, online, and with headlines by e-mail.

OIL AND GAS JOURNAL
1421 S. Sheridan Rd.
(918) 835-3161
www.ogj.com

In business since 1902, the *Oil and Gas Journal* is the most widely read publication on petroleum industry issues in the world. Covering all facets of the industry from production to marketing, international petroleum news, and technology, with analysis of issues and events, it is read throughout the industry by engineers, managers, and executives.

OWASSO REPORTER

202 East 2nd Ave., Owasso
(918) 272-1155
www.owassoreporter.com
Published Tuesday and Thursday, the Owasso Reporter is the best source for school, community, and city government news. It is available in a print edition, online, and with headlines by e-mail.

TULSA BUSINESS JOURNAL

20 E. 5th St., Ste. 105
(918) 585-6655
www.tulsabusiness.com
Published every other Monday, this paper covers issues that affect the Tulsa business community. Industries covered include aviation, government, gaming, energy, real estate, and many more.

TULSA COUNTY NEWS

3704 Southwest Blvd.
(918) 447-8882
www.thetulsacountynews.com
This weekly newspaper, published on Tuesday afternoons, carries news of interest to residents of southwest Tulsa, Berryhill, Carbondale, Garden City, Oakhurst, Red Fork, South Haven, and West Tulsa. It covers state and city issues pertaining to the area, District Two council and county commissioners, and local schools

URBAN TULSA WEEKLY

Renegade Publishing, Inc.
710 S. Kenosha Ave.
(918) 592-5550
www.urbantulsa.com
This is a pick-up-free tabloid and a must for anyone who wants to be in the know about the hottest bands, the newest venues, entertainment, restaurants, and controversial issues. It's edgy, sometimes irritating, but essential.

MAGAZINES AND MONTHLY PUBLICATIONS

THE CURRENT

326 E. Downing St., Tahlequah
(417) 890-1222
www.currentland.com
Self-described as "Oklahoma's Alternative Source for News, Entertainment and Green Living," this monthly, tabloid-style publication can be picked up free on local news racks. And it does what it says. You'll find lots and lots of information about entertainment in Green Country—pretty much the northeast quarter of Oklahoma. Tulsa is well covered but you'll also find information on what's going on in Muskogee, Eufala, Talequah, and other towns. There are also columns on sustainable living.

GREATER TULSA REPORTER (GTR) NEWSPAPERS

7116 S. Mingo Rd, Ste. 103
(918) 254-1515
www.gtrnews.com
GTR publishes monthly newspapers—*Union Boundary, Midtown Monitor, Jenks District Gazette, Broken Arrow Express, Owasso Rambler,* and *Bixby Breeze*—highly targeted to specific areas. While news of general interest is also covered, the papers are good at highlighting individuals in the communities, students, locals in the military, new businesses, sports, and upcoming events. They also publish features on subjects—for example, oil history in Tulsa or the heritage of the Perrymans, the prominent Creek family—and they let their reporters give some depth to their stories.

Ayn Robbins, a lyricist who's written the words to two Academy Award–nominated songs, now lives in Tulsa and writes on fashion and culture trends for the papers.

While these are "pick-up-free" papers, about 70 percent of those printed are driveway-delivered.

LIFE'S VINTAGE NEWSMAGAZINE
5950 E. 31st St.
(918) 664-9000
www.seniorline.org
This is a monthly magazine that can be picked up free at various locations around town or delivered by subscription. It focuses on topics of interest to seniors as well as their families, caregivers, and anyone interested in aging issues. Regular features include columns with opportunities for volunteering, consumer issues, Medicare questions, and health information. Feature articles range from travel to tips for green living.

OKLAHOMA MAGAZINE
2424 E. 21st St.
(918) 744-6205
www.okmag.com
Oklahoma Magazine covers not only Tulsa but other parts of the state including Oklahoma City. It features celebrity interviews and articles on home and gardens, health, fashion, arts and entertainment, and charitable and community events. Features range from stories about Oklahoma entrepreneurs to unsolved crimes.

OKLAHOMA SPORTS AND FITNESS
6945 E. 38th St.
(918) 587-7223
www.oksportsandfitness.com
Re-branded in 2009, this magazine was formerly named *Oklahoma Runner and Triathlete*. Over the last few years, the scope of coverage of the magazine expanded to encompass not only runners and triathletes but also walkers, endurance athletes, cyclists, and anyone interested in a healthier lifestyle. The magazine includes articles on training techniques, nutrition, and cooking, as well as race results and a calendar of regional events.

TULSAPEOPLE
1603 S. Boulder Ave.
(918) 585-9924
www.tulsapeoplemagazine.com
TulsaPeople is published monthly and is distributed around town. You can pick one up at no charge or buy a subscription to have it home-delivered. The magazine is chock-full of the who, why, when, where, and how in Tulsa. Everything from fashion and decor to sports and city leaders is covered in this well-done publication. You'll always find something you didn't know or something you need to know in this magazine.

TULSAKIDS
1820 S. Boulder Ave.
(918) 582-8504
www.tulsakids.com
The name says it all. The free magazine concentrates on parenting, family issues, health, traveling with children, and local events aimed at this audience. In addition, the business directory is a good resource for finding shops and services aimed at families and kids.

TELEVISION STATIONS

With local broadcast, cable, satellite, and DirecTV, Tulsans can glue themselves to their TV sets 24 hours a day. The listing below will tell you where to find the most popular local and cable channels—the ones you'll probably look for when you travel.

Channels are given for local and cable.

KJRH (NBC), CHANNEL 2 OR 9
3701 S. Peoria Ave.
(918) 743-2222
www.teamtulsa.com

KOED (PBS), CHANNEL 11
811 N. Sheridan Rd.
(918) 838-7611
www.onenet.net

KOKI (FOX), CHANNEL 23 AND 5
2625 S. Memorial Dr.
(918) 491-0023
www.fox23.com

KOTV (CBS), CHANNEL 6
302 S. Frankfort Ave.
(918) 732-6000
www.newson6.com

KTUL (ABC), CHANNEL 8
3333 S. 29th Ave. West
(918) 445-8888
www.ktul.com

OTHER CHANNELS OF INTEREST INCLUDE:
CNBC, Channel 49
CNN, Channel 41
ESPN, Channel 25
ESPN2, Channel 26
MSNBC, Channel 50

RADIO

AM Stations

KAKC 1300 (TALK)
www.1300kakc.com

KFAQ 1170 (TALK)
www.1170kfaq.com

KRMG 740 (NEWS/TALK)
www.krmg.com

KTBZ 1430 (SPORTS TALK)
www.1430thebuzz.com

KXRO 1530 (HISPANIC)
www.quebuenatulsa.com

FM Stations

KBEZ 92.9 (ADULT CONTEMPORARY)
www.kbez.com

KHTT 106.9 (CONTEMPORARY)
www.khits.com

KIZS 101.5 (CLASSIC HISPANIC)
http://tulsa.lapreciosa.com

KKCM 102.3 (NEWS/TALK)
www.spirit1023.com

KMOD 97.5 (ROCK)
www.kmod.com

KOSU 107.5 (PUBLIC RADIO, CLASSICAL)
www.kosu.org

KQLL 106.1 (TOP 40 CLASSICS)
www.kooltulsa.com

KTBT 92.1 (CONTEMPORARY)
www.921thebeat.com

KVOO 98.5 (MODERN COUNTRY)
www.kvoo.com

KWGS 89.5 (PUBLIC RADIO)
www.publicradiotulsa.org

KWTU 88.7 (CLASSICAL)
www.publicradiotulsa.org

KXBL 99.5 (CLASSIC COUNTRY)
www.bigcountry995.com

RETIREMENT

There are so many reasons to live and work in Tulsa. And there are just as many reasons to retire here. The cost of living in the area is attractive and you'll have access to a wide variety of cultural and educational opportunities. There are innumerable places to utilize your talents—whether it's guiding guests through one of the city's fine museums, mentoring young people, or planting a garden. Have time to learn something new? The educational opportunities in Tulsa are amazing, affordable, and convenient. If you don't want to enroll in a regular class, check out the continuing education offerings, short courses, and seminars. Looking for social activities and fun? Consider the senior center programs through the city Parks Department—join a bridge group, play bunko, or learn how to dance the Salsa.

Let's face it, though, the golden years aren't always so golden—sometimes health and family issues create problems. Even in these circumstances, there's a silver lining. Tulsa has an amazing service that provides help and information to get you through tough times. Life Services has done a lot of your legwork for you and can help you find solutions and services to deal with difficulties.

All in all, in good times and not so good times, it's good to be in Tulsa—a friendly place, an affordable place, and an attractive place—a good place to call "home."

SENIOR ACTIVITIES

Many Tulsa activities are available for multiage groups. You will find a number of these throughout the book. Some programs designed specifically for seniors are listed below.

Tulsa Parks Community Centers

CENTRAL CENTER
1028 E. 6th St.
(918) 596-1444

HICKS CENTER
3443 S. Mingo Rd.
(918) 669-6355

MCCLURE CENTER
7440 E. 7th St.
(918) 669-6678

WHITESIDE CENTER
4009 S. Pittsburg Ave.
(918) 746-5040
Classes and services for the 50-plus age group have included Aerobics/ Senior Cardio Sculpt, Fit and Fun, Prime Time Conditioning, Balance Testing/Training, Over 50 Basketball, and preventive screening with the cooperation of the University of Oklahoma Medical School. Central is also a nutrition site. All seniors, regardless of income, are eligible for these meals.

i The public library is your best friend. There are classes and discussion groups offered if you are able to get out; and their research resources both at the library and online are quite helpful. There is also a book delivery service for homebound readers and tapes for people with visual problems. Contact the library at (918) 596-7922 or online at www.tulsa library.org.

LIFE Services Senior Centers

LIFE'S SENIOR CENTER AT EAST SIDE CHRISTIAN CHURCH
East 15th St. and South Indianapolis Avenue
(918) 744-6760
www.lifeseniorservices.org

LIFE'S SENIOR CENTER AT SOUTHMINSTER PRESBYTERIAN CHURCH
3500 S. Peoria Ave.
(918) 749-2623
www.lifeseniorservices.org
Seniors 55 and older enjoy fun, friendship, and food at these two centers. Whether it's breakfast, brunch, or lunch, most stay for activities that include music, classes, movies, cards and games, exercise, and community outings.

YMCA OF GREATER TULSA
2405 E. Skelly Dr.
(918) 747-9622
www.ymcatulsa.org
Check here for specific programs for seniors and locations.

YWCA
Patti Johnson Wilson Center
1910 S. Lewis Ave.
(918) 749-2519
www.ywcaoftulsa.org

EAST CENTER
8145 E. 17th St.
(918) 628-1030
Both of these centers have warm-water indoor pools with ramps and pool lifts. More programs designed for seniors are offered at Patti Johnson Wilson—Water Seniorcise, the Arthritis Foundation Aquatics Program, and Senior Chair Aerobics. They also offer ai chi (water) and tai chi, designed to improve balance, posture, and coordination. The East Center offers an Arthritis Aquatics class.

NEATS
3817 S. Lewis Ave.
(918) 743-1303
www.neacco.org/NEATs.html
NEATs, which stands for Northeast Active Times, provides programs and services in an ecumenical religious setting for adults 55 and older, with special emphasis and recognition for centenarians. Included in the programs are bus trips to theaters and musical presentations, luncheons, and other activities. The Web site is not particularly helpful so call for information and a newsletter. This group has a lot of fun and makes it possible to stay active and involved in community events with other interesting people. While the group has a connection to the Christian Church, Disciples of Christ, the organization is ecumenical.

OKLAHOMA SENIOR GAMES/OLYMPICS
1829 W. Honolulu St., Broken Arrow
(918) 455-1894
www.oklahomaseniorgames.org
The senior games festival is a multiday event for men and women 50 and older. Competitions include archery, running, swimming, and track and field events. Success in the State Games qualifies competitors to attend the National Senior Games.

VOLUNTEER OPPORTUNITIES

RSVP OF TULSA (RETIRED SENIOR VOLUNTEER PROGRAM)
5756 E. 31st St.
(918) 280-8656
www.rsvptulsa.org
RSVP matches senior volunteers' skills with organizations needing those skills. Some of the entities utilizing senior volunteers include the Airport Ambassadors, Volunteers in the Courts, Hospitality House for families with members in medical facilities, the Arthritis Foundation, Meals on Wheels, and Grandfriends. Volunteers are also used to teach computer classes and serve as consultants in a number of areas.

SENIOR SERVICES

LIFE SENIOR SERVICES
5950 E. 31st St.
(918) 664-9900 (Senior Line)
www.lifeseniorservices.org

The number above is your lifeline to all sorts of information. It will help you access hundreds of services through information and referrals to local, state, and national programs and services that help seniors and their families solve problems

Among the things they do themselves, you'll find adult day-care services, two senior centers, caregiver support and community education, senior centers, and publications like their *Vintage Newsmagazine* and *Vintage Guide to Housing and Services* that will supply you with listings of agencies and facilities too numerous to mention. But the best thing they do is help you sort through all the information. There's so much out there, it can be overwhelming. Through their case-management service, they will help you match your needs with resources. Whether it's finding services to help you stay independent in your home or finding a facility to meet special needs, this is the place to turn when you don't know where to turn. They can even help walk you through the mysteries of Medicare and the prescription drug program! Save yourself a lot of time and frustration and make this your first call.

And, in case you were wondering, this marvelous agency is funded by the Oklahoma State Department of Health, the Veterans Administration, the Department of Human Service, the Advantage Program, the State Department of Education, the Tulsa Area United Way, and charitable contributions.

MEALS ON WHEELS OF METRO TULSA
12620 E. 31st St.
(918) 627-4103
www.mealsonwheelstulsa.org

This volunteer service delivers hundreds of meals a day to homebound seniors in the Tulsa area. In addition to the regular nutritious hot meals, they can accommodate individuals whose diets call for vegetarian, diabetic, or low-sodium foods.

SENIOR INFO-LINE (800) 211-2116
This is another good place to turn for information. One of its most valuable programs is the Ombudsman service. Ombudsmen are volunteers who visit nursing homes, assisted living, and residential care facilities on a regular basis. They respond to and attempt to resolve complaints of residents and advocate for the rights of individuals in these facilities. They are given extensive training and are under the supervision of a Tulsa Area Agency on Aging (TAAA) professional. While the agency will not make specific recommendations on the facility you should choose, they can help you choose more wisely by informing you of any history of problems at a particular place.

TAAA also oversees a senior nutrition program, providing healthy, nutritious food at nutrition sites (often in a senior center) across the area. Like Life Services, they provide information, assistance, and case management.

TULSA AREA AGING AGENCY
175 E. 2nd St., Ste. 480
(918) 596-7688
www.cityoftulsa.org/community/taaa

OTHER HELPFUL ORGANIZATIONS AND NUMBERS

There are so many in the Tulsa area. Here are several that will help address specific needs.

ALZHEIMER'S ASSOCIATION
6465 S. Yale Ave., Ste. 312
(918) 481-7741
www.alz.org/alzokar

The Alzheimer's Association in Tulsa provides a 'round-the-clock telephone help line, support groups, Safe Return registration, education programs, and referrals. Anyone who has dealt with this disease knows that caregivers need as much care as the Alzheimer's patient. The support systems available through this resource are invaluable.

LIFE'S ADULT DAY SERVICES
5950 E. 31st St.
(918) 664-9000
www.lifeseniorservices.org

Central Tulsa
LIFE's Adult Day Center
5950 E. 31st St.

North Tulsa
LIFE's Donald W. Reynolds Adult Day Center
902 E. Pine St.

Broken Arrow
LIFE's Donald W. Reynolds Adult Day Center
3106 S. Juniper Ave.

Adult day centers are for people age 18 and older who have Alzheimer's disease or other dementia, are frail or physically impaired, have chronic health conditions that require routine management, are socially isolated and/or experience depression, need assistance with activities of daily living, have chronic mental health disorders, have a developmental disability, or for whom being at home alone all day is not a good option.

Care is provided seven days a week at a reasonable rate that includes meals, activities, and nursing care. Some financial aid is available for qualifying participants.

In addition to stimulating activities and good food, staff can assist with showers, health care, medication, and physical therapy. There's also an in-house beauty/barbershop. Not only does the day center provide opportunities for interaction for the participants, it provides needed respite for caregivers.

DRIVING RESOURCES

AARP DRIVER SAFETY PROGRAM
(888) 227-7669
www.aarp.org/drive

This driver education program is scheduled periodically and is a good refresher for drivers 50 and older. Not only will it remind you of road rules and safety issues, it will address some of the particular problems faced by senior drivers. Comple-tion of the course may entitle you to a discount on your auto insurance premiums.

DRIVING EVALUATION PROGRAM AT ST. FRANCIS HOSPITAL AT BROKEN ARROW
3000 S. Elm Place, Broken Arrow
(918) 451-5119
www.saintfrancis.com

For a $200 fee (subject to change), your strength, range of motion, coordination, vision, visual perception, cognition, and in-vehicle skills will be evaluated. Recommendations for adaptive devices and referrals for on-road assessment will be given.

DRIVING EVALUATION–KAISER MEDICAL CENTER, HILLCREST
1125 S. Trenton Ave.
(918) 579-7100

This program uses a driving simulator to determine reaction speed and other components of driving skill, identifying specific limitations that could impair driving ability. There is a $137.50 fee (subject to change).

TULSA TRANSIT
510 S. Rockford Ave.
(918) 582-2100
www.tulsatransit.org

Among the programs sponsored by the city transit system are the Super Seniors Program in which individuals 75 and older can ride free on the fixed-route bus system; the Reduced Fare Program, which allows individuals 62 and over and persons with disabilities to use the bus system at half price; and the Lift Program, which provides curb-to-curb paratransit services for a minimal fee.

SENIOR HOUSING

There are many options for assisted living and nursing homes. Independent living is a bit trickier. As more of the population ages, and desires to age in their own communities, there should be more choices coming. Many people who are still independent choose to settle in continuum of

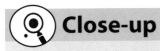

Close-up

Is It Time to Stop Driving?

Just because you're getting older, doesn't mean you're not a good driver. However, some functions do slow down as we age. Use the following checklist if you're concerned—or someone else is—about your driving.

Does driving make you nervous?

Have you experienced frequent close calls?

Do you have new scrapes, dents, or dings on your car?

Are you relying solely on rearview mirrors to help you back up or change lanes?

Are you easily distracted and having difficulty concentrating on signs, signals, and pavement markings?

Do you have difficultly gauging traffic gaps before entering the roadway or turning left?

Do your friends and family not want to ride with you when you're driving?

This last question could be the most telling. Often friends and family will try to drop hints with their comments. As difficult as it is, ask them for an honest assessment. Then consider going to one of the facilities that will evaluate the situation scientifically.

care communities, also called life-care communities. Most of these are not inexpensive and are usually privately paid. Long-term care insurance may help with assisted living and nursing care. Some facilities accept Medicare, others don't. A few will accept Medicaid. This is where LIFE Services comes in handy. They will help you assess facilities and determine which ones are going to fit your financial plan.

It's not feasible for a book like this to give you up-to-the-minute information on facilities. Situations and staff changes can quickly alter the information you need. We are listing here several life-care communities that have solid reputations and good histories in the community. This is just a starting place.

INVERNESS VILLAGE
3800 W. 71st St.
(918) 388-4235 (877) 481-9988
www.invernessvillage.com
In far west Tulsa, Inverness Village has a wonderful rural setting but isn't that far from city services. The community offers cottage and garden homes and apartments for independent living, and the entrance fee is 95 percent refundable

to your estate. There are substantial tax benefits available, and you're assured continued care while being protected from rising health costs.

Amenities on the 190-ace campus include 24-hour security in a gated community, tennis courts, and a putting green, bank, ATM and business center with a computer lab, a convenience store and ice-cream parlor, walking trails, and a center for cultural events, lectures, and group activities. Assisted living and skilled nursing care are available if they become necessary, and there is a Memory Care unit for residents with Alzheimer's or dementia.

OKLAHOMA METHODIST MANOR
4134 E. 31st St.
(918) 346-6663
www.ommtulsa.org
Handily located near midtown Tulsa, the Oklahoma Methodist Manor has been serving the community since 1956. There are 33 cottages, 44 garden apartments, and 6 garden homes on the campus. There is a sizeable nonrefundable deposit required and monthly fees. Residents pay for their own electricity, gas, and telephone services and provide their own washers, dryers,

and refrigerators. Benefits provided include lawn care, city water and sewer, and trash and ambulance service. There is a community nurse's office with 24-hour response, pastoral care, worship services and Bible studies, activity programming, and weekly group shopping trips. Residents are given priority consideration for admission to the assisted-living facility or health-care center. Independent-living apartments are also available for monthly rental.

At the present time, there is no special area for memory care.

ST. SIMEON'S EPISCOPAL HOME
3701 N. Cincinnati Ave.
(918) 425-3583
www.saintsimeons.org

St. Simeon's has a 50-acre, tree-shaded campus on the north side of Tulsa. Walking paths and courtyards help residents connect with nature. Attractive one- and two-bedroom cottages provide independent living, and residents can take

advantage of services like housekeeping, lawn maintenance, and scheduled transportation, which are included in the monthly fee.

The assisted-living facility offers three levels of care based on personal preferences and need, while the health-care center provides total nursing care. St. Simeon's Memory Center, for people who suffer from Alzheimer's or related forms of dementia, provides a safe, homelike setting for residents. This area is divided into six home units surrounding a central common area, used for group activities and visiting entertainment. This area has 24-hour staffing by a medical professional, continuous camera, infrared and Wander System security, recreational and social activities, housekeeping and laundry services, and individual care plans created by an interdisciplinary team.

The new Wellness Center features an indoor, warm-water pool, an exercise room, a massage room, activity areas, and a wellness coordinator.

WORSHIP

Religion plays a large role in life in Oklahoma. Visitors are often surprised that the first question they're asked after being introduced to an Oklahoman is "Where do you go to church?" or some variation on the theme. For the most part, this is not meant to be intrusive or to be a prelude to proselytizing. For many Oklahomans, a church is the center of their social network. The question is the Okie version of six degrees of separation. It's a way to connect someone new with someone you know.

The majority of Oklahomans identify themselves with a church—whether they attend regularly or not. Unfortunately, religion and politics often get tangled together here. Tulsa has a more diverse population than most of Oklahoma, and Tulsans seem to be more open to a variety of expressions of religion—or no religion.

Does this mean Tulsans aren't religious? No, it just means most of them are willing to make their own choices and allow others to do the same. One of the best indications of this openness is the history of the Tulsa Council of Churches, which was started in 1937. Originally, the group was exclusively Christian—of the Protestant persuasion. In the 1960s some members of the Catholic clergy joined the group. When members of the Jewish faith joined the council, the name was changed to Tulsa Metropolitan Ministry. The membership now includes Muslims, Buddhists, and representatives of the Native American church. Do these people agree theologically? Certainly not. But they have agreed to work together as an interfaith community for understanding, cooperation, and service.

They're only following in the footsteps of Tulsa's founders.

OVERVIEW

Tulsa's first Sunday School was an ecumenical effort. Shortly after the railroad building crew reached the Tulsa area, one of the worker's wives invited two of the other early settlers to her tent. Mrs. Slater was a Congregationalist; one of the men, Dr. W. P. Booker, was a Baptist; the other man, J. M. Hall, was Presbyterian. Together they formed a "union" Sunday school.

That was in 1883. In 1885 the Presbyterians, meeting at a school started by the Presbyterian Church Missions Board to serve Indian children, organized their own congregation. Shortly after, Methodist Episcopal communicants did the same. Catholics organized in 1890, and Southern Methodists started meeting together in 1893. The two tiny Methodist congregations were the cradles for First Methodist Church and Boston Avenue

Methodist Church. Why two Methodist congregations? The Methodist Church, like many others, had split over the question of slavery. At the time of Tulsa's founding, the church was still divided; the branches were not united until 1939.

Once oil was discovered, Tulsa's population jumped and more people from more faith heritages moved in. Churches were being built, outgrown, rebuilt, or sold to start over again. Tulsa has an unusual number of churches in its downtown area, and they all seem to be quite active. It's been said, though probably without accuracy, that there are more people in downtown Tulsa on Sunday mornings than any other time of week. More accurately, you'll probably see more people on the streets in downtown Tulsa as they come to and leave church than you'll see at any other time of the week.

And while the opposite is true for the rest

i The Tulsa Interfaith Alliance, (918) 292-8457, www.tulsainterfaith.org, is a faith-based, nonpartisan, grassroots organization promoting the positive and healing role of religion in the community. The organization challenges religious intolerance and promotes compassion, civility, and mutual respect for human dignity in a diverse society.

of the town, the streets around churches certainly have traffic on them. There are between 300 and 400 houses of worship in Tulsa. And they divide themselves into approximately 70 denominations—even the ones that call themselves nondenominations. There are around 80 Baptist churches—Southern, American, Free Will, Independent-Fundamental, Missionary, and National. Just over 50 churches declare themselves nondenominational. In numbers, the Methodists come next, followed by the Catholics.

All of this is just to tell you that if you're looking for a church home, you'll have lots of choices. Even within the same denomination, there are differences in worship style and even disagreements on questions of faith.

While you're exploring the possibilities, consider visiting the historic downtown churches. Historically and architecturally, these buildings have a lot to say. Holy Family Catholic Church was dedicated in 1914 and at that time was the tallest building in the state. Built in northern Italian Renaissance style, the church has one of the largest Gothic altars in the United States.

Trinity Episcopal Church is the oldest Episcopal church in Tulsa. They purchased the property in 1906. The current building was built in 1926. The stained-glass windows illustrate the Apostles' Creed.

i If you're looking for a church that is open and affirming, check the Oklahomans for Equality Web site, www.okeq .org. Eighteen Christian churches, a Jewish congregation, and the Islamic Society are committed to inclusion.

The two Methodist churches couldn't be more different in architectural style. First Methodist is said to be the tallest perpendicular Gothic building west of the Mississippi. Boston Avenue Methodist is one of the finest examples of art deco design in the country. Its architecture is so significant that the church offers tours after the 11 a.m. service each Sunday.

First Presbyterian Church is also a Gothic-style building. Its pipe organ is quite possibly the largest in the state. The Church of Christ, Scientist, may have the oldest pipe organ in the state. Built in 1923 in a combination of Greek and Roman styles, its interior was redecorated in 1943 by Adah Robinson, the talented Quaker lady who designed Boston Avenue Methodist.

First Christian Church, built in 1919, is an amalgam of styles, too. It has Greek columns but the mission-style, quatrefoil windows add an unusual touch, and you can't miss the slightly flattened, modified octagonal dome with its green tile. Inside, there's an interesting stained-glass interior dome.

First Baptist Church has grown and grown. Church members have been generous in meeting the needs of the downtown community. In 1972 they built a gym—the only church gym downtown.

Just north and east of downtown is Vernon AME Church. Founded in 1905, the church burned in the 1921 riot. The present building was completed in 1928.

Of course, you're not going to choose a church based on its architecture. You'll have to do it like everyone else does—by visiting churches. In Tulsa that could take a while.

INDEX

ABOUT THE AUTHOR

Elaine Warner has enjoyed traveling since the days she and her brother fought over the invisible line in the backseat of the car. Writing was reserved for school projects and, later, in preparing press releases for favorite nonprofit organizations. It wasn't until 1991 that she combined the two. She was taking a summer class in photography and, on a trip to Jefferson (Texas) with a friend, made the offhand comment, "I ought to write an article to go with my photos."

Having traveled to Europe, Hong Kong, and Singapore, she had visions of writing about far-off places. The reality was an offer to write a column on Oklahoma for her local paper, which turned out to be even better! Elaine has been writing Oklahoma travel stories for eighteen years and is still discovering new and exciting things about the state.

So far Elaine has traveled to all fifty states and twenty-one countries but still thinks there's no place like Okla-HOME-a.

THE INSIDER'S SOURCE

With more than 540 West-related titles, we have the area covered. Whether you're looking for the path less traveled, a favorite place to eat, family-friendly fun, a breathtaking hike, or enchanting local attractions, our pages are filled with ideas to get you from one state to the next.

For a complete listing of all our titles, please visit our Web site at www.GlobePequot.com. The Globe Pequot Press is the largest publisher of local travel books in the United States and is a leading source for outdoor recreation guides.

FOR BOOKS TO THE WEST